Microsoft® Windows NT® 4.0
Administrator's Pocket Consultant

William R. Stanek

***Microsoft* Press**

PUBLISHED BY
Microsoft Press
A Division of Microsoft Corporation
One Microsoft Way
Redmond, Washington 98052-6399

Copyright © 1999 by William R. Stanek

All rights reserved. No part of the contents of this book may be reproduced or transmitted in any form or by any means without the written permission of the publisher.

Library of Congress Cataloging-in-Publication Data
Stanek, William R.
    Microsoft Windows NT Server 4.0 Administrator's Pocket Consultant / William Stanek.
       p. cm.
    ISBN 0-7356-0574-2
    1. Operating systems (Computers) 2. Client/server computing.
    3. Microsoft Windows NT Server. I. Title.
    QA76.76.O63S7345   1999
    005.4'469--dc21   99-10308
                                                                                                       CIP

Printed and bound in the United States of America.

1 2 3 4   MLML   9 8

Distributed in Canada by Penguin Books Canada Limited.

A CIP catalogue record for this book is available from the British Library.

Microsoft Press books are available through booksellers and distributors worldwide. For further information about international editions, contact your local Microsoft Corporation office or contact Microsoft Press International directly at fax (425) 936-7329. Visit our Web site at mspress.microsoft.com.

Macintosh is a registered trademark of Apple Computer, Inc. used under license. Microsoft, Microsoft Press, MS-DOS, Win32, Windows, and Windows NT are either registered trademarks or trademarks of Microsoft Corporation in the United States and/or other countries. Other product and company names mentioned herein may be the trademarks of their respective owners.

The example companies, organizations, products, people, and events depicted herein are fictitious. No association with any real company, organization, product, person, or event is intended or should be inferred.

Acquisitions Editor: Juliana Aldous
Project Editor: Maureen Williams Zimmerman

Contents at a Glance

Part I
Windows NT Administration Fundamentals 1

1 Overview of Windows NT System Administration 3

2 Managing Windows NT Workstations and Servers 13

3 Monitoring Windows NT Processes, Services, and Security 35

Part II
Windows NT User Administration 57

4 Understanding User and Group Accounts 59

5 Creating User and Group Accounts 79

6 Managing Existing User and Group Accounts 107

Part III
Windows NT Data Administration 125

7 Managing File Systems and Drives 127

8 Administering Volume Sets and RAID Arrays 149

9 Managing Files and Directories 161

10 Sharing Files, Directories, and Drives 177

11 Data Backup and Recovery 193

Part IV
Windows NT Network Administration 209

12 Managing TCP/IP Networking 211

13 Administering Network Printers and Print Services 231

14 Running DHCP Clients and Servers 253

15 Managing WINS and NetBIOS Over TCP/IP 267

16 Optimizing DNS 287

Table of Contents

Acknowledgments	xix
Introduction	xxi

Part I
Windows NT Administration Fundamentals

1 Overview of Windows NT System Administration   3

Windows NT Workstations and Servers	3
Other Windows NT Resources	4
Frequently Used Tools	5
Using Control Panel Utilities	6
Using Graphical Administrative Tools	7
Tools and Configuration	8
Using Administrative Wizards	10
Using Command-Line Utilities	11
Using NET Tools	11

2 Managing Windows NT Workstations and Servers   13

Managing Network Systems	13
Selecting a Computer or Domain to Manage	15
Managing Windows NT Properties	15
Sending Messages to Users	21
Managing Domain Controllers	21
Managing System Environments, Profiles, and Properties	22
Determining System Information	23
Configuring Application Performance and Virtual Memory	23
Configuring System and User Environment Variables	26
Configuring System Startup and Recovery	27
Configuring Hardware Profiles	29
Configuring User Profiles	31
Managing Replication	31
Creating Replication Accounts	31

	Configuring the Directory Replicator Service	32
	Setting Up the Export Server	33
	Setting Up Import Computers	33
3	**Monitoring Windows NT Processes, Services, and Security 35**	
	Managing Applications, Processes, and Performance	35
	Task Manager	36
	Administering Applications	36
	Administering Processes	37
	Viewing System Performance	38
	Managing System Services	40
	Common Windows NT Services	41
	Starting, Stopping, and Pausing Services	42
	Configuring Service Startup	42
	Configuring Service Logon	43
	Auditing System Resources	43
	Setting Auditing Policies for System Security	43
	Auditing for Directory and File Security	45
	Auditing for Printer Security	46
	Event Logging and Viewing	48
	Accessing and Using the Event Logs	48
	Setting Event Log Options	49
	Clearing the Event Logs	51
	Archiving the Event Logs	51
	Viewing Events on Remote Computers	52
	Diagnosing System Problems	52
	Determining OS Build and Service Pack Version	53
	Determining BIOS Version and CPU Clock Speed	53
	Determining Video Drivers, Adapters, and BIOS Version	53
	Obtaining Disk Drive Information	54
	Determining Memory Page File Usage	54
	Troubleshooting Service and Device Problems	55
	Determining IRQ, I/O Port, and DMA Usage	55

Part II
Windows NT User Administration

4 Understanding User and Group Accounts 59
- The Windows NT Security Model — 59
- Granting and Denying Access — 59
- Differences Between User and Group Accounts — 60
  - User Accounts — 60
  - Group Accounts — 60
  - Tools for Working with User and Group Accounts — 61
- Built-In Accounts — 64
  - Built-In User Accounts — 64
  - Built-In Group Accounts — 67
- Account Priveleges and Permissions — 68
  - User Rights for Domain Controllers — 69
  - Built-In Capabilities for Domain Controllers — 70
  - User Rights for Non-Domain Controllers — 71
  - Built-In Capabilities for Non-Domain Controllers — 72
- Using the Built-In Group Accounts — 73
  - Groups Used by Administrators — 73
  - Groups Used by Operators — 74
  - Groups Used by Users — 76
  - Implicit Groups — 78

5 Creating User and Group Accounts 79
- User Account Setup and Organization — 79
  - User Name Policies — 79
  - Password and Account Policies — 80
  - User Rights Policies — 86
- Adding a User Account — 89
- Adding a Group Account — 91
  - Creating a Local Group — 91
  - Creating a Global Group — 93
- Handling Group Membership — 94
  - Making a User a Member of a Group — 95
  - Removing a User from a Group — 95

Setting the Primary Group for a User	96
Working with User Profiles	96
System Environment Variables	97
Local, Roaming, and Mandatory Profiles	98
Logon Scripts	101
Assigning Home Directories	102
Managing Logon Hours	103
Setting Permitted Logon Workstations	104
Setting Account Information and Dial-In Privileges	105

6 Managing Existing User and Group Accounts 107

Updating User and Group Accounts	107
Renaming User Accounts	108
Copying User and Group Accounts	109
Deleting User and Group Accounts	110
Changing and Resetting Passwords	110
Enabling User Accounts	110
Troubleshooting Logon Problems	111
Managing User Profiles	112
Using the System Utility to Manage Local Profiles	112
Deleting a Local Profile and Assigning a New One	113
Copying a Profile	114
Changing the Profile Type	115
Managing Multiple User Accounts	115
Setting Group Membership for Multiple Accounts	117
Setting Profiles for Multiple Accounts	118
Setting Logon Hours for Multiple Accounts	119
Setting Permitted Logon Workstations for Multiple Accounts	119
Setting Account Type and Expiration for Multiple Accounts	119
Setting Dial-In Privileges for Multiple Accounts	120
Customizing User Logons	120

Part III
Windows NT Data Administration

7 Managing File Systems and Drives 127

Adding Hard Drives	127
Physical Drives	128
Preparing a Drive for Use	129
Understanding Drive Partitions	132
Partitioning a Drive	134
Creating Primary Partitions	135
Creating Extended Partitions with Logical Drives	136
Formatting Partitions	136
Managing Existing Partitions and Drives	138
Assigning Drive Letters	138
Changing or Deleting the Volume Label	139
Deleting Partitions and Drives	140
Converting a Volume to NTFS	140
Checking a Drive for Errors and Bad Sectors	141
Defragmenting Disks	143
Compressing Drives and Data	143
Creating an Emergency Boot Disk	145
Creating an Emergency Repair Disk	145
Recovering a Boot Failure	146

8 Administering Volume Sets and RAID Arrays 149

Using Volume Sets	149
Creating a Volume Set	149
Deleting a Volume Set	150
Extending a Volume Set or Logical Drive	150
Improved Performance and Fault Tolerance with RAIDs	151
Implementing RAID on Windows NT Servers	152
Implementing RAID 0: Disk Striping	152
Implementing RAID 1: Disk Mirroring	154
Implementing RAID 5: Disk Striping with Parity	155

	Managing RAIDs and Recovering from Failures	157
	Breaking a Mirrored Set	157
	Repairing a Mirrored Set	157
	Repairing a Mirrored System Partition to Enable Boot	158
	Repairing a Stripe Set without Parity	159
	Regenerating a Stripe Set with Parity	159

9 Managing Files and Directories 161

Windows NT File Structures		161
	Major Features of FAT and NTFS	161
	File Naming	162
	Accessing Long File Names Under MS-DOS	162
Manipulating Files and Directories		164
	Using Windows NT Explorer	164
	Selecting Files and Directories	170
	Copying and Moving Files	171
	Renaming Files and Directories	173
	Deleting Files and Directories	173
	Creating Folders	173
	Examining Drive Properties	174
	Examining File and Folder Properties	175

10 Sharing Files, Directories, and Drives 177

Sharing Directories on Local and Remote Systems		177
	Creating Shared Directories	177
	Creating Additional Shares on an Existing Share	179
	Creating a Web Share	179
Managing Share Permissions		180
	The Different Share Permissions	181
	Viewing Share Permissions	181
	Adding User and Group Permissions to Shares	182
	Modifying Existing Share Permissions for Users and Groups	183
	Removing Share Permissions for Users and Groups	184

Managing Existing Shares	184
Understanding Special Shares	184
Connecting to Special Shares	185
Viewing Shares on Local and Remote Systems	186
Stop Sharing Files and Directories	186
Connecting to Network Drives	186
Mapping a Network Drive	186
Disconnecting a Network Drive	187
Managing Directory and File Permissions	187
Taking Ownership of Files	187
File and Directory Permissions	188
Setting File and Directory Permissions	191

11 Data Backup and Recovery 193

Creating a Backup and Recovery Plan	193
Figuring Out a Backup Plan	193
The Basic Types of Backup	194
Differential and Incremental Backups	195
Selecting Backup Devices and Media	196
Common Backup Solutions	196
Buying and Using Tapes	197
Installing Backup Devices	198
Installing a SCSI Adapter and Backup Device Driver	198
Installing a Tape Device	200
Using the Windows NT Backup Utility	201
Backing Up File Systems, Directories, and Files	202
Recovering Data from Backups	205
Backing Up and Restoring the Windows NT Registry	207
Backing Up and Restoring Data on Remote Systems	207
Automating and Scheduling Backups	207

Part IV
Windows NT Network Administration

12 Managing TCP/IP Networking   211

Installing TCP/IP Networking	211
Installing Network Adapters	212
Installing the TCP/IP Protocol Service	213
Configuring TCP/IP Networking	215
Configuring Static IP Addresses	215
Configuring Dynamic IP Addresses	217
Configuring Multiple IP Addresses and Gateways	218
Configuring DNS Resolution	220
Configuring WINS Resolution	221
Configuring DHCP Relays	223
Configuring IP Forwarding and Dynamic Routing	225
Connecting Computers to a Domain	225
Adding a Computer to a Domain	225
Removing a Computer from a Domain	226
Configuring Additional TCP/IP Services	227
Using the Services Tab	228
Testing the TCP/IP Configuration	229

13 Administering Network Printers and Print Services   231

Troubleshooting Printer Problems	231
Installing and Configuring Printers	233
Installing Network Print Devices	234
Installing Local Print Devices	238
Connecting to Printers Created on the Network	239
Solving Spooling Problems	240
Configuring Printer Properties	241
Adding Comments and Location Information	241
Changing Printer Drivers	242
Setting a Separator Page and Changing Print Device Mode	243

Changing the Printer Port	243
Scheduling and Prioritizing Print Jobs	243
Starting and Stopping Printer Sharing	245
Setting Printer Access Permissions	245
Auditing Print Jobs	247
Setting Document Defaults	247
Configuring Print Server Properties	247
Viewing and Creating Printer Forms	248
Locating the Spool Folder and Enabling Printing on NTFS	248
Logging Printer Events	249
Removing Print Job Completion and Notification	249
Managing Print Jobs on Local and Remote Printers	249
Using the Print Management Window	250
Pausing the Printer and Resuming Printing	250
Emptying and Purging the Printer	251
Pausing, Resuming, and Restarting Individual Document Printing	251
Removing a Document and Canceling a Print Job	251
Checking the Properties of Documents in the Printer	251
Setting the Priority of Individual Documents	252
Scheduling the Printing of Individual Documents	252

14 Running DHCP Clients and Servers   253

Understanding DHCP	253
The DHCP Client and the IP Address	253
Installing a DHCP Server	254
Managing DHCP Scopes	254
Using the DHCP Manager	254
Creating a Scope	256
Setting Scope Options	257
Setting Default WINS Servers for DHCP Clients	259

xiv | Table of Contents

    Setting Default WINS Node Type for DHCP Clients ... 260
    Setting Default DNS Servers for DHCP Clients ... 260
    Setting Default Routers and Gateways for DHCP Clients ... 260
    Modifying a Scope ... 261
    Activating and Deactivating Scopes ... 261
    Removing a Scope ... 261
    Configuring Multiple Scopes on a Network ... 262
Managing Client Leases and Reservations ... 262
    Managing Client Leases ... 262
    Reserving DHCP Addresses ... 263
    Modifying Lease and Reservation Properties ... 265
    Deleting Leases and Reservations ... 265
Backing Up and Restoring the DHCP Database ... 266
    The Backup Directory ... 266
    Restoring the Database from Backup ... 266

15 Managing WINS and NetBIOS Over TCP/IP   267

Understanding WINS and NetBIOS Over TCP/IP ... 267
    Using DNS ... 267
    Configuring WINS Clients and Servers ... 268
    Name Resolution Methods ... 268
Installing WINS Servers ... 270
Using WINS Manager ... 270
    Getting to Know WINS Manager ... 270
    Adding a WINS Server to WINS Manager ... 271
    Refreshing and Clearing Server Statistics ... 272
    Viewing Detailed Server Information ... 272
    Setting WINS Manager Preferences ... 273
    Configuring WINS Servers ... 274
Configuring WINS Database Replication ... 276
    Setting Default Replication Parameters ... 276
    Creating Push and Pull Partners ... 277
    Forcing Database Replication ... 279
Managing Static Mappings for Non-WINS Clients ... 280

Viewing Static Mappings	280
Creating Static Mappings	280
Importing Static Mappings from Other WINS Servers	282
Editing Static Mappings	282
Managing the WINS Database	282
Showing WINS Database Mappings	283
Cleaning and Scavenging the WINS Database	284
Compacting the WINS Database	284
Backing Up and Restoring the WINS Database	284

16 Optimizing DNS   287

Understanding DNS	287
Root Domains and Parent Domains	287
DNS and WINS	288
Enabling DNS on the Network	288
Installing DNS Servers	289
Installing the Microsoft DNS Service	289
Configuring a Primary Server	289
Configuring a Secondary DNS Server	291
Configuring Reverse Lookups	291
Managing DNS Servers	293
Adding Remote Servers to DNS Manager	293
Working with the Cache Zone	294
Examining Server Statistics	295
Removing a Server from DNS Manager	295
Deleting a Zone	296
Creating a Domain within a Zone	296
Delegating an Existing Domain to a New Server	296
Managing DNS Records	297
Adding Address and Pointer Records	298
Adding DNS Aliases with CNAME	299
Adding Mail Exchange Servers	300
Adding Name Servers	301

Viewing and Updating DNS Records	301
Updating Zone Properties and the SOA Record	302
Modifying the Start of Authority Record	302
Notifying Secondaries of Changes	304
Restricting Access to the Primary Zone Database	305
Managing DNS Server Configuration and Security	305
Enabling and Disabling IP Addresses for a DNS Server	305
Controlling Access to DNS Servers Outside the Organization	306
Integrating WINS with DNS	308
Configuring WINS Lookups in DNS	308
Configuring Reverse WINS Lookups in DNS	308
Setting Caching and Timeout Values for WINS in DNS	310
Configuring Full WINS and DNS Integration	310

Tables

1 1-1. Quick Reference for Key Windows NT Administration Tools — 8

3 3-1. Default Services That May Be Installed on Windows NT Systems — 41

4 4-1. Quick Reference for Using Account Administration Tools and Working with Accounts — 64
4-2. Availability of Built-In Groups Based on the Type of Network Resource — 67
4-3. Default User Rights for Groups on Windows NT Domain Controllers — 69
4-4. Built-In Capabilities for Groups on Domain Controllers — 71
4-5. Default User Rights for Other Computers in Windows NT Domains — 71
4-6. Built-In Capabilities for Other Computers in Windows NT Domains — 72
4-7. The Administrators Group Overview — 73
4-8. Domain Admins Group Overview — 74
4-9. Account Operators Group Overview — 74
4-10. Backup Operators Group Overview — 75
4-11. Print Operators Group Overview — 75
4-12. Server Operators Group Overview — 75
4-13. Replicator Group Overview — 76
4-14. Users Group Overview — 76
4-15. Domain Users Group Overview — 76
4-16. Power Users Group Overview — 77
4-17. Guests Group Overview — 77
4-18. Domain Guests Group Overview — 78

5 5-1. Basic and Advanced User Rights on Windows NT Systems — 86
5-2. Logon Hours Features — 104

6 6-1. Omitting the Name of the Last User to Log On — 121
6-2. Shutdown without Logon — 121
6-3. Powerdown After Shutdown — 121
6-4. Configuring Automatic Logon — 122
6-5. Sync Logon with Script — 122
6-6. Displaying a Custom Logon Message — 122

	6-7.	Setting Default Screen Saver Options	123
	6-8.	Wallpaper Settings for the Default User	124
8	8-1.	Windows NT Server Support for RAID	152
9	9-1.	Availability and Description of Drive Property Tabs	175
	9-2.	Availability and Description of Common File and Folder Tabs	176
10	10-1.	Special Shares Used by Windows NT	184
	10-2.	Basic Permissions Used by Windows NT	189
	10-3.	Access Types Used with Files	190
	10-4.	Access Types Used with Directories	190
11	11-1.	Incremental and Differential Backup Techniques	195
	11-2.	Using Incremental Backups	198
	11-3.	Options in the Backup Information Dialog Box	203
	11-4.	Options in the Restore Information Dialog Box	206
12	12-1.	Network Services Available on Windows NT	227
13	13-1.	Groups That Can Configure Printers, According to System Type	234
	13-2.	Printer Permissions Used by Windows NT	246
15	15-1.	WINS Database Files	282
16	16-1.	DNS Server Statistics	295

Acknowledgments

Wow, writing this book was a great experience that *really* put my years of Windows NT administration and consulting knowledge to the test. It is gratifying to see techniques I've used time and again to solve problems put into a printed book so that others may benefit from them. But no man is an island, and this book couldn't have been written without help from some very special people.

The team at Microsoft Press is top-notch. I'd like to offer a big thanks to Anne Hamilton, who helped get this project rolling, and throw in a big hug for Juliana Aldous, who shepherded the book through the acquisition and writing processes. Juliana did a terrific job of managing the project, especially since this is the first book in a new series.

Unfortunately for the writer (but fortunately for readers), writing is only one part of the publishing process, to be followed by editing and author review. I must say, Microsoft Press has the most thorough editorial and technical review process I've seen anywhere—and I've written a lot of books for many different publishers. Maureen Zimmerman watched over the editorial process from the Microsoft Press side and Sarah Kimnach headed up the editorial process for nSight, Inc. Richard and Darian Taha from FTA Computer Consultants were the technical editors and Joseph Gustaitis was the copy editor for the book. Together with a few pinch hitters—like Jim Kramer—they did a bang-up job!

Thanks also to Studio B literary agency and my agent, David Rogelberg. After going through several agents in the past, it is refreshing to finally find one that is willing to go the distance for his clients. But David, are you *really* sending out those proposals?

Before I forget, I'd also like to thank a few of my fellow techies at Intel Corporation's e-commerce division: Jack Story (IS/IT Director), Chris Aloia (Systems Programmer/DBA), Randy Rees (Ops Manager), and Tomas Vetrovsky (Windows NT Engineer). The challenging problems you've presented over the past many months have helped me stay sharp and hone my networking, administration, and problem-solving skills. Thanks!

Hopefully, I haven't forgotten anyone but, if I have, it was an oversight. *Honest*. ;-)

Introduction

Microsoft® Windows NT® 4.0 Administrator's Pocket Consultant is designed to be a concise and usable resource for Microsoft Windows NT administrators. This is the readable resource guide you'll want on your desk at all times. The book covers everything you need to perform the core administrative tasks for Windows NT server and workstation systems. Because the focus is on giving you maximum value in a pocket-sized guide, you don't have to wade through hundreds of pages of extraneous information to find what you're looking for. Instead, you'll find exactly what you need to get the job done.

In short, the book is designed to be the one resource you turn to whenever you have questions regarding Windows NT administration. To this end, the book zeroes in on daily administration procedures, frequently used tasks, documented examples, and options that are representative while not necessarily inclusive. One of the goals is to keep the content so concise that the book remains compact and easy to navigate while at the same time ensuring that the book is packed with as much information as possible—making it a valuable resource. Thus, instead of a hefty 1,000-page tome or a lightweight 100-page quick reference, you get a valuable resource guide that can help you quickly and easily perform common tasks, solve problems, and implement advanced Windows NT technologies like DHCP, WINS, and DNS.

Who Is This Book For?

Microsoft® Windows NT® 4.0 Administrator's Pocket Consultant covers the workstation and server versions of Windows NT 4.0. The book is designed for

- Current Windows NT 4.0 system administrators
- Accomplished users who have some administrator responsibilities
- Administrators migrating to Windows NT 4.0
- Administrators transferring from other platforms

To pack in as much information as possible, I had to assume that you have basic networking skills and a basic understanding of Windows NT, and that Windows NT is already installed on your systems. With this in mind, I don't devote entire chapters to understanding Windows NT architecture, installing Windows NT 4.0, or Windows NT startup and shutdown. I do, however, cover Windows NT workstation and server configuration, managing system services, processes, and tasks, and much more.

I also assume that you are fairly familiar with Windows NT commands and procedures as well as the Windows NT user interface. If you need help learning Windows NT basics, you should read other resources (many of which are available from Microsoft Press).

How Is This Book Organized?

Microsoft® Windows NT® 4.0 Administrator's Pocket Consultant is designed to be used in the daily administration of Windows NT networks. Consequently, the book is organized by job-related tasks rather than by Windows NT features. If you are reading this book, you should be aware of the relationship between Pocket Consultants and Administrator's Companions. Both types of books are designed to be part of an administrator's library. While Pocket Consultants are the down-and-dirty, in-the-trenches books, Administrator's Companions are the comprehensive tutorials and references that cover every aspect of deploying a product or technology in the enterprise.

Speed and ease of reference is an essential part of this hands-on guide. The book has an expanded table of contents and an extensive index for finding answers to problems quickly. Many other quick reference features have been added as well. These features include quick step-by-step instructions, lists, tables with fast facts, and extensive cross-references. The book is broken down into both parts and chapters. Each part contains an opening paragraph or two about the chapters contained in that part.

Part I, "Windows NT Administration Fundamentals," covers the fundamental tasks you need for Windows NT administration. Chapter 1 provides an overview of Windows NT administration tools, techniques, and concepts. Chapter 2 explores the tools you'll need to manage Windows NT systems. The final chapter in this part covers monitoring system processes, services, and security.

In Part II, "Windows NT User Administration," you'll find the essential tasks for administering user and group accounts. Chapter 4 explains how to operate system accounts, built-in groups, user rights, built-in capabilities, and implicit groups. You'll find extensive tables that tell you exactly when you should use certain types of accounts, rights, and capabilities. The core administration tasks for creating user and group accounts are covered in Chapter 5, with a logical follow-up for managing existing user and group accounts covered in Chapter 6.

The book continues with Part III, "Windows NT Data Administration." Chapter 7 starts by explaining how to add hard drives to a system and how to partition drives. Then the chapter dives into common tasks for managing file systems and drives, such as defragmenting disks, creating emergency boot disks, and more. In Chapter 8, you'll find tools for managing volume sets and RAID arrays, as well as detailed advice on repairing damaged arrays. Chapter 9 focuses on managing files and directories and all of the tasks that go along with that. You'll even find tips for performing advanced file searches and for working with drag and drop operations. Chapter 10 details how to enable file, drive, and directory sharing for remote network and Internet users. The final chapter in this part explores data backup and recovery.

Part IV, "Windows NT Network Administration," covers advanced administration tasks. Chapter 12 provides the essentials for installing, configuring, and testing TCP/IP networking on NT systems—covering everything from installing network adapter cards to actually connecting a computer to a Windows NT domain. Chapter 13 begins with a troubleshooting guide for common printer problems and then goes on to cover tasks for installing and configuring local printers and network print servers. The final three chapters in this section focus on the key Windows NT services: DHCP, WINS, and DNS. DHCP (Dynamic Host Configuration Protocol) is used to assign dynamic IP addresses to network clients. WINS (Windows Internet Name Service) is used to resolve computer names to IP addresses. DNS (Domain Name Service) is used to resolve host names to IP addresses.

Conventions Used in This Book

I've used a variety of elements to help keep the text clear and easy to follow. You'll find code terms and listings in monospace type. Anything that the user should enter appears in **bold** type. When using an unfamiliar term, I put it in *italics*.

Other conventions include

Note An item that provides additional details on a particular point that needs emphasis

Tip An item that offers helpful hints or additional information

Caution An item that warns you of potential problems

More Info A pointer to more information on the subject

Real World An item designed to provide real-world advice when discussing advanced topics

Best Practice An item designed to point out the best way to configure or work with an advanced feature

I truly hope you find that Microsoft® *Windows NT® 4.0 Administrator's Pocket Consultant* provides everything you need to perform essential administrative tasks on Windows NT workstations and servers quickly and efficiently. Your thoughts are welcome at nt-consulting@tvpress.com. Thank you.

Part I
Windows NT Administration Fundamentals

The fundamental tasks you need for Microsoft Windows NT 4.0 administration are covered in Part I. Chapter 1 provides an overview of Windows NT administration concepts, tools, and techniques. Chapter 2 explores the tools you'll need to manage Windows NT workstations and servers. Chapter 3 covers monitoring system processes, services, and security.

Chapter 1
Overview of Windows NT System Administration

Windows NT Workstations and Servers

Microsoft Windows NT 4.0 is distributed in two main formats: workstation versions and server versions. Windows NT Workstation is designed primarily for use by end users. Windows NT Server is designed to provide services and resources to other systems on the network.

When you install a Windows NT system, you configure the system according to its role on the network:

- Workstations and servers are generally assigned to be part of a workgroup or a domain.
- Workgroups are loose associations of computers where each individual computer is managed separately.
- Domains are collections of computers that can be managed collectively via domain controllers, which are Windows NT servers responsible for user authentication and similar tasks.

When you install Windows NT Server on a new system, you can designate the system as

- A primary domain controller
- A backup domain controller
- A stand-alone server

Primary domain controllers have overall responsibility for the domain. While Windows NT domains can only have one primary domain controller, multiple backups can be configured. Backup domain controllers provide a fail-safe mechanism that ensures the availability of authentication services in case the primary fails. Additional backup domain controllers can speed up the logon process from remote locations. Stand-alone servers have no controller responsibilities and must be reinstalled if you want to give them controller responsibilities. Backup options are covered in Chapter 11.

While Windows NT domains can only have one primary domain controller, multiple backups can be—and should be—configured on the domain. If the primary domain controller fails, you can designate a backup as a primary. This process, called promoting the backup, is handled in Server Manager—a key system administration tool you'll use often.

Other Windows NT Resources

Before we take a look at administration tools, let's look at other Windows NT resources that you can use to make Windows NT administration easier. One of the system administrator's greatest resources is the Windows NT distribution disks. They contain all the system information you'll need whenever you make changes to a Windows NT system. Keep the disks handy whenever you modify a system's configuration. You'll probably need them.

To avoid having to access the Windows NT distribution disk whenever you make system changes, you may want to copy the system resource directory to a network drive. For example, on an Intel system you would copy the \I386 directory to a network drive. When you are prompted to insert the CD-ROM and specify the source directory, you simply point to the directory on the network drive. This technique is convenient and saves time.

> **More Info** Two key add-ins are available for Windows NT: Windows NT 4.0 Resource Kit and Windows NT 4.0 Option Pack. Windows NT 4.0 Resource Kit contains a collection of unsupported utilities for handling everything from system diagnostics to network monitoring. Versions of the resource kit are available for Windows NT Workstation and Windows NT Server. Windows NT 4.0 Option Pack contains internetworking products and includes

- **Certificate Server** A server for creating and managing digital certificates
- **Index Server** A server that provides index and search facilities for a Web site or intranet site
- **Internet Connection Services for Microsoft Remote Access Service** A set of enhancements to the current Windows NT 4.0 Server remote access service
- **Internet Information Server** A full-featured server for Internet and intranet publishing that includes support for Web, FTP, and SMTP services
- **Microsoft Message Queue Server** A server that provides asynchronous network communications services
- **Microsoft Transaction Server** A component-based transaction processing system for enterprise applications
- **Site Server Express** A server that provides site analysis and Web posting facilities

Service Packs

Service packs for Windows NT are also available. Service packs contain updates that should be applied to the operating system. When you install a Windows NT computer, you should also install the latest service pack—provided it is proven to be stable. Service packs are numbered sequentially, with the latest service pack having the highest number. By installing a service pack, you can ensure that your workstations and servers operate smoothly.

Hot Fixes

In addition to service packs, you can also find hot fixes for Windows NT. Hot fixes are used to patch specific problems you are encountering with the operating system. Because most hot fixes haven't been regression tested, if you are not encountering the referenced problem, you shouldn't install the hot fix.

You can find current service packs and hot fixes for Windows NT at the Microsoft FTP site *(ftp://ftp.microsoft.com/bussys/winnt/winnt-public/fixes)*. When you access this directory, you will need to further navigate country, language, and product subdirectories. You can also look for the US version of Service Pack 4 for Intel systems at the *http://www.microsoft.com/support/winnt/default.htm* site. The US version of hot fixes that came out after Service Pack 4 are available in the directory of *ftp://ftp.microsoft.com/bussys/winnt/winnt-public/fixes/usa/nt40/hotfixes-postSP4*.

Most hot fixes are provided as self-installing executable files. Before you install a hot fix, you should read the ReadMe.txt file located in the hot fix directory. This file details what the hot fix is used for and also contains instructions for applying the hot fix. If you want to extract the hot fix and examine the files it contains before installation, follow the executable file name with the /x option. You can then apply the hot fix using the enclosed HotFix utility.

Frequently Used Tools

Windows NT provides many utilities for administrating Windows NT workstations and servers. The tools you'll use the most include

- **Control Panel**   A collection of tools for managing Windows NT workstation and server configuration. You can access these tools by selecting Start, then choosing Settings, and then selecting Control Panel.
- **Graphical administrative tools**   The key tools for managing network computers and their resources. You can access these tools by selecting them individually on the Administrative Tools (Common) submenu, which is on the Programs submenu on the Start menu.
- **Administrative Wizards**   Tools designed to automate key administrative tasks. You can access these tools by selecting Start, then choosing Programs, then choosing Administrative Tools (Common), and then using the Administrative Wizards menu. These are available on the Windows NT Server only.
- **Command-line utilities**   Most administrative utilities can be launched from the command line. In addition to these utilities, Windows NT provides others that are useful for working with Windows NT systems.

The following sections provide brief introductions to these administrative utilities. Additional details for key tools are provided throughout this book. Keep in mind that to use these utilities you may need an account with administrator privileges.

6 | Part I Windows NT Administration Fundamentals

Using Control Panel Utilities

If you've worked with Windows NT for a while, you are probably very familiar with Control Panel. Control Panel contains utilities for working with a system's setup and configuration. Figure 1-1 shows the Control Panel.

The key utilities you'll use in system administration are shown below. To run any of them, simply double-click on its icon in Control Panel.

- **Add/Remove Programs** Used to install programs and automatically remove all components of software that supports this utility. Also used to modify Windows NT setup components. For example, if you didn't install a communications component such as HyperTerminal during installation of the operating system, you can use this utility to add it later.

- **Date/Time** Used to view or set a system's date, time, and time zone. Rather than manually setting the time on individual computers in the domain, you can use the NET TIME command to automatically synchronize time. You can use NET TIME in the user logon script for the domain. In the logon script, insert the command **net time*servername*/set** where *servername* is the computer name of the server with which you want to synchronize time. Logon scripts are discussed in Chapter 4.

- **Display** Used to configure backgrounds, screen savers, video display mode, and video settings. You can also use this utility to install or update video drivers for a system. To do this, click on the Display Type button on the Settings tab and then click Change. If the video driver you need isn't listed in the Change Display dialog, click on the Have Disk button and follow the prompts.

- **Licensing** On a workstation, this utility is used to manage licenses on a local system. On a server, it also allows you to change the

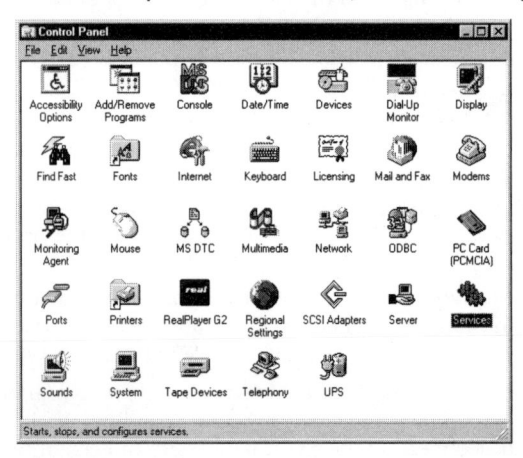

Figure 1-1. *Control Panel utilities are used to manage a system's setup and configuration.*

software-licensing mode of installed products, such as Windows NT Server or Microsoft SQL Server.

- **Multimedia** Used to manage a system's multimedia components. These components include audio, video, MIDI, and CD music. This is where you can install or update sound drivers for a system. To do this, click on the Add button in the Devices tab. Now if the driver you need isn't listed in the Add dialog box, select the first option (which is labeled as Unlisted or Updated Driver) and follow the prompts.
- **Network** Used to manage network services, adapters, protocols, and bindings. You can also use this utility to change a system's computer name and domain. See Chapter 12 for details.
- **Ports** Used to manage serial ports and add new ports.
- **Printers** Provides quick access to the Printers folder, which you can use to manage printers on a system. See Chapter 13 for more information on managing network printers.
- **SCSI Adapters** Used to install SCSI adapters and controller cards. See Chapter 11 for more information.
- **Server** On a Windows NT server, this tool provides quick access to system resource usage for users, shares, replication, and files. This dialog box is also accessible from the Server Manager utility. Using Server Manager is discussed in Chapter 2.
- **Services** Used to stop, start, and pause system services and to configure whether they start up automatically at boot time. Managing services is covered in Chapter 3.
- **System** Used to display and manage system properties, including properties for startup/shutdown, environment, hardware profiles, and user profiles. This utility is explored in Chapter 2.
- **Tape Devices** Used to add and configure a system's tape devices as well as drivers for tape devices. See Chapter 11 for more information.
- **UPS** Windows NT has built-in support for UPS (uninterruptible power supply). Use this utility to configure and manage UPS.

Using Graphical Administrative Tools

Windows NT provides several types of tools for system administration. The GUI-based tools are the ones you'll use the most. You can access these tools by selecting Start, then choosing Programs, and then using the Administrative Tools (Common) menu.

Most of the graphical administrative tools can be used to manage the system to which you are currently logged on, as well as systems throughout Windows NT domains. For example, in Server Manager you specify the computer or domain you want to work with using the Select Domain option of the Computer menu. Table 1-1, on the following page, lists the key graphical administrative tools and their uses.

Part I Windows NT Administration Fundamentals

Table 1-1. Quick Reference for Key Windows NT Administration Tools

Administrative Tool	File Name	Purpose
Backup	NTBACKUP.EXE	Backup and restore files on tape devices.
DHCP Manager	DHCPADMN.EXE	Manage dynamic IP addressing with DHCP (Dynamic Host Configuration Protocol).
DNS Manager	DSNADMIN.EXE	Manage DNS (Domain Name Service).
Disk Administrator	WINDISK.EXE	Manage disks, disk partitions, volumes, and software RAID arrays.
Event Viewer	EVENTVWR.EXE	View status messages for the system, security, and applications logs.
License Manager	LLSMGR.EXE	Manage software licenses for the network.
Network Client Administrator	NCADMIN.EXE	Manage network installation of clients and client updates.
Network Monitor	NETMON.EXE	Monitor network activity levels at the Frame and the Packet level.
Performance Monitor	PERFMON.EXE	Monitor system usage as an aid in performance tuning.
Remote Access Administrator	RASADMIN.EXE	Manage Remote Access Services.
Remoteboot Manager	RPOMGR.EXE	Administer remoteboot clients.
Server Manager	SRVMGR.EXE	Manage network computers, resources, services, and domain controllers.
System Policy Editor	POLEDIT.EXE	Manage system policies, which specify the permitted actions for users on a system.
Task Manager	TASKMGR.EXE	Manage system tasks and processes. You can also view system performance.
User Manager	USRMGR.EXE	Manage local user and group accounts.
User Manager for Domains	MUSRMGR.EXE	Manage domain user and group accounts.
Windows NT Diagnostics	WINMSD.EXE	View system settings and properties for the purpose of troubleshooting.
WINS Manager	WINSADMIN.EXE	Manage WINS (Windows Internet Naming Service).

Tools and Configuration

The administrative tools available on your system depend on its configuration. By default, Windows NT workstations and servers have different sets of tools. For example, User Manager is installed on Windows NT workstations and User Manager for Domains is installed on Windows NT servers.

Tools can also be installed when you add services to a system. For example, if you install the Microsoft DHCP Server service on a Windows NT server, DHCP Manager is installed as well.

Installing Tools on a Windows NT Workstation

Additional network administration tools can be installed on Windows clients from the Windows NT distribution CD-ROM. The goal is to allow administrators to manage network services and resources from their primary computer whether it runs Windows NT Workstation or Windows 95 (these tools are not available for Windows 98). If you want to install additional tools on a Windows NT workstation, follow these steps:

1. Log on to the workstation using an account with administrator privileges.
2. Insert the Windows NT Server 4.0 CD-ROM into the CD-ROM drive.
3. Execute the SETUP.BAT file in the \Clients\Srvtools\Winnt directory on the CD. The Windows NT Server management tools are installed on your workstation.
4. Once you install the client tools on a workstation, you can run them from the command line or the Run utility. The tools installed are DHCP Manager, Remote Access Server Administrator, Remoteboot Manager, Server Manager, User Manager for Domains, and WINS Manager.

Seeing the Administrative Tools

If you want the tools to appear in the Administrative Tools (Common) menu, follow these steps:

1. Administrative tools are installed in the *%SystemRoot%*\system32 directory. Access this directory in Windows NT Explorer.

Note Throughout the text, you'll see references to *%SystemRoot%*. This is an environment variable used by Windows NT to designate the base directory for the Windows NT operating system, such as C:\WINNT. For more information on environment variables, see Chapter 5.

2. Create shortcuts for the administrative tools in the *%SystemRoot%*\Profiles\All Users\Start Menu\Programs\Administrative Tools (Common) directory. Drag the icon for each tool from the system32 folder to this directory.
3. Rename the shortcuts as appropriate.

On a Windows 95 system, you can install the administrative tools as follows:

1. Insert the Windows NT Server 4.0 CD-ROM into the CD-ROM drive.
2. Access the Control Panel and then start the Add/Remove Programs utility.
3. Choose the Windows Setup tab, then click on the Have Disk button.
4. Enter the path to the Clients\Srvtools\Win95 directory (such as H:\Clients\Srvtools\Win95) on the CD-ROM.
5. Choose OK, then select the Windows NT Server Tools check box.

6. Select Install, then click OK.
7. The administrative tools are installed in the \Srvtools directory on the same drive as the Windows 95 operating system. In the Windows NT Server Tools folder, you'll find icons for using the tools.

Using Administrative Wizards

Administrative wizards are designed to automate key system administration tasks. Wizards are presented as a series of dialog boxes that you can use to manage local and remote systems. To access the wizards, select Start, then choose Administrative Wizards from the Administrative Tools (Common) submenu on the Programs menu.

Figure 1-2 shows the main dialog box for the administrative wizards. As you can see, eight wizards are available. These are

- **Add Printer** Configures local and network printers.
- **Add User Accounts** Creates new user accounts in a specified Windows NT domain.
- **Add/Remove Programs** Starts the Add/Remove Programs Control Panel utility.
- **Group Management** Manages local and global group accounts.
- **Install New Modem** Starts the Modems Control Panel utility.
- **License Compliance** Checks a system's license compliance.
- **Managing File and Folder Access** Manages folder permissions and share resources on local and remote systems.
- **Network Client Administrator** Starts the Network Client Administrator utility, which is normally located in the Administrative Tools (Common) folder.

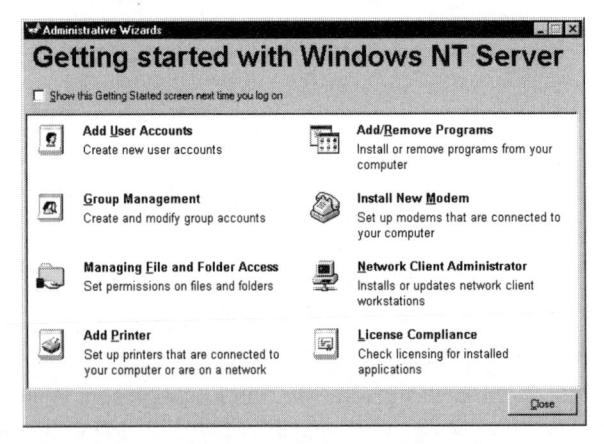

Figure 1-2. *Administrative wizards help you accomplish key administration tasks.*

Using Command-Line Utilities

Many command-line utilities are included with Windows NT. Most of the utilities you'll work with as an administrator rely on the TCP/IP Protocol. Because of this you should install TCP/IP networking, as explained in Chapter 12, before you experiment with these tools.

As an administrator, you should familiarize yourself with the following command-line utilities:

- **AT**   Schedules programs to run automatically.
- **FTP**   Starts the built-in FTP client.
- **HOSTNAME**   Displays the computer name of the local system.
- **IPCONFIG**   Displays the TCP/IP properties for network adapters installed on the system. Can also be used to renew and release DHCP information.
- **NBTSTAT**   Displays statistics and current connections for NetBIOS over TCP/IP.
- **NET**   Displays a family of useful networking commands.
- **NETSTAT**   Displays current TCP/IP connections and protocol statistics.
- **NSLOOKUP**   Checks the status of a host or IP address when used with DNS.
- **PING**   Tests the connection to a remote host.
- **ROUTE**   Manages the routing tables on the system.
- **TRACERT**   During testing, determines the network path taken to a remote host.

Using NET Tools

Most of the tasks performed with the NET commands are more easily managed using graphical administrative tools and Control Panel utilities. However, some of the NET tools are very useful for performing tasks quickly or obtaining information, especially during telnet sessions to remote systems. These commands include

- **NET SEND**   Sends messages to users logged in to a particular system.
- **NET START**   Starts a service on the system.
- **NET STOP**   Stops a service on the system.
- **NET TIME**   Displays the current system time or synchronizes the system time with another computer.
- **NET USE**   Connects and disconnects from a shared resource.
- **NET VIEW**   Displays a list of network resources available to the system.

To learn how to use any of the command-line tools, type the command name at the prompt without any flags. Windows NT will then provide an overview of how the command is used.

Chapter 2

Managing Windows NT Workstations and Servers

Workstations, servers, and domains are the heart of any Microsoft Windows NT 4.0 network. As an administrator, one of your primary responsibilities is to manage these resources. The key tool you'll use is Server Manager. Server Manager handles such core system administration tasks as

- Synchronizing and promoting domain controllers
- Managing user sessions and connections
- Managing file, directory, and share usage
- Setting administrative alerts
- Replicating directories and files to other systems in the domain

While Server Manager is great for remote management of network resources, you also need a tool that gives you fine control over system environment settings and properties. This is where the System utility comes into the picture. You'll use this utility to

- Determine general system information
- Configure application performance, virtual memory, and registry settings
- Manage system and user environment variables
- Set system startup and recovery options
- Manage hardware and user profiles

Managing Network Systems

Server Manager is designed to handle core system administration tasks like synchronizing domain controllers, managing user sessions, and determining file and directory usage. You run Server Manager by going to Start, selecting Programs, then Administrative Tools, and then Server Manager. This opens the dialog box shown in Figure 2-1, on the following page. In Server Manager, the currently selected domain or computer name is always listed at the top of the dialog box. Double backslashes before the name indicate that a single computer is selected. If there are no double backslashes displayed, an actual Windows NT domain controller is selected.

The main window of Server Manager lists computers by Computer, Type, and Description.

- **Computer** Simply the computer name assigned to the system during installation or configuration
- **Type** The type of computer
- **Description** An optional description that can be defined for a computer using Server Manager

Common computer types you will see include

- **Windows NT Workstation or Server** A standard workstation or server computer
- **Windows NT 4.0 Primary** A primary domain controller running Windows NT 4.0
- **Windows NT 4.0 Backup** A backup domain controller running Windows NT 4.0
- **Windows 95 Workstation** A workstation running Windows 95
- **Windows 98 Workstation** A workstation running Windows 98

> **Tip** You can use the View menu to specify what types of computers to display in Server Manager. Select Workstations to display workstations only. Select Servers to display servers only. Select All to display both workstations and servers. Select Show Domain Members Only to display only computers that are members of the domain. Double click on any computer listed on the screen and you will see an additional dialog box with the properties of that computer. Adding and removing computers to or from a domain is covered in Chapter 12.

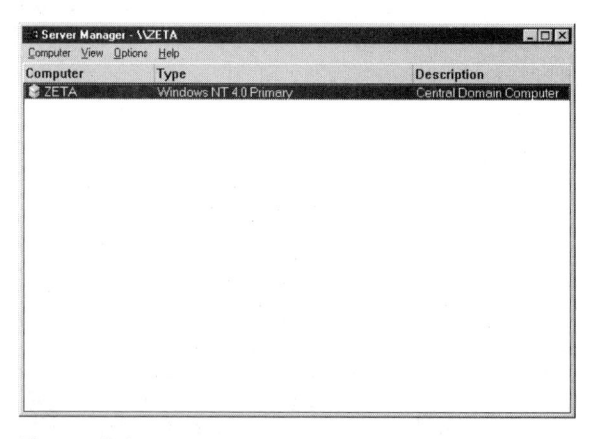

Figure 2-1. *Use Server Manager to manage network computers and resources.*

Selecting a Computer or Domain to Manage

In Server Manager you can select a computer or domain to manage by using the Select Domain option on the Computer menu. Choosing this option opens the Select Domain dialog box and you can now

- Choose the domain you want to work with in the Select Domain list.
- Enter the computer name or IP address of a computer you want to work with in the Domain field. Be sure to precede the name with a double backslash, such as \\ZETA.

Managing Windows NT Properties

You manage the properties of remote computers using the dialog box shown in Figure 2-2. Display the Properties dialog box using one of the following techniques:

- Select the computer you want to work with, then choose Properties from the Computer menu.
- Double-click on the entry for the computer you want to work with.

You can now manage Windows NT workstation and server properties for users, shares, open resources, replication, and alerts. You can also enter a new description for a computer in the Description field. This description is displayed in Server Manager's main window. The Usage Summary area of this dialog box provides the following information:

- **Sessions** The total number of user sessions open for the system's shared resources
- **File Locks** The total number of file locks for the system's shared resources
- **Open Files** The total number of open files on the system's shared resources
- **Open Named Pipes** The total number of named pipes on the system's shared resources

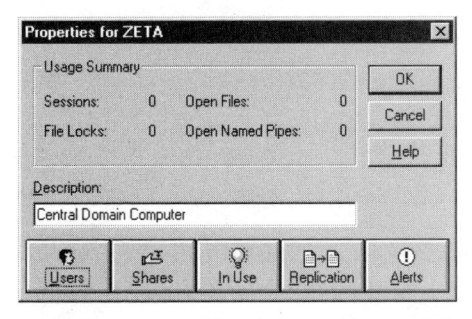

Figure 2-2. *Computer properties are managed using the Properties dialog box.*

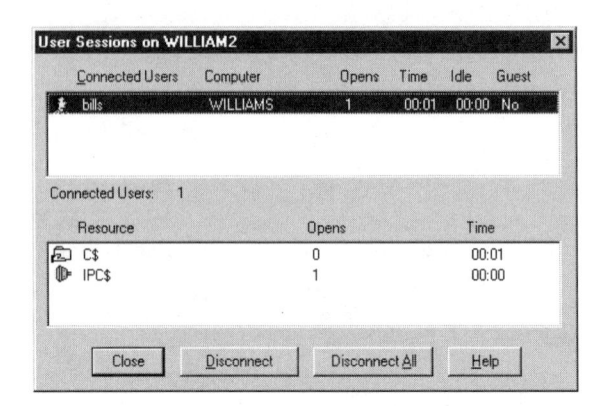

Figure 2-3. *Viewing user connections on a per user basis.*

Viewing User Connections and Shared Resources

Server Manager can track all connections to shared resources on a Windows NT system. Whenever a user connects to a shared resource, a user connection is listed in the computer's Properties dialog box. You can view and manage these connections on a per user or per share basis.

Viewing connections by user name To view connections to shared resource by user name, follow these steps:

1. Find the computer you want to work with in Server Manager, then double-click on its entry.
2. Select the Users button in the Properties dialog box. This opens the User Sessions dialog box shown in Figure 2-3.
3. You can now view connections on a per user basis.

The User Sessions dialog box provides important information about user connections. The dialog box is divided into two key areas. The top area shows connected users. The bottom area shows resources to which the currently selected user is connected. The fields of this dialog box provide the following information:

- **Connected Users** The names of users connected to shared resources
- **Computer** The computer being used by the user
- **Opens** The number of files the user has opened
- **Time** The time that has elapsed since the connection was established
- **Idle** The time that has elapsed since the connection was last used
- **Guest** Specifies whether the user is logged on as a guest
- **Resource** Shared resources to which the currently selected user is connected

Viewing connections by share name To view connections to shared resource by share name, follow these steps:

1. Find the computer you want to work with in Server Manager, then double-click on its entry.

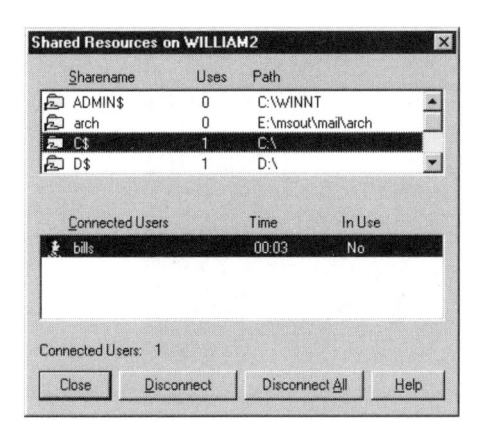

Chapter 2 Managing Windows NT Workstations and Servers | 17

Figure 2-4. *Viewing user connections on a per share basis.*

2. Select the Shares button in the Properties dialog box. This opens the Shared Resources dialog box shown in Figure 2-4.
3. You can now view connections on a per share basis.

The Shared Resources dialog box is divided into two key areas. The top area shows shared resources. The bottom area shows users that are connected to the currently selected share. The fields of this dialog box provide the following information:

- **Sharename** The name of the shared resource
- **Uses** The number of connections to the resource
- **Path** The location of the shared resource on the remote system
- **Connected Users** The names of users connected to shared resources
- **Time** The time that has elapsed since the connection was established
- **In Use** Specifies whether the resource is currently in use

Tip The dialog box as shown in Figure 2-4 above may not be wide enough to show the full path of shared resources. If so, to see the full path, go to Start, select Programs, and then select Command Prompt. Type **Net Share** and press Enter. See Figure 2-5, on the following page.

Managing User Connections and Shares

Managing user connections and shares is a common administrative task. Before you shut down a server or an application running on a server, you may want to disconnect users from shared resources. You may also need to disconnect users when you plan to change access permissions or delete a share entirely. Another reason to disconnect users is to break file locks.

Server Manager lets you manage connections on a per user or a per share basis.

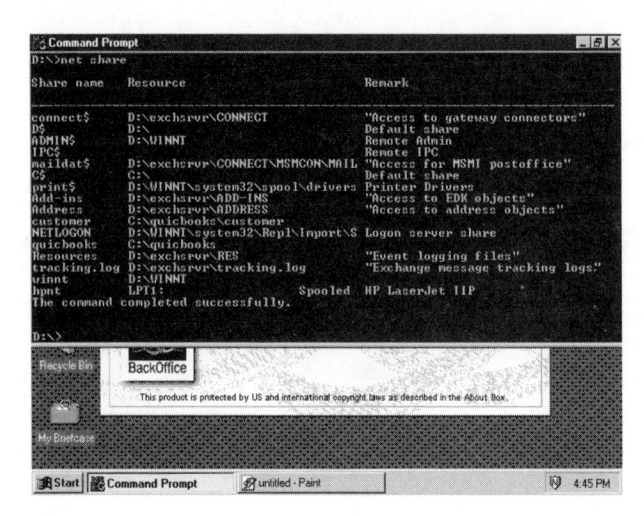

![Screenshot of Command Prompt showing net share output]

```
D:\>net share

Share name   Resource                              Remark

connect$     D:\exchsrvr\CONNECT                   "Access to gateway connectors"
D$           D:\                                   Default share
ADMIN$       D:\WINNT                              Remote Admin
IPC$                                               Remote IPC
maildat$     D:\exchsrvr\CONNECT\MSMCON\MAIL       "Access for MSMI postoffice"
C$           C:\                                   Default share
print$       D:\WINNT\system32\spool\drivers       Printer Drivers
Add-ins      D:\exchsrvr\ADD-INS                   "Access to EDK objects"
Address      D:\exchsrvr\ADDRESS                   "Access to address objects"
customer     C:\quickbooks\customer
NETLOGON     D:\WINNT\system32\Repl\Import\S       Logon server share
quickbooks   C:\quickbooks
Resources    D:\exchsrvr\RES                       "Event logging files"
tracking.log D:\exchsrvr\tracking.log              "Exchange message tracking logs"
winnt        D:\WINNT
hpnt         LPT1:                        Spooled  HP LaserJet IIP
The command completed successfully.

D:\>
```

Figure 2-5. *Viewing user connections on a per share basis from Command Prompt.*

Disconnecting users on a per user basis To disconnect users from shared resources on a per user basis, follow these steps:

1. Select the computer you want to work with in Server Manager, then choose Properties from the Computer menu.
2. Click on the Users button in the Properties dialog box.
3. You can now disconnect users from shared resources. Use Disconnect to disconnect individual users. Use Disconnect All to break all user connections.

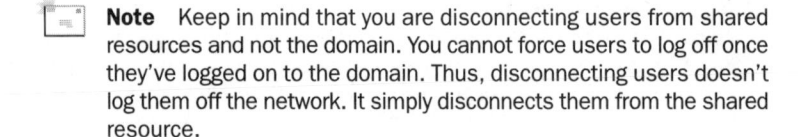

Disconnecting users on a per share basis To disconnect users from shared resources on a per share basis, follow these steps:

1. Select the computer you want to work with in Server Manager, then choose Properties from the Computer menu.
2. Click on the Shares button in the Properties dialog box.
3. You can now disconnect users from shared resources. Use Disconnect to disconnect individual users. Use Disconnect All to break all user connections.

> **Note** Keep in mind that you are disconnecting users from shared resources and not the domain. You cannot force users to log off once they've logged on to the domain. Thus, disconnecting users doesn't log them off the network. It simply disconnects them from the shared resource.

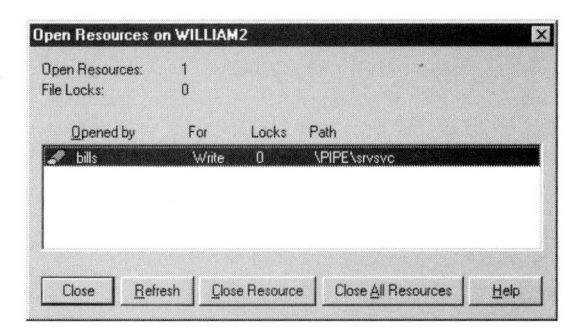

Chapter 2 Managing Windows NT Workstations and Servers | 19

Figure 2-6. *You can manage open resources by using the Open Resources dialog box.*

Managing Open Resources

Anytime users connect to shares, the individual file and object resources they are working with are displayed in the Open Resources dialog box. You can access this dialog box by completing the following steps:

1. Select the computer you want to work with in Server Manager, then choose Properties from the Computer menu.
2. Choose In Use from the Properties dialog box. This displays the Open Resources dialog box shown in Figure 2-6.

The open resources dialog box The Open Resources dialog box provides the following information about resource usage:

- **Open Resources** The total number of open resources on the system.
- **File Locks** The total number of file locks.
- **Opened By** Displays the type of resource and the name of the user accessing it. A document icon indicates a file. A pipe icon indicates a named pipe. A printer icon indicates a print job. A communications port icon indicates a communication-device queue. A question mark indicates an unknown resource type.

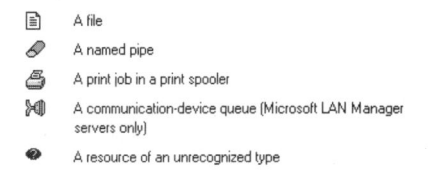

    - A file
    - A named pipe
    - A print job in a print spooler
    - A communication-device queue (Microsoft LAN Manager servers only)
    - A resource of an unrecognized type

- **For** Indicates the permission granted when the resource was opened, such as Read or Write permission.
- **Locks** Displays the number of locks on the resource.
- **Path** The location of the resource on the remote system.

The buttons on the open resources dialog box The information provided by the Open Resources dialog box is useful when you are trying to determine who is accessing a file and is thus preventing it from being modified, deleted, or copied. The buttons on the bottom of the dialog box allow you to manage open resources and are used as follows:

- **Refresh** Used to refresh the list of open resources to reflect current changes
- **Close Resource** Closes the currently selected resource
- **Close All Resources** Closes all open resources

Viewing Replication Properties

The Replication button on the Properties dialog box is used to set up directory replication. With directory replication, you can automatically copy files between systems in a Windows NT domain. For complete details on replication, see the section of this chapter titled "Managing Replication."

Computer Alerts

You can configure network computers to alert you whenever administrative alerts are generated by the operating system. Administrative alerts provide useful information about the state of the computer and can provide warnings related to security, file usage, low drive space, and more.

Setting up alerts To set up alerts, follow these steps:

1. Select the computer you want to work with in Server Manager, then choose Properties from the Computer menu.
2. Choose Alerts from the Properties dialog box. This displays the dialog box shown in Figure 2-7.

Configuring alerts You can now configure alerts on the system

- To configure a computer or user to receive alerts, type the computer or user name in the New Computer Or Username field, then choose Add.
- To disable alerts for a computer or user, select the computer or user name in the Send Administrative Alerts To list, then click Remove.

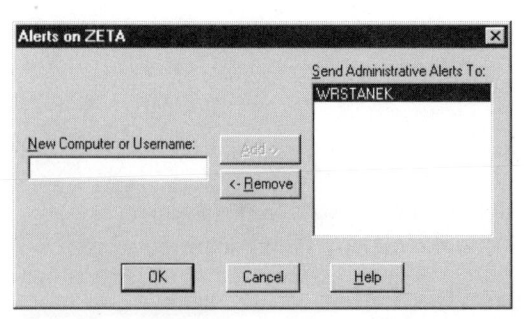

Figure 2-7. *Alerts lets you configure computers and users so they can receive administrative alerts.*

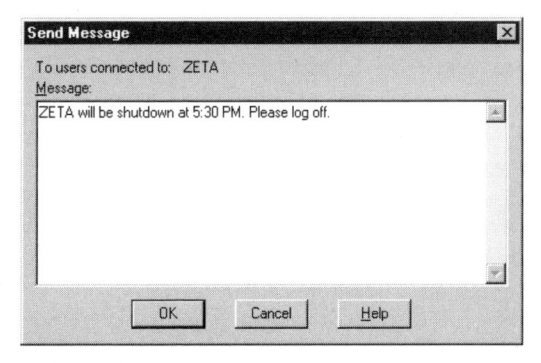

[Screenshot of Send Message dialog box showing "To users connected to: ZETA" and message "ZETA will be shutdown at 5:30 PM. Please log off." with OK, Cancel, and Help buttons.]

Figure 2-8. *To send a message to a remote user, open the Send Message dialog box, enter the text of the message, and click OK.*

Note The Alerter and Messenger services must be running on the system generating alerts. Additionally, the Messenger service must be running on the client computer receiving the alerts. Configuring services is covered in the section of Chapter 3 titled "Managing System Services."

Sending Messages to Users

You can use Server Manager to send messages to users logged in to remote systems. These messages appear in a dialog box that the user must click on to close.

You send messages to remote users by doing the following:

1. In Server Manager, select the computer you want to send messages to, then choose Send Message from the Computer menu. This opens the dialog box shown in Figure 2-8.
2. Enter the text of the message and click OK.

Note Only users logged in to the selected system receive the message. Other users do not.

Managing Domain Controllers

Domain controllers are responsible for managing access to Windows NT domains. Two types of domain controllers are used:

- **Primary domain controller (PDC)** A Windows NT server that has overall responsibility for the domain and on which the primary domain user database is stored. Windows NT domains can have only one primary domain controller.
- **Backup domain controller (BDC)** A Windows NT server that maintains a backup copy of the domain user database and provides a fail-safe mechanism that ensures the availability of authentication services in case the primary domain controller fails or is otherwise unavailable.

Windows NT domains can have multiple BDCs. (BDCs are recommended but not required.)

Promoting a Domain Controller

The only time you can designate a Windows NT server as a domain controller is during installation, when you can designate the server as either a primary or a backup. However, you cannot install a computer as a BDC unless there is already an active PDC computer on the subnet. Anytime after installation, you can promote a BDC to a primary. When you do, the current primary is demoted and the BDC is promoted to the primary.

You promote a backup to a primary by doing the following:

1. Start Server Manager by going to the Start menu, selecting Programs, then Administrative Tools, and then Server Manager.
2. Select the BDC in Server Manager, then choose Promote To Primary Domain Controller from the Computer menu.

Synchronizing the User Database Throughout the Domain

Promoting a backup is only one of two key tasks you'll perform with domain controllers. The other is to synchronize backups with the primary. You only need to synchronize backups with the primary when automatic synchronization fails or when you need user and trust changes to be immediately reflected throughout the domain.

You synchronize a single BDC with the primary by doing the following:

1. Start Server Manager by going to the Start menu, selecting Programs, then Administrative Tools, and then Server Manager.
2. Select the BDC in Server Manager, then choose Synchronize With Primary Domain Controller from the Computer menu.

You synchronize all BDCs with the primary by completing these steps:

1. Start Server Manager by going to the Start menu, selecting Programs, then Administrative Tools, and then Server Manager.
2. Select the PDC in Server Manager, then choose Synchronize Entire Domain from the Computer menu.

> **Tip** For faster synchronization you can go to Start, select Programs, and then select Command Prompt. This will open the Command Prompt windows. Type **NET ACCOUNTS /SYNC** and press the Enter key.

Managing System Environments, Profiles, and Properties

The System utility is used to manage system environments, profiles, and properties. Start it by double-clicking on the System icon in the Control Panel. This opens the dialog box shown in Figure 2-9. As you see, the dialog box is divided into six tabs. Each of these tabs is discussed in the sections that follow.

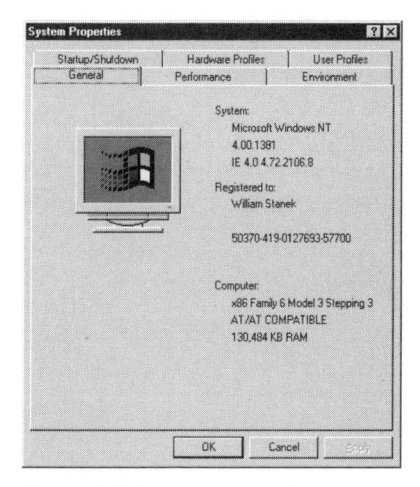

Figure 2-9. *The System utility is used to manage system environment variables, profiles, and properties.*

Determining System Information

General system information is available for any Windows NT workstation or server via the System utility's General tab shown in Figure 2-9.

The information provided by the General tab helps you determine the following:

- Operating system version
- Registered owner
- Windows NT serial number
- Computer type
- Amount of RAM installed on the computer

To access the General tab, start the System utility by double-clicking on the System icon in the Control Panel. Then click on the General tab.

Note If you are trying to determine the service pack version installed on the system, check the Version tab of Windows NT Diagnostics. For more information, see the section of Chapter 3 titled "Diagnosing System Problems."

Configuring Application Performance and Virtual Memory

Application performance and virtual memory are configured via the System utility's Performance tab shown in Figure 2-10, on the following page. To access the Performance tab, start the System utility by double-clicking on the System icon in the Control Panel, then click on the Performance tab.

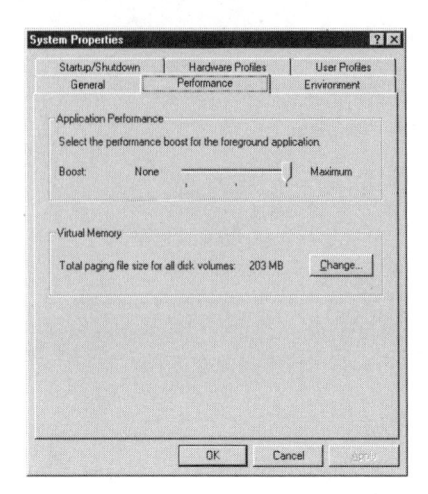

Figure 2-10. *The Performance tab lets you configure application performance and virtual memory.*

Setting Application Performance

Application performance determines the responsiveness of the current active application (as opposed to background applications that may be running on the system). You control application performance with the Performance tab's Boost slider, which works as follows:

- Set Boost to Maximum to give the active application the best response time and the greatest share of available resources.

- Set Boost to an intermediate value to give background applications a better response time but still give the active application more processing time.

- Set Boost to None to give all applications equal response time and equal amounts of processing time.

Setting Virtual Memory

Virtual memory allows you to use disk space to extend the amount of available RAM on a system. This feature of Intel 386 and later processors writes RAM to disks using a process called paging. With paging, a set amount of RAM, such as 32 MB, is written to the disk as a paging file where it can be accessed from the disk when needed.

An initial paging file is created automatically for the drive containing the operating system. By default, other drives do not have paging files, and you must create these paging files manually if you want them. When you create a paging file, you set an initial size and a maximum size. Paging files are written to the volume as a file called PAGEFILE.SYS.

Chapter 2 Managing Windows NT Workstations and Servers | 25

Best Practice Microsoft recommends that you create a paging file for each volume on the system. On most systems, multiple paging files can improve the performance of virtual memory. Thus instead of a single large paging file, it is better to have many small paging files. Keep in mind that removable drives do not need paging files.

Configuring virtual memory You can configure virtual memory by completing the following steps:

1. Start the System utility by double-clicking on the System icon in the Control Panel, then click on the Performance tab.
2. Choose Change in the Virtual Memory area to display the dialog box shown in Figure 2-11.
   - The Drive header shows how virtual memory is configured currently on the system. Each volume is listed with its associated paging file (if any). The paging file range shows the initial and maximum size values set for the paging file.
   - Paging File Size For Selected Drives provides information on the currently selected drive and allows you to set its paging file size. Current Space Available tells you how much space is available on the drive.
   - Total Paging File Size For All Drives provides a recommended size for virtual RAM on the system and tells you the amount currently allocated. If this is the first time you are configuring virtual RAM, you'll note that the recommended amount has already been given to the system drive (in most instances).

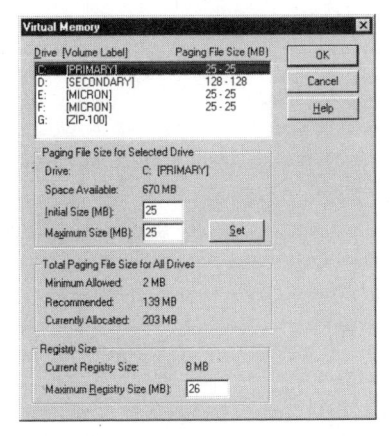

Figure 2-11. *Virtual memory extends the amount of RAM on a system.*

26 | Part I Windows NT Administration Fundamentals

> **Tip** Although Windows NT can expand paging files incrementally as needed, this can result in fragmented files, which slow system performance. For optimal system performance, set the initial size and maximum size to the same value. This ensures that the paging file is consistent and can be written to a single contiguous file (if possible, given the amount of space on the volume).

3. Select the volume you want to work with in the Drive list box.
4. Use the Paging File Size For Selected Drive area to configure the paging file for the drive. Enter an initial size and a maximum size, then choose Set to save the changes.

> **Note** The paging file is also used for debugging purposes when a STOP error occurs on the system. If the paging file on the system drive is smaller than the minimum amount required to write the debugging information to the paging file, this feature will be disabled. If you want to use debugging, the minimum size should be set the same as the amount of RAM on the system. For example, a system with 128 MB of RAM would need a page file of 128 MB on the system drive.

5. Repeat steps 3 and 4 for each volume you want to configure.
6. Click OK, and if prompted to overwrite an existing pagefile.sys file, click Yes.
7. Close the System utility and choose Yes to restart the system when prompted.

Setting Registry Size

Windows NT allows you to control the maximum amount of memory and disk space used by the registry. Setting a size limit on the registry doesn't allocate space or guarantee that space is available if needed. Instead, space is used only as required up to the maximum allowable value. You set a limit on the registry by following these steps:

1. Log on to the system using an account with administrator privileges.
2. Start the System utility by double-clicking on the System icon in the Control Panel, then click on the Performance tab.
3. Choose Change in the Virtual Memory area. In the Virtual Memory dialog box enter a new maximum registry size using the Maximum Registry Size field.

Configuring System and User Environment Variables

System and user environment variables are configured via the System utility's Environment tab shown in Figure 2-12. To access the Environment tab, start the System utility by double-clicking on the System icon in the Control Panel, then click on the Environment tab.

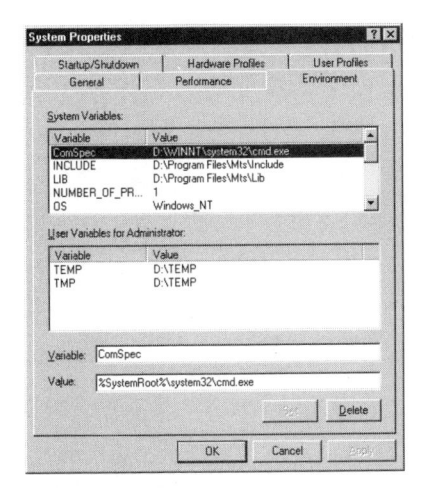

Chapter 2 Managing Windows NT Workstations and Servers | 27

Figure 2-12. *The Environment tab lets you configure system and user environment variables.*

Creating an environment variable   You can create environment variables by doing the following:

1. Select an item in the System Variables or User Variables list box.
2. Enter the variable name in the Variable field and then enter the variable value in the Value field.
3. Choose Set.

Editing an environment variable   You can edit an existing environment variable by doing the following:

1. Select the variable in the System Variables or User Variables list box.
2. Enter a new value in the Value field.
3. Choose Set.

Deleting an environment variable   You can delete an environment variable by selecting the variable and then choosing Delete.

Note When you create or modify *system environment* variables, the changes take effect when you restart the computer. When you create or modify *user environment* variables, the changes take effect the next time the user logs on to the system.

Configuring System Startup and Recovery

System startup and recovery properties are configured via the System utility's Startup/Shutdown tab shown in Figure 2-13, on the following page. To access the Startup/Shutdown tab, start the System utility by double-clicking on the System icon in the Control Panel. Then click on the Startup/Shutdown tab.

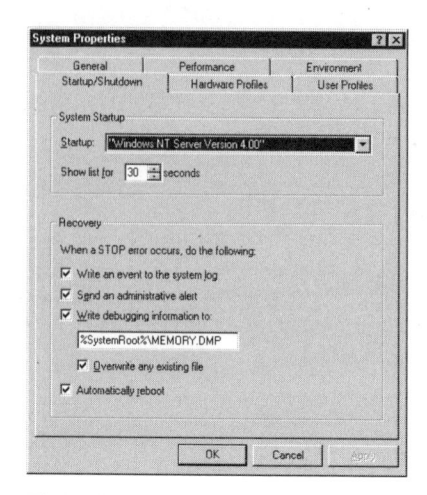

Figure 2-13. *The Startup/Shutdown tab lets you configure system startup and recovery procedures.*

Setting Startup Options
The System Startup area of the System utility's Startup/Shutdown tab controls system startup. To set the default operating system, select one of the operating systems listed in the Startup field. These options are obtained from the operating system section of the system's BOOT.INI file.

At startup, Windows NT displays the startup configuration menu for 30 seconds by default. You can change this value by using the Show List For field. Generally, on most systems you will want to use a value of 3–5 seconds. This is long enough to be able to make a selection, yet short enough to expedite the system startup process.

Setting Recovery Options
Recovery options allow administrators to control precisely what happens when the system encounters a fatal system error (also known as a STOP error). You can set these options via the System utility's Startup/Shutdown tab. The available options include:

- **Write an event to the system log**   Logs the error in the system log, which allows administrators to review the error later using the Event Viewer.

- **Send an administrative alert**   Sends an alert to the recipients specified in the Alert dialog box. For more information, see the section of this chapter titled "Setting Up Alerts."

- **Write debugging information to**   Instructs the system to write debugging information to a dump file, which can be used to diagnose the problem. If you set this option, you must specify a file name.

- **Overwrite any existing file**   Check this option to ensure that any existing dump files are overwritten if a new stop error occurs. Generally, it's a good idea to select this option, especially if you have limited drive space.

- **Automatically reboot** Check this option to have the system attempt to reboot when a fatal system error occurs.

Best Practice The dump file can only be created if the system is properly configured. The system drive must have a sufficiently large memory paging file (as set for virtual memory via the Performance tab), and the drive where the dump file is written must have free space of equal size. For example, my server has 128 MB of RAM and requires a paging file on the system drive of the same size—128 MB. Since the same drive is used for the dump file, the drive must have at least 256 MB of free space to create the debugging information correctly (that's 128 MB for the paging file and 128 MB for the dump file).

Note Configuring automatic reboots isn't always a good thing. Sometimes you may want the system to halt rather than reboot, which should ensure that the system gets proper attention. Otherwise, you can only know that the system rebooted when you view the System logs or if you happen to be in front of the system's monitor when it reboots.

Configuring Hardware Profiles

Windows NT workstations and servers can use multiple hardware profiles. Hardware profiles are most useful for mobile computers, such as laptops. Using hardware profiles, you can configure one profile for when the computer is connected to the network (called *docked*) and one profile for when the computer is mobile (called *undocked*).

Configuring the Way Hardware Profiles Are Used

Hardware profiles are configured via the System utility's Hardware Profiles tab shown in Figure 2-14. As with systems with multiple operating

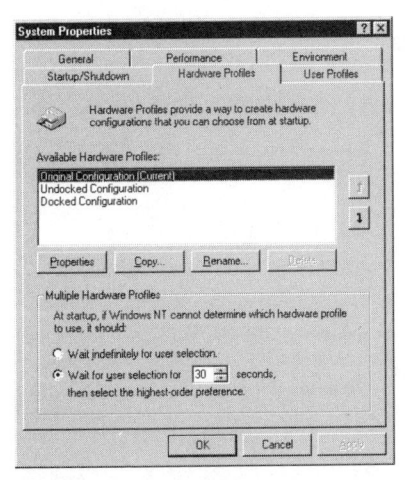

Figure 2-14. *Multiple hardware profiles can be configured for any Windows NT system.*

systems, Windows NT allows you to configure the way hardware profiles are used:

- Set a default profile by changing the profile's position in the Available Hardware Profiles list. The top profile is the default profile.
- Determine how long the system displays the startup hardware profile menu by setting a value using the Wait For User Selection For field. The default value is 30 seconds.
- Have the system wait indefinitely for user input by selecting Wait Indefinitely For User Selection.

Configuring for Docked and Undocked Profiles

To configure a computer for docked and undocked profiles, follow these steps:

1. Select Original Profile in the Available Hardware Profiles list, then click on Copy.
2. In the Copy Profile dialog box, enter a name for the Docked profile in the To field.
3. Select the new profile, then click on the Properties button.
4. Check the This Is A Portable Computer check box, then choose The Computer Is Docked.
5. Click on the Network tab and make sure the Network-disabled hardware profile check box is not selected. Alternately, you can enable and disable services for the profile via the HW Profiles button of the Service utility.

> **Note** You can enable or disable services in the Service utility as follows: Select the service and then click HW Profiles. Next, choose the profile you want to work with, then click Enable or Disable as appropriate.

6. Click OK.
7. Select Original Profile in the Available Hardware Profiles list, then click on Copy.
8. In the Copy Profile dialog box, enter a name for the Undocked profile in the To field.
9. Select the new profile, then click on the Properties button.
10. Check the This Is A Portable Computer check box, then choose The Computer Is Undocked.
11. Click on the Network tab and select the Network-disabled Hardware Profile check box. Alternately, you can enable and disable services for the profile via the HW Profiles button of the Service utility.
12. Click OK.

13. Now set the default hardware profile as appropriate for the computer's current state as either docked or undocked.
14. You're done. Click OK.

When the system is booted, the hardware profiles now are displayed and the user can select the appropriate profile.

Configuring User Profiles

User profiles are configured via the System utility's User Profiles tab. The various types of user profiles are discussed in the section of Chapter 5 titled "Local, Roaming, and Mandatory Profiles." Managing existing user profiles in the System utility is covered in the section of Chapter 6 titled "Managing User Profiles."

Managing Replication

Windows NT Directory Replication Service is used to automatically copy files between systems in a Windows NT domain. You configure this service via the Server Manager by specifying export directories and import directories for computers in the domain. Export directories are used as the originator for file copies and import directories are the destination to which files are copied.

The service is primarily designed to replicate logon scripts on the primary domain controller to backup domain controllers. Because of this, the export directory is set by default to *%SystemRoot%*\System32\Repl\Export and the import directory is set by default to *%SystemRoot%*\System32\Repl\Import. Any subdirectories of Export can be imported to other systems. For example, if Export contained Scripts and Samples subdirectories, these could be made available to other systems.

As you'll see when you work with directory replication, one of the major shortcomings is that you can only export and import a single directory tree structure.

Setting up directory replication is a four-step process:

1. Create replication accounts.
2. Configure the Directory Replicator service.
3. Set up the Export server.
4. Set up the Import workstations or servers, or both.

Creating Replication Accounts

Before you can enable replication, you need to create a domain user account in User Manager for Domains with the following properties:

- Select Password Never Expires.
- Allow all logon hours.

- Make the user a member of the domain Backup Operators group.

This account is known as the replication user account. You will need to refer to this account when you set up the replication service.

> **Note** Repeat this process if you are working with multiple domains. For complete details on working with User Manager for Domains, see Chapter 5.

Configuring the Directory Replicator Service

On each computer that will use replication, use Server Manager to configure the Directory Replicator service to start up automatically and to log on using the replication user account. You can configure the service by following these steps:

1. Select the computer you want to work with in Server Manager, then choose Services from the Computer menu.
2. In the Services utility, double-click on the entry for Directory Replicator. This opens the dialog box shown in Figure 2-15.
3. In the Startup Type area, select the Automatic radio button.
4. In the Log On As area, select the This Account radio button. Then enter the replication account name or use the associated button to select the account.
5. Enter the password for the account, then confirm the password by entering it again.
6. Click OK.
7. Repeat as necessary for other computers that will use replication.

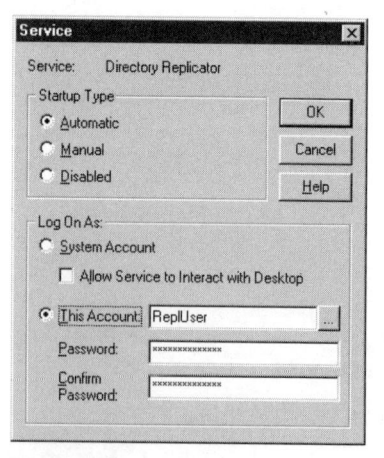

Figure 2-15. *Configure the Directory Replicator service to use the replicator user account.*

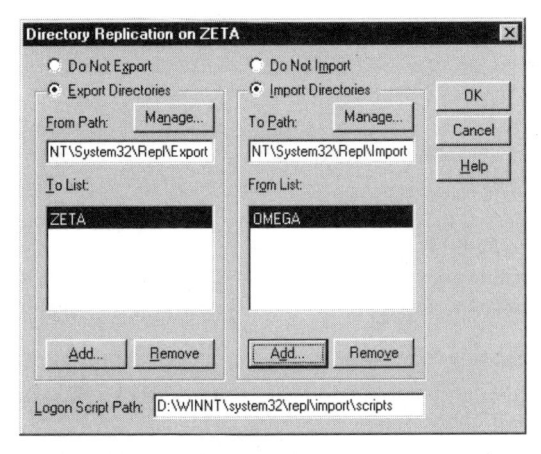

Figure 2-16. *With this dialog box you can create and manage directory replication on Windows NT servers.*

Setting Up the Export Server

Only Windows NT servers can export directories. Select the server that will export directories in Server Manager, then open its Properties dialog box. You can now configure the server to export directories as follows:

1. In the Properties dialog box, click on the Replication button. This opens the dialog box shown in Figure 2-16.
2. Select the Export Directories radio button, then enter the path you want to export in the From Path field. The default path is *%SystemRoot%\ System32\Repl\Export*.
3. The To List on the left side of the dialog box lists import destinations. You must specify at least one computer or domain in this list. Click on the Add button to display the Select Domain dialog box. You can now select a domain or enter a computer name. Computer names must be preceded by the double backslash, such as \\ZETA.
4. When you are finished adding the import destination, click OK. Add additional import destinations as necessary.
5. Choose OK to complete the configuration of the export server.

Setting Up Import Computers

Both Windows NT servers and workstations can import directories. Select the computer that will import directories in Server Manager, then open its Properties dialog box. You can now configure the computers to import directories as follows:

1. In the Properties dialog box, click on the Replication button. This opens the dialog box shown in Figure 2-16. Windows NT workstations

can only import directories. They cannot export directories. Because of this, if you are replicating to a Windows NT workstation the dialog box is different, as shown in Figure 2-17.

2. Select the Import Directories radio button, then enter the path you want to import in the From Path field. The default path is *%SystemRoot%\System32\Repl\Import*.

3. The From List on the right side of the dialog box lists export destinations (this applies to Windows NT Server only). You must specify at least one computer or domain in this list. Click on the Add button to display the Select Domain dialog box. You can now select a domain or enter a computer name. Computer names must be preceded by a double backslash, such as \\ZETA.

4. When you are finished adding the export destination, click OK. Add additional export destinations as necessary.

5. Choose OK to complete the configuration of the import server.

6. The Directory Replicator service should be started automatically on the Import and Export computers. Once the export directory is stabilized, the import directory should contain an exact mirror of the export directory.

Once you set up replication, you can control replication by starting and stopping the Directory Replicator service via the Services Control Panel utility. To replicate additional files, place them in subdirectories of the export path. To manage the way in which directories are replicated, use the Manage buttons found in the Directory Replication dialog box.

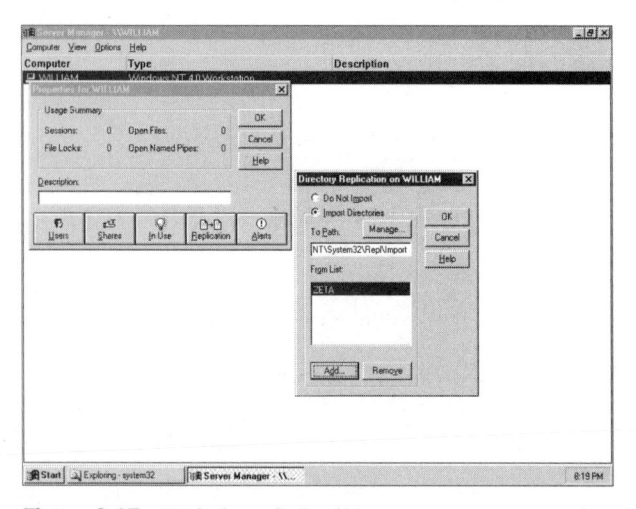

Figure 2-17. *With these dialog boxes you can create and manage directory replication on Windows NT workstations.*

Chapter 3
Monitoring Windows NT Processes, Services, and Security

As an administrator, it's your job to keep an eye on the network systems. Over time, the status of system resources and usage can change dramatically. Services may stop running. File systems may run out of space. Applications may throw exceptions, which in turn can cause system problems. Unauthorized users may try to break into the system. The techniques discussed in this chapter will help you find and resolve these and other system problems.

Managing Applications, Processes, and Performance

Anytime you start an application or enter a command on the command line, Microsoft Windows NT 4.0 starts one or more processes to handle the related program. Generally, processes that are started by the user in this manner are called *interactive* processes. That is, the processes are started *interactively* via the keyboard or mouse. If the application or program is active and selected, the related interactive process has control over the keyboard and mouse until you switch control by selecting a different program or by terminating the program. When a process has control, it is said to be running *in the foreground*.

Processes can also run *in the background*. With processes started by users, this means that programs that aren't currently active can continue to operate—only they generally aren't given the same priority as the current active process. Background processes can also be configured to run independently of the user login session; such processes are usually started by the operating system. An example of this type of background process is a batch file started with an At command. The At command tells the system to run the file at a specified time and (if permissions are configured correctly) the At command can do so regardless of whether a user is logged on to the system.

Task Manager

The key tool you'll use to manage system processes and applications is Task Manager. You can access Task Manager using any of the following techniques:

- Press Ctrl+Shift+Esc
- Press Ctrl+Alt+Del, and then select the Task Manager button
- Enter **taskmgr** into the Run utility or a command prompt
- Right-click on the taskbar and select Task Manager from the pop-up menu

Techniques you'll use to work with the Task Manager are covered in the sections that follow.

Administering Applications

Task Manager's Applications tab is shown in Figure 3-1. This tab shows the status of the programs that are currently running on the system. You can use the buttons on the bottom of this tab as follows:

- Stop an application by selecting the application and then clicking End Task.
- Switch to an application and make it active by selecting the application and then clicking Switch To.

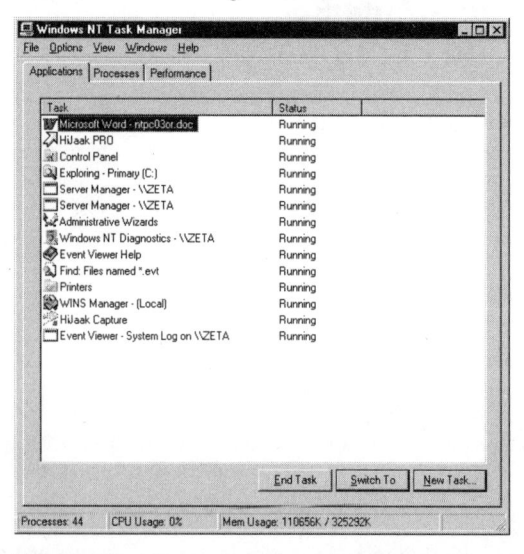

Figure 3-1. *The Applications tab of the Windows NT Task Manager reveals the status of programs currently running on the system.*

- Start a new program by selecting New Task and then enter a command to run the application. New Task functions like the Start menu's Run utility.

Tip Application status tells you if the application is running normally or if the application has gone off into the ozone. A status of Not Responding is an indicator that an application may be frozen and you may want to end its related task. However, some applications may not respond to the operating system during certain process-intensive tasks. Because of this, you should be certain the application is really frozen before you end its related task.

Right-Clicking on a Listing

Right-clicking on an application's listing displays a pop-up menu that allows you to

- Switch to the application and make it active
- Bring the application to the front of the display
- Minimize and maximize the application
- Tile or end the application
- Go to the related process in the Processes tab

Note Go To Process is very helpful when you are trying to find the primary process for a particular application. Selecting this option highlights the related process in the Processes tab.

Administering Processes

Task Manager's Processes tab is shown in Figure 3-2, on the following page. This tab provides detailed information on running processes. As you examine processes, note that although applications have a main process, a single application may start multiple processes. Generally, these processes are dependent on the main application process and are normally stopped when you terminate the main application process or use End Task. Because of this, you will usually want to terminate the main application process or the application itself rather than dependent processes.

The fields of the Processes tab provide lots of information about running processes. You can use this information to determine which processes are hogging system resources such as CPU time and memory. Additional uses for the tab include

- Stopping a process by selecting it and then choosing End Process
- Setting a process's priority by right-clicking on it and then choosing Set Priority from the pop-up menu

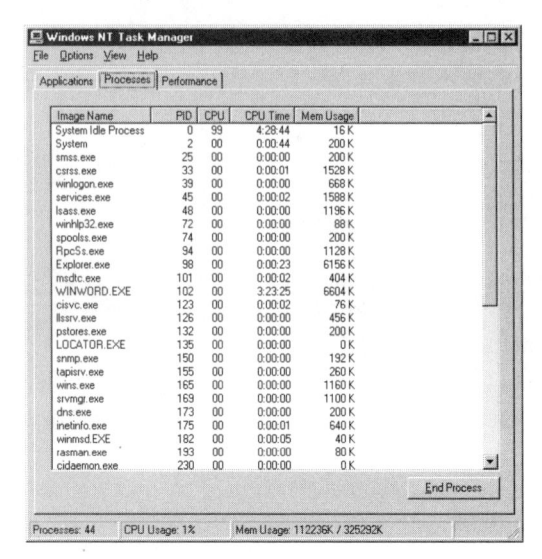

Figure 3-2. *The Processes tab provides detailed information on running processes.*

> **Note** If you examine processes running in Task Manager, you'll note a process called System Idle Process. You can't set the priority of this process. Unlike other processes that track resource usage, System Idle Process tracks the amount of system resources that aren't used. Thus, a 99 in the CPU column for the process means 99% of the system resources currently aren't being used.

Priority determines how much of the system resources are allocated to a process. Most processes have a normal priority by default. To increase priority, set the priority to high. To decrease priority, set the priority to low. The highest priority is given to real-time processes.

Viewing System Performance

Task Manager's Performance tab provides an overview of CPU and memory usage. As shown in Figure 3-3, the tab displays graphs as well as statistics. This information provides a quick check on system resource usage. For more detailed information, use Performance Monitor.

Graphs on the Performance Tab

The graphs on the Performance tab provide the following information:

- **CPU Usage**   The percentage of processor resources being used
- **CPU Usage History**   A history graph on CPU usage plotted over time
- **Mem Usage**   The amount of memory currently being used on the system
- **Memory Usage History**   A history graph on memory usage plotted over time

Chapter 3 Monitoring Windows NT Processes, Services, and Security | 39

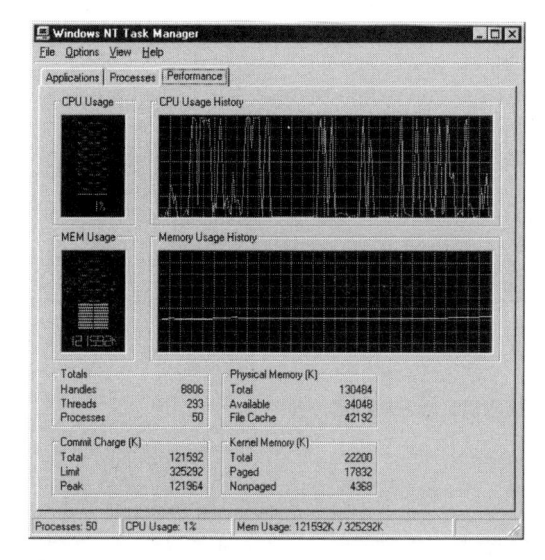

Figure 3-3. *The Performance tab provides a quick check on system resource usage.*

Tip To view a close-up of the CPU graphs, double-click within the Performance tab. Double-clicking again returns you to normal viewing mode.

Customizing and Updating the Graph Display

To customize or update the graph display, use the following options on the View menu:

- **Update Speed** Allows you to change the speed of graph updating as well as to pause the graph.
- **CPU History** On multiprocessor systems, allows you to specify how CPU graphs are displayed.
- **Show Kernel Times** Allows you to display the amount of CPU time used by the operating system kernel.

Beneath the graphs you'll find several lists of statistics. These statistics provide the following information:

- **Commit Charge** Provides information on the total memory used by the operating system. *Total* lists all physical and virtual memory currently in use. *Limit* lists the total physical and virtual memory available. *Peak* lists the maximum memory used by the system since bootup.
- **Kernel Memory** Provides information on the memory used by the operating system kernel. Critical portions of kernel memory must operate in RAM and cannot be paged to virtual memory. This type of kernel memory is listed as *Nonpaged*. The rest of kernel memory can be paged to virtual memory and is listed as *Paged*. The total amount of memory used by the kernel is listed under *Total*.

- **Physical Memory** Provides information on the total RAM on the system. *Total* shows the amount of physical RAM. *Available* shows the RAM not currently being used and available for use. *File Cache* shows the amount of memory used for file caching.
- **Totals** Provides information on CPU usage. *Handles* shows the number of I/O handles in use. *Threads* shows the number of threads in use. *Processes* shows the number of processes in use.

> **Note** For detailed information on paged memory usage, refer to the Memory tab of Windows NT Diagnostics. This utility is discussed in the "Diagnosing System Problems" section of this chapter.

Managing System Services

Services provide key functions to Windows NT workstations and servers. To manage system services, you'll use the Services utility, which is started as follows:

- In the Control Panel: by double-clicking on the Services icon. This is used to manage services on the local system.
- From Server Manager: by selecting the computer you want to work with and then choosing Services from the Computers menu. This is used to manage services on remote systems.

Figure 3-4 shows the Services dialog box. The key fields of this dialog box are used as follows:

- **Service** The name of the service. Only services installed on the system are listed here. Double-click on an entry to configure its startup options. If a service you need isn't listed, you can install it via the Services tab of the Network utility.
- **Status** The status of the service as started, paused, or stopped. (Stopped is indicated by a blank entry.)
- **Startup** The startup setting for the service. Automatic services are started at bootup. Manual services are started by users or other services. Disabled services are turned off and cannot be started.

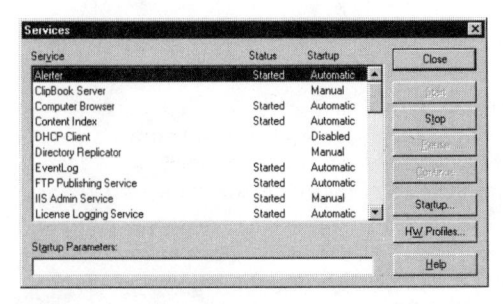

Figure 3-4. *Use Services to manage services on Windows NT workstations and servers.*

Note Services can be disabled by the operating system and by users. Generally, Windows NT disables services if there is a possible conflict with another service.

Common Windows NT Services

Table 3-1 shows the services that are installed by default on Windows NT systems. Keep in mind that the type and number of services running on a Windows NT system depend on its configuration. For a list of additional services you can install, as well as for installation instructions, see the section of Chapter 12 titled "Configuring Additional TCP/IP Services."

Table 3-1. Default Services That May Be Installed on Windows NT Systems

Service Name	Description
Alerter	Sends administrative alert messages to designated recipients. Depends on the messenger service. For more information, see the section of Chapter 2 titled "Setting Up Alerts."
ClipBook Server	Enables remote viewers to see local pages with ClipBook Viewer.
Computer Browser	Enables computer browsing; maintains a list of resources used for network browsing.
Directory Replicator	Enables directory and file replication. For details, see the section of Chapter 2 titled "Managing Replication."
EventLog	Used to log system, application, and security events.
License Logging Service	Used to track license usage and compliance.
Messenger	Relays messages sent by the Alerter service and Send Message from Server Manager.
Net Logon	Authenticates user logons. On domain controllers, the service also is used to synchronize the domain user database.
Network DDE	Supports DDE (dynamic data exchange) between applications.
Network DDE DSDM	DSDM (data share database manager) manages dynamic data exchanges on the network.
NT LM Security port Provider	Supports security services for RPC applications that don't use name pipes.
Plug and Play	Supports automatic configuration updates when you add or remove components from a system.
Remote Procedure Call (RPC) Locator	Locates RPC clients and servers on the network.
Remote Procedure Call (RPC) Service	The RPC name service for distributed applications.
Schedule	Enables job scheduling with the At service.
Server	Provides services for Windows NT servers including file sharing, printer spooling, and named pipes.
Spooler	Enables printer spooling.
UPS	Enables UPS (uninterruptible power supply) support.
Workstation	Provides services for Windows NT workstations.

Starting, Stopping, and Pausing Services

As an administrator, you'll often have to start, stop, or pause Windows NT services. To start, stop, or pause, follow these steps:

1. In Server Manager, select the computer you want to work with.
2. Select Services from the Computer menu. This opens the Services utility for the selected computer.
3. Choose the Service you want to manipulate, and then select Start, Stop, or Pause as appropriate. After you pause a service, select the service and click Continue to resume normal operation.

> **Note** When services that are set to start automatically fail: the status is listed as blank, and you'll usually receive notification in a pop-up dialog box. Service failures can also be logged to the system's event logs.

Configuring Service Startup

Windows NT services can be set to start manually or automatically. They can also be turned off permanently by disabling them. You configure service startup as follows:

1. In Server Manager, select the computer you want to work with.
2. Select Services from the Computer menu. This opens the Services utility for the selected computer.
3. Choose Startup to display a dialog box similar to the one shown in Figure 3-5. In this example, the Telephony Service was selected.
4. Select the service startup option using the Startup Type radio button. Use Automatic to start services at bootup. Use Manual to allow the services to be started manually. Use Disabled to turn off the service.
5. Click OK.

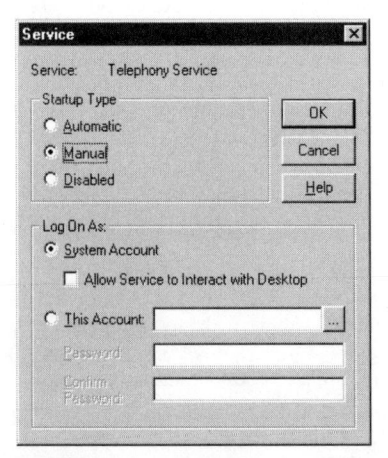

Figure 3-5. *This dialog box is used to configure service startup options.*

Configuring Service Logon

Key Windows NT services can be configured to log on as a system account or as a specific user. To do this, follow these steps:

1. In Server Manager, select the computer you want to work with.
2. Select Services from the Computer menu. This opens the Services utility for the selected computer.
3. Temporarily stop the service by clicking Stop.
4. Choose Startup to display the dialog box shown previously in Figure 3-5.
5. Select System Account if the service should log on using the system account (which is the default for most services).
6. Select This Account if the service should log on using a specific user account. Be sure to enter an account name and password in the fields provided. Use the ellipsis button to search for a user account if necessary.
7. Click OK.
8. Restart the service by clicking Start.

Auditing System Resources

Auditing is the best way to track what is happening on your Windows NT systems. You can use auditing to collect information related to resource usage, such as file access, system logon, and system configuration changes. Anytime an action occurs that you've configured for auditing, the action is written to the system's security log, where it is stored for your review. The security log is accessible from Event Viewer.

Note For most auditing changes, you'll need to be logged on using an account that is a member of the Administrators group.

Setting Auditing Policies for System Security

Auditing policies for system security are essential to ensure the security and integrity of your systems. Just about every computer system on the network should be configured with some type of security logging. You can configure system security settings as follows:

- For the entire domain (domain-wide auditing):

    When you configure domain-wide auditing, you set auditing policies for the entire domain. Afterward, all Windows NT domain controllers in the domain will use these auditing policies.

- For an individual workstation or server (system-level auditing):

    When you configure system-level auditing policies, you set auditing policies on an individual Windows NT workstation or server. Afterward, these policies are only used on that system.

To set security auditing policies, follow these steps:

1. Start User Manager for Domains.
2. To set domain-wide auditing policies, choose the domain you want to work with, using the Select Domain option of the User menu.
3. To set system-level auditing policies, choose the individual computer you want to work with, using the Select Domain option of the User menu. Be sure to enter the double backslashes before the computer name, such as \\ZETA.
4. Select Audit from the Policies menu to display the dialog box shown in Figure 3-6.
5. Choose Audit These Events, then select the Success or Failure check boxes, or both, for each of the events you want to audit. Success logs successful events, such as successful logon attempts. Failure logs failed events, such as failed logon attempts. The events you can audit are

   - **Logon and Logoff** Tracks events related to user logon, logoff, and remote connections to network systems.
   - **File and Object Access** Tracks system resource usage for files, directories, shares, and system-level objects.
   - **Use of User Rights** Tracks the use of user rights, such as the right to back up files and directories. User rights are configured with the User Rights option on the User menu.

     Note Use of User Rights does not track system access-related events, such as the use of the right to log on interactively or the right to access the computer from the network. These events are tracked with the Logon and Logoff auditing.

   - **User and Group Management** Tracks account management via User Manager or User Manager For Domains. Events are generated anytime user or group accounts are created, modified, or deleted.

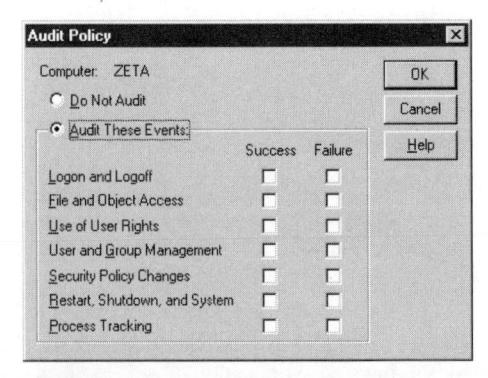

Figure 3-6. *Set domain-wide and system-level auditing policies using the Audit Policy dialog box.*

- **Security Policy Changes** Tracks changes to user rights, auditing, and trust relationships.
- **Restart, Shutdown, and System** Tracks system startup, shutdown, and restart as well as actions that affect system security or the security log.
- **Process Tracking** Tracks system processes and the resources they use.

6. Click OK when you are finished.

Auditing for Directory and File Security

If you configure a domain or system to audit file and object access, you can set the level of auditing for individual directories and files as well. This allows you to precisely control how directory and file usage is tracked. Auditing of this type is only available on NTFS volumes.

To configure directory and file auditing, follow these steps:

1. In Windows NT Explorer, right-click on the directory or file to be audited.
2. Select Properties from the pop-up menu.
3. Choose the Security tab, then click Auditing. For directories, this opens the dialog box shown in Figure 3-7. A similar dialog box is used for files.
4. If you want to audit the same events for all subdirectories of the current directory, select Replace Auditing On Subdirectories.
5. If files in these directories should have the same auditing, select Replace Auditing On Existing Files.
6. Use the Name list box to select the users whose actions you want to audit. To add specific users, click on the Add button, then select the user names to add. To remove a user, select the user in the Name list box, and then click Remove.

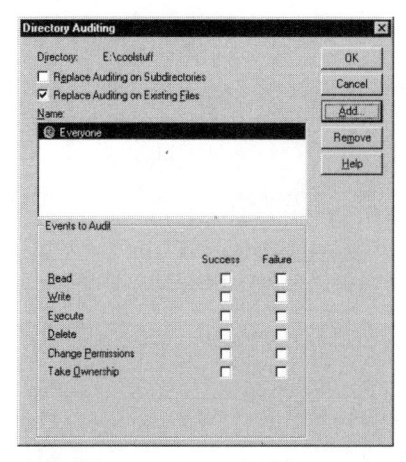

Figure 3-7. *Set directory and file auditing policies using the Directory Auditing dialog box.*

> **Note** If you want to audit actions for all users, use the special group Everyone. Otherwise, select the specific user groups and/or users you want to audit.

7. Select the Success or Failure check boxes, or both, for each of the events you want to audit. Success logs successful events, such as successful file reads. Failure logs failed events, such as failed file deletions.
8. Choose OK when you're finished.

The actions that are audited depend on whether you are working with files or directories.

Actions Audited with Directory Events
The following actions are audited with directory events:

- **Read**   Audits display of filenames, attributes, permissions, and owner.
- **Write**   Audits changes to attributes, display of permissions and owner, and creation of subdirectories and files.
- **Execute**   Audits changes to subdirectories and display of attributes, permissions, and owner.
- **Delete**   Audits deletion of a directory.
- **Change Permissions**   Audits changes to directory permissions.
- **Take Ownership**   Audits changes to directory ownership.

Actions Audited with File Events
The following actions are audited with file events:

- **Read**   Audits display of file data, attributes, permissions, and owner.
- **Write**   Audits changes to file data or attributes and display of permissions and owner.
- **Execute**   Audits running programs and display of attributes, permissions, and owner.
- **Delete**   Audits deletion of the file.
- **Change Permissions**   Audits changes to file permissions.
- **Take Ownership**   Audits changes to file ownership.

Auditing for Printer Security

With printer auditing, you can track events related to printer usage and printer administration. Printer auditing is only enabled if you configure a domain or system to audit file and object access.

You can configure printer auditing by completing the following steps:

1. In Control Panel, double-click on the Printers folder. This opens the Printers folder.

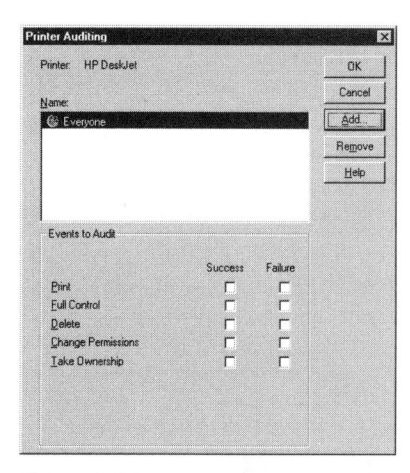

Figure 3-8. *Set printer auditing policies using the Printer Auditing dialog box.*

2. Right-click on the printer you want to audit, and then select Properties from the pop-up menu.
3. Choose the Security tab, then click Auditing. This opens the dialog box shown in Figure 3-8.
4. Use the Name list box to select the users whose actions you want to audit. To add specific users, click on the Add button, then select the user names to add. To remove a user, select the user in the Name list box, then click Remove.

Note To audit actions for all users, use the special group Everyone. Otherwise, select the specific user groups and/or users you want to audit.

5. Select the Success or Failure check boxes, or both, for each of the events you want to audit. Success logs successful events, such as successful printing. Failure logs failed events, such as failed print jobs.
6. Choose OK when you're finished.

Auditing Printer Events
The printer events that can be audited are

- **Print** Tracks document printing.
- **Full Control** Tracks changes to printer and document settings in Print Manager.
- **Delete** Tracks when a printer is deleted.
- **Change Permissions** Tracks changes to permissions.
- **Take Ownership** Tracks when a user takes ownership of a printer.

Event Logging and Viewing

Event logs provide historical information that can help you track down system and security problems. The event-logging service controls whether events are tracked on Windows NT systems. When this service is started, the following user actions and system resource usage events can be tracked via the system's event logs:

- **Application Log** Records events logged by applications, such as the failure of MS SQL to access a database.
- **Security Log** Records events you've set for auditing in User Manager for Domains.
- **System Log** Records events logged by the operating system or its components, such as the failure of a service to start at bootup.

Accessing and Using the Event Logs

You access the event logs by completing the following steps:

1. Go to Start, select Programs, then Administrative Tools (Common), and then Event Viewer.
2. Choose System, Security, or Application from the Log menu. This opens the related log, as shown in Figure 3-9.

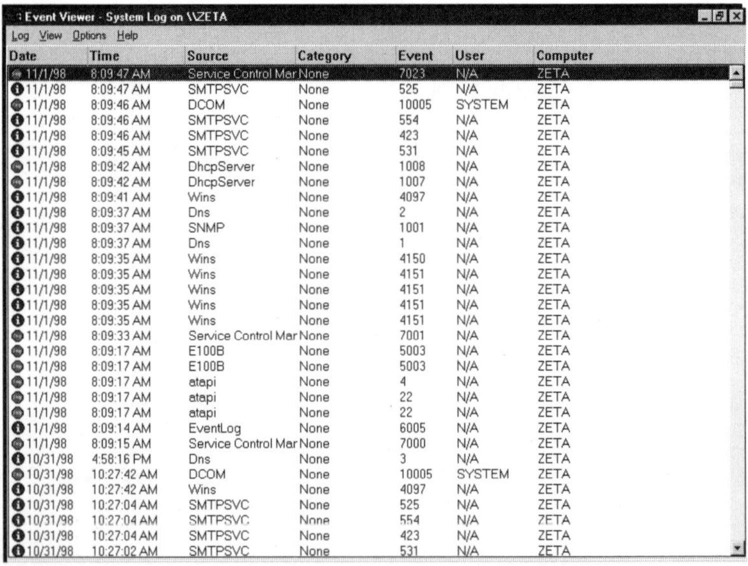

Date	Time	Source	Category	Event	User	Computer
11/1/98	8:09:47 AM	Service Control Mar	None	7023	N/A	ZETA
11/1/98	8:09:47 AM	SMTPSVC	None	525	N/A	ZETA
11/1/98	8:09:46 AM	DCOM	None	10005	SYSTEM	ZETA
11/1/98	8:09:46 AM	SMTPSVC	None	554	N/A	ZETA
11/1/98	8:09:46 AM	SMTPSVC	None	423	N/A	ZETA
11/1/98	8:09:45 AM	SMTPSVC	None	531	N/A	ZETA
11/1/98	8:09:42 AM	DhcpServer	None	1008	N/A	ZETA
11/1/98	8:09:42 AM	DhcpServer	None	1007	N/A	ZETA
11/1/98	8:09:41 AM	Wins	None	4097	N/A	ZETA
11/1/98	8:09:37 AM	Dns	None	2	N/A	ZETA
11/1/98	8:09:37 AM	SNMP	None	1001	N/A	ZETA
11/1/98	8:09:37 AM	Dns	None	1	N/A	ZETA
11/1/98	8:09:35 AM	Wins	None	4150	N/A	ZETA
11/1/98	8:09:35 AM	Wins	None	4151	N/A	ZETA
11/1/98	8:09:35 AM	Wins	None	4151	N/A	ZETA
11/1/98	8:09:35 AM	Wins	None	4151	N/A	ZETA
11/1/98	8:09:35 AM	Wins	None	4151	N/A	ZETA
11/1/98	8:09:33 AM	Service Control Mar	None	7001	N/A	ZETA
11/1/98	8:09:17 AM	E100B	None	5003	N/A	ZETA
11/1/98	8:09:17 AM	E100B	None	5003	N/A	ZETA
11/1/98	8:09:17 AM	atapi	None	4	N/A	ZETA
11/1/98	8:09:17 AM	atapi	None	22	N/A	ZETA
11/1/98	8:09:17 AM	atapi	None	22	N/A	ZETA
11/1/98	8:09:14 AM	EventLog	None	6005	N/A	ZETA
11/1/98	8:09:15 AM	Service Control Mar	None	7000	N/A	ZETA
10/31/98	4:58:16 PM	Dns	None	3	N/A	ZETA
10/31/98	10:27:42 AM	DCOM	None	10005	SYSTEM	ZETA
10/31/98	10:27:42 AM	Wins	None	4097	N/A	ZETA
10/31/98	10:27:04 AM	SMTPSVC	None	525	N/A	ZETA
10/31/98	10:27:04 AM	SMTPSVC	None	554	N/A	ZETA
10/31/98	10:27:04 AM	SMTPSVC	None	423	N/A	ZETA
10/31/98	10:27:02 AM	SMTPSVC	None	531	N/A	ZETA

Figure 3-9. *Event Viewer displays events for the selected log.*

Chapter 3 Monitoring Windows NT Processes, Services, and Security

Note Windows NT Service Pack 4 updates the Event Log service and requires that the Security privilege be enabled in order to view and manage the security event log. Under SP4, any user who needs access to the security logs must be granted the privilege to manage the security log. This change also effects members of the Administrators group.

Entries in the main window of Event Viewer provide a quick overview of when, where, and how an event occurred. To obtain detailed information on an event, double-click on its entry. A summary icon that tells you the event type precedes the date and time of the event. Event types include

- **Information** An informational event which is generally related to a successful action.
- **Success Audit** An event related to the successful execution of an action.
- **Failure Audit** An event related to the failed execution of an action.
- **Warning** A noncritical error that provides a warning. Details for warnings are often useful in preventing future system problems.
- **Critical Error** A critical error, such as the failure of a service to start.

Note Warnings and critical errors are the two key types of events that you'll want to examine closely. Whenever these types of events occur and you are unsure of the cause, double-click on the entry to view the detailed event description.

In addition to the date, time, and icon, the summary and detailed event entries provide the following information:

- **Source** The application, service, or component that logged the event.
- **Category** The category of the event, which is sometimes used to further describe the related action.
- **Event** An identifier for the specific event.
- **User** The user account that was logged on when the event occurred.
- **Computer** The computer name where the event occurred.
- **Description** In the detailed entries, this provides a text description of the event.
- **Data** In the detailed entries, this provides any data or error code output by the event.

Setting Event Log Options

Log options allow you to control the size of the event logs as well as how logging is handled. By default, event logs are set with a maximum file size of 512 KB, then, when a log reaches this limitation, events older than seven days are overwritten to prevent the log from exceeding the maximum file size.

To set the log options, follow these steps:

1. Start Event Viewer, then select Log Settings from the Log menu. This opens the dialog box shown in Figure 3-10.
2. Choose a log using the Change Settings For . . . Log drop-down list box.
3. Enter a maximum size in the Maximum Log Size field. Make sure that the drive containing the operating system has enough free space for the maximum log size you select. Log files are stored in the *%SystemRoot%*\system32\config directory by default.
4. Select an event log wrapping mode. The options available are
   - **Overwrite Events As Needed**   Events in the log are overwritten when the maximum file size is reached. Generally, this is the best option on a low priority system.
   - **Overwrite Events Older Than . . . Days**   When the maximum file size is reached, events in the log are overwritten only if they are older than the setting you select. If the maximum size is reached and the events cannot be overwritten, the system generates error messages telling you the event log is full.
   - **Do Not Overwrite Events (Clear Log Manually)**   When the maximum file size is reached, the system generates error messages telling you the event log is full.
5. Click OK when you're finished.

Note   On critical systems where security and event logging is very important, you may want to use Overwrite Events Older Than . . . Days or Do Not Overwrite Events (Clear Log Manually). When you use these methods, you may want to periodically archive and clear the log file to prevent the system from generating error messages.

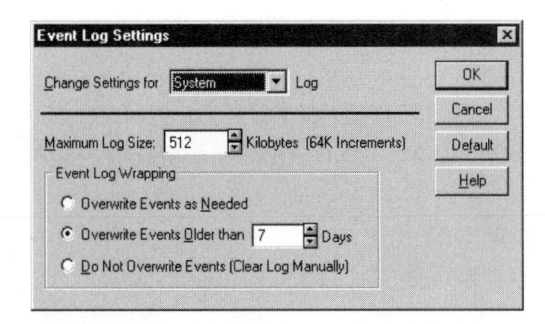

Figure 3-10. *Log settings should be configured according to the level of auditing on the system.*

Clearing the Event Logs

When an event log is full, you need to clear it. To do that, complete the following steps:

1. Start Event Viewer, and then select the log to be cleared from the Log menu.
2. Select Clear All Events from the Log menu.
3. Choose Yes to save the log before clearing it. Choose No to continue without saving the log file.
4. When prompted to confirm that you want to clear the log, click Yes.

Archiving the Event Logs

On key systems such as domain controllers and application servers, you'll want to keep several months worth of logs. However, it usually isn't practical to set the maximum log size to accommodate this. Instead, you should periodically archive the event logs.

Archive Log Formats

Logs can be archived in three formats:

- Event log format for access in Event Viewer
- Text format for access in any text editor or word processor
- Comma-delimited text format for import into spreadsheets or databases

When you save log files to a comma-delimited file, each field in the event entry is separated by a comma. The event entries look like this:

```
1/1/99,8:09:47 AM,Ci,Error,CI Service ,4147,N/A,ZETA,
The IISADMIN service is not available, so virtual roots
cannot be indexed.
1/1/99,8:09:46 AM,JET,Information,General ,9,N/A,ZETA,
((169) ) The database engine stopped.
```

The format for the entries is as follows:

```
Date, Time, Source, Type, Category, Event, User, Computer,
Description.
```

Creating Log Archives

To create a log archive, follow these steps:

1. Start Event Viewer, then select the log to be archived from the Log menu.
2. Select Save As from the Log menu.
3. In the Save As dialog box, select a directory and a log file name.
4. Select a log format using the Save As Type drop-down list box.
5. Choose Save.

> **Note** If you plan to archive logs regularly, you may want to create an archive directory. This way you can easily locate the log archives. You should also name the log file so that you can easily determine the log file type and the period of the archive. For example, if you are archiving the system log file for January 1999, you may want to use the file name System Log Jan. 99.

Viewing Log Archives

Log archives in text format can be viewed in any text editor or word processor. Log archives in the event log format should be viewed in the Event Viewer. You can view log archives in Event Viewer by doing the following:

1. Start Event Viewer, then Open from the Log menu.
2. Use the Open dialog box to select the archive file, then click Open.
3. In the Open File Type dialog box, choose the log file type: System, Security, or Application.
4. Click OK.

Viewing Events on Remote Computers

Event Viewer can access the event logs on any Windows NT system in the domain. To access an event log, do the following:

1. Start Event Viewer using an account that has access to the computers you want to work with.
2. Choose Select Computer from the Log menu.
3. In the Select Computer dialog box, enter the computer name beginning with the double backslashes (\\), such as \\ZETA. Or select a computer name in Select Computer dialog box.
4. Click OK.

When you work with event logs on remote computers, the Open, Save As, and Clear All Events options of the Log menu behave slightly differently. To use these options, you may need access to the local file system on the remote computer.

Diagnosing System Problems

Windows NT Diagnostics (WINMSD.EXE) is a limited-use tool for checking system configuration. Use the information the utility provides to help you diagnose system problems. Figure 3-11 shows the utility's main window.

You work with the utility by doing the following:

- Run the utility by going to Start, selecting Programs, then Administrative Tools (Common), and then Windows NT Diagnostics.
- Select the Windows NT computer you want to work with using the Select Computer option of the File menu.
- Print any of the utility's windows using the Print button.

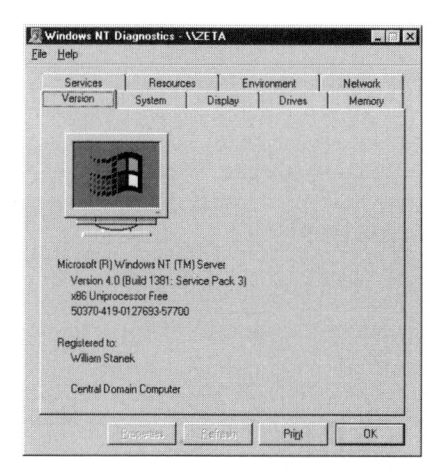

Figure 3-11. *Windows NT Diagnostics provides information on the system's configuration. You can use this information to troubleshoot system problems.*

Rather than detailing each and every tab of the utility, the following sections focus on the tasks you can accomplish with the utility. Note that many of these tasks can be accomplished in other ways. However, to obtain all of the information available in Windows NT Diagnostics, you'd have to use many different tools.

Determining OS Build and Service Pack Version

Most Windows NT systems should have the most recent OS version and service pack installed on them. The Version tab of Windows NT Diagnostics provides information on the OS version including the OS build and service pack version. You'll find additional information on the CPU and the system's registered owner.

Determining BIOS Version and CPU Clock Speed

Many computers are shipped with updateable BIOS. If you need to check the system's current BIOS version before updating it, use the System tab of Windows NT Diagnostics. You can also use this tab to determine if the system has multiple processors. Each processor is listed separately in the Processor(s) list box.

Determining Video Drivers, Adapters, and BIOS Version

Video driver and adapter conflicts are common causes of system problems. Use the Display tab of Windows NT Diagnostics to obtain information on the system's video card, including

- BIOS version
- Current display setting mode
- Type and available memory

- Chip architecture
- Driver version and driver file name(s)

> **Note** Similar information is available in the Display utility. Select the Settings tab, and then click on the Display Type button.

Obtaining Disk Drive Information

The Drives tab of the Windows NT Diagnostics provides a way to quickly obtain information on all of the drives available to the system. You can check the available drive space, the permissible file naming conventions, and more.

Once you access the Drives tab, you examine drive information as follows:

1. Select Drives by type to display a list of available drives by type. You can now double-click on the drive type listings to show listings for individual drives.
2. Select Drives by letter to list available drives by letter.
3. Double-click on the entry for the drive you want to work with. This opens the drive's Properties dialog box.

The Properties dialog box has two tabs. The General tab provides information on the drive's label, sector byte size, cluster size, drive space free, and drive space used. The File System tab provides information on the file system type, the maximum file name size (based on file system type), and flag settings for the file system.

On FAT volumes, the flag settings usually read as follows:

- Case is preserved in filenames
- Unicode characters are allowed in filenames

On NTFS volumes, the flag settings usually read as follows:

- Case is preserved in filenames
- Supports case-sensitive filenames
- Unicode characters are allowed in filenames
- File-based compression is supported
- Security is preserved and enforced

Determining Memory Page File Usage

For optimal system performance, paged memory should be spread across all fixed system drives, and there should be adequate additional paged memory available to handle system tasks. To view paged memory usage, use the Memory tab of Windows NT Diagnostics. Once you access this tab, use the following statistics of the Pagefile Space area:

- **Total** The total amount of pagefile space available
- **Total In Use** The total amount of pagefile space in use

- **Peak Use** The highest amount of pagefile space used by the system since startup
- **Pagefile** A list box showing the usage breakdown and location for each pagefile on the system

Tip If you find that a system is running out of pagefile space, you may want to increase the amount of virtual memory. For details, see the section of Chapter 2 titled "Setting Virtual Memory."

Troubleshooting Service and Device Problems

Settings, flags, and dependencies can help you determine why a service or device isn't running properly. To troubleshoot service problems, follow these steps:

1. Start Windows NT Diagnostics, then click on the Services tab.
2. Click on the Services button to examine system services. Double-click on the service you want to examine.
3. Click on the Devices button to examine system devices (as well as a few system services that depend on devices). Double-click on the device you want to examine.
4. If properties are available for the service or device, a Properties dialog box is displayed. Use this dialog box to examine the service or device.

The General Tab

In the General tab, examine the service settings and flags. The following settings must be configured properly:

- **Pathname** Provides the complete path to the service's executable or DLL.
- **Start type** Provides service startup type: Automatic, Manual, or Disabled.
- **Service Account Name** The account the service runs as. LocalSystem is the default.
- **Service flags** Provide insight into how the service runs and its permissible actions. For example, some services must be able to interact with the desktop; if they can't, they won't run properly. Thus, if this flag isn't available you'll need to reconfigure the service.

The Dependencies Tab

In the Dependencies tab, determine if the service or device is dependent on any other service, file, or system component. Generally, any item listed in this tab must be running in order for the service or device to start and run properly.

Determining IRQ, I/O Port, and DMA Usage

Conflicts with IRQ, I/O ports, and DMA are less common on Windows NT systems, but they do occur. If you need to examine these resources and check for possible conflicts, start Windows NT Diagnostics and then click on the Resources tab. The buttons of this tab are used as follows:

- **IRQ**   Displays IRQ settings, bus, and bus type for installed devices.
- **I/O Port**   Displays I/O port addresses used by installed devices.
- **DMA**   Displays DMA channel, port, bus, and bus type for any DMA-driven device installed on the system.
- **Memory**   Displays memory dedicated to any of the system's installed devices.
- **Devices**   Displays a list of installed devices.

Once you select the type of resource you want to view, you can view properties of individual items. Simply double-click on their entry.

Part II
Windows NT User Administration

In this part, you'll find essential tasks for administering user and group accounts. Chapter 4 provides insight into using system accounts, built-in groups, user rights, built-in capabilities, and implicit groups. Core administration tasks for creating user and group accounts are covered in Chapter 5. A logical follow-up for managing existing user and group accounts is covered in Chapter 6.

Chapter 4
Understanding User and Group Accounts

One of your primary tasks as a Microsoft Windows NT administrator is to manage accounts. Accounts enable individual users to log on to the network and access network resources. The permissions and privileges you assign to accounts determine the actions users can perform, as well as which computer systems and resources they can access.

Although you may be tempted to give users wide access, you need to balance the user's need for job-related resources against your need to protect sensitive resources or privileged information. For example, you wouldn't want everyone in the company to have access to payroll data. Consequently, you would make sure that only those who need it have access to that information.

The Windows NT Security Model

You control access to network resources with the components of the Microsoft Windows NT security model. These components include

- Interactive logon processes
- Local security authority
- Security account manager
- Security reference monitor

Granting and Denying Access

The Windows NT security model components work together to grant or deny access to resources based on the permissions and privileges of user accounts as follows:

- Logon processes restrict access to resources based on user accounts, which have names and passwords.
- Local security authority verifies that the user has authority to access the local system.
- Security account manager validates rights and authorities using its database containing information about users and groups.
- Security resource monitor validates access to files, folders, and other system objects.

Differences Between User and Group Accounts

Windows NT provides accounts for users and groups. User accounts are designed for individuals. Group accounts are designed to ease administration for multiple users. While you can log on to user accounts, you cannot log on to a group account.

User Accounts

User accounts are identified with user names and passwords. User names are text labels for accounts. Passwords are authentication strings for accounts. Although Windows NT displays user names to describe privileges and permissions, the key identifiers for accounts are SIDs (security identifiers). SIDs are unique identifiers that are generated when accounts are created. Windows NT uses SIDs to track accounts independently from user names.

SIDs serve many purposes, the most important of which are to allow you to easily change user names and to allow you to delete accounts without worrying that someone may gain access to resources simply by re-creating an account.

When you change a user name, you tell Windows NT to map a particular SID to a new name. When you delete an account, you tell Windows NT that a particular SID is no longer valid. Afterward, even if you create an account with the same user name, the new account will not have the same privileges and permissions as the previous one. That's because the new account will have a new SID.

Group Accounts

In addition to user accounts, Windows NT provides group accounts. You use group accounts to grant permissions to similar types of users and to simplify account administration. If a user is a member of a group that can access a resource, that particular user can access the resource. Thus, you can give a user access to various work-related resources just by making the user a member of the correct group. Note that while you can log on to a computer with a user account, you cannot log on to a computer with a group account.

> **Real World** Employees in a marketing department probably need access to all marketing-related resources. Instead of granting access to these resources individually, you could make users members of a Marketing group so the users automatically obtain the group's privileges. Later, if a user moves to a different department, you simply remove the user from the group and all access permissions are revoked. Compared to having to revoke access for each individual resource, this technique is pretty easy—so you'll want to use group accounts whenever possible.

Windows NT also uses unique security identifiers to track group accounts. This means that you cannot delete a group account, re-create it, and expect all the permissions and privileges to remain the same. The new group will have a new security identifier, and all the permissions and privileges of the old group will be lost.

Tools for Working with User and Group Accounts

Windows NT provides several tools for working with user and group accounts:

- Add User Accounts Wizard
- User Manager
- User Manager for Domains
- A group of command-line tools

The administration tools you will use the most are User Manager and User Manager for Domains. User Manager (MUSRMGR.EXE) is a Windows NT Workstation tool for managing the resources of a single workstation. User Manager for Domains (USRMGR.EXE) is a Windows NT Server tool for administering accounts throughout a Windows NT domain.

You may wonder why there are two account administration tools that seem to do the same thing. Basically, User Manager is a streamlined version of User Manager for Domains. When you work with a single workstation, many of the options for Windows NT domains don't apply, so you don't need the extra features that the Windows NT Server tool provides. On the other hand, when you work with many computers within a domain, you'll need these extra features. You'll find these applications in the Administrative Tools folder for their respective systems.

Run User Manager by going to Start, selecting Programs, then Administrative Tools, and then User Manager. Figure 4-1, on the following page, shows the User Manager for Domains.

Tip If your primary computer is a Windows NT workstation and you will regularly administer domain accounts, you can install the User Manager for Domains on your workstation. To do this, complete the following steps:

1. Access the Windows NT Server 4.0 CD-ROM.
2. Execute the SETUP.BAT file in the \Clients\Srvtools\Winnt directory on the CD. This will install Windows NT Server management tools on your workstation.
3. You'll now have access to User Manager for Domains. The executable for this tool is USRMGR.EXE. You can launch it from the command line or the Run utility. You can also create a shortcut for easy access.

Part II Windows NT User Administration

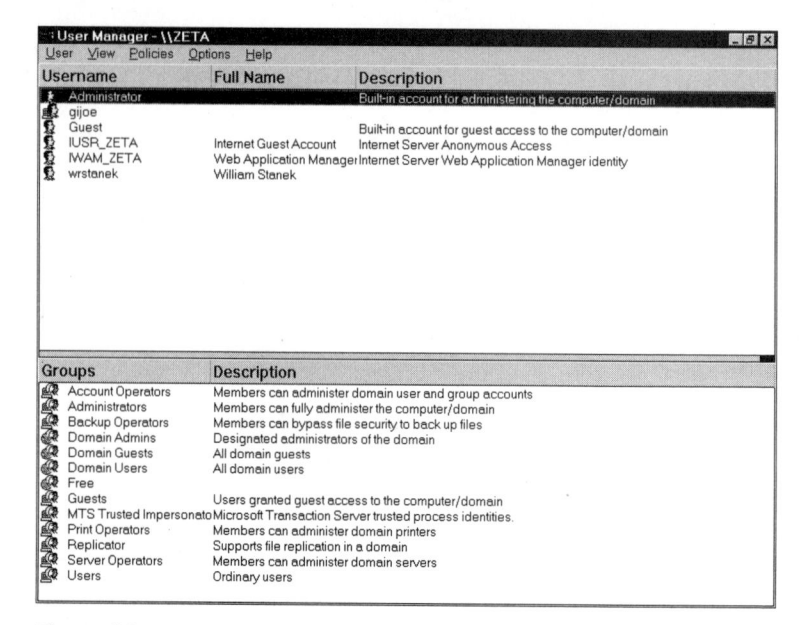

```
User Manager - \\ZETA
User  View  Policies  Options  Help
```

Username	Full Name	Description
Administrator		Built-in account for administering the computer/domain
gijoe		
Guest		Built-in account for guest access to the computer/domain
IUSR_ZETA	Internet Guest Account	Internet Server Anonymous Access
IWAM_ZETA	Web Application Manager	Internet Server Web Application Manager identity
wrstanek	William Stanek	

Groups	Description
Account Operators	Members can administer domain user and group accounts
Administrators	Members can fully administer the computer/domain
Backup Operators	Members can bypass file security to back up files
Domain Admins	Designated administrators of the domain
Domain Guests	All domain guests
Domain Users	All domain users
Free	
Guests	Users granted guest access to the computer/domain
MTS Trusted Impersonato	Microsoft Transaction Server trusted process identities.
Print Operators	Members can administer domain printers
Replicator	Supports file replication in a domain
Server Operators	Members can administer domain servers
Users	Ordinary users

Figure 4-1. *User Manager for Domains is the Windows NT Server tool for administering user accounts. The top part of the screen lists user accounts. The bottom part lists group accounts.*

When you start User Manager for Domains, the tool displays the domain in which your user account is defined. If you manage multiple Windows NT domains, you can select a different domain to administer by doing the following:

1. Choose the Domain option on the User menu.
2. Click on the domain name in the list of domains or enter the name of the domain, then click OK.

To have User Manager for Domains start up with a different domain, you can modify its shortcut on the Administrative Tools menu or create a new shortcut. To modify an existing shortcut, do the following:

1. Right-click on the taskbar's Start button, then select Open All Users.
2. Drill down to the tools shortcuts by double-clicking on the Programs folder and then the Administrative Tools folder.
3. Right-click on the User Manager for Domains shortcut and choose Properties from the Context menu.
4. Click on the Shortcut tab.
5. Now you can edit the command in the Target field to include the domain name as a parameter. Simply follow the current entry with a

Chapter 4 Understanding User and Group Accounts | 63

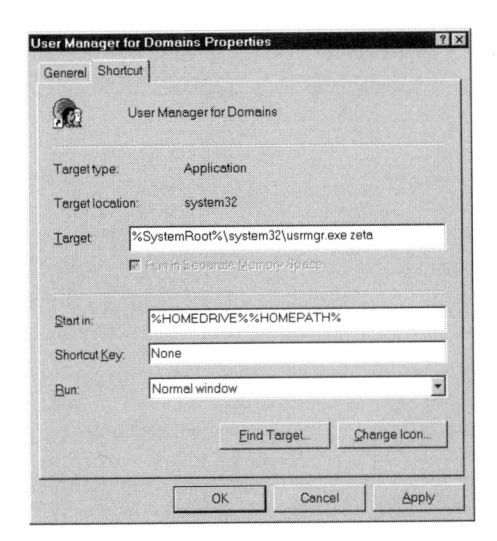

Figure 4-2. *By editing the target for the shortcut, you can determine which domain is set when the tool starts. Add the domain name to the entry in the Target field.*

space and then the domain name. Figure 4-2 shows how to do this for a domain called ZETA.

Global and Local Scope

Once you are pointing to the domain you want to administer, you can create new accounts or edit existing accounts. Depending on how you create them, user and group accounts can have different scopes—*global* or *local*. That is, the accounts have different areas in which they are valid.

- When you create accounts with the User Manager tool on a Windows NT workstation, the accounts are valid only on that single workstation. This means that the accounts have a *local scope*.

- When you create accounts with User Manager for Domains, the accounts are by default usable throughout the currently selected domain. This means that the accounts have a *global scope*.

NT allows you to create both local and global group accounts with User Manager for Domains. Don't let this confuse you. Local groups still have only a local scope and are valid only for the computer you're currently using. Global groups still have a global scope and are valid throughout the currently selected domain. Table 4-1, on the following page, provides a quick reference for account types and their uses. For complete details on working with the User Manager, see Chapter 5, "Creating User and Group Accounts."

Table 4-1. Quick Reference for Using Account Administration Tools and Working with Accounts

Tool	Account Type	Scope	Use
User Manager (Windows NT Workstation)	User	Local	Single computer; for workgroups or computers not part of a Windows NT domain.
	Group	Local	Single computer; for workgroups or computers not part of a Windows NT domain.
User Manager for Domains (Windows NT Server)	User	Global (by default)	Many computers; for use throughout the currently selected domain.
	Local Group	Local	Single computer; for workgroups or computers not part of a Windows NT domain.
	Global Group	Global	Many computers; for use throughout the currently selected domain.

Built-In Accounts

When you install Windows NT, the operating system installs the built-in user and group accounts. These accounts are designed to provide the basic setup necessary to grow your network. Although you can modify these user and group accounts, you can't delete them.

> **Note** The reason you can't delete built-in accounts is that you wouldn't be able to re-create them. The SIDs of the old and new accounts wouldn't match, and the permissions and privileges of these accounts would be lost. Because of this, Windows NT doesn't let you delete built-in accounts.

Built-In User Accounts

Built-in user accounts are installed with all Windows NT workstations and servers. These accounts are local to the individual system they are installed on and may have domain-wide access depending on how the computer is set up. The built-in accounts include Administrator, Guest, and System.

The Administrator Account

Administrator provides complete access to files, directories, services, and other facilities. The account cannot be deleted or disabled. If a computer is connected to a domain, the Administrator account has domain-wide access and privileges. Otherwise, the Administrator account generally has access only to the local system. Although files and directories can be protected from the Administrator temporarily, the Administrator can take control of these resources at any time by changing the access permissions. For more information, see Chapter 9, "Managing Files and Directories."

Chapter 4 Understanding User and Group Accounts | 65

Tip To prevent unauthorized access to the system, be sure to give the account an especially secure password. Also, because this is a known Windows NT account, as an extra security precaution you may want to rename the account.

Figure 4-3 shows the User Properties dialog box for the Administrator account on a newly installed system. In most instances you won't need to change the basic settings for this account. However, you may need to change the advanced settings for the account, such as membership in particular groups. By default, the Administrator is a member of these groups: Administrators, Domain Admins, and Domain Users. You'll find more information on these groups in the next section.

Real World In a domain environment, you will use the Administrator account primarily to manage the system when you first install it. [You need this account to] set up the system without getting locked out. You [should rarely u]se the account once the system has been installed. [Instead, you'll pr]obably want to make your administrators members [of the Administra]tors group. This ensures that you can revoke admin[istrative privilege]s without having to change the passwords for all [administrative ac]counts.

[If the computer] is part of a workgroup where each individual com[puter is manage]d separately, you'll typically rely on this account [and password] to perform your system administration duties. [You typical]ly won't want to set up individual accounts for each person who has administrative access to a system. Instead, you'll use a single Administrator account on each computer.

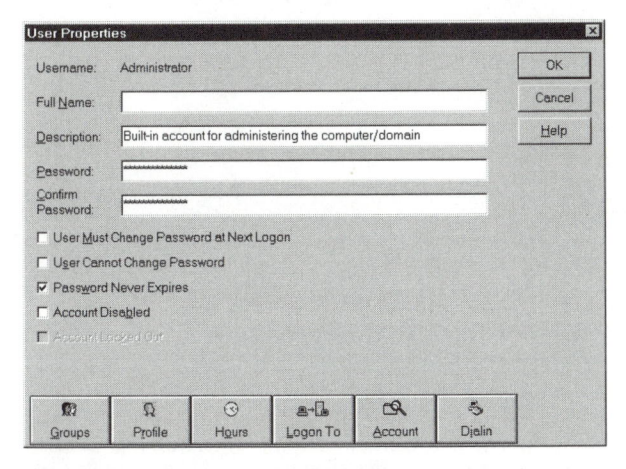

Figure 4-3. *When you install Windows NT, the Administrator account has these basic settings. To ensure that the account remains valid, the Password Never Expires check box should remain checked.*

The Guest Account

Guest is designed for users who need one-time or occasional access. While guests have limited system privileges, you should be very careful about using this account. Whenever you use this account, you open the system up to potential security problems. The potential is so great that the account is initially disabled when you install Windows NT 4.0.

> **Tip** If you decide to enable the Guest account, be sure to restrict its use and to change the password regularly. As with the Administrator account, as an added security precaution you may want to rename the account.

Figure 4-4 shows the User Properties dialog box for the Guest account on a newly installed system. If you decide to use the account, you will need to deselect the Account Disabled check box. By default, the Guest account is the *only* member of the group Domain Guests. Domain Guests are in turn members of the Guests group. Because of these settings, the Guest account has domain-wide access in a Windows NT domain.

> **Caution** The Guest account can inadvertently provide access to the default shares on a computer. When you install a new Windows NT system, the network drives are shared by default so they can be accessed from other systems. If a user attempts to log on to a computer and the attempt fails, Windows NT tries to use the Guest account to access the shares. If the Guest account doesn't have a password, the user is connected to the shared drive automatically.

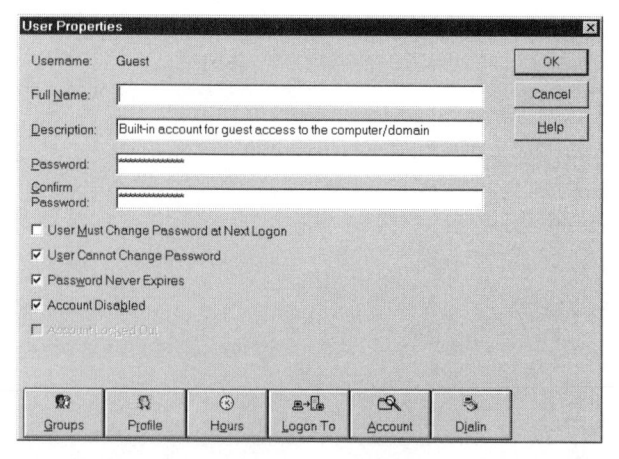

Figure 4-4. *When you first install Windows NT, the Guest account has these basic settings. As you see, the account is disabled by default. To enable the account, deselect the Account Disabled check box.*

As an administrator, you'll be dealing with account privileges on a daily basis. To help track built-in capabilities and default user rights, refer to Tables 4-3, 4-4, 4-5, and 4-6. These tables summarize the built-in capabilities and rights for groups. As you study the tables, please note how they are organized. Capabilities and rights are listed in alphabetical order. Groups are listed according to their level of privilege. Administrators have the most privileges and are listed on the far left. Guests have the fewest privileges and are listed on the far right.

Keep in mind that while you can't change the built-in capabilities of a group, you can change the default rights of a group. For example, an administrator could revoke network access to a computer by removing a group's right to access the computer from the network.

User Rights for Domain Controllers

Table 4-3 shows the default user rights on Windows NT servers that are acting as primary or backup domain controllers. As you read the table, note that all user rights—both basic and advanced—are shown. An X in a column means the group has the privilege. If the column is empty, it means the group does not have the privilege. For example, using the table, you can see that only Administrators have permission to add workstations to a Windows NT domain.

Table 4-3. Default User Rights for Groups on Windows NT Domain Controllers

User Rights	Administrators	Server Operators	Account Operators	Backup Operators	Print Operators	Everyone	Users	Guests
Access computer from network	X					X		
Act as part of operating system								
Add workstations to domain	X							
Backup files and directories	X	X		X				
Bypass directory traverse checking						X		
Change system time	X	X						
Create a pagefile	X							
Create a token object								
Create permanent shared objects								
Debug programs	X							

(continued)

Table 4-3. (continued)

User Rights	Administrators	Server Operators	Account Operators	Backup Operators	Print Operators	Everyone	Users	Guests
Force shutdown from remote system	X	X						
Generate security audits								
Increase quotas	X							
Increase scheduling priority	X							
Load and unload device drivers	X							
Lock pages in memory								
Log on as a batch job								
Log on as a service								
Log on locally	X	X	X	X	X			
Manage auditing and security log	X							
Modify firmware	X							
Profile single process	X							
Profile system performance	X							
Replace a process level token								
Restore files and directories	X	X		X				
Shutdown the system	X	X	X	X	X			
Take ownership of files	X							

Built-In Capabilities for Domain Controllers

Table 4-4 shows the built-in capabilities for Windows NT servers acting as primary or backup domain controllers. As you study the table, note that restricted accounts include the Administrator user account, the user accounts of administrators, and the group accounts for Administrators, Server Operators, Account Operators, Backup Operators, and Print Operators. Because these accounts are restricted, Account Operators can't create or modify them.

Chapter 4 Understanding User and Group Accounts | 71

Table 4-4. Built-In Capabilities for Groups on Domain Controllers

Built-In Capabilities	Administrators	Server Operators	Account Operators	Backup Operators	Print Operators	Everyone	Users	Guests
Assign user rights	X							
Create and manage restricted groups and users	X							
Create and manage unrestricted groups and users	X		X					
Create common program groups	X	X						
Format server's disk drive	X	X						
Have local profile	X	X	X	X	X			
Lock server	X	X				X		
Manage auditing of system events	X							
Override server lock	X	X						
Share directories	X	X						
Share printers	X	X			X			

User Rights for Non-Domain Controllers

Table 4-5 shows the default user rights on stand-alone Windows NT servers and Windows NT workstations. Note that on these systems, Power Users have privileges that normal users don't. Note also that any action that is available to the Everyone group is available to all groups, including the Guests group. This means that although the Guests group does not have explicit permission to access the computer from the network, Guests can still access the system because the Everyone group has this right.

Table 4-5. Default User Rights for Other Computers in Windows NT Domains

User Rights	Administrators	Power Users	Backup Operators	Everyone	Users	Guests
Access computer from network	X	X		X		
Act as part of operating system						
Add workstations to domain	X					
Backup files and directories	X		X			
Bypass traverse checking				X		

(continued)

Table 4-5. *(continued)*

User Rights	Administrators	Power Users	Backup Operators	Everyone	Users	Guests
Change system time	X	X				
Create a pagefile	X					
Create a token object						
Create permanent shared objects						
Debug programs	X					
Force shutdown from remote system	X	X				
Generate security audits						
Increase quotas	X					
Increase scheduling priority	X					
Load and unload device drivers	X					
Lock pages in memory						
Log on as a batch job						
Log on as a service						
Log on locally	X	X	X	X	X	X
Manage auditing and security log	X					
Modify firmware	X					
Profile single process	X					
Profile system performance	X					
Replace a process level token						
Restore files and directories	X		X			
Shutdown the system	X	X	X	X	X	
Take ownership of files	X					

Built-In Capabilities for Non-Domain Controllers

Table 4-6 shows the built-in capabilities for stand-alone Windows NT servers and workstations. Note that members of the Users group can only modify local groups they create. Note also that although Power Users can work with user and group accounts, there are many restrictions. Power Users can only modify user accounts that they create. Further, although they can create new local groups, they can only modify these local groups and the groups for Users, Guests, and Power Users.

Table 4-6. *Built-In Capabilities for Other Computers in Windows NT Domains*

Built-In Capabilities	Administrators	Power Users	Backup Operators	Everyone	Users	Guests
Assign user rights	X					
Create and manage local groups	X	X			X	

(continued)

Table 4-6. *(continued)*

Built-In Capabilities	Administrators	Power Users	Backup Operators	Everyone	Users	Guests
Create and manage users	X	X				
Create common program groups	X	X				
Format computer's disk drive	X					
Have local profile	X	X	X		X	
Lock computer	X	X		X		
Manage auditing of system events	X					
Override computer lock	X					
Share directories	X	X				
Share printers	X	X				

Using the Built-In Group Accounts

The built-in group accounts are designed to be versatile. By assigning users to the right groups, you can make managing your Windows NT workgroup or domain a lot easier. Unfortunately, with so many different groups, understanding the purpose of each isn't easy. To help, let's divide the groups into four categories: those used by administrators, those used by operators, those used by users, and those that are implicitly created.

Groups Used by Administrators

An administrator is someone who has wide access to network resources. Administrators can create accounts, modify user rights, install printers, manage shared resources, and more. The main administrator groups are Administrators and Domain Admins.

Table 4-7. The Administrators Group Overview

Network Environment	Group Type	Membership	Account Administration
NT Domains	Local	Administrator, Domain Admins	Administrators
Workgroups, computers not part of a Windows NT domain	Local	Administrator	Administrators

Administrators is a local group that provides full administrative access to a workstation or server. Because this account has complete access, you should be very careful about adding users to this group. To make someone an administrator for a local computer, all you need to do is make that person a member of this group. Only members of the Administrators group can modify this account (see Table 4-7).

Tip The local group Administrator and the global group Domain Admins are members of this group. The Administrator user membership is used to access the local computer. The Domain Admins membership allows other administrators to access the system from elsewhere in the domain. Thus, if you want to isolate a server, you could remove Domain Admins from this group.

Table 4-8. Domain Admins Group Overview

Network Environment	Group Type	Membership	Account Administration
Servers and Workstations in Windows NT Domains	Global	Administrator	Administrators

Domain Admins is a global group designed to help you administer all the computers in a domain. This group has administrative control over all computers in a domain because it is by default a member of the Administrators group. To make someone an administrator for a domain, make that person a member of this group. When you add a stand-alone server or workstation to a domain, the Domain Admins group is automatically added to the computer's Administrators group (see Table 4-8).

Tip In a Windows NT domain, the Administrator local user is a member of Domain Admins by default. This means that if someone logs on to a computer as the administrator and the computer is a member of the domain, the user will have complete access to all resources in the domain. To prevent this, you can remove the local Administrator account from the Domain Admins group.

Groups Used by Operators

Operators are users who have privileges to perform very specific administrative tasks, such as creating accounts or backing up file systems. By default, no other group or user accounts are members of the operator groups. This is primarily to ensure that you grant explicit access to these accounts. Additionally, because these are local groups, operators can only perform the tasks on a specific computer.

The operator groups are Account Operators, Backup Operators, Print Operators, Server Operators, and Replicator.

Table 4-9. Account Operators Group Overview

Network Environment	Group Type	Membership	Account Administration
Windows NT Domain Controllers	Local	None	Administrators

Account Operators is a local group that grants limited account creation privileges to a user. Members of this group can create and modify most types of accounts, including those of users, local groups, and global groups. They can also log on locally to domain controllers. However, Account Operators can't manage the Administrator user account, the user accounts of administrators, or the group accounts Administrators, Server Operators, Account Operators, Backup Operators, and Print Operators. Account Operators also can't modify user rights (see Table 4-9).

Table 4-10. Backup Operators Group Overview

Network Environment	Group Type	Membership	Account Administration
Any server or workstation	Local	None	Administrators

Backup Operators is a local group that enables a user to back up and restore files and directories on workstations and servers in a Windows NT domain. Members of this group can log on to a computer, back up or restore files, and shut down the computer. Because of how the account is set up, they can back up files regardless of whether they have read/write access to the files. However, they can't change access permissions of the files or perform other administrative tasks (see Table 4-10).

Table 4-11. Print Operators Group Overview

Network Environment	Group Type	Membership	Account Administration
Windows NT Domain Controllers	Local	None	Administrators

Print Operators is a local group for managing network printers. Members of this group can manage printers running in a Windows NT domain. They can define which printers are shared, which printers aren't, and other related printer privileges. Print Operators can also log on to a server locally and shut it down (see Table 4-11).

Table 4-12. Server Operators Group Overview

Network Environment	Group Type	Membership	Account Administration
Windows NT Domain Controllers	Local	None	Administrators

Server Operators is a local group that allows a user to perform general administrator tasks. These tasks include creating common program groups, sharing server resources, performing file backup and recovery, formatting the server's disk drives, and more. As with other operator accounts, Server Operators can also log on to a server locally and shut it down. Server Operators can perform most common server administration tasks (see Table 4-12).

Table 4-13. Replicator Group Overview

Network Environment	Group Type	Membership	Account Administration
Any server or workstation	Local	None	Administrators, Account Operators, Server Operators

Replicator, a special group account, is used with the directory replication service. Administrators and operators can set up this service to manage the replication of files and directories in a domain. If you do this, you'll need to set up a special user account for the replication service and make the account a member of this group (see Table 4-13).

Groups Used by Users

Windows NT provides many different types of user accounts. These accounts are designed to meet the needs of diverse networking environments. The user groups are Users, Domain Users, Power Users, Guests, and Domain Guests.

Table 4-14. Users Group Overview

Network Environment	Group Type	Membership	Account Administration
Servers and workstations in Windows NT domains	Local	Domain Users, Administrator	Administrators, Account Operators
Computers not part of a Windows NT domain	Local	User account selected during installation of the operating system	Administrators, Power Users

Users are the people who do most of their work on a single Windows NT workstation. Because of this, members of the Users group have more restrictions than privileges. By default, members of the Users group cannot log on locally to a Windows NT server acting as a domain controller. However, they can access the controller's resources over the network.

On Windows NT workstations, members of the Users group can log on to a workstation locally, keep a local profile, lock the workstation, and shut down the workstation. Users can also create local groups and manage those groups.

In Windows NT domains, the local Administrator and the global Domain Users are members of this group by default. For workgroups or isolated workstations, there are no predefined members of this group (see Table 4-14).

Table 4-15. Domain Users Group Overview

Network Environment	Group Type	Membership	Account Administration
Servers and Workstations in Windows NT domains	Global	Administrator	Administrators, Account Operators

Chapter 4 Understanding User and Group Accounts | 77

Domain users is a global group for users in a Windows NT domain. When new domain users are created, they are added to this group automatically. By default, the local Administrator is a member of this group (see Table 4-15).

Table 4-16. Power Users Group Overview

Network Environment	Group Type	Membership	Account Administration
Non-domain controllers and computers not part of a Windows NT domain	Local	None	Administrators, Power Users

Power Users exist only on computers that are not domain controllers. Power Users have all the privileges of members of the Users group, as well as a few additional privileges. They can create accounts and modify the accounts they create. They can also modify the groups for Users, Guests, and Power Users. Beyond this, Power Users can also create common program groups, lock the workstation, have a local profile, and share system resources.

To give users of a Windows NT workstation extra control, Microsoft recommends that you make them members of the Power Users group. This allows users to perform limited administration on their workstations (see Table 4-16).

Table 4-17. Guests Group Overview

Network Environment	Group Type	Membership	Account Administration
Server or workstation in a Windows NT domain	Local	Domain Guests, Guest	Administrators, Account Operators
Computers not part of a Windows NT domain	Local	Guest	Administrators, Power Users

Guests are users with very limited privileges. Members of the Guests group can access the system and its resources remotely, but they can't perform most other tasks, such as logging on locally.

For Windows NT domains, the only member of this group is Domain Guests. On workgroups or isolated computers, there are no default members for this group (see Table 4-17).

Note Keep in mind that any action available to the group Everyone is available to the Guests group. This means that if someone is a member of the local Guests account, they can lock a Windows NT domain controller or workstation, access a Windows NT domain controller or workstation remotely, and shut down a workstation.

Table 4-18. Domain Guests Group Overview

Network Environment	Group Type	Membership	Account Administration
Servers and Workstations in Windows NT Domains	Global	Guest	Administrators, Account Operators

Domain Guests are users with guest privileges throughout a domain. By default, the local Guest user is a member of this account. Therefore, anytime you create a local guest account in a Windows NT domain, the guest user gains access to the entire domain (see Table 4-18).

Implicit Groups

Windows NT defines a set of implicit groups that can be used to handle directory and file permissions in certain situations. These groups are not available in the User Manager. The implicit groups are Interactive, Network, Everyone, System, and Creator Owner.

The Interactive Group
Any user logged in to the local system is a member of the Interactive group. This group is used to allow *only* local users to access a resource.

The Network Group
Any user accessing the system through a network is a member of the Network group. This group is used to allow *only* remote users to access a resource.

The Everyone Group
All interactive and network users are members of the Everyone group. This group is used to give wide access to a system resource.

The System Group
The Windows NT Operating System itself is the member of this group. This group is used when the operating system needs to perform a system-level function.

The Creator Owner Group
The person who created the file or directory is a member of this group. This group is used by Windows NT to automatically grant access permissions to the creator of a file or directory.

Chapter 5

Creating User and Group Accounts

A key part of your job as an administrator is to create user accounts, and in this chapter you'll learn how to do that.

User accounts allow Microsoft Windows NT to track and manage information about users, including permissions and privileges. When you create user accounts, you use the Windows NT administration tools. The primary account administration tool is the User Manager, which comes in two versions:

- The Windows NT Workstation version, User Manager (MUSRMGR.EXE), is designed to administer accounts on a single computer.
- The Windows NT Server version, User Manager for Domains (USRMGR.EXE), is designed to administer accounts throughout a Windows NT domain.

For details on getting started with User Manager, see Chapter 4, "Understanding User and Group Accounts." Note that for ease of reference this chapter uses the term User Manager to refer to both User Manager and User Manager for Domains (unless otherwise noted).

User Account Setup and Organization

Account setup and organization are the most important aspects of account creation. Without appropriate policies in place, you could quickly find that you need to rework all the user accounts in your company. So before you create accounts, determine the policies you want to use for setup and organization.

User Name Policies

A key policy you'll need to set is the naming scheme for accounts. In Windows NT, user names must follow these rules:

- Local user names must be unique on a workstation.
- Global user names must be unique throughout a domain.
- User names must be no more than 20 characters in length.
- User names cannot contain certain characters. Invalid characters include:
  " / \ [ ] : ; | = , + * ? < >

User names can contain all other special characters, including spaces, periods, dashes, and underscores. But it's generally not a good idea to use spaces in account names. On some non-Windows NT systems, such as UNIX, spaces aren't valid in user names and the user may have difficulty accessing these systems.

> **Note** Although Windows NT stores user names in the case you enter, user names are not case-sensitive. For example, you can access the Administrator account with the user name Administrator or administrator. Thus, user names are case-aware but not case-sensitive.

You'll find that most small organizations tend to assign account names that use the first or last name of the user. But you can have several Toms, Dicks, and Harrys in a company of any size. So rather than having to rework your account naming scheme when you run into problems, select a good naming scheme now and make sure other administrators use it. For naming accounts, you should use a consistent procedure that

1. Allows your user base to grow and limits the possibility of name conflicts.
2. Ensures that your accounts have secure names that aren't easily exploited.

If you follow these guidelines, the types of naming schemes you may want to use include:

- **User's first name and last initial** You take the user's first name and combine it with the first letter of the last name to create the account name. For William Stanek, you would use *williams* or *bills*. This naming scheme is not practical for large organizations.
- **User's first initial and last name** You take the user's first initial and combine it with the last name to create the account name. For William Stanek, you would use *wstanek*. This naming scheme is not practical for large organizations, either.
- **User's first initial, middle initial, and last name** You combine the user's first initial, middle initial, and last name to create the account name. For William R. Stanek, you would use *wrstanek*.
- **User's first initial, middle initial, and first five characters of the last name** You combine the user's first initial, middle initial, and the first five characters of the last name to create the account name. For William R. Stanek, you would use *wrstane*.
- **User's first name and last name** You combine the user's first and last name. To separate the names, you could use the underscore character (_) or hyphen (-). For William Stanek, you could use *william_stanek* or *william-stanek*.

Password and Account Policies

Windows NT accounts use passwords to authenticate access to network resources. A password is a case-sensitive string that can contain up to 14 characters. Valid characters for passwords are letters, numbers, and symbols. When you set a password for an account, Windows NT stores the password in an encrypted format in the account database.

Simply having a password isn't enough. The key to preventing unauthorized access to network resources is to use *secure* passwords. The difference between an average password and a secure password is that secure passwords are difficult to guess and crack. You make passwords difficult to crack by using combinations of all the available character types including lowercase letters, uppercase letters, numbers, and symbols. For example, instead of using **happydays** for a password you would use **haPPy2Days&**, **Ha**y!dayS**, or even **h*PPY%d*ys**.

Unfortunately, no matter how secure you initially make a user's password, eventually the password is usually chosen by the user. Because of this, you'll want to set account policies. On a Windows NT domain, you can set a domain-wide account policy with User Manager for Domains. To do this, complete the following steps:

1. Start User Manager for Domains.
2. Select Account from the Policies menu.
3. You should now see the Account Policy dialog box shown in Figure 5-1. Use the areas of this dialog box to configure your account policy, and then click OK.

The Account Policy dialog box is divided into two main areas: Password Restrictions and Account Lockouts. Password Restrictions set the characteristics of passwords. Account Lockouts control access to the account. The No Account Lockout and Account Lockout radio buttons determine

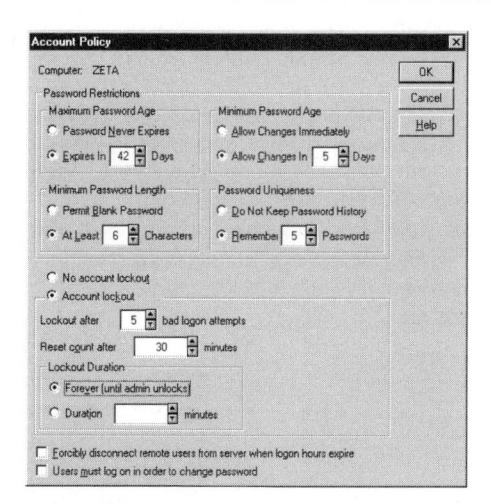

Figure 5-1. *Use the Account Policy dialog box to set policies for passwords and general account use. The top line of the dialog box shows the name of the computer or domain you are configuring. Be sure that this is the appropriate network resource to configure.*

whether account lockout controls are active. Select the Account Lockout button to set lockout controls.

The fields in the Account Policy are these:

- Maximum Password Age
- Minimum Password Age
- Minimum Password Length
- Password Uniqueness
- Lockout After X Bad Logon Attempts
- Reset Count After
- Lockout Duration
- Forcibly Disconnect Remote Users From Server When Logon Hours Expire
- Users Must Log On In Order To Change Password

Their uses are discussed in the following sections.

Maximum Password Age

Maximum Password Age determines how long users can keep a password before they have to change it. The aim is to periodically force users to change their passwords. When you use this feature, set a value that makes sense for your network. Generally, you use a shorter period when security is very important and a longer period when security is less important.

By default, this field is set to 42 days. However, you can set it to any value from 1 to 999. Good values where security is a concern are 30, 60, or 90 days. Good values where security is less important are 120, 150, or 180 days.

Although you may be tempted to set no expiration date, there is a check box on the main User Properties dialog box that allows you to specify whether this policy should be enforced for a particular user. Ideally, you should use the check box to override the expiration on a case-by-case basis rather than set a blanket policy that passwords don't expire. Users should change passwords regularly to ensure the security of the network.

> **Note** Windows NT notifies users when they are getting close to the password expiration date. Anytime the expiration date is less than 30 days away, users see a warning when they log on that they have to change their password within X days.

Minimum Password Age

Minimum Password Age determines how long users must keep a password before they can change it. You can use this field to prevent users from cheating the password system by entering a new password and then changing it right back to the old one.

By default, Windows NT lets users change their passwords immediately. To prevent this, set a specific minimum age. Reasonable settings are from three to seven days. In this way, you make sure that users are less inclined to switch back to an old password but are able to change their passwords in a reasonable amount of time if they want to.

Minimum Password Length

Minimum Password Length sets the minimum number of characters for a password. If you haven't changed the default setting, you'll want to do so immediately. The default is to allow empty passwords (passwords with zero characters), which is definitely not a good idea.

For security reasons, you will generally want passwords of at least eight characters. The reason for this is that long passwords are usually harder to crack than short passwords. If you want greater security, set the minimum password length to 14 characters.

Password Uniqueness

Password Uniqueness sets how frequently old passwords can be reused. You can use this control to discourage users from changing back and forth between a set of common passwords. Windows NT can store up to 24 passwords for each user in the password history. Windows NT does not, however, keep a password history by default.

To use this feature, set the size of the password history using the Remember Passwords field. Windows NT will then track old passwords using a password history that is unique for each user and users will not be allowed to reuse any of the stored passwords.

Note To discourage users from cheating the Password Uniqueness control, you shouldn't allow them to change passwords immediately. This will prevent users from changing their passwords several times to get back to their old passwords.

Lockout After X Bad Logon Attempts

Lockout After X Bad Logon Attempts sets the number of logon attempts to allow before locking out an account. If you decide to use lockout controls, you should set this field to a value that balances the need to prevent account cracking against the needs of users who are having difficulty accessing their accounts.

The main reason users may not be able to access their accounts properly the first time is that they forgot their passwords. If this is the case, it may take them several attempts to log on properly. Users could also have problems accessing a remote system where their current passwords don't match the passwords the remote system expects. If this happens, several bad logon attempts may be recorded by the remote system before the user ever gets a prompt to enter the correct password. The reason is that Windows NT may attempt to automatically log on to the remote system.

The field accepts values from 1 to 999. However, the higher the value, the higher the risk that a hacker may be able to break into your system. A reasonable range of values for this field is between 7 and 15. This is high enough to rule out user error and low enough to deter hackers.

Reset Count After

Every time a logon attempt fails, Windows NT raises the value of a counter tracking the number of bad logon attempts. The field accepts values from 1 to 99,999. As with the Lockout field, you need to select a value that balances security needs against valid user access needs. A good value is from one to two hours. This waiting period should be long enough to force hackers to wait longer than they want to before trying to access the account again.

The lockout counter is reset in one of two ways. If a user logs on successfully, the counter is reset. If the waiting period for the Reset Count After field has elapsed since the last bad logon attempt, the counter is reset.

> **Note** Bad logon attempts to a workstation against a password-protected screen saver do not increase the lockout counter. Similarly, if you lock a server or workstation using Ctrl+Alt+Delete, bad logon attempts against the Unlock dialog box do not count.

Lockout Duration

If someone violates the lockout controls, Lockout Duration sets the length of time the account is locked. You can set the lockout duration to a specific length of time using the Duration field or to an indefinite length of time using the Forever field.

The best security policy is to lock the account indefinitely. When you do, only an administrator can unlock the account. This will prevent hackers from trying to access the system again and will force users who are locked out to seek help from an administrator, which is usually a good idea. By talking to the user, you can determine what the user is doing wrong and help the user avoid future problems.

> **Tip** When an account is locked out, the Account Locked Out check box is displayed in the Properties dialog box for the user. To unlock an account, all you need to do is uncheck this check box.

Forcibly Disconnect Remote Users From Server When Logon Hours Expire

This field ensures that users can only connect to servers during their valid logon hours. Valid logon hours can be set for each individual user account using the Logon Hours dialog box (which is covered in detail later in this chapter).

If you do *not* select this field, a user who logs on during normal logon times can remain on the network after hours. If you do, all current network connections remain open but any new connection attempts are rejected.

Note If this policy is set, remote users will see a warning to log off the system. Users who do not log off are disconnected when the logon time expires (if Windows NT systems are used). On non-Windows NT systems, users are not forcibly disconnected. Here, they simply cannot log on to the domain during the restricted hours.

Users Must Log On In Order To Change Password

This field is used to determine what happens when a user's password expires. If the field is *not* checked, users can still log on after their account has expired—the catch is that they will have to change their password immediately. On the other hand, if the field is checked, users cannot log on if their account has expired. The user is denied access to the system and only an administrator can change the user's password, which effectively resets the account.

Additional Password Controls

Beyond the basic password and account policies, Windows NT includes facilities for creating additional password controls. These facilities are available in the Password Change Filter DLL (PASSFILT.DLL). When you install Service Pack 3 or later, this linked library is copied to your *%SystemRoot%*\System32 directory, where *%SystemRoot%* is the base directory for the Windows NT operating system. You can use the Password Change Filter DLL to set strong password filtering. This filtering enforces the use of secure passwords that follow these guidelines:

- Passwords must be at least six characters long.
- Passwords cannot contain the user name, such as stevew, or parts of the user's full name, such as Steve.
- Passwords must use three of the four available character types: lowercase letters, uppercase letters, numbers, and symbols.

To set up strong password filtering, you need to:

1. Make sure that the file Passfilt.dll is in the *%SystemRoot%*\System32 directory.

   Add the value PASSFILT to the registry key:

   ```
   HKEY_LOCAL_MACHINE
       \System
           \CurrentControlSet
               \Control
                   \Lsa
                       \Notification  Packages
   ```

   As shown in Figure 5-2, on the following page, be sure to place the PASSFILT value on its own line without altering the current entry for FPNWCLNT.

2. Use the PassProp Utility in the Windows NT Resource Kit to manage the strong password filtering once it's enabled.

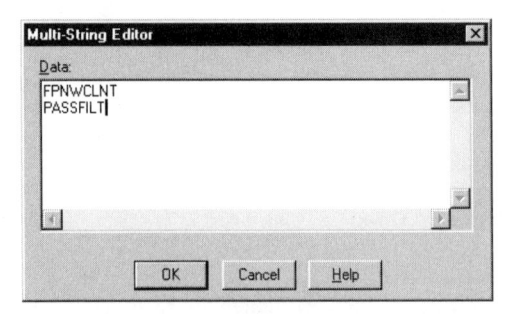

Figure 5-2. *In the Multi-String Editor, be sure to place the value PASSFILT on its own line. When you are finished, there should be two entries for the Notification Packages key: FPNWCLNT and PASSFILT.*

User Rights Policies

Chapter 4 covered built-in capabilities and default user rights. Although you cannot change built-in capabilities for accounts, you can administer user rights for accounts. Normally, you grant user rights to users by making them members of the appropriate group or groups. However, you can also grant rights directly, and you do this by managing the user rights for the user's account.

> **Note** Keep in mind that changes you make to user rights can have a far-reaching effect. Because of this, only experienced administrators should make changes to the user rights policy.

Table 5-1 provides an overview of the basic and advanced user rights on Windows NT. Use this table to help you understand the meaning of various rights. For a domain, rights generally apply to all domain controllers in the domain. For a workstation, rights generally apply only to the single workstation.

> **Note** Any user who is a member of a group assigned a right also has the right. For example, if the Backup Operators has the right and GIJOE is a member of this group, GIJOE has this right as well.

Table 5-1. Basic and Advanced User Rights on Windows NT Systems

User Rights	Type of Right	Description
Access computer from network	Basic	The user can connect to the computer through the network.
Act as part of operating system	Advanced	Allows user to perform operations as a trusted and secure part of the Windows NT operating system. Some Windows NT subsystems have this right, as does the pseudo-account system.

(continued)

Table 5-1. *(continued)*

User Rights	Type of Right	Description
Add workstations to domain	Basic	Allows a user to add workstations to the domain. This right can be granted to users who are not members of the Administrators, Operators, or Power Users groups. However, you cannot revoke this right for privileged groups, such as Administrators.
Back up files and directories	Basic	The user can back up files and directories on the computer. The user can do this regardless of the permissions on the files and directories.
Bypass directory traverse checking	Advanced	Users can change directories and traverse directory trees even if they don't have permission to access a particular directory.
Change system time	Basic	Allows user to set the time for the internal clock on the computer.
Create a pagefile	Advanced	The user can create pagefiles. Security for pagefiles is in accordance with the registry key \CurrentControlSet\Control\Session.
Create a token object	Advanced	Used to create the user token for logon. Although you can assign this right, only the local security authority can use this right properly.
Create permanent shared objects	Advanced	A system right used to grant the right to create permanent shared resources, such as devices used by Windows NT.
Debug programs	Advanced	Allows user to debug low-level objects, such as threads.
Force shutdown from remote system	Basic	The user can shut down a remote system.
Generate security audits	Advanced	Allows the user to generate security audit trails, which are written to the security log.
Increase quotas	Advanced	Enables user to increase object quotas.
Increase scheduling priority	Advanced	Enables user to increase the priority of a process, such as a scheduled printer job.
Load and unload device drivers	Basic	The user can load and unload Windows NT device drivers.
Lock pages in memory	Advanced	Allows the user to lock pages in memory so they cannot be written out to PAGEFILE.SYS.
Log on as a batch job	Advanced	Enables the user to log on using a batch queue facility.

(continued)

Table 5-1. *(continued)*

User Rights	Type of Right	Description
Log on as a service	Advanced	The user can log on as a service. Generally, you set service options using the Services utility on Control Panel or through the Server Manager.
Log on locally	Basic	Allows the user to log on using the computer's keyboard.
Manage auditing and security log	Advanced	The user can manage the auditing and security log.
Modify firmware	Advanced	Enables the user to modify system environment variables.
Profile single process	Advanced	The user can measure system performance by profile capabilities on individual processes.
Profile system performance	Advanced	The user can measure system performance using profile capabilities.
Replace a process level token	Advanced	Allows the user to change a process's security access token. Changing security can open your system up to attack. Thus, this right should only be used by Windows NT or the System account.
Restore files and directories	Basic	Enables the user to restore files and directories. The user can do this regardless of the permissions on the files and directories.
Shut down the system	Basic	Allows a user at the computer to shut it down.
Take ownership of files	Basic	The user can take ownership of files, regardless of the permissions on the files.

Administering the User Rights Policy

To administer the user rights policy, start User Manager and then select User Rights from the Policy menu. You should now see the User Rights Policy dialog box shown in Figure 5-3. Use the Right selection menu to select the user right you want to modify. As you select rights, the Grant To list box shows you the users and groups who have been assigned this right.

To grant a right to a user or group, do the following:

1. Select the user right you want to modify using the Right selection menu. Display advanced user rights by selecting the Show Advanced User Rights check box (if necessary).

2. Click Add, and then use the Add Users and Groups dialog box to grant the right to additional users and groups.

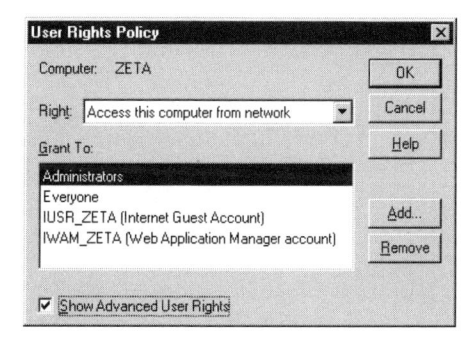

Figure 5-3. *The User Rights Policy dialog box lets you modify the default user rights policy for domains and individual computers. The domain or computer you are modifying is shown at the top of the dialog box.*

To revoke an existing right, do the following:

1. Select the user right you want to modify using the Right selection menu. Display advanced user rights by selecting the Show Advanced User Rights check box (if necessary).

2. Select the users or groups for whom you want to revoke the right, and then click Remove.

Adding a User Account

You need to create a user account for each user that wants to use your network resources. User accounts are created in User Manager. Generally, there are two ways to create new accounts:

- **Create a completely new user account** Create a completely new account by selecting New User from the User menu. This opens the New User dialog box shown in Figure 5-4, on the following page. When you create a new account, the default system settings are used.

- **Base the new account on an existing account** Select the user account you want to copy in the User Manager window, then select the Copy option of the User menu. This opens the Copy Of dialog box, which is essentially the same as the New User dialog box. However, when you create a copy of an account, the new account gets most of its environment settings from the existing account. For more information on copying accounts, see Chapter 6.

After you enter all the information for the account, click Add to create the account. Each of the fields in the dialog box are used as follows:

- **Username** The name for the user account. This name should follow the conventions for your user name policy.

- **Full Name** The full name of the user, such as William R. Stanek. Keep in mind that the full name may be used by some system utilities. Because of this, you should use a consistent naming convention for full names.

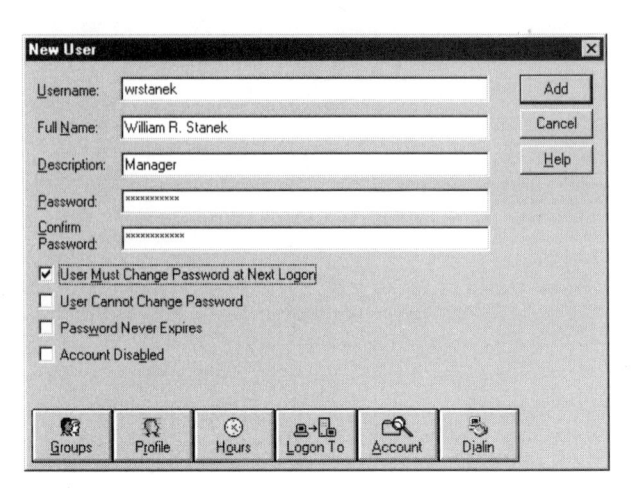

Figure 5-4. *The New User dialog box allows you to set basic account properties. If you want to set advanced properties, you'll need to use the buttons at the bottom of the dialog box. When you are finished creating the account, click the Add button.*

- **Description**   A description of the user. Normally you'd enter the user's job title, such as Webmaster. You could also enter the user's job title and department.
- **Password**   The password for the account. This password should follow the conventions of your password policy.
- **Confirm Password**   A field to ensure that you assign the account password correctly. Simply reenter the password to confirm it.
- **User Must Change Password at Next Logon**   If selected, the user must change the password upon logon. This check box is selected by default for all new users.
- **User Cannot Change Password**   If checked, the user cannot change the password.
- **Password Never Expires**   If selected, the password for this account never expires. This setting overrides the domain account policy. Generally, it is not a good idea to set a password so it doesn't expire because this defeats the purpose of having passwords in the first place.
- **Account Disabled**   If checked, the account is disabled and cannot be used. Use this field to temporarily prevent anyone from using an account.
- **Account Locked Out**   If checked, the account is locked by the system because the user broke the general account policy for bad logon attempts. You can unlock the account by unchecking the check box. This field is not visible when you create new users. It is, however, visible, but shaded, on existing users.

You'll also find a row of buttons at the bottom of the New User dialog box. These buttons open dialog boxes that let you set advanced properties for user accounts. These dialog boxes are discussed later in the chapter.

Adding a Group Account

Group accounts are used to manage privileges for multiple users. In User Manager, the currently defined groups are shown in the lower section of the main window. As discussed in Chapter 4, Windows NT supports both local and global group types. While local groups are valid only for a single computer, global groups are valid throughout a Windows NT domain.

Tip In User Manager, you can easily tell the difference between a global group and a local group. The icon for global groups shows a globe in the background. The icon for local groups shows a computer in the background.

Group accounts names are not case-sensitive and can be up to 20 characters long. Illegal characters for group names are the same as those for user names and include:

" / \ [ ] : ; | = , + * ? < >

As you set out to create group accounts, remember that you create group accounts for similar types of users. Following this, the types of groups you may want to create include the following:

- **Groups for departments within the organization** Generally, users who work in the same department need access to similar resources. Because of this, you can create groups that are organized by department, such as Business Development, Sales, Marketing, or Engineering.
- **Groups for users of specific applications** Often, users will need access to an application and resources related to the application. If you create application-specific groups, you can be sure that users get proper access to the necessary resources and application files.
- **Groups for roles within the company** Groups could also be organized by the user's role within the company. For example, executives probably need access to different resources than supervisors and general users. Thus, by creating groups based on roles within the company, you can ensure that proper access is given to the users that need it.

Creating a Local Group

Local groups can include local users, domain users, and global groups from the current domain as well as local users, domain users, and global

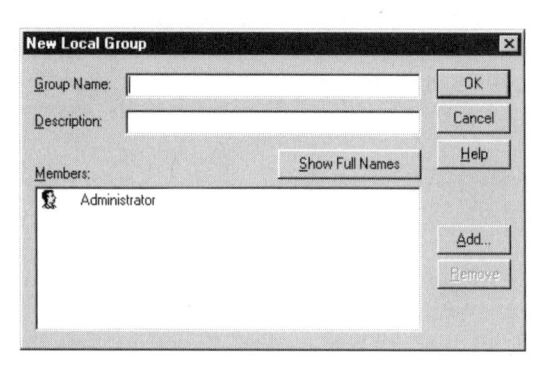

Figure 5-5. *The New Local Group dialog box allows you to add a new local group to the workstation or server.*

groups from other trusted domains. To create a local group, do the following:

1. Start User Manager. Highlight any group in the bottom pane of User Manager. Select New Local Group from the User menu. This opens the New Local Group dialog box shown in Figure 5-5.

   Note Windows NT includes the name(s) of the currently selected user(s) in the Members list box. You can use this feature to preselect users who should be members of the new local group. In Figure 5-5, Administrator was selected prior to opening the New Local Group dialog box.

   Note By default, Windows NT includes the name of the currently selected user in the Members list box. Because of this, a completely new group may have an initial group member.

2. After you enter a name and description of the group, use the Add button to add names to the group. This opens the Add Users and Groups window shown in Figure 5-6. You can now add members to the group. The fields of this dialog box can be used as follows:

   - **List Names From** To access account names from other domains, click on the List Names From the drop-down list box. You should now see a list that shows the current domain, trusted domains, and other computers that you can access. An asterisk following a domain or computer name indicates that the global groups of that domain or computer can be listed in the Names list box. If no asterisk is displayed, local groups cannot be displayed for that domain or computer.

     Note Only domains that have specifically been designated as trusted are available in the List Names From drop-down menu.

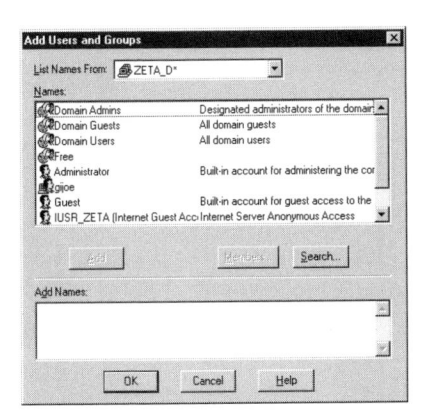

Figure 5-6. *Add members to the group using the Add Users and Groups dialog box. Note that the Names field shows the Domain name as well as the account name. This ensures you can tell the ZETA\GIJOE account from GAMMA\GIJOE account.*

- **Names** The Names list box shows the available accounts of the currently selected domain or computer. For a domain, user accounts and global group accounts are shown. For a computer, only user accounts are shown.
- **Add** Add selected names to the Add Names list.
- **Members** Shows the members of a global group. When you select a global group in the Names list box, you can use this button to show group members. You can then select individual members of the group and add them to the Add Names list.
- **Search** Allows you to search for a user or group name.
- **Add Names** The list of users and groups to add to the local group.

3. After you select the account names to add to the group, click OK. The New Local Group dialog box should now show these accounts as members of the group. If you made a mistake, select a name and remove it with the Remove button.
4. Choose OK when you are finished adding or removing group members.

Creating a Global Group

Global groups can only include user accounts. To create a global group, do the following:

1. Start User Manager. Highlight any group in the bottom pane of User Manager. Select New Global Group from the User menu. This opens the New Global Group dialog box shown in Figure 5-7, on the following page.

94 | Part II Windows NT User Administration

[Screenshot of New Global Group dialog box]

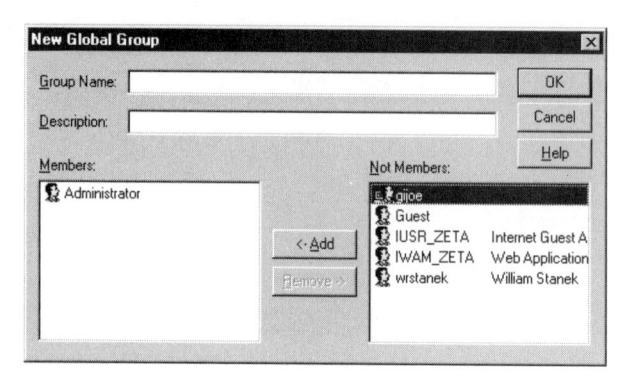

Figure 5-7. *The New Global Group dialog box allows you to add a new local group to the workstation or server.*

> **Note** As with new local groups, if you preselect users who should be members of the group, they'll be added to the group automatically. In Figure 5-7, Administrator was selected prior to opening the dialog box.

2. Enter a name and description of the group. The remaining fields in this dialog box are used as follows:

   - **Members** Shows the current members of the group.
   - **Not Members** Shows users that are not currently members of the group.
   - **Add** Adds a user to the Members list. To add users, select a name in the Not Members list, then click on the Add button.
   - **Remove** Removes a user from the Members list. To remove users, select a name in the Members list, then click on the Remove button.

3. After you select the account names to add to the group, click OK.

Handling Group Membership

The Group Memberships dialog box allows you to configure which groups a user is a member of. Click on the Groups button to access this dialog box from the New User, User Properties, and Copy Of dialog boxes.

Figure 5-8 shows the Group Memberships dialog box. Note that normally the current user you're working with is shown at the top of the dialog box and the primary group of the user is shown at the bottom. In this example, however, the user name is blank because this is a new account. Additionally, because all new domain users are members of the group Domain Users, the Primary group is specified as Domain users.

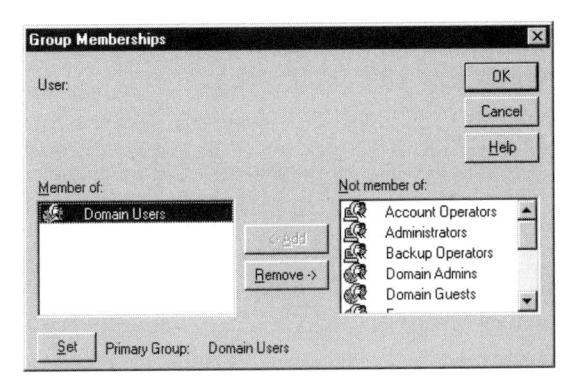

Figure 5-8. *The Group Memberships dialog box shows which groups a user is a member of.*

Making a User a Member of a Group

The Member Of list box shows which groups a user belongs to. The Not Member Of list box shows which groups the user doesn't belong to. To make a user a member of a group, do one of the following:

- Select the group name in the Not Member Of list box and click Add.
- Double-click on the group name in the Not Member Of list box.

Windows NT also lets you select multiple group names. To do this, use one of these techniques:

- **Select multiple groups individually in the Not Member Of list box** Hold down the Ctrl key and click the left mouse button on each group you want to select, then click the Add button.
- **Select a range of groups in the Not Member Of list box** Hold down the Shift key and select the first group, then click on the last group in the range. Then click the Add button.

Removing a User from a Group

The Member Of list box shows which groups a user belongs to. If you want to remove a group membership:

- Select the group name in the Member Of list box and click Remove.
- Double-click on the group name in the Not Member Of list box.

Using the Ctrl and Shift keys, you can remove users from multiple groups by doing the following:

- **Select multiple groups individually in the Member Of list box** Hold down the Ctrl key and click the left mouse button on each group you want to select, then click the Remove button.
- **Select a range of groups in the Member Of list box** Hold the Shift key and select the first group, then click on the last group in the range. Then click the Remove button.

Setting the Primary Group for a User

Primary groups are used by users who access Windows NT through services for Macintosh and for POSIX applications that log on to Windows NT systems. When a Macintosh user or POSIX application creates files or directories on a Windows NT system, the primary group is assigned to these files or directories. All user accounts must have a primary group regardless of whether the accounts access Windows NT systems through Macintosh or POSIX. This group must be a global group, such as the global group Domain User. To set the primary group, do the following:

1. Select a global group in the Member Of list box.
2. Click Set.

All users must be a member of at least one primary group. You cannot revoke membership in a primary group without first assigning the user to another primary group. To do this, complete the following steps:

1. Select a global group in the Member Of list box, and then click Set.
2. In the Member Of list box, double-click on the former primary group to revoke membership.

Working with User Profiles

The User Environment Profile dialog box allows you to configure a user's network environment. To configure these optional settings, click on the Profile button in the New User, User Properties, or Copy Of dialog boxes.

Figure 5-9 shows the User Environment Profile dialog box. As with the Groups dialog box, the user you are working with is shown at the top. In this dialog box, you can set the following fields:

- **User Profile Path**   The path to the user's profile. Profiles provide the environment settings for users. Each time a user logs on to a computer,

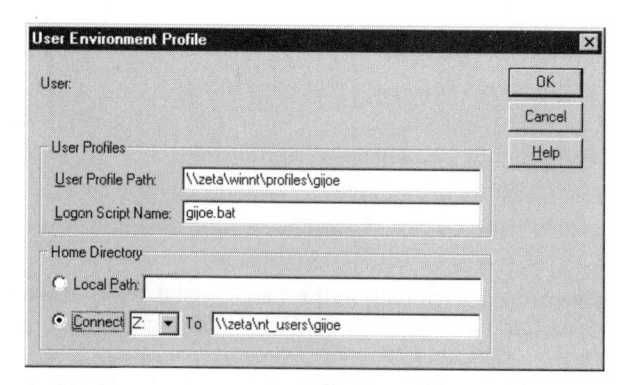

Figure 5-9. *The User Environment Profile dialog box allows you to create a user profile. Profiles let you configure the network environment for a user.*

that user's profile is used to determine desktop and control panel settings, the availability of menu options and applications, and more.

- **Logon Script Name** The name or path to the user's logon script. Logon scripts are batch files that run whenever a user logs on. You use logon scripts to set commands that should be executed each time a user logs on.
- **Home Directory** The directory the user should use for storing files. Here, you assign a specific directory for the user's files. If the directory is available to the network, the user can access the directory from any computer on the network.

System Environment Variables

System environment variables often come in handy when you are setting up the user's environment, especially when you work with logon scripts. You'll use environment variables to specify path information that can be dynamically assigned. The environment variables you'll use the most are:

- *%SystemRoot%* The base directory for the Windows NT operating system, such as C:\WINNT. Use with the User Environment Profile dialog box and logon scripts.
- *%UserName%* The user account name, such as GIJOE. Use with the User Environment Profile dialog box and logon scripts.
- *%HomeDrive%* The driver letter of the user's home directory, such as C:. Use with logon scripts.
- *%HomePath%* The full path to the user's home directory on the respective home drive, such as \USERS\MKG\GIJOE. Use with logon scripts.
- *%Processor_Architecture%* The processor architecture of the user's computer, such as x86 or ALPHA. Use with logon scripts.

Figure 5-10 shows how you might use environment variables when creating user accounts. Note that by using the %UserName% variable, you

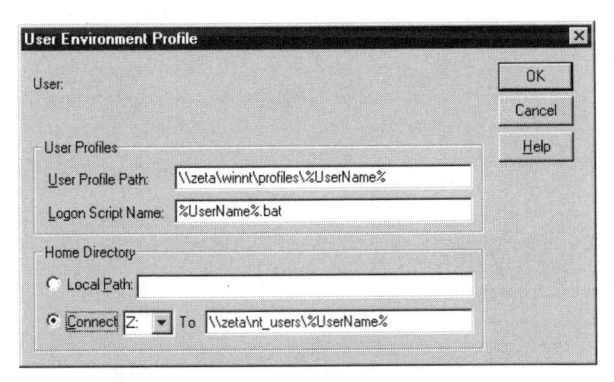

Figure 5-10. *Environment variables can save you typing, especially when you create an account based on another account.*

allow the system to determine the full path information on a user-by-user basis. If you use this technique, you can use the same path information for multiple users and all the users will have unique settings.

Local, Roaming, and Mandatory Profiles

In Windows NT, every user has a profile. Profiles control startup features for the user's session, the types of programs and applications that are available, the desktop settings, and a lot more. Each computer that a user logs on to has a copy of the user's profile. Because this profile is stored on the computer's hard disk, users who access several computers will have a profile on each computer. Another computer on the network cannot access a locally stored profile, called a local profile, and, as you might expect, this has some drawbacks. For example, if a user logs on to three different workstations, the user could have three very different profiles on each system. As a result, the user may get confused about what network resources are available on a given system.

To solve the problem of multiple profiles and reduce confusion, you may want to create a profile that can be accessed by other computers. This type of profile is called a *roaming profile*. With a roaming profile, users can access the same profile no matter which computer within the domain they are using. Roaming profiles are server-based and can only be stored on a Windows NT server. When a user with a roaming profile logs on, the profile is downloaded, which creates a local copy on the user's computer. When the user logs off, changes to the profile are updated both on the local copy and on the server.

As an administrator, you can control user profiles or let users control their own profiles. One reason to control profiles is to make sure that all users have a common network configuration, which can reduce the number of environment-related problems.

Profiles controlled by administrators are called *mandatory profiles*. Users who have a mandatory profile can only make transitory changes to their environment. Here, any changes users make to the local environment are not saved, and the next time they log on they are back to the original profile. The idea is that if users can't permanently modify the network environment, they can't make changes that cause problems. A key drawback to mandatory profiles is that the user can only log on if the profile is accessible. If, for some reason, the server that stores the profile is inaccessible or the profile itself is inaccessible, the user will not be able to log on. On Windows NT Workstation the user will receive a warning message and will be logged into the local Windows NT workstation using the workstation's cached profile.

Creating Local Profiles

The User Profile Path field in the User Environment Profile dialog box is used to set the location of user profiles. On Windows NT 4.0, user profiles are maintained in a directory. By default, this directory is located at *%SystemRoot%*\Profiles*%UserName%* where *%SystemRoot%* is the root directory for the system, such as C:\WINNT, and *%UserName%* is the user name, such as wrstanek. If you do not change the default location, the user will have a local profile.

Creating Roaming Profiles

Roaming profiles are stored on Windows NT servers. If you want a user to have a roaming profile, you must set a server-based location for the profile directory by doing the following:

1. Create a shared directory on a Windows NT server and make sure that the group Everyone has access to it.
2. Enter the path to the shared directory in the User Profile Path field. The path should have the form \\server name\profile folder name\user name. An example is \\ZETA\USERPROFILES\GIJOE where ZETA is the server name, USERPROFILES is the shared directory, and GIJOE is the user name.

Note Generally, you do not need to create the profile directory. The directory is created automatically when the user logs on.

3. As an optional step, you can create a profile for the user or copy an existing profile to the user's profile folder. If you do not create an actual profile for the user, the next time the user logs on, the user will use the default local profile. Any changes the user makes to this profile will be saved when the user logs off. Thus, the next time the user logs in the user can have a personal profile.

Creating a Profile by Hand In some cases, you may want to create the profile by hand. You do this by logging on to the user account, setting up the environment, and then logging out. As you might guess, creating accounts in this manner is time-consuming. A better way to handle account creation is to create a base user account. Here, you create the base user account, set up the account environment, and then use this account as the basis of other accounts.

Copying an Existing Profile to a New User Account If you have a base user account or a user account that you want to use in a similar manner, you can copy an existing profile to the new user account. To do this, you will use the System control panel utility as follows:

1. Start the System control panel utility and open the User Profile tab.
2. Select the existing profile you want to copy using the Profiles Stored On This Computer list box (see Figure 5-11, on the following page).
3. Copy the profile to the new user's account by clicking on the Copy To button. Next, enter the path to the new user's profile directory in the Copy Profile To field (see Figure 5-12, on the following page). For example, if you were creating the profile for our user, GIJOE, you would enter **\\ZETA\USERPROFILES\GIJOE**.
4. Now you need to give the user permission to access the profile. Click on the Change button in the Permitted To Use area, then use the Choose

100 | **Part II** Windows NT User Administration

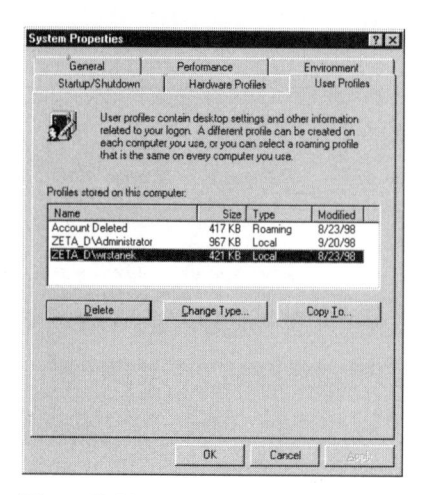

Figure 5-11. *Select the existing profile you want to copy to the new user account.*

User dialog box to grant access to the new user account. By default, the Choose User dialog box only shows the names of group accounts. If you want to grant access to a group the new user is a member of, select this group, then use the Add button to copy the group to the Add Name field. Alternately, to grant access to a specific user, click on the Show Users button. This should add a list of available user accounts to the dialog box. Select the user account, then use the Add button to copy the user name to the Add Name field.

5. Close the Copy To dialog box by clicking OK. Windows NT will then copy the profile to the next location.

Tip If you know the name of the user or group you want to use, you can type this directly into the Add Name field. This will save you time.

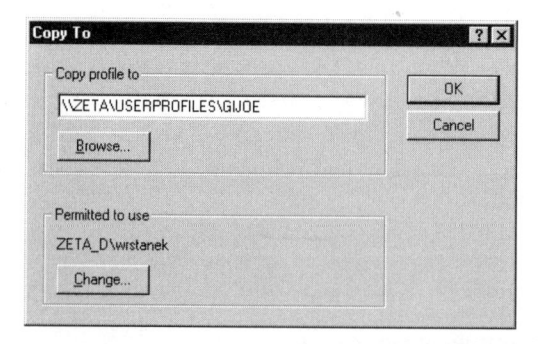

Figure 5-12. *Use the Copy To dialog box to enter the location of the profile directory and to assign access permissions to the user.*

Creating Mandatory Profiles

Mandatory profiles are stored on Windows NT servers. If you want a user to have a mandatory profile, you define the profile as follows:

1. Follow steps 1–3 described in the "Creating Roaming Profiles" section.
2. Create a mandatory profile by renaming the file *%USERNAME%\ NTUSER.DAT* as *%USERNAME%\NTUSER.MAN*. Now when the user logs in the next time, the user will have a mandatory profile.

Note NTUSER.DAT contains the registry settings for the user. When you change the extension for the file to NTUSER.MAN, you tell Windows NT to create a mandatory profile.

Logon Scripts

Logon scripts set commands that should be executed each time a user logs on. You can use logon scripts to set the system time, network drive paths, network printers, and more. While you can use logon scripts to execute one-time commands, logon scripts should not be used to set environment variables. Any environment settings used by scripts are not maintained for subsequent user processes. Additionally, logon scripts should not be used to specify applications that should run at startup. You should set startup applications by placing the appropriate shortcuts in the user's Startup folder.

Normally, logon scripts contain Windows NT commands. However, logon scripts can be batch files with the .BAT extension, command files with the .CMD extension, or executable programs with the .EXE extension. One user or many users can use a single logon script, and as the administrator, you control which users use which scripts. As the name implies, logon scripts are accessed when users log on to their accounts. In a Windows NT domain, the location of logon scripts is relative to the server authenticating the logon. On the authenticating server, the default location of logon scripts is *%SystemRoot%*\System32\REPL\IMPORT\SCRIPTS.

To set the logon script name, you use the Logon Script Name field in the User Environment Profile dialog box. Any directory path information associated with the logon script name is relative to the default path for logon scripts. Because you can set a relative path, you have two ways of setting the logon script name:

- Specify only the file name, such as MARKETING.CMD. Here the complete path to the script is *%SystemRoot%*\System32\REPL\IMPORT\ SCRIPTS\MARKETING.CMD.
- Specify a relative path and file name, such as MKG\DOMUSERS.BAT. Here the complete path to the script is *%SystemRoot%*\System32\ REPL\IMPORT\SCRIPTS\MKG\DOMUSERS.BAT.

Tip In a Windows NT domain, domain controllers are responsible for authenticating log on. Using the directory Replicator service, you can replicate the SCRIPTS directory on the primary domain controller on the backup domain controllers. In this way, logon scripts should be available throughout the domain.

Creating logon scripts is easier than you might think, especially when you use the Windows NT command language. Just about any command you can type into a command prompt can be set to run in a logon script. The most common tasks you'll want logon scripts to handle are to set the default printers and network paths for users. You can set this information with the NET USE command. The following net use commands define a network printer and a network drive:

```
net use lpt1: \\zeta\deskjet
net use g: \\gamma\corp\files
```

If these commands were in the user's logon script, the user would have a network printer on LPT1 and a network drive on G:.

Assigning Home Directories

Windows NT lets you assign a home directory for each user account. Users can use this directory to store and retrieve their personal files. Many applications use the home directory as the default for File Open and Save As operations, which helps users find their resources easily. The command prompt also uses the home directory as the initial current directory.

Home directories can be located on a user's local hard disk drive or on a shared network drive. On a local drive, the directory is only accessible from a single workstation. On the other hand, shared network drives can be accessed from any computer on the network, which makes for a more versatile user environment.

Note Although users can share home directories, this isn't a good idea. You'll usually want to provide each user with a unique home directory.

You do not need to create the user's home directory ahead of time. User Manager automatically creates the directory for you. But if there's a problem creating the directory, User Manager will instruct you to create it manually.

To specify a local home directory:

- Click on the Local Path radio button, and then enter the path to the home directory in the associated field. Here's an example: C:\Home*%UserName%*

To specify a network home directory:

1. Click on the Connect radio button, and then select a drive letter for the home directory. For consistency, you should use the same drive letter for all users. Also, be sure to select a drive letter that will not conflict with any currently configured physical or mapped drives. To avoid problems, you may want to use Z: as the drive letter.
2. Enter the complete path to the home directory using the UNC notation, such as: \\GAMMA\USER_DIRS*%UserName%*. You include the server name in the drive path to ensure the user can access the directory from any computer on the network.

Note If you do not assign a home directory, Windows NT uses the default local home directory. On systems where Windows NT is installed as an upgrade, this directory is \Users\Default. Otherwise, this directory is the root directory.

Managing Logon Hours

Windows NT allows you to control when users can log on to the network. You do this by setting their valid logon hours. You can use logon hour restrictions to tighten security and prevent system cracking or malicious conduct after normal business hours.

During valid logon hours, users can work as they normally do. They can log on to the network and access network resources. During restricted logon hours, users can't work normally. They can't log on to the network or make connections to network resources. If users are logged on when their logon time expires, the action taken depends on the Account Policy set for users. Generally, one of two things happens to the user:

- **Forcibly disconnected** You can set a policy that tells Windows NT to forcibly disconnect Windows NT users when their logon hours expire. If this policy is set, remote Windows NT users are disconnected from all network resources and logged off the system when their hours expire. (For more information, see the section of this chapter titled, "Password and Account Policies.")
- **Not disconnected** Users are not disconnected from the network when they enter the restricted hours. Instead, Windows NT simply doesn't allow them to make any new network connections.

To configure the logon hours, click on the Hours button in the New User, User Properties, or Copy Of dialog boxes. You can now set the valid and invalid logon hours using the Logon Hours dialog box shown in Figure 5-13, on the following page. Logon Hours features are listed in Table 5-2, on the following page.

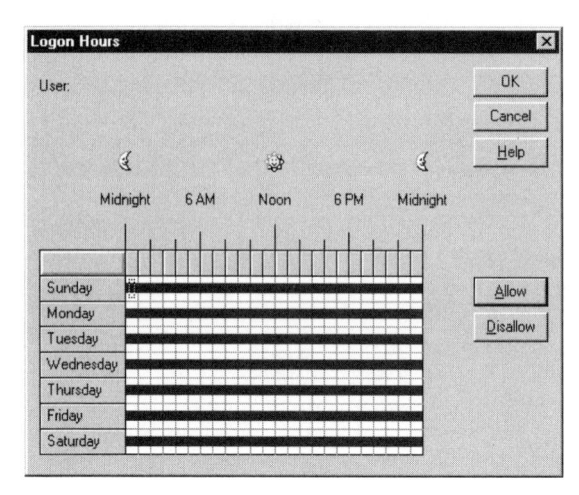

Figure 5-13. *Select the existing profile you want to copy to the new user account.*

In this dialog box each hour of the day or night is a field that you can turn on and off.

- Hours that are allowed are filled in with a dark bar—you can think of these hours as being turned on.
- Hours that are disallowed are blank—you can think of these hours as being turned off.

To change the setting for an hour, click on it, then use either the Allow or Disallow button.

Table 5-2. Logon Hours Features

Feature	Function
Button above Sunday	Allows you to select all the time periods.
Day of week buttons	Allow you to select all the hours in a particular day.
Hourly buttons	Allow you to select a particular hour for all the days of the week.
Allow button	Sets the allowed logon hours.
Disallow button	Sets the disallowed logon hours.

> **Tip** When setting logon hours, you'll save yourself a lot of work in the long run if you give users a moderately restricted time window. For example, rather than explicit 9–5 hours, you may want to allow a few hours on either side of the normal work hours. This will let the early birds onto the system and allow the night owls to keep working until they finish for the day.

Setting Permitted Logon Workstations

Windows NT has a formal policy that allows users to log on to systems locally. This policy controls whether or not a user can sit at the computer's

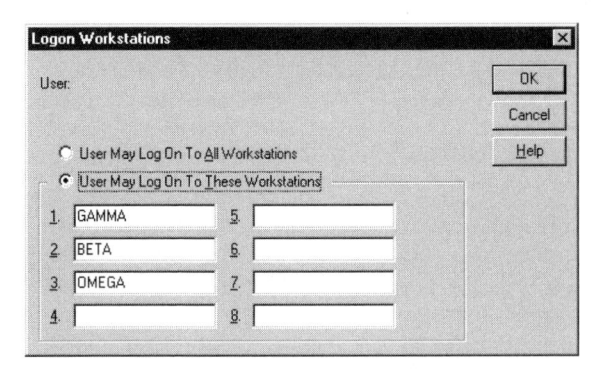

Figure 5-14. *To restrict access to workstations, specify the permitted logon workstations.*

keyboard and log on. By default, on Windows NT workstations you can use any valid user account to log on locally, including the guest account.

As you might imagine, allowing users to log on to any workstation is a big security no-no. Unless you restrict workstation use, anyone who obtains a user name and password can use it to log on to any workstation in the domain. By defining a permitted workstation list, you close the opening in your domain and reduce the security risk. Now hackers must not only find a user name and password, they must also find the permitted workstations for the account.

Note The permitted logon workstation restrictions only affect Windows NT computers in the domain. If there are any non-Windows NT computers in the domain, they are not subject to the restrictions, which means you only need a valid user name and password to log on to these systems.

For domain users, you define permitted logon workstations as follows:

- Open the Logon Workstations dialog box by clicking the Logon To button in the New User, User Properties, or Copy Of dialog boxes.
- Select the User May Log On To These Workstations radio button, then specify up to eight logon workstations (see Figure 5-14).

Setting Account Information and Dial-In Privileges

The Account Information dialog box allows you to specify an expiration date for an account and whether an account is local or global. By default, accounts do not expire. If you set an expiration date, the account will be disabled on the expiration date and the user will not be able to log on. To open this dialog box, click the Account button in the New User, User Properties, or Copy Of dialog boxes.

Windows NT lets you set dial-in privileges for accounts using the Dial In Information dialog box. Access this dialog box by clicking on the Dial In button in the New User, User Properties, or Copy Of dialog boxes. By default, dial-in privileges are disabled for new user accounts. To allow users to dial in, select the Grant Dial-In Permission To User check box, then define the call back parameters. Call back parameters are used as follows:

- **No Call Back** The user is allowed to dial in directly and remain connected. The user pays the long-distance telephone charges if applicable.
- **Set by Caller** The user is allowed to dial in directly, and then the server prompts the user for a call back number. Once entered, the user is disconnected and the server dials the user back at the specified number to reestablish the connection. The company pays the long-distance telephone charges if applicable.

> **Note** You should not assign call back for users who dial in through a switchboard. The switchboard may not allow the user to properly connect to the network.

- **Preset To** Allows you to set a predefined call back number for security purposes. When a user dials in, the server calls back the preset number. The company pays the long-distance telephone charges if applicable and reduces the risk of an unauthorized person accessing the network.

> **Note** You should not use preset call back numbers with multilinked lines. The multilinked lines will not function properly.

Chapter 6
Managing Existing User and Group Accounts

In a perfect world, you could create user and group accounts and never have to touch them again. Unfortunately, we live in the real world. After you create accounts, you'll spend a lot of your time managing them. This chapter provides guidelines and tips to make that task easier.

Note For ease of reference this chapter uses the term User Manager to refer to both User Manager and User Manager for Domains, unless otherwise noted.

Updating User and Group Accounts

User Manager is usually the tool to use when you want to update an account. Because you'll be working with User Manager quite a bit, you'll want to learn how to get the most out of it. Here are some tips for working with accounts in User Manager:

- Double-click on a user or group name to open it for editing.
- Resize user and group areas within User Manager by, first, clicking on the small black box midway down the right-hand side of the window and, second, holding the mouse button as you resize the window by moving up or down.
- Use Font from the Options menu to select a font that's easy for you to read. Be sure to select the Save Settings On Exit option from the same menu. This ensures that your User Manager settings are saved for next time.
- Do not use the low-speed connection settings unless you have to. If you do, the available information is severely restricted and you are limited in what you can do.

Renaming User Accounts

User Manager lets you rename user accounts using the Rename option on the User menu. To do this, complete the following steps:

1. Select the account you want to rename in the main window of User Manager.
2. Choose Rename from the User menu and then enter the new account name when prompted.

SIDs

When you rename a user account, you give the account a new label. As discussed in Chapter 4, text labels are meant to make managing and using accounts easier. Behind the scenes, Microsoft Windows NT uses SIDs (security identifiers) to identify, track, and handle accounts independently from user names. SIDs are unique identifiers that are generated when accounts are created.

Because SIDs are mapped to account names internally, you don't need to change the privileges or permissions on the renamed account. Windows NT simply maps the SID to the new account name as necessary.

Marriage is a common reason for changing the name on an account. For example, if Jane Williams (JANEW) gets married, she may want her user name to be changed to Jane Marshall (JANEM). When you change the user name from JANEW to JANEM, all associated privileges and permissions will reflect the name change. Thus, if you view the permissions on a file that JANEW had access to, JANEM will now have access (and JANEW will no longer be listed).

Changing Other Information

When you change JANEW to JANEM, the user properties and names of files associated with the account are not changed. This means you should update the account information. The information you *may* need to change includes:

- **Full Name**   Change the user account's Full Name in User Manager.
- **User Profile Path**   Change the User Profile Path in User Manager, then rename the corresponding directory on disk.
- **Logon Script Name**   If you use individual logon scripts for each user, you'll need to change the Logon Script Name in User Manager and then rename the logon script on disk.
- **Home Directory**   Change the home directory path in User Manager, then rename the corresponding directory on disk.

> **Note**   Changing directory and file information for an account when a user is logged on may cause problems. So you may want to update this information after-hours or ask the user to log off for a few minutes and then log back on.

Copying User and Group Accounts

Creating accounts from scratch every time can be tedious. Instead of starting anew each time, you may want to use an existing account as a starting point. To do this, follow these steps:

1. Select the account you want to copy in the main window of User Manager.
2. Press F8 or choose Copy from the User menu. For user accounts, this opens the Copy Of dialog box. For group accounts, this opens the appropriate dialog box for the type of group you are copying. If you are copying a local group, you'll see the New Local Group dialog box. Otherwise, you'll see the New Global Group dialog box.
3. Update the properties of the account as appropriate.

As you might expect, when you create a copy of an account, User Manager doesn't retain all the information from the existing account. Instead, User Manager tries to copy only the information you'll need and discards the information that you'll need to update.

Properties Retained
For user accounts, the properties that are retained include

- Account description
- Check box selections for User Must Change Password, User Can't Change Password, and Password Never Expires
- Group account memberships
- Profile settings
- Logon hours
- Permitted logon workstations
- Account type and expiration
- Dial-in privileges

Note If you used environment variables to specify the profile settings in the original account, the environment variables are used for the copy of the account as well. For example, if the original account used the *%UserName%* variable, the copy of the account will also use this variable.

Properties Not Retained
For user accounts, the properties that are not retained include

- User Name
- Full Name
- Check box selections for Account Disabled
- Password and Confirm Password
- Rights and Permissions

Deleting User and Group Accounts

Deleting an account permanently removes the account. Once you delete an account, you can't create an account with the same name to get the same permissions. That's because the SID for the new account won't match the SID for the old account.

Because deleting built-in accounts could have far-reaching effects on the domain, Windows NT does not let you delete built-in user accounts or group accounts. You *could* remove other types of accounts by selecting them and pressing the Del key or by using the Delete option on the User menu. When prompted, click OK and then click Yes.

> **Note** When you delete a user account, Windows NT doesn't delete the user's profile, personal files, or home directory. If you want to delete these files and directories, you'll have to do it manually.

Changing and Resetting Passwords

As an administrator, you'll often have to change or reset user passwords. This usually happens when users forget their passwords or their passwords expire.

To change or reset a password, follow these steps:

1. Start User Manager, then double-click on the user's account name.
2. Enter a new password for the user and confirm it. The password should conform to the password policy for the domain.
3. Deselect the Account Disabled and Account Locked Out check boxes as necessary.

Enabling User Accounts

User accounts can become disabled for several reasons. If a user forgets the password and tries to guess it, the user may exceed the account policy for bad logon attempts. Another administrator could have disabled the account while the user was on vacation. Or the account could have expired. What to do when an account is disabled, locked out, or expired is described in the following sections.

Account Disabled
When an account is disabled, do the following:

1. Start User Manager, then double-click on the user's account name.
2. Deselect the Disable Account check box in User Manager.

Account Locked Out
When an account is locked out, do the following:

1. Start User Manager, then double-click on the user's account name.
2. Deselect the Account Locked Out check box in User Manager.

Account Expired

When an account is expired, do the following:

1. Start User Manager, then double-click on the user's account name.
2. Click on the Account button, then set a new expiration date for the account using the fields in the Account Expires area.

Note If users are frequently locked out of their accounts, you may want to consider adjusting the account policy for the domain. Here, you may want to increase the value for acceptable bad logon attempts and reduce the duration for the associated counter. For more information on setting account policy, see Chapter 5.

Troubleshooting Logon Problems

The previous section listed ways in which accounts can become disabled. Beyond the typical reasons for an account being unavailable, some system settings can also cause access problems. Specifically, you should look for the following:

- **User gets a message that says that the user can't log on interactively.** The user right to log on locally is not set for this user and the user is not a member of a group that has this right.

    The user may be trying to log on to a server or domain controller. If so, keep in mind that the right to log on locally applies to all domain controllers in the domain. Otherwise, this right only applies to the single workstation.

    If the user should have access to the local system, follow these steps:

    1. Start User Manager, then double-click on the user's account name.
    2. Click on the Groups button, then make the user a member of a group that has local logon privileges.

- **User gets a message that the system could not log the user on.** If you've already checked the password and account name, you may want to check the account type. The user may be trying to access the domain with a local account. If the user should have a domain account, change the account type by doing the following:

    1. Start User Manager, then double-click on the user's account name.
    2. Click on the Account button, then select the Global Account radio button.

    On the other hand, if the user should have a local account, tell the user to select the local computer name rather than the domain name when logging on.

- **User has a mandatory profile and the computer storing the profile is unavailable.** When a user has a mandatory profile, the computer storing the profile must be accessible during the logon process.

If the computer is shut down or otherwise unavailable, users with mandatory profiles will not be able to log on.

- **User gets a message saying the account has been configured to prevent the user from logging on to the workstation.** The user is trying to access a workstation that is not defined as a permitted logon workstation. If the user should have access to this workstation, change the logon workstation information by doing the following:

    1. Start User Manager, then double-click on the user's account name.
    2. Click on the Logon To button, then add the workstation to the permission list.

Managing User Profiles

User profiles contain settings for the network environment, such as desktop configuration and menu options. Problems with a profile can sometimes prevent a user from logging on. For example, if the display size in the profile isn't available on the system being used, the user may not be able to log on properly. In fact, the user may get nothing but a blank screen when trying to log on. You could reboot the machine, go into VGA mode, and then reset the display manually, but solutions for profile problems aren't always this easy and you may need to update the profile itself.

Windows NT provides several ways to manage user profiles:

- You can assign profile paths in User Manager.
- You can copy, delete, and change the type of an existing local profile with the System utility in the Control Panel.
- You can set system policies that prevent users from manipulating certain aspects of their environment

In this section you'll learn how to manage existing profiles with the System utility. For complete information on profile types and setting initial profile paths, see Chapter 5. To learn how to set system policies, see Chapter 3, "Monitoring Windows NT Processes, Services, and Security."

Using the System Utility to Manage Local Profiles

To manage local profiles, you will need to log on to the user's computer. Afterward, you can use the System utility in the Control Panel to manage local profiles. To view current profile information, start the System utility, and then click on the User Profiles tab.

As shown in Figure 6-1, the User Profiles tab displays various information about the profiles stored on the local system. You can use this information to help you manage profiles. The fields have the following meanings:

- **Name** The name of the local profile, which generally includes the name of the originating domain or computer and the user account

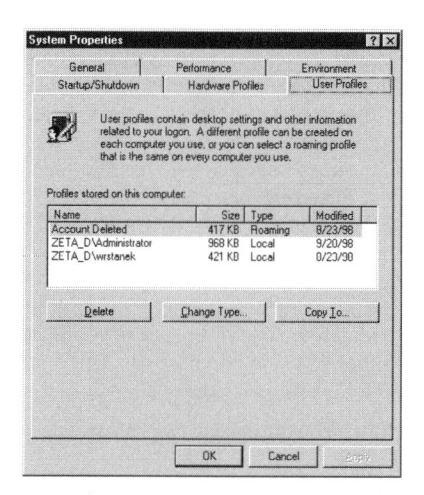

Chapter 6 Managing Existing User and Group Accounts | 113

Figure 6-1. *The User Profiles tab in the System Properties dialog box lets you manage existing local profiles.*

name. For example, the name ZETA_D\GIJOE tells you the original profile is from the domain ZETA_D and the user account is GIJOE.

If you delete an account but don't delete the associated profile, you may also see an entry that says Account Deleted. Don't worry, the profile is still available for copying if you need it.

- **Size** The size of the profile. Generally, the larger the profile, the more the user has customized the environment.
- **Type** The profile type, which is either local or roaming.
- **Modified** Tells you the date when the profile was last modified.

Deleting a Local Profile and Assigning a New One

Profiles are accessed when a user logs on to a computer. Windows NT uses local profiles for all users who do not have roaming profiles. Generally, local profiles are also used if the local profile has a more recent modification date than the user's roaming profile. Because of this, there are instances when you may need to delete a user's local profile. For example, if a user's local profile becomes corrupt, you can delete the profile and assign a new one. Keep in mind that when you delete a local profile that is not stored anywhere else on the domain, you can't recover the user's original environment settings.

To delete a user's local profile, follow these steps:

1. Log on to the user's computer.
2. Start the System utility and then click on the User Profiles tab.
3. Select the profile you want to delete and then click on the Delete button. When asked to confirm that you want to delete the profile, click Yes.

> **Note** You can't delete a profile that is currently in use. If the user is currently logged on to the local system (the computer you are deleting the profile from), the user will need to log off. In some instances Windows NT marks profiles as in use when they are not. This is typically a result of an environment change for the user that has not been properly applied. To correct this, you may need to reboot the computer.

Now the next time the user logs in, Windows NT will do one of two things. Either the operating system will give the user the default local profile for that system or it will retrieve the user's roaming profile stored on another computer. To prevent the use of either of these profiles, you will need to assign a new profile to the user. To do this, you can

- Copy an existing profile to the user's profile directory. Copying profiles is covered in the next section.
- Update the profile settings for the user in User Manager. Setting the profile path is covered in Chapter 5.

Copying a Profile

When you work with workgroups where each computer is managed separately, you'll often have to copy a user's local profile from one computer to another. Copying a profile allows users to maintain environment settings when they use different computers. Of course, in a Windows NT domain you can use a roaming profile to create a single profile that can be accessed from anywhere within the domain. The catch is that sometimes you may need to copy an existing local profile over the top of a user's roaming profile (when the roaming profile is corrupt) or you may need to copy an existing local profile to a roaming profile in another domain.

You can copy an existing profile to a new location by doing the following:

1. Log on to the user's computer, then start the System Control Panel utility and open the User Profile tab.
2. Select the existing profile you want to copy using the Profiles Stored On This Computer list box.
3. Copy the profile to the new location by clicking on the Copy To button, then enter the path to the new profile directory in the Copy Profile To field. For example, if you are creating the profile for JANEW, you could enter: **\\GAMMA\USERPROFILES\JANEW** (see Figure 6-2).
4. Now you need to give the user permission to access the profile. Click on the Change button in the Permitted To Use area, then use the Choose User dialog box to grant access to the appropriate user account. By default, the Choose User dialog box only shows the names of group accounts. If you want to grant access to a *group* the new user is a member of, select this group and then use the Add button to copy the group to the Add Name field. To grant access to a *specific user*, click on the Show Users button.

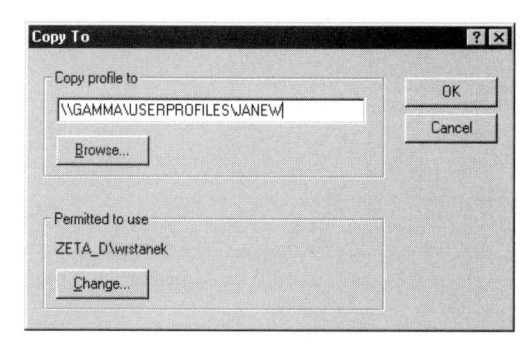

Chapter 6 Managing Existing User and Group Accounts | 115

Figure 6-2. *Use the Copy To dialog box to enter the new location of the profile directory and assign access permissions to the appropriate user.*

This should add a list of available user accounts to the dialog box. Select the user account and then use the Add button to copy the user name to the Add Name field.

5. When you are finished, close the Copy To dialog box by clicking OK. Windows NT will then copy the profile to the next location.

Changing the Profile Type

With roaming profiles, the System utility lets you change the profile type on the user's computer. To do this, select the profile and then click on the Change Type button. The options of this dialog box allow you to

- **Change a roaming profile to a local profile** If you want the user to always work with the local profile on this computer, set the profile for local use. Here, all changes to the profile are made locally and the original roaming profile is left untouched.

- **Change a local profile (that was defined originally as a roaming profile) to a roaming profile** The user will use the original roaming profile for the next logon. Afterward, Windows NT will treat the profile like any other roaming profile, which means that any changes to the local profile will be copied to the roaming profile.

- **Specify that a roaming profile should be cached locally** Instead of downloading the roaming profile when the user logs on, Windows NT will use a cached copy of the profile. Updates to the profile may be copied back to the original roaming profile.

Note If these options aren't available, the user's original profile is defined locally.

Managing Multiple User Accounts

A little-known fact about User Manager is that you can use it to modify the properties of multiple accounts simultaneously. Any changes you make to the property settings are made for all the selected accounts.

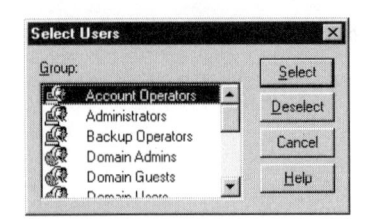

Figure 6-3. *Select Users allows you to select multiple users based on group membership. When you are finished selecting accounts, click Close and then choose Properties from the User menu.*

You can select multiple accounts by doing the following:

- Select multiple user names for editing by holding down the Ctrl key and clicking the left mouse button on each account you want to select.
- Select a range of user names by holding down the Shift key, selecting the first account name, and then clicking on the last account in the range.
- Use the Select Users dialog box to select multiple users based on group membership. To do this, open the dialog box shown in Figure 6-3 using the Select Users option on the User menu. Now, if you highlight a group and choose Select, members of that group are added to the selected users in the main window. On the other hand, if you highlight a group and choose Deselect, members of that group are added to the deselected users in the main window. When you are finished selecting accounts, click on the Close button.

When you are finished selecting accounts for management, choose Properties from the User menu. This opens the main User Properties window. As you can see, the User Properties dialog box has a different interface (see Figure 6-4). You should note the following changes:

- The dialog box now has a Users field that shows the user account names that you are modifying.
- The Full Name, Password, and Confirm Password fields are no longer available.
- The Description field now sets a description for all the accounts.
- If you see a selected check box that is partially shaded, this option is set for one or more of the accounts.
- If you see a selected check box that is *not* partially shaded, all of the selected accounts currently have this option set.

Any changes you make to the main dialog box window are applied to all the accounts you are working with. For example, if you deselect a partially shaded check box, this option will be deselected for all the accounts. You can also use the Groups, Profile, Hours, Logon To, Account, and Dialin buttons. In the sections that follow you'll learn ways to set these properties for multiple accounts.

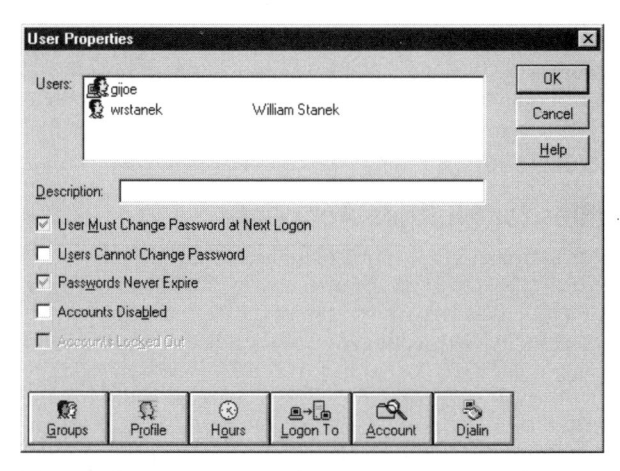

Chapter 6 Managing Existing User and Group Accounts | 117

Figure 6-4. *The User Properties dialog box has a different interface when you work with multiple accounts.*

Setting Group Membership for Multiple Accounts

When you work with group membership for multiple accounts, the Group Memberships dialog box has a slightly different interface (see Figure 6-5). Be careful, because this new interface can be misleading. The dialog box only shows group membership when *all* of the users are members of a particular group. Because of this, the main list boxes are renamed as

- **All Are Members Of** This list box only lists groups that all users are a member of.
- **Not All Are Members Of** This list box shows all groups that aren't already assigned to all the users listed in the Users area.

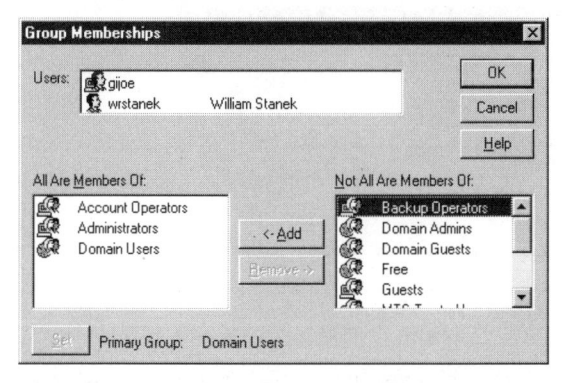

Figure 6-5. *Group Memberships for multiple users is broken down into groups all users are members of and groups all users aren't members of.*

To configure group memberships, click on the Groups button in the User Properties dialog box. As with single account management, you can add and remove group membership using the Add and Remove buttons. When you're finished assigning or removing group membership, click the OK button. For complete information on setting group membership, see Chapter 5.

Setting Profiles for Multiple Accounts

You set the profile information for multiple accounts using the User Environment Profile dialog box, which is displayed when you select the Profile button in the User Properties dialog box. One of the best reasons to work with multiple accounts in User Manager is to set all their environment profiles using a single interface. To do this, you will usually rely on the *%UserName%* environment variable, which lets you assign paths and file names that are based on individual user names. For example, if you assign the logon script name as *%USERNAME%*.CMD, Windows NT replaces this value with the user name—and it does so for each user you are managing. Thus, BOBS, JANEW, and ERICL would all be assigned unique logon scripts and those scripts would be named BOBS.CMD, JANEW.CMD, and ERICL.CMD.

An example of setting environment profile information for multiple accounts is shown in Figure 6-6. Note that the *%UserName%* variable is used to assign the user profile path, the user logon script name, and the home directory.

While you may want all users to have unique files and paths, there are times when you want users to share this information. For example, if you're using mandatory profiles for users, you may want to assign a specific user profile path rather than one that is dynamically created. For detailed information on setting user profiles, see Chapter 5.

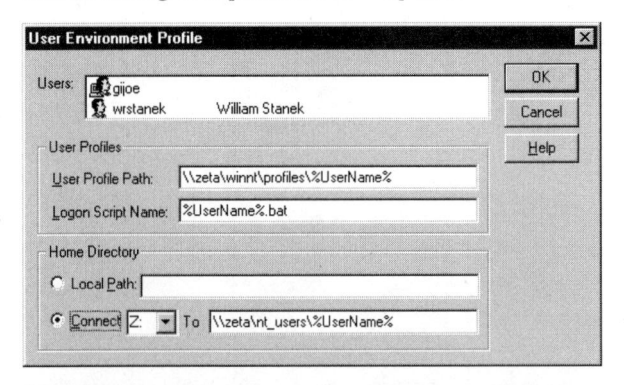

Figure 6-6. *Use the* %UserName% *environment variable to assign paths and filenames that are based on individual user names.*

Setting Logon Hours for Multiple Accounts

When you select multiple user accounts in User Manager, you can manage their logon hours collectively. To do this, select the Hours button in the User Properties dialog box.

User Manager warns you if the selected users have different logon settings. If you see the warning, you can cancel the operation or continue. If you choose to continue, the logon hours for all selected users are reset and you will need to reconfigure the logon hours as explained in Chapter 5. When you click OK, these settings are applied to all the selected user accounts.

Setting Permitted Logon Workstations for Multiple Accounts

You set the permitted logon workstations for multiple accounts using the Logon Workstations dialog box, which you get to by clicking on the Logon To button in the User Properties window. This dialog box has two radio buttons that let you configure the permitted logon workstations. If all the selected users share the same settings, these settings will be shown in the dialog box. Otherwise, neither radio button will be initially selected.

If you want to allow the users to log on to any workstation, select the User May Log On To All Workstations radio button. On the other hand, if you want to specify which workstations users are permitted to use, select the User May Log On To These Workstations radio button and then enter the names of up to eight workstations. When you click OK, these settings are applied to all the selected user accounts. For more information, see Chapter 5.

Note Users on systems other than Windows NT are not subject to these restrictions. This means that MS-DOS or Mac users could log on to their system even if it is not specifically listed as a permitted workstation.

Setting Account Type and Expiration for Multiple Accounts

Account type and expiration is set using the Account Information dialog box. To open it, click on the Account button in the User Properties window. This dialog box has two pairs of radio buttons that let you configure the account type and expiration for all the users. If all the selected users share the same settings, these settings are shown in the dialog box. Otherwise, the affected pair of radio buttons will not be selected. In the example shown in Figure 6-7, on the following page, all users share the same account expiration—never—but there is a conflict in the account type settings so neither account type radio button is initially selected.

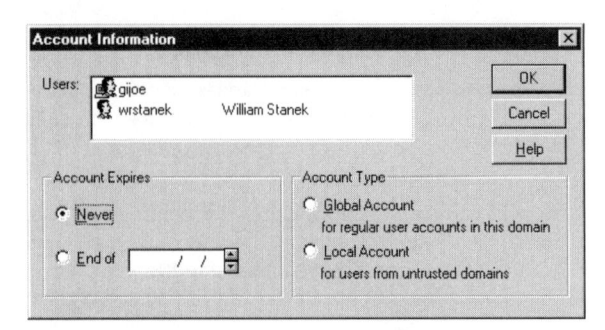

Figure 6-7. *Set the account type and expiration date using the Account Information dialog box. Because multiple accounts are affected, the initial settings reflect shared settings and conflicts in the settings.*

As outlined in Chapter 5, use the radio buttons to configure the account type and expiration date. When you are finished, click OK and the settings will be applied to all the selected user accounts.

Setting Dial-In Privileges for Multiple Accounts

You set dial-in privileges for multiple accounts using the Dial-in Information dialog box, which is accessible by clicking on the Dialin button in the User Properties window. This dialog box has a check box and a set of radio buttons that let you configure dial-in privileges. If all the selected users share the same settings, these settings will be shown in the dialog box. Otherwise, if there is a conflict, the conflicting element will be deselected initially.

As described in Chapter 5, use the check box and the radio buttons to configure dial-in privileges. When you are finished, click OK to apply the settings to all the selected user accounts.

Customizing User Logons

To optimize workstations and servers for different workplaces and needs, Windows NT lets you customize the logon process. Most of the customizations involve modifying registry settings. In Windows NT you modify the registry using the 32-bit registry editor (REGEDT32.EXE).

This section discusses setting values for two keys in the registry.

- The Winlogon key:
```
HKEY_LOCAL_MACHINE
    \SOFTWARE
        \Microsoft
            \Windows NT
                \CurrentVersion
                    \WinLogon
```

Chapter 6 Managing Existing User and Group Accounts | 121

- The Desktop key:

    HKEY_USERS

        \Default

            \Control Panel

                \Desktop

Table 6-1. Omitting the Name of the Last User to Log On

Key	Entry	Omit Name	Display Name
Winlogon	DontDisplayLastUserName	0	1

By default, Windows NT displays the name of the last user to log on to a computer. Although this is convenient if the same users access a computer repeatedly, this capability presents a potential security problem—anyone with access to the computer can use the logon dialog box to obtain a valid user name for the computer.

To omit the name of the last user logon, you need to change the Winlogon key entry for DontDisplayLastUserName. By default, the entry is set to 0, which displays the last logon user name. Change the value to 1 to omit the user name (see Table 6-1).

Note This value may not be present in your Registry. In this case, add the field and set its value.

Table 6-2. Shutdown without Logon

Key	Entry	Disable	Enable
Winlogon	ShutdownWithoutLogon	0	1

The Winlogon key entry ShutdownWithoutLogon determines whether the Shutdown button is enabled in the logon dialog box. If available, anyone with physical access to the computer can use the Shutdown button to halt the system without logging on first.

By default, this button is enabled on Windows NT workstations and disabled on Windows NT servers. You can change the setting through the registry entry. A value of 0 disables the button and a value of 1 enables the button (see Table 6-2).

Table 6-3. Powerdown After Shutdown

Key	Entry	Disable	Enable
Winlogon	PowerdownAfterShutdown	0	1

Some computers have BIOS that allows the computer to be powered off by software. The PowerdownAfterShutdown entry lets you take advantage of this feature. If you enable this feature, a radio button labeled Shutdown and Power Off is added to the Shutdown dialog box.

By default, the value of this entry is 0 and the button is not available on the Shutdown dialog box. To enable powerdown after shutdown, set the value to 1 (see Table 6-3).

Table 6-4. Configuring Automatic Logon

Key	Entry	Value
Winlogon	AutoAdminLogon	0 to disable; 1 to enable
	DefaultUserName	Username
	DefaultDomainName	Domainname
	DefaultPassword	Password

Normally, Windows NT prompts you for a user name and password before you can log on to a system. However, there are times when you may want to log on automatically after the system boots. For example, if you are working with servers in a locked server room, you may want to set automatic logons (see Table 6-4). To do this, you will need to make several changes to the Winlogon key:

1. Add the AutoAdminLogon value with a data type of REG_SZ. Afterward, set this value entry to 1, which enables the feature.

2. Double-check the values for the DefaultUserName and DefaultDomainName entries. DefaultUserName should be set to a valid user name with administrator privileges. DefaultDomainName should be set to the current domain name.

3. Add the DefaultPassword value with a data type of REG_SZ. Then set this value to the current password for the default user.

Note You can disable this feature at any time by changing the value of the AutoAdminLogon entry to 0.

Table 6-5. Sync Logon with Script

Key	Entry	Disable	Enable
Winlogon	RunLogonScriptSync	0	1

The RunLogonScriptSync determines whether the user is allowed to log on before the logon script finishes executing. This is disabled by default, which allows users to log on before the script finishes executing. To enable the feature, set the RunLogonScriptSync value to 1 (see Table 6-5).

Table 6-6. Displaying a Custom Logon Message

Key	Entry	Value
Winlogon	LegalNoticeCaption	Caption to display
	LegalNoticeText	Text of the custom message

Sometimes you may want to display a message to all users before they can log on. This message could be a system use policy, a disclaimer, or any other custom message you want users to see. You can create a custom logon message using the LegalNoticeCaption and LegalNoticeText values.

LegalNoticeCaption sets the caption of the message's dialog box. LegalNoticeText sets the text of the message.

When you set these entries for the Winlogon key, your custom message is displayed after Ctrl+Alt+Del is pressed and before the logon process (see Table 6-6).

Table 6-7. Setting Default Screen Saver Options

Key	Entry	Value
Desktop	ScreenSaveActive	0 to deactivate; 1 to activate
	ScreenSaveTimeOut	Timeout in seconds
	SCRNSAVE.EXE	Screen saver executable

When no one is logged into a computer, the computer uses the default settings in the registry to determine how the screen saver is used. You can modify these settings using the Desktop key (see Table 6-7).

ScreenSaveActive determines whether the default screen saver is active. Set this value to 0 to disable the screen saver or 1 to enable the screen saver. The default is 1.

ScreenSaveTimeOut determines the number of seconds before the screen saver is activated. The default value is 900. You can set this to any value that suits your organization.

You can also specify the screen saver program that Windows NT uses. By default, the system uses LOGON.SCR, which is in the *%SystemRoot%*\System32 folder. If you want to specify a different screen saver program, copy its executable to the *%SystemRoot%*\System32 folder and then use the appropriate setting for the SCRNSAVE.EXE value. If you look in the System32 folder, you'll find there are other screen savers available. These screen savers were installed with the Windows NT operating system and they include

- **SCRNSAVE.SCR**   Default screen saver
- **SS3DFO.SCR**   3-D flying objects
- **SSBEZIER.SCR**   Beziers
- **SSFLWBOX.SCR**   Flower box
- **SSMARQUE.SCR**   Marquee display
- **SSMAZE.SCR**   3-D maze
- **SSMYST.SCR**   Mystify
- **SSPIPES.SCR**   3-D pipes
- **SSTARS.SCR**   Starfield simulation
- **SSTEXT3D.SCR**   3-D text

Caution   You should not modify the screen saver when performing key network tasks and services on Windows NT servers. Screen savers can be processor intensive and may seriously affect the performance of the system.

Another feature you may want to set is the image that is displayed by the screen saver. By default, Windows NT stores the standard screen saver images in the *%SystemRoot%* folder. For workstations, the image file names are WINNT256.BMP and WINNT.BMP. For servers, the image file names are LANMAN256.BMP and LANMANNT.BMP. These represent the 256-color and the true color images used by Windows NT. Be sure to replace the default images with images of similar size and color depth.

Table 6-8. Wallpaper Settings for the Default User

Key	Entry	Value
Desktop	TileWallPaper	0 to disable; 1 to enable
	Wallpaper	Filename

Through the registry, you can also define the wallpaper settings for the default user. You assign wallpaper settings using the Desktop key.

TileWallPaper lets you tile the wallpaper to fill the background. By default, this value is set to 0. To enable tiling, set the value to 1.

Wallpaper lets you define the file to use as wallpaper. By default, Windows NT uses the default wallpaper. You can change this to any valid BMP file that is in the *%SystemRoot%* folder. Be sure to use a color depth that is appropriate for the system (see Table 6-8).

Part III
Windows NT Data Administration

This part of the book covers Microsoft Windows NT data administration. Chapter 7 starts by detailing how to add hard drives to a system and how to partition drives. It then dives into common tasks for managing file systems and drives, such as defragmenting disks and creating emergency boot disks. Chapter 8 covers tools for managing volume sets and RAID arrays and also provides detailed advice on repairing damaged arrays. Chapter 9 focuses on managing files and directories and the associated tasks. You'll even find quick tips for performing advanced file searches and dragging files. Chapter 10 details how to enable file, drive, and directory sharing for remote network and Internet users. Chapter 11 explores data backup and recovery.

Chapter 7

Managing File Systems and Drives

A hard drive is the most common storage device used on network workstations and servers. Users depend on hard drives to store their word-processing documents, spreadsheets, and other types of data. Drives are organized into file systems that users can access either locally or remotely:

- **Local file systems** Local file systems are installed on a user's computer and don't require remote network connections to access. An example of a local file system is the C drive available on most workstations and servers. You access the C drive using the file path C:\.
- **Remote file systems** Remote file systems, on the other hand, are accessed through a network connection to a remote resource. You can connect to a remote file system using the Map Network Drive feature of Microsoft Windows NT Explorer.

Wherever disk resources are located, it's your job as a system administrator to manage them. The tools and techniques you use to manage file systems and drives are discussed in this chapter. Chapter 8 looks at fault tolerance and drive arrays. Chapter 9 tells you how to manage files and directories.

Adding Hard Drives

Before you make a hard drive available to users, you'll need to configure it and consider the way it will be used. Windows NT makes it possible to configure hard drives in a variety of ways. The technique you choose depends primarily on the type of data you're working with and the needs of your network environment. For general user data stored on workstations, you may want to configure individual drives as stand-alone storage devices. In that case, user data is stored on a workstation's hard drive, where it can be accessed and stored locally.

Although storing data on a single drive is convenient, it isn't the most reliable way to store data. To improve reliability and performance, you may want a set of drives to work together. Windows NT supports drive sets and arrays using RAID (redundant array of inexpensive disk) technology, which is built into the operating system. RAID arrays are usually installed on Windows NT servers rather than on workstations.

Physical Drives

Whether you use individual drives or drive sets, you'll need physical drives. Physical drives are the actual hardware devices that are used to store data. The amount of data a drive can store depends on its size and whether compression is used. Typical drives have capacities of 500 megabytes to 10 gigabytes. The two drive types most commonly used on Windows NT are

- SCSI (small computer systems interface)
- IDE (integrated drive electronics)

The terms SCSI and IDE are designators for the interface type used by the hard drives. This interface is used to communicate with a drive controller. SCSI drives use SCSI controllers. IDE drives use IDE controllers. In general, you'll find that SCSI drives are more expensive than IDE but offer more options and are faster.

SCSI Drives

With SCSI, you can connect up to seven drives to a single controller. Each drive connected to the primary controller is given a numeric designation from 0 to 6. This designation is the drive's SCSI ID, meaning drive 0 is SCSI ID 0, drive 1 is SCSI ID 1, and so on. The drive controller itself is usually designated as SCSI ID 7. Designators for drives on secondary controllers start where the first controller leaves off. For example, if the first controller has seven drives, the first drive on the second controller would normally be SCSI ID 8.

Generally, you set a drive's SCSI ID number before you install it. This is done by using the jumpers on the back of the drive. Instead of jumpers, some drives have a push button or similar mechanism for setting the SCSI ID. If you change the ID of a SCSI device, you must power cycle the drive. This ensures that the change takes effect.

SCSI devices are connected to the controller in a daisy chain, with each device serially in a single line. The first and last device in the chain must be terminated properly. Typically, the SCSI controller terminates the first device itself, and the last device in the chain uses an actual terminator.

> **Tip** If you're installing an additional SCSI-2 disk drive on a computer with SCSI devices, the system should already have a terminator. Simply remove the terminator from the existing drive, hook up the new drive, and then plug the terminator into the new drive to complete the chain.

Before you can use a hard drive, it must be low-level formatted. With SCSI, the manufacturer normally performs this task before shipping the drive. If you need to do a low-level format on site, you'll usually find that the manufacturer has supplied a utility for this purpose. If necessary, use this utility to format the drive.

IDE Drives

With IDE, you can connect up to two drives to a controller. Each drive connected to the primary controller is given a numeric designation from 0 to 1. The first drive has a designator of 0. The second drive has a designator of 1. Designators for drives on secondary controllers start where the first controller leaves off. For example, if the first controller has two drives, the first drive on the second controller normally would have a designator of 3.

As with SCSI drives, you should set an IDE drive's designator before you install it. If this is the first IDE drive on a controller, you must set it up as the master device. If there are two drives on a controller, one drive must be set up as a master device and the other as a slave device. Generally, if you're installing a new drive, the existing drive becomes the master device and the new drive becomes the slave device.

Note Generally, you can't perform a low-level format of an IDE drive. The manufacturer performs this task before shipping the drive.

Preparing a Drive for Use

Once you install a drive, you'll need to configure it for use. You configure the drive by partitioning it and creating file systems in the partitions as needed. A partition is a section of a physical drive that functions as if it were a separate unit. After you create a partition, you can create a file system in the partition.

Disk Administrator

The tool you'll use to configure drives is Disk Administrator. Disk Administrator makes it easy to work with the internal and external drives on a local system. To use it, you'll need to log on to the workstation or server you want to configure. Run Disk Administrator by going to Start, selecting Programs, then Administrative Tools, and then Disk Administrator. Disk Administrator has two main dialog box windows: Disk Configuration and Volumes.

The Disk Configuration Window

The Disk Administrator window shown in Figure 7-1, on the following page, provides an overview of all the drives installed on the system. In this example, there are three disk devices installed on the system: Disk 0, a fixed drive of 8056 MB, Disk 1, a zip drive, and a CD-ROM device. Drive 0 is further broken down into sections: a primary partition, three logical drives, and a section of free space. The information provided for these drive sections can tell you the following information:

- Drive letter for the section
- The text label for the section (known as a volume label)
- The file system type, either FAT or NTFS
- The size of the drive section in megabytes

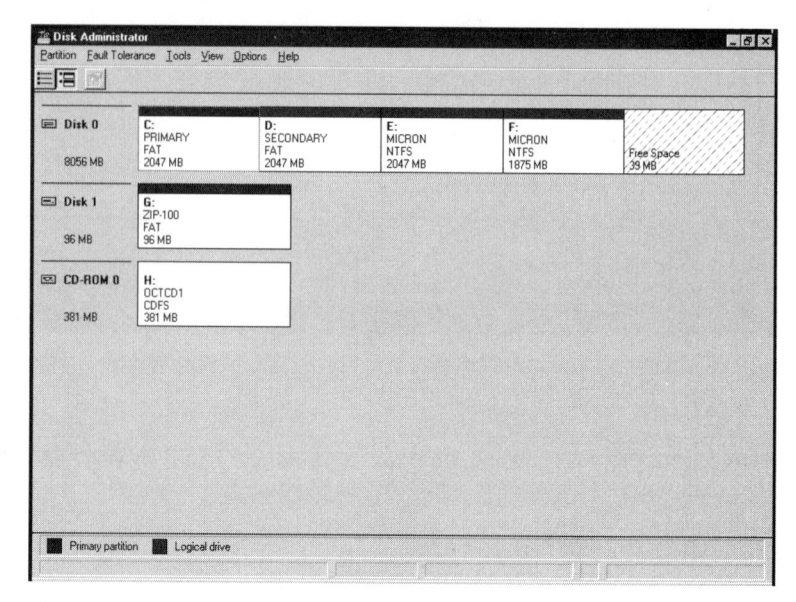

Figure 7-1. *The Disk Administrator window shown here provides an overview of all the drives installed on the system.*

> **Note** The first time you run Disk Administrator, the utility will display a dialog box telling you that the system configuration will be updated. Click OK. Windows NT is simply updating the system configuration information for your drives in Disk Administrator. You'll see the same dialog box anytime you install a new drive on the system and try to manage it with Disk Administrator.

More Detailed Drive Information

From the Disk Administrator window, you can get more detailed information on a drive section by right-clicking on it and then selecting Properties from the pop-up menu. Alternately, you can click on the drive section and then select the Properties button on the menu bar. When you do this, you'll see a dialog box much like the one shown in Figure 7-2. This is the same dialog box that you can access from Windows NT Explorer (by selecting the top-level folder for the drive and then choosing Properties from the File menu). The information provided on the General tab of the Properties dialog box tells you the following:

- Drive letter for the section.
- The text label for the section (known as a volume label).
- The disk type. A local disk is a disk on the current computer system. A network drive is a disk located on a remote computer system that is accessible through a network connection. You may also see floppy, CD-ROM, and RAM drive types.
- The file system type, either FAT or NTFS.

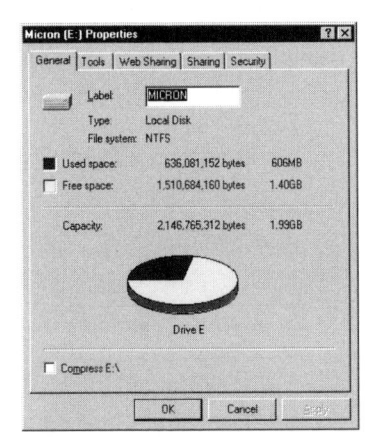

Figure 7-2. *The General tab of the Properties dialog box provides detailed information about a drive.*

- The amount of free space on the disk.
- The amount of used space on the disk.
- The total capacity of the disk.

The Volumes Window

Within Disk Administrator, you can also access a window that depicts volumes installed on the system. Click on the Volumes button on the menu bar or select Volumes from the View menu. As you can see from Figure 7-3, on the following page, the Volumes window provides a detailed summary of all the drives on the computer. Clicking on a column label, such as Name, allows you to sort the disk information based on that column. The column labels are used as follows:

- **Volume** The drive letter of the volume
- **Name** The text label (volume name)
- **Capacity** The amount of data the volume can hold
- **Free Space** The amount of free space in megabytes
- **% Free** The amount of free space as a percentage of total drive capacity
- **Format** The file system type, either FAT or NTFS
- **Fault Tolerant** Whether the drive uses Windows NT fault tolerant features, such as mirroring or striping
- **Volume Type** The type of volume used, such as a mirror set or stripe set
- **Fault Tolerant Overhead** The total additional drive space required as a result of the fault tolerant feature used
- **Status** The status of the volume, such as running or failed

Note Volume sets and fault tolerance are discussed in Chapter 8.

![Disk Administrator screenshot]

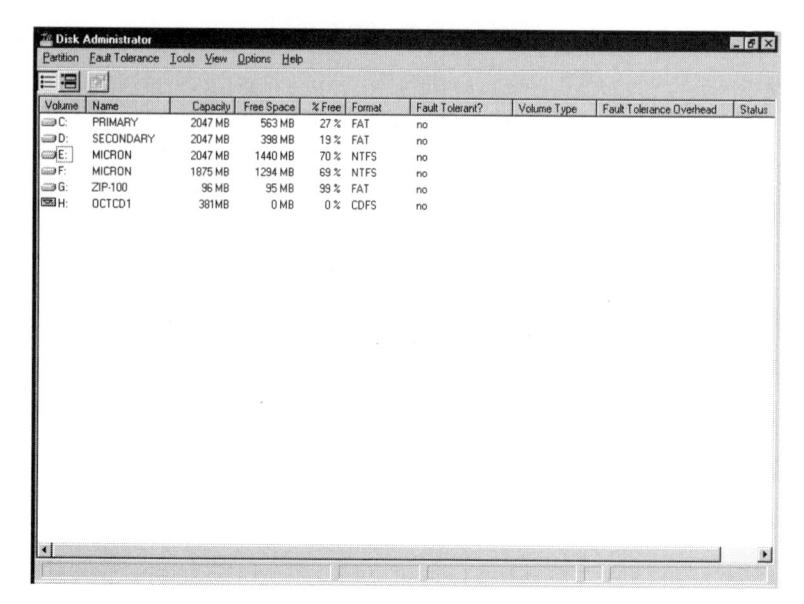

Volume	Name	Capacity	Free Space	% Free	Format	Fault Tolerant?	Volume Type	Fault Tolerance Overhead	Status
C:	PRIMARY	2047 MB	563 MB	27 %	FAT	no			
D:	SECONDARY	2047 MB	398 MB	19 %	FAT	no			
E:	MICRON	2047 MB	1440 MB	70 %	NTFS	no			
F:	MICRON	1875 MB	1294 MB	69 %	NTFS	no			
G:	ZIP-100	96 MB	95 MB	99 %	FAT	no			
H:	OCTCD1	381MB	0 MB	0 %	CDFS	no			

Figure 7-3. *In Disk Administrator, click on the Volume button or select Volume from the View menu to access the Volume window and get a detailed summary of all the drives on the computer.*

Understanding Drive Partitions

Windows NT uses two types of partitions: primary and extended.

- **Primary partitions**   Drive sections that can be used directly for file storage. Each physical drive can have up to four primary partitions. You make a primary partition accessible to users by creating a file system on it.

- **Extended partitions**   Unlike primary partitions, these can't be accessed directly. Instead, extended partitions can be configured with one or more logical drives that are used to store files. Being able to divide extended partitions into logical drives allows you to divide a physical drive into more than four sections.

On Windows NT, a physical drive can have up to four primary partitions and up to one extended partition. This allows you to configure drives in one of two ways:

- Using one to four primary partitions
- Using one to three primary partitions and one extended partition

> **Note**   With MS-DOS, a physical drive can have only one primary partition. This partition is the boot partition. If you plan to boot a Windows NT system in MS-DOS, you should use only one primary partition and then use an extended partition to create additional logical drives.

Assigning Drive Letters

After you partition a drive, you format the partitions to assign drive letters. This is a high-level format that creates the file system structure rather than a low-level format that sets the drive up for initial use.

You're probably very familiar with the C drive used by Windows NT. Well, the C drive is simply the designator for a disk partition. If you partition a disk into multiple sections, each section can have its own drive letter. You use the drive letters to access file systems in various partitions on a physical drive. Unlike MS-DOS, which assigns drive letters automatically starting with the letter C, Windows NT lets you specify drive letters. Generally, the drive letters C through Z are available for your use.

Note The drive letter A is usually assigned to the system's floppy drive. If the system has a second floppy drive, the letter B is assigned to it, meaning you can only use the letters C through Z. Don't forget that CD-ROMs, Zip drives, and other types of media drives need drive letters as well.

The total number of drive letters you can use at one time is 24. This means you can have 24 active volumes on a single Windows NT system. If you need additional volumes, you can create them without assigning a drive letter. These volumes won't, however, be accessible until you assign them a drive letter.

Figure 7-4 shows the primary and extended partitions for a sample system in Disk Administrator. Disk 0 has two partitions: one primary partition and one extended partition. The primary partition is designated by the drive letter C. The extended partition is divided into three logical drives, which

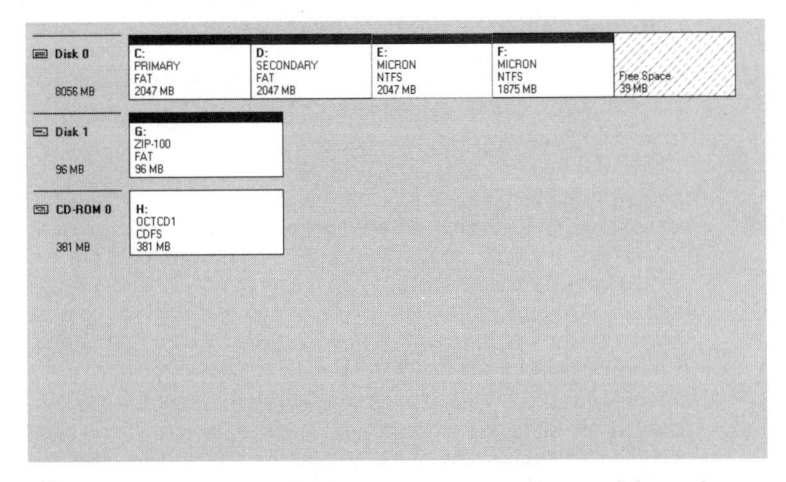

Disk 0 8056 MB	C: PRIMARY FAT 2047 MB	D: SECONDARY FAT 2047 MB	E: MICRON NTFS 2047 MB	F: MICRON NTFS 1875 MB	Free Space 39 MB
Disk 1 96 MB	G: ZIP-100 FAT 96 MB				
CD-ROM 0 381 MB	H: OCTCD1 CDFS 381 MB				

Figure 7-4. *Disk Administrator shows a system with several drives that are partitioned.*

are designated with the drive letters D, E, and F. Disk 1 is a removable Zip drive. The third disk in the example is a CD-ROM drive, which also has a letter designator.

Color-Coding Partitions

To help you differentiate between primary partitions and extended partitions with logical drives, Disk Administrator color-codes the partitions. For example, primary partitions may be color-coded with a dark-blue band and logical drives in extended partitions may be color-coded with a light-blue band. The key for the color scheme is shown at the bottom of the Disk Administrator window. You can change the colors by using the Colors dialog box that is displayed when you select Colors and Patterns from the Options menu.

Note Before you work with Disk Administrator, there are several things you should know. If you create a partition but don't format it, the partition may be labeled as Unknown or Unformatted. If you haven't assigned a portion of the disk to a partition, this section of the disk is labeled Free Space. In Figure 7-4, both disk 0 and disk 1 have free space.

Partitioning a Drive

When you install a new computer or update an existing computer, you'll often need to partition the drives on the computer. You partition drives using Disk Administrator.

Tip In the Windows NT environment, the partition known as the System partition contains the following files: NTLDR, NTDETECT.COM, BOOT.INI, and, optionally, BOOTSECT.DOS and NTBOOTDD.SYS. The partition containing the operating system and the NTOSKRNL.EXE is called the Boot Partition. This may not be intuitive to some users.

Caution Before you make any changes to hard drives, consider the consequences. Changing partition information for drives may result in data loss, and improper configuring of partitions may even prevent system boot. To ensure that you can recover the drive information, Disk Administrator doesn't actually make changes until you commit them using the Commit Changes Now feature on the Partition menu. This feature allows you to discard unwanted changes.

Anytime you add partitions to a physical drive that contains the Windows NT operating system, you may inadvertently change the number of the partition containing the system files. This partition is known as the boot partition. If you change the partition number, Windows NT will display a prompt warning you that the number of the boot partition has changed. Because of this, you may need to edit the BOOT.INI file and update the designator for the boot partition as instructed.

Chapter 7 Managing File Systems and Drives | 135

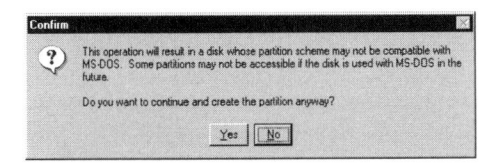

Figure 7-5. *Disk Administrator warns you with a Confirm notice if you try to create more than one primary partition.*

Creating Primary Partitions

Each physical drive can have up to four primary partitions. A primary partition can fill an entire disk or be sized as appropriate for the workstation or server you're configuring.

You can create primary partitions in Disk Administrator. To do this, select an area marked Free Space by clicking on it and then choose Create from the Partition menu. When you attempt to create more than one primary partition on a disk, Disk Administrator displays the warning shown in Figure 7-5. This warning tells you that if you create the partition, the drive may not be compatible with MS-DOS. Generally, if you plan to use the drive with MS-DOS, you shouldn't create additional primary partitions. If you click Yes, you'll be able to create the partition.

Next, you should see the Create Primary Partition dialog box shown in Figure 7-6. This dialog box specifies the minimum and maximum size for the partition in megabytes and lets you size the partition within these limits. Size the partition using the Create Partition Of Size field and then repeat this procedure for other primary partitions you want to make.

New primary partitions are designated as New Unformatted. Once you commit the changes for the partition, these partitions are given a default drive letter and marked as Unformatted.

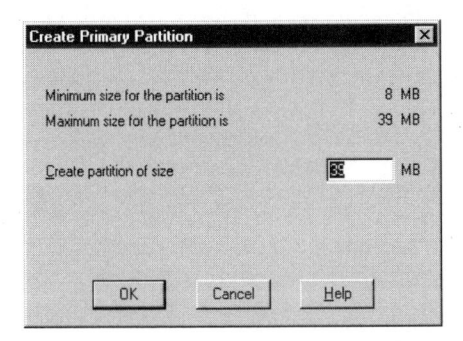

Figure 7-6. *Size the primary partition within the minimum and maximum size limits and then click OK.*

Creating Extended Partitions with Logical Drives

Each physical drive can have one extended partition. This extended partition can contain one or more logical drives, which are simply sections of the partition with their own file system. You can create extended partitions in Disk Administrator. To do this, select an area marked Free Space by clicking on it and then choose Create Extended from the Partition menu.

> **Note** If a drive already contains an extended partition, the Create Extended option won't be available. You'll need to delete the existing extended partition and create a new one, which will result in data loss.

Next, you should see the Create Extended Partition dialog box (which has the same options as the Create Primary Partition dialog box shown in Figure 7-6). This dialog box specifies the minimum and maximum size for the partition in megabytes and lets you size the partition within these limits. Size the partition using the Create Partition Of Size field.

New extended partitions are still designated as Free Space. However, Disk Administrator changes the pattern used within the area to help you tell the difference between free space that is unassigned and free space that is assigned to an extended partition. With unassigned free space, the background pattern has stripes going from the lower left to the upper right. With assigned free space that is part of an extended partition, the background pattern has stripes going from the upper left to the lower right.

Creating Logical Drives

After you create the partition, you need to create logical drives within the partition. You create a logical drive by selecting an area of free space within an extended partition and then choosing Create from the Partition menu. This opens the Create Logical Drive dialog box where you can size the logical drive using the Create Partition Of Size field. When you click OK, the drive is given a default letter and is marked as Unformatted. Any unassigned space in the extended partition remains marked as Free Space.

> **Tip** Although you can size the logical drive any way you want, you may want to take a moment to consider how you'll use logical drives on the current workstation or server. Generally, you use logical drives to divide a large drive into manageable sections. With this in mind, you may want to divide a 3 GB extended partition into 3 logical drives of 1 GB each.

Formatting Partitions

New partitions are marked as unformatted. Before you can format new partitions, you need to commit the changes you've made using the Commit Changes Now option on the Partition menu. When you commit the changes, Disk Administrator creates the new partitions on the chosen drives. To discard unwanted changes, simply exit Disk Administrator and respond

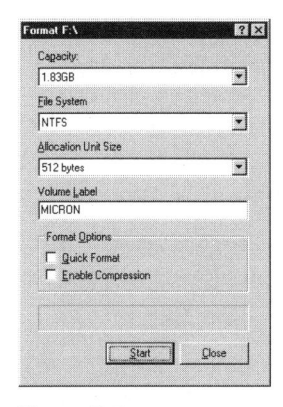

Figure 7-7. *Format a partition by specifying its file system type and volume label.*

No to the prompt that asks if you want to save the changes made to the disk configuration.

After you commit the changes, you can format the new partitions. Select the partition by clicking on it, then chose Format from the Tools menu. This opens the Format dialog box shown in Figure 7-7.

Note Formatting creates a file system in the partition. This is a high-level formatting that creates the file system structure rather than a low-level formatting that initializes a drive for use.

The fields in the Format dialog box are used as follows:

- **Capacity** Specifies how much data the disk or partition can hold. With removable disks, such as a floppy, you can use the drop-down list to select a different capacity.
- **File System** Specifies the file system type, either FAT or NTFS. FAT (file allocation table) is the file system type supported by MS-DOS and Microsoft Windows 3.1, Microsoft Windows 95, and Microsoft Windows 98. NTFS (Windows NT file system) is the native file system type for Windows NT. In the section of Chapter 9 titled "Windows NT File Structures," you'll learn more about NTFS and the advantages of using it with Windows NT.

Tip If you create a file system as FAT, you can later convert it to NTFS by using the Windows NT Convert utility. You can't, however, convert NTFS partitions to FAT. Often, you'll want your boot partition to be FAT and other partitions to be NTFS. With Intel x86 systems, having your system partition as FAT is often a good idea. This gives you freedom to boot the system under MS-DOS if necessary.

With RISC-based systems, you don't have the option of using NTFS. The boot partition must be FAT. For details on creating partitions, see the section of this chapter titled "Understanding Drive Partitions."

- **Allocation Unit Size** Specifies the cluster size for the file system. This is the basic unit in which disk space is allocated. The default allocation unit size is 4 KB (4096 bytes). Microsoft recommends that you use the default allocation unit size for general use. The default allocation unit size (4 KB) is also necessary if you plan to compress the drive.

  That said, there are times when you may want to change this setting. If you use lots of small files, you may want to use a smaller cluster size, such as 512 or 1024 bytes. With these settings, small files use less disk space.

- **Volume Label** Specifies a text label for the partition. This label is the partition's volume name.

- **Quick Format** Tells Windows NT to format without checking the partition for errors. With large partitions, this option can save you a few minutes. However, it is more prudent to check for errors, which allows Disk Administrator to mark bad sectors on the disk and lock them out.

- **Enable Compression** Turns on compression for the disk. Built-in compression is only available for NTFS. Under NTFS, compression is transparent to users and compressed files can be accessed just like regular files. If you select this option, files and directories on this drive are compressed automatically. For more information on compressing drives, files, and directories, see the section of this chapter titled "Compressing Drives and Data."

When you're ready to proceed, click OK. Because formatting a partition destroys any existing data, Disk Administrator gives you one last chance to abort the procedure. Click Yes to start formatting the partition. Disk Administrator displays a bar graph to show the progress of the formatting. When formatting is complete, you'll see a prompt that tells you so.

Managing Existing Partitions and Drives

Disk Administrator provides many useful functions for managing existing partitions and drives. You can use these features to assign drive letters, delete partitions, set the active partition, and more. In addition, Windows NT provides other utilities to carry out common tasks such as converting a volume to NTFS or checking a drive for errors.

Assigning Drive Letters

Windows NT assigns default drive letters when you create new primary partitions and logical drives. Generally, these drive letters are assigned consecutively, but you can change the drive letter or remove the drive letter designator. For details on working with drive letters, see the section of this chapter titled "Understanding Drive Partitions."

To assign a drive letter or remove a drive letter designator, complete the following steps:

1. Select the drive you want to change by clicking on it in Disk Administrator.
2. Choose Drive Letter from the Tools menu. This opens the Assign Drive Letter dialog box shown in Figure 7-8.

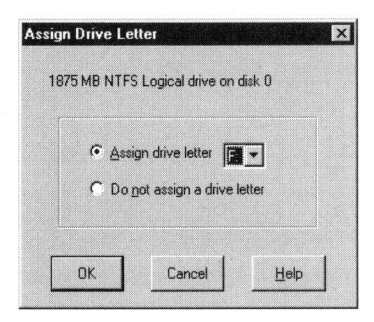

Figure 7-8. *To assign a drive letter, select the letter from the list box and click OK.*

3. Assign a drive letter by choosing the Assign Drive Letter button and then selecting a letter from the list box. Remove a drive letter assignment by choosing the Do Not Assign A Drive Letter button.
4. Click OK after you make your selection.

Note If you try to change the letter of a drive in use, Windows NT displays a warning. You'll need to exit programs that are using the drive and try again or allow Disk Administrator to make the change and reboot the system.

Changing or Deleting the Volume Label

The volume label is a text descriptor for a drive. Because this label is displayed when the drive is accessed in various Windows NT utilities, such as Windows NT Explorer, you can use the label to help provide information about the contents of a drive. You can change or delete a volume label using Disk Administrator or Windows NT Explorer.

- Using Disk Administrator, you can change or delete a label by doing the following:
  1. Select the partition or drive by clicking on it and then choose Properties from the Tools menu.
  2. In the General tab of the Properties dialog box, use the Label field to enter a new label for the volume or delete the existing label.
  3. Click OK.
- Using Windows NT Explorer, you can change or delete a label by doing the following:
  1. Select the top-level folder for the drive by clicking on it and then choose Properties from the File menu.
  2. In the General tab of the Properties dialog box, use the Label field to enter a new label for the volume or delete the existing label.
  3. Click OK.

Deleting Partitions and Drives

To change the configuration of an existing drive that is fully allocated, you may need to delete existing partitions and logical drives. Deleting a partition or drive removes the associated file system, and all data in the file system is lost. So before you delete a partition, you should backup any files and directories the partition contains.

You can delete a primary partition or logical drive as follows:

1. In Disk Administrator, select the partition or drive by clicking on it and then choose Delete from the Partition menu.
2. Confirm that you want to delete the partition by clicking Yes.
3. Commit the change by selecting Commit Changes Now from the Partition menu or by exiting Disk Administrator and choosing Yes when prompted.

To delete an extended partition, complete the following steps:

1. Delete all the logical drives on the partition following the steps outlined above.
2. You should now be able to select the extended partition area itself (designated as Free Space with a background pattern of stripes that run from the upper left to the lower right).

Converting a Volume to NTFS

Windows NT provides a utility for converting FAT volumes to NTFS. This utility, called Convert (CONVERT.EXE), is located in the %SystemRoot% folder. When you convert a volume using this tool, the file and directory structure is preserved and no data is lost. Keep in mind, however, that Windows NT doesn't provide a utility for converting NTFS to FAT. The only way to go from NTFS to FAT is to delete the partition by following the steps outlined in the previous section and then to recreate the partition as a FAT volume.

The Convert Utility

Convert is a command-line utility run at the Command prompt. If you want to convert a drive use the follow syntax:

```
convert   drive_designator   /FS:NTFS
```

where *drive_designator* is the drive letter followed by a colon. For example, if you wanted to convert the D drive to NTFS, you would use the following command:

```
convert   D:   /FS:NTFS
```

Before you use the Convert utility, double-check to see if the partition is being used as the active boot partition or a system partition containing the operating system. With Intel x86 systems, you can convert the active boot partition to NTFS. Doing so requires that the system gain exclusive access to this partition, which can only be obtained during startup. Thus, if you try to convert the active boot partition to NTFS, Windows NT displays a

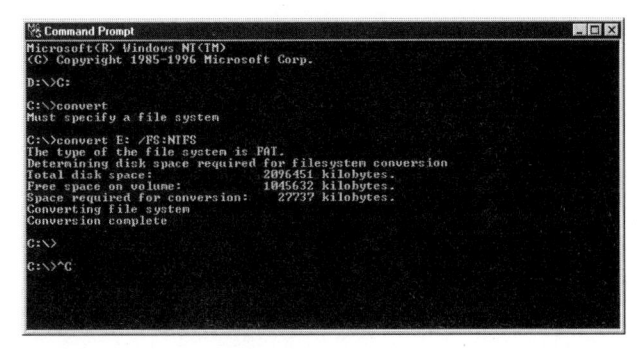

```
Command Prompt
Microsoft(R) Windows NT(TM)
(C) Copyright 1985-1996 Microsoft Corp.

D:\>C:

C:\>convert
Must specify a file system

C:\>convert E: /FS:NTFS
The type of the file system is FAT.
Determining disk space required for filesystem conversion
Total disk space:            2096451 kilobytes.
Free space on volume:        1045632 kilobytes.
Space required for conversion:    27737 kilobytes.
Converting file system
Conversion complete

C:\>
C:\>^C
```

Figure 7-9. *Before you use the Convert utility to convert a FAT file system to NTFS, you should make sure that the drive has enough free space. Don't attempt to use the drive while the conversion is in progress.*

prompt asking if you want to schedule the drive to be converted the next time the system starts. If you click Yes, you can restart the system to begin the conversion process.

Tip Often it will take several restarts of a system to completely convert the active boot partition. Don't panic. Let the system proceed with the conversion.

RISC-Based Systems

RISC-based systems are hardware configured and do not use an active boot partition. RISC computers, however, do use a system partition that contains the necessary files for the operating system. This partition must be a FAT file system, so you shouldn't convert the system partition to NTFS on RISC-based computers.

Figure 7-9 shows the output from an actual drive conversion. Before Convert actually converts a drive to NTFS, the utility checks to see if the drive has enough free space to perform the conversion. Generally, Convert needs a block of free space that is roughly equal to 25 percent of the total space used on the drive. For example, if the drive stores 100 MB of data, Convert needs about 25 MB of free space. If there isn't enough free space, Convert aborts and tells you that you need to free up some space. On the other hand, if there is ample free space, Convert initiates the conversion. Be patient. The conversion process takes several minutes (longer for large drives). Don't access files or applications on the drive while the conversion is in progress.

Checking a Drive for Errors and Bad Sectors

The Windows NT utility for checking the integrity of a disk is Check Disk (CHKDSK.EXE). You'll find this utility in the *%SystemRoot%* folder. Use Check Disk to check for and optionally repair problems found on both FAT and NTFS volumes.

While Check Disk can check for and correct many types of errors, the utility primarily looks for inconsistencies in the file system and its related metadata. One of the ways Check Disk locates errors is by comparing the volume bitmap to the disk sectors assigned to files in the file system. But beyond this, Check Disk's usefulness is rather limited. For example, Check Disk can't repair corrupted data within files that appear to be structurally intact.

You can run Check Disk from the command line or within other utilities. At the Command prompt you can test the integrity of the E drive, by entering the command:

chkdsk E:

To find and repair errors that are found in the E drive, use the command:

chkdsk /f E:

> **Note** Check Disk can't repair volumes that are in use. If the volume is in use, Check Disk displays a prompt that asks if you want to schedule the volume to be checked the next time you restart the system. Answer Yes to the prompt to schedule this.

Two ways you can also run Check Disk interactively are by using either Windows NT Explorer or Disk Administrator.

- Using Disk Administrator, you can access Check Disk by doing the following:
  1. Select the drive by clicking on it and then choose Properties from the Tools menu.
  2. In the Tools tab of the Properties dialog box, click on the Check Now button.
- Using Windows NT Explorer, you can access Check Disk by doing the following:
  1. Select the top-level folder for the drive by clicking on it and then choose Properties from the File menu.
  2. In the Tools tab of the Properties dialog box, click on the Check Now button.

Figure 7-10 shows the dialog box for the interactive version of Check Disk. You can use the dialog box to check a disk for errors and then to repair them if you like.

- To check for errors without repairing them, click on the Start button without selecting either of the check boxes.
- To check for errors and fix them, make the appropriate selections in the check boxes to fix file system errors or to recover bad sectors, or both.

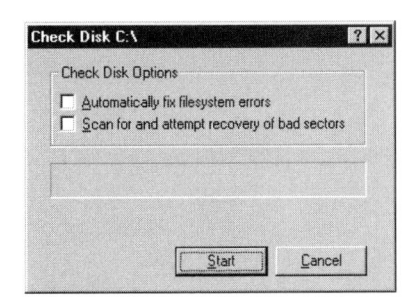

Figure 7-10. *Check Disk is available by clicking the Check Now button on the Properties dialog box. Use it to check a disk for errors and repair them if you wish.*

Defragmenting Disks

Anytime you add files to or remove files from a drive, the data on the drive can become fragmented. When a drive is fragmented, large files can't be written to a single continuous area on the disk. As a result, the operating system must write the file to several smaller areas on the disk, which means more time is spent reading the file from the disk. To reduce fragmentation, use a defragmenter, such as Disk Keeper—a network-aware utility for repairing and defragmenting disks on local and remote systems.

When you install a defragmenter on a system, you can access it in the Tools tab of the disk's Properties dialog box. Simply click on the Defragment Now button.

Compressing Drives and Data

When you format a drive for NTFS, Windows NT allows you to turn on the built-in compression feature. Using built-in compression, all files and directories stored on a drive are automatically compressed when they are created. Because this compression is transparent to users, compressed data can be accessed just like regular data. The difference is that you can store more information on a compressed drive than you can on an uncompressed drive.

Compressing Directories and Files

If you decide not to compress a drive, Windows NT lets you selectively compress directories and files. To compress a file or directory, select the file or directory in Windows NT Explorer. Then, in the General tab of the related property dialog box, select the Compress check box as shown in Figure 7-11, on the following page. Then click Apply or OK.

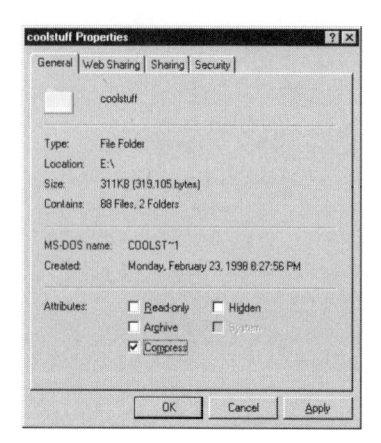

Figure 7-11. *With NTFS, you can compress a file or directory by selecting the Compress check box on the General tab of the Properties window.*

For an individual file, Windows NT marks the file as compressed and then compresses it. For a directory, Windows NT marks the directory as compressed and then compresses all files in it. If the directory contains subfolders, Windows NT displays the dialog box shown in Figure 7-12. This dialog box allows you to compress all the subfolders associated with the directory. Simply select the Also Compress Subfolders check box and then click OK. Once you compress a directory, any new files added to the directory are compressed automatically.

Expanding Compressed Files and Directories

If you decide later that you want to expand a compressed file or directory, simply reverse the process by completing the following steps:

1. Choose the file or directory in Windows NT Explorer.
2. In the General tab of the related Property dialog box, deselect the Compress check box.
3. Click Apply or OK.

With files, Windows NT removes compression and expands the file. With directories, Windows NT expands all files within the directory. If the

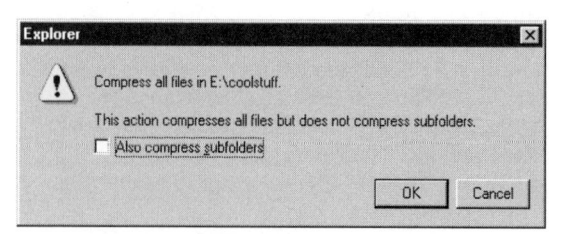

Figure 7-12. *If you compress a directory that contains subfolders, Windows NT asks if you want to compress the subfolders. To do so, select the Also Compress Subfolders check box and then click OK.*

directory contains subfolders, you'll also have the opportunity to remove compression from the subfolders. To do this, select the Also Uncompress Subfolders check box when prompted and then click OK.

Tip Windows NT also provides command-line utilities for compressing and decompressing your data. The compression utility is called Compact (COMPACT.EXE). The decompression utility is called Expand (EXPAND.EXE).

The Windows NT 4 Resource Kit has enhanced utilities for working with compressed files as well. Use Compress (COMPRESS.EXE) to compress sets of files and store them in separate directories. Use ExpndW32 to expand distribution files from the Windows NT CD-ROM.

Creating an Emergency Boot Disk

An emergency boot disk is handy when you have problems booting a system. You can create an emergency boot disk for an Intel x86 system by doing the following:

1. Insert a new floppy disk into your floppy drive.
2. Right-click on the floppy drive icon in Windows NT Explorer and then select Format from the pop-up menu.
3. Select the appropriate formatting options and then click Start to format the floppy.
4. Copy these files from the boot drive's base directory (normally C:\) to the floppy:
   - BOOT.INI
   - NTDETECT.COM
   - NTLDR
   - BOOTSECT.DOS (in dual boot systems)
   - NTBOOTDD.SYS (if used on this system)

The BOOT.INI file tells the computer the location of the boot partition. You can edit this file to have the computer load an operating system from a different partition. For example, if you mirrored the boot partition and the primary mirror drive fails, you can point BOOT.INI to the boot partition on the secondary mirror drive and boot your system. The actual procedure for recovering a mirrored boot partition is covered in Chapter 8.

Creating an Emergency Repair Disk

Anytime you change the configuration of your system, Windows NT may display a message telling you to update your emergency repair disk. An emergency repair disk contains important system and registry information that can be used to recover a Windows NT system in case of boot failure. Because the problems that the emergency disk can resolve are extensive,

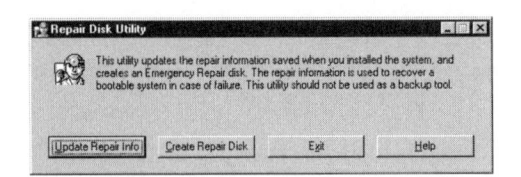

Figure 7-13. *Repair disks are essential for recovering the system in case of failure. Update the repair disk anytime you make system changes.*

it should be your first line of defense in recovering a system from boot failure. Creating and updating this disk often is a good idea.

To create or update an emergency repair disk, you'll use the Repair Disk Utility (RDISK.EXE). You can start the Repair Disk Utility by typing **rdisk** at the Command prompt or from the Run dialog box. Figure 7-13 shows the main window for the utility. You can now

- **Create a new repair disk by selecting the Create Repair Disk button** The Repair Disk Utility asks you to label a floppy disk "Emergency Repair Disk" and insert it into the floppy drive. When you do this, click OK to continue. The utility will format the floppy disk and then copy configuration files to the disk.

  Afterward, you'll see a final prompt telling you to store the disk in a safe location. The disk contains sensitive information, such as registry data containing security and user information. You'll also find that some files have been created in the *%SystemRoot%*\repair folder. These files are also used to recover the system in case of failure.

- **Update an existing repair disk by selecting the Update Repair Info button** The Repair Disk Utility tells you that the repair information last saved will be deleted. If you want to do this, click OK to continue. The utility will then copy configuration files to the disk. You'll also find that files in the *%SystemRoot%*\repair folder have been updated.

Recovering a Boot Failure

The Emergency Repair Disk created with the Repair Disk Utility (RDISK.EXE) can recover the system from most types of boot failures. To do this, you'll need the Windows NT Setup Disks and the Emergency Repair Disk created for this system.

> **Note** If the floppy drive is not configured as a boot drive, you'll need to edit the configuration settings of your system. During boot you should see a message that tells you which key you should press to enter system setup. Typically, this button is the Del key or a function key, such as F5. Once you're in the system setup, you'll need to enable boot from floppy.

To recover the system, insert the Windows NT Setup Disk A into the floppy drive and boot the system. Windows NT won't actually begin the installation process unless you tell it to. You should see an option menu that allows you to "Repair a Damaged NT Installation." Select this option, then follow the prompts.

Windows NT will attempt to repair the system using the repair data in the *%SystemRoot%*\repair folder and the Emergency Repair Disk (as necessary). When prompted, insert the Emergency Repair Disk. This disk will reflect the most recent system configuration settings if possible.

Chapter 8

Administering Volume Sets and RAID Arrays

When you work with Microsoft Windows NT servers, you'll often need to perform advanced disk setup procedures, such as creating a volume set or setting up a RAID array.

- With a *volume set*, you can create a volume that uses multiple partitions on multiple drives. Users can access this volume as if it were a single drive, regardless of how many drives the actual volume is spread over.
- With *RAID arrays*, you can protect important business data and, sometimes, improve the performance of drives. Microsoft Windows NT supports three different levels of RAID: 0, 1, and 5.

Using Volume Sets

By using volume sets, you can create volumes that span several drives. To do this, you use free space on different drives to create what users see as a single volume. Files are stored on the volume set segment by segment, with the first segment of free space being used first to store files. When this segment fills up, the second segment is used, and so on.

You can create a volume set using free space on up to 32 hard drives. The key advantage to volume sets is that they let you tap into unused free space and create a usable file system. The key disadvantage is that if any hard drive in the volume set fails, the volume set can no longer be used—which means that essentially all the data on the volume set is lost.

Note Some operating systems, such as MS-DOS, do not support volume sets. If you dual boot your system to one of these noncompliant operating systems, your volume set will be unusable.

Creating a Volume Set

To create a volume set, you use Disk Administrator. The steps follow:

1. Select an area designated as Free Space. Then hold down the Ctrl key and select additional areas of free space. You must select at least two areas of free space.
2. Select Create Volume Set from the Partition menu.

3. You should see the Create Volume Set dialog box. This dialog box specifies the minimum and maximum size for the volume set in megabytes and lets you size the volume set within these constraints. Size the volume set using the Create Volume Set Of Total Size field.
4. When you're finished, click OK.
5. Choose Commit Changes Now from the Partition menu to create the volume set.
6. The volume set areas are designated as Unformatted. To format the volume set, select any area of the volume set, and then choose Format from the Tools menu. You format a volume set as you would a standard partition. For details, see the section titled "Formatting Partitions" in Chapter 7.

Deleting a Volume Set

You delete a volume set as you would a normal partition. Deleting a volume set removes the associated file system and all associated data is lost. Thus, before you delete a volume set you should back up any files and directories that the volume set contains.

To delete a volume set in Disk Administrator, follow these steps:

1. Select the volume set you want to delete by clicking on one of the areas assigned to the set.
2. Choose Delete from the Partition menu.
3. Confirm that you want to delete the partition by clicking Yes.
4. Commit the change by selecting Commit Changes Now from the Partition menu or by exiting the Disk Administrator and choosing Yes when prompted.

Extending a Volume Set or Logical Drive

Windows NT provides several different ways to extend NTFS volumes that are not part of a mirror set or stripe set. You can extend an individual volume—such as a logical drive—to create a volume set, and you can extend existing volume sets. When you extend volumes, you add free space to them.

> **Note** When extending volume sets, there are many things you can't do. You can't extend boot or system partitions. You can't extend the active partition on drive 0 or on any volumes that use mirroring or striping. Additionally, you can't extend FAT volumes. As you work with volume sets, please keep these exceptions in mind.

To extend an NTFS volume, complete the following steps:

1. Select the individual volume or volume set, and then hold down the Ctrl key and select an area of free space to add.

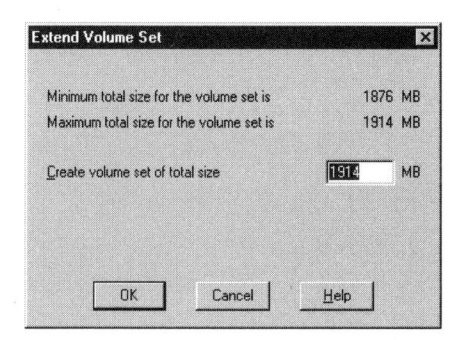

Figure 8-1. *Extend volumes using the Extend Volume Set dialog box. The minimum size reflects the current size of the volume or volume set.*

2. Select Extend Volume Set from the Partition menu.
3. You should see the Extend Volume Set dialog box shown in Figure 8-1. The minimum size reflects the current size of the volume or volume set. Set the new size for the volume set using the Create Volume Set Of Total Size field.
4. Click OK when you're finished.
5. You do not need to format the new set, but you do need to commit the changes. Commit the changes by selecting Commit Changes Now from the Partition menu or by exiting the Disk Administrator and choosing Yes when prompted.

Improved Performance and Fault Tolerance with RAIDs

You'll often want to give important data increased protection from drive failures. To do this, you can use RAID (redundant array of independent disks) technology to add fault tolerance to your file systems. With RAID you increase data integrity and availability by creating redundant copies of the data. You can also use RAID to improve the performance of your disks.

Different implementations of RAID technology are available. These implementations are described in terms of levels. Currently, RAID levels 0 to 5 are defined. Each RAID level offers different features. Windows NT supports RAID levels 0, 1, and 5.

- RAID 0 can be used to improve the performance of your drives.
- RAID 1 and 5 are used to provide fault tolerance for data.

Table 8-1, on the following page, provides a brief overview of the supported RAID levels. This support is completely software-based and is only available on Windows NT servers.

Table 8-1. Windows NT Server Support for RAID

RAID Level	RAID Type	Description	Major Advantages
0	Disk striping	Two or more partitions, each on a separate drive, are configured as a stripe set. Data is broken into blocks, called stripes, and then written sequentially to all drives in the stripe set.	Speed/Performance
1	Disk mirroring	Two partitions on two drives are configured identically. Data is written to both drives. If one drive fails, there is no data loss because the other drive contains the data. (Does not include disk striping.)	Redundancy. Better write performance than disk striping with parity.
5	Disk striping with parity	Uses three or more partitions, each on a separate drive, to create a stripe set with parity error checking. In the case of failure, data can be recovered.	Fault tolerance with less overhead than mirroring. Better read performance than disk mirroring.

The most common RAID levels in use on Windows NT servers are level 1 disk mirroring and level 5 disk striping with parity. Disk mirroring is the least expensive way to increase data protection with redundancy. Here, you use two identically sized partitions on two different drives to create a redundant data set. If one of the drives fails, the data can still be obtained from the other drive.

On the other hand, disk striping with parity requires more disks—a minimum of three—but offers fault tolerance with less overhead than disk mirroring. If any of the drives fail, the data can be recovered by combining blocks of data on the remaining disks with a parity record. Parity is a method of error checking that uses an exclusive OR operation to create a checksum for each block of data written to the disk. This checksum is used to recover data in case of failure.

Implementing RAID on Windows NT Servers

For server systems, Windows NT supports disk mirroring, disk striping, and disk striping with parity. Implementing these RAID techniques is discussed in the sections that follow.

> **Note** Some operating systems, such as MS-DOS, do not support RAID. If you dual boot your system to one of these noncompliant operating systems, your RAID-configured drives will be unusable.

Implementing RAID 0: Disk Striping

RAID level 0 is disk striping. With disk striping, two or more partitions—each on a separate drive—are configured as a stripe set. Data written to the stripe set is broken into blocks that are called stripes. These stripes are written sequentially to all drives in the stripe set. You can place partitions for a stripe set on up to 32 drives, but in most circumstances sets with 2–5 partitions offer the best performance improvements. Beyond this, the performance improvement decreases significantly.

The major advantage of disk striping is speed. Data can be accessed on multiple disks using multiple drive heads, which improves performance considerably. However, this performance boost comes with a price tag. As with volume sets, if any hard drive in the stripe set fails, the stripe set can no longer be used, which means that essentially all data in the stripe set is lost. You will need to re-create the stripe set and restore the data from backups. Data backup and recovery is discussed in Chapter 11.

Note The boot and system partitions can't be part of a striped set. Do not use disk striping with these partitions.

When you create stripe sets, you'll want to use partitions that are approximately the same size. Disk Administrator bases the overall size of the stripe set on the smallest partition size. Specifically, the maximum size of the stripe set is a multiple of the smallest partition size. For example, if the smallest partition is 50 MB and you've selected three free space areas, the maximum size for the stripe site is 150 MB.

To maximize performance of the stripe set, there are several things you can do:

- Use disks that are on separate disk controllers. This allows the system to simultaneously access the drives.
- Do not use the disks containing the stripe set for other purposes. This allows the disk to dedicate its time to the stripe set.

In Disk Administrator, you can create a stripe set by doing the following:

1. Select a free space area, and then hold down the Ctrl key and select additional free space areas to add to the stripe set. Each free space area must be on a separate disk.
2. Select Create Stripe Set from the Partition menu.
3. You should see the Create Stripe Set dialog box (which is essentially the same as the dialog box shown in Figure 8-1). Disk Administrator displays the minimum and maximum size for the stripe set and lets you size the stripe set within these constraints.

   Use the Create Stripe Set Of Total Size field to size the stripe set. Partitions are sized equally and assigned a single drive letter. To size the individual partitions, Disk Administrator divides the total size by the number of areas you've selected. These partitions are unformatted and labeled as such.
4. Click OK when you're finished.
5. Commit the change by selecting Commit Changes Now from the Partition menu.

6. Select an area within the stripe set by clicking on it, and then choose Format from the Tools menu to format partitions in the stripe set. The stripe set can be formatted as FAT or NTFS.

Once you create a stripe set, users can use the set just like they would a normal drive. You can't expand a stripe set once it is created. Because of this, you should carefully consider the setup before you implement it.

Implementing RAID 1: Disk Mirroring

RAID level 1 is disk mirroring. With disk mirroring, you use identically sized partitions on two different drives to create a redundant data set. Here, the drives are written with identical sets of information and, if one of the drives fails, the data can still be obtained from the other drive.

Disk mirroring offers about the same fault tolerance as disk striping with parity. Because mirrored disks don't need to write parity information, they can offer better write performance in most circumstances. However, disk striping with parity usually offers better read performance because read operations are spread out over multiple drives.

The major drawback to disk mirroring is that it effectively cuts the amount of storage space in half. For example, to mirror a 1 GB drive, you need another 1 GB drive. That means you use 2 GB of space to store 1 GB of information.

> **Note** Unlike disk striping, with disk mirroring you can mirror any partition. This means you can mirror the boot and system partitions if you want.

As with disk striping, you'll often want the mirrored disks to be on separate controllers. This provides increased protection against failure of the disk controller. If one of the disk controllers fails, the disk on other controller is still available. Technically, when you use two separate disk controllers to duplicate data, you're using a technique known as disk duplexing. Figure 8-2 shows the difference between the two techniques. Where disk mirroring typically uses a single drive controller, disk duplexing uses two drive controllers.

If one of the mirrored drives in a set fails, disk operations can continue. Here, when users read and write data, the data is written to the remaining disk. You'll need to break the mirror before you can fix it. To learn how, see the section of this chapter titled "Managing RAIDs and Recovering from Failures."

Creating a Mirror Set in Disk Administrator

In Disk Administrator, you create a mirror set by completing the following steps:

1. Select the partition you want to duplicate.
2. Hold down the Ctrl key and select an equally sized or larger area of free space on another disk.
3. Select Establish Mirror on the Fault Tolerance menu.

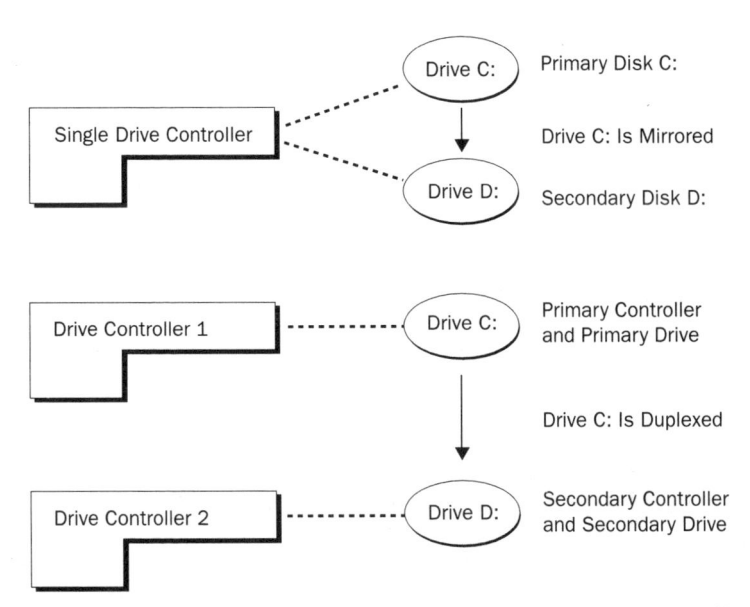

```
                                    ┌─────────┐    Primary Disk C:
                              ┌─────│ Drive C:│
┌──────────────────────┐      │     └─────────┘
│ Single Drive Controller │───┤                   Drive C: Is Mirrored
└──────────────────────┘      │     ┌─────────┐
                              └─────│ Drive D:│
                                    └─────────┘   Secondary Disk D:


┌──────────────────────┐            ┌─────────┐   Primary Controller
│  Drive Controller 1  │────────────│ Drive C:│   and Primary Drive
└──────────────────────┘            └─────────┘

                                                  Drive C: Is Duplexed

┌──────────────────────┐            ┌─────────┐   Secondary Controller
│  Drive Controller 2  │────────────│ Drive D:│   and Secondary Drive
└──────────────────────┘            └─────────┘
```

Figure 8-2. *While disk mirroring typically uses a single drive controller to create a redundant data set, disk duplexing uses two drive controllers. Other than this, the two techniques are essentially the same.*

4. Commit the change by selecting Commit Changes Now from the Partition menu.

When you commit the changes, Disk Administrator creates the mirror and assigns the same drive letter to both partitions. You can use the Volumes window (by clicking on the Volumes button or selecting Volumes from the View menu) to see the status of the mirror. As with other RAID techniques, mirroring is transparent to users and they can access the mirrored set just as they would any other drive.

Note The status of a normal mirror is Healthy. During the creation of a mirror, you may see a status of Initializing. This tells you that Disk Administrator is setting up the mirror.

Note Windows NT automatically synchronizes mirrored drives. If the mirrored drives get out of sync, Disk Administrator's Disk Configuration window may show one of the mirrored partitions in red. This tells you that Windows NT is attempting to resynchronize the drives.

Implementing RAID 5: Disk Striping with Parity

RAID level 5 is disk striping with parity. With this technique, you need a minimum of three hard drives to set up fault tolerance. The partitions on these drives are sized identically by Disk Administrator. Although you can place partitions for a stripe set on up to 32 drives, in most circumstances sets with 2–5 partitions offer the best performance improvements. Beyond this, the performance improvement decreases significantly.

RAID 5 is essentially an enhanced version of RAID 1—with the key addition of fault tolerance. Fault tolerance ensures that the failure of a single drive won't bring down the entire drive set. Instead, the set continues to function with disk operations directed at the remaining partitions in the set.

To allow for fault tolerance, RAID 5 writes parity checksums with the blocks of data. If any of the drives in the stripe set fails, the parity information can be used to recover the data. (This process, called regenerating the striped set, is covered in the section of this chapter titled "Managing RAIDs and Recovering from Failures.") If two disks fail, however, the parity information is not sufficient to recover the data and you will need to rebuild the striped set from backup.

> **Note** The boot and system partitions can't be part of a striped set. Do not use disk striping with parity on these partitions.

Creating a Stripe Set with Parity in Disk Administrator

In Disk Administrator, you can create a stripe set with parity by doing the following:

1. Stripe sets with parity are created in free space areas on a minimum of three separate disks. Select a free space area and then hold down the Ctrl key and select at least two additional free space areas to add to the stripe set.
2. Select Create Stripe Set with Parity from the Fault Tolerance menu.
3. You should see the Create Stripe Set with Parity dialog box (which is essentially the same as the dialog box shown in Figure 8-1). Disk Administrator displays the minimum and maximum size for the stripe set and lets you size the stripe set within these constraints.

    Use the Create Stripe Set Of Total Size field to size the stripe set. Partitions are sized equally and assigned a single drive letter. To size the individual partitions, Disk Administrator divides the total size by the number of areas you've selected. These partitions are unformatted and labeled as such.
4. Click OK when you're finished.
5. Commit the change by selecting Commit Changes Now from the Partition menu.
6. Select an area within the stripe set by clicking on it, and then choose Format from the Tools menu to format partitions in the stripe set. The stripe set can be formatted as FAT or NTFS.

Once you create a stripe set, users can use the set just like they would a normal drive. Keep in mind that you can't expand a stripe set once it's created. Because of this, you should carefully consider the setup before you implement it.

Managing RAIDs and Recovering from Failures

Managing mirrored drives and stripe sets is somewhat different from managing other drive partitions, especially when it comes to recovering from failure. The techniques you'll need to manage RAID arrays and to recover from failure are covered in this section.

Breaking a Mirrored Set

There are two reasons you may want to break a mirror:

- If one of the mirrored drives in a set fails, disk operations can continue. Here, when users read and write data, these operations use the remaining disk. Still, at some point you'll need to fix the mirror, and to do this, you must first break the mirror and then reestablish it.

- If you no longer want to mirror your drives, you may also want to break a mirror. This allows you to use the disk space for other purposes.

Note Although breaking a mirror doesn't delete the data in the set, you should always back up the data before you perform this procedure. This ensures that if you have problems, you can recover your data.

In Disk Administrator, you can break a mirrored set by doing the following:

1. Select one of the partitions in the mirrored set.
2. Choose Break Mirror from the Fault Tolerance menu.
3. Confirm that you want to break the mirror by clicking Yes. This creates two independent partitions.
4. Commit the change by selecting Commit Changes Now from the Partition menu or by exiting the Disk Administrator and choosing Yes when prompted.

Repairing a Mirrored Set

Before you can repair a mirrored set with a failed drive, you need to break the mirror. Once you do, you can follow these steps to repair the mirror:

1. Remove or repair the broken drive.
2. Start Disk Administrator and make sure that the working drive in the original mirror set has the drive letter that was previously assigned to the complete mirror. If it doesn't, assign the appropriate drive letter. This allows users to access the drive using the original file path.
3. Create a new mirror set by mirroring the working drive. When you do this, data from the remaining mirrored drive will be copied to the new drive to create a mirror set.

Repairing a Mirrored System Partition to Enable Boot

The failure of a mirrored drive may prevent your system from booting. Typically, this happens when you're mirroring the system or boot partition, or both, and the primary mirror drive has failed. To correct this problem, you need to replace the failed drive and then use an emergency boot disk for the system or a similarly configured system to enable system boot. Creating an emergency boot disk is covered in Chapter 7.

Once you have an emergency boot disk, you need to edit the BOOT.INI file it contains so that the operating system loads from the secondary mirror. This file contains entries that look like this:

```
[boot loader]
timeout=30
default=multi(0)disk(0)rdisk(0)partition(2)\WINNT
[operating systems]
multi(0)disk(0)rdisk(0)partition(2)\WINNT="Windows
NT Server Version 4.00"
multi(0)disk(0)rdisk(0)partition(2)\WINNT="Windows
NT Server Version 4.00
[VGA mode]"/basevideo /sos
```

Entries like this tell Windows NT where to find the operating system:

```
multi(0)disk(0)rdisk(0)partition(2)\WINNT
```

How Designators Are Used

The designators for this entry are used as follows:

- **multi(0)** Designates the controller for the drive, which in this case is controller 0. If the secondary mirror is on a different controller, enter the number of the controller. Controllers are numbered from 0 to 3.

> **Note** The format for the BOOT.INI entries is the ARC (Advanced RISC Computer) name format. On SCSI systems that don't use SCSI BIOS, the first field in the entry is scsi(n), where *n* is the controller number.

- **disk(0)** Designates the SCSI bus adapter, which in this case is adapter 0. On most systems, this is always 0. The exception is for systems with multiple bus SCSI adapters. These systems use the scsi(n) syntax.

- **rdisk(0)** Designates the ordinal number of the disk on the adapter, which in this case is drive 0. With SCSI drives that use SCSI BIOS, you'll see numbers from 0 to 6. With other SCSI drives, this is always 0. With IDE, you'll see either 0 or 1. In most cases, you'll need to change this field—so be sure to enter the number of the secondary mirror drive.

- **partition(2)** The partition that contains the operating system, which in this case is 2. Primary partitions are numbered 1 to 4. Extended partitions and unused partitions are not numbered.

If the secondary mirror was on drive 1, you could update the BOOT.INI file shown earlier as follows:

```
[boot loader]
timeout=30
default=multi(0)disk(0)rdisk(1)partition(2)\WINNT
[operating systems]
multi(0)disk(0)rdisk(1)partition(2)\WINNT="Windows
NT Server Version 4.00"
multi(0)disk(0)rdisk(1)partition(2)\WINNT="Windows
NT Server Version 4.00
[VGA mode]"/basevideo /sos
```

Booting and Rebooting the System

Once you update the BOOT.INI file, you can use the emergency boot disk to boot your system. When the system boots, you will need to complete the following steps:

1. Break the mirror set and then recreate the mirror on the drive you replaced, which is usually drive 0.
2. Reboot again using the emergency boot disk. The system will then rebuild the mirror.
3. When the mirror is completely rebuilt, use Disk Administrator to break the mirror again. Make sure that the primary drive in the original mirror set has the drive letter that was previously assigned to the complete mirror. If it doesn't, assign the appropriate drive letter.
4. Commit the changes when you exit Disk Administrator.
5. You should now be able to boot using the original system partition. Remove the emergency boot disk from the floppy drive and reboot the system.
6. Recreate the mirror set for the original system partition.

Repairing a Stripe Set without Parity

A stripe set without parity doesn't have fault tolerance. If a drive that is part of a stripe set fails, the entire stripe set is unusable. Before you try to restore the stripe set, you should repair or replace the failed drive. Afterward, you need to recreate the stripe set and then recover the data contained on the stripe set from backup.

Regenerating a Stripe Set with Parity

With RAID 5 you can recover the stripe set if a single drive fails. You'll know that a stripe set with parity drive has failed when you see a system error message stating that a disk that is part of a fault-tolerant volume can no longer be accessed. If you see this message, you should repair or replace the failed drive. Afterward, you can attempt to regenerate the stripe set.

> **Note** You should always back up the data before you perform this procedure. This ensures that if you have problems, you can recover your data.

In Disk Administrator, you can regenerate a stripe set with parity as follows:

1. Select the stripe set with parity that you're attempting to regenerate.
2. Hold down the Ctrl key and select an equally sized or larger area of free space on the new disk or any other disk that isn't a member of the striped set.
3. Choose Regenerate from the Fault Tolerance menu.
4. Restart the server. Windows NT will then regenerate the data in the new area.

When this is finished, you may need to assign the original drive letter to the stripe set. This ensures that users can access the drive using the same path information.

Chapter 9
Managing Files and Directories

Microsoft Windows NT provides a robust environment for working with files and directories. At the core of this environment are the two basic file system types:

- FAT (file allocation table)
- NTFS file system

When you work with files and directories on a Windows NT system you'll usually work with one of these file system types. To help you better administer FAT and NTFS volumes, this chapter explains how to implement common file and directory tasks. It also offers ways of troubleshooting problems.

Windows NT File Structures

This section covers the core information you'll need to work with files. An understanding of file basics can make your job as an administrator a lot easier.

Major Features of FAT and NTFS

What you can or can't do with files and directories in Windows NT depends on the file system type. Windows NT servers and workstations provide direct support for FAT and NTFS.

FAT Volumes

FAT volumes rely on an allocation table to keep track of the status of files and directories. Although FAT is adequate for most file and directory needs, it is rather limited. With FAT

- You can't control local access to files and directories using Windows NT access permissions.
- You can't compress files using Windows NT compression.
- You can use Windows NT file sharing.
- You have limited control over remote access to files and directories. (You do this with file sharing.)
- You can use long file names (file and directory names with up to 255 characters).

Using NTFS

On the other hand, NTFS offers a robust environment for working with files and directories. With NTFS

- You can use Windows NT file access permissions to control local access to files.
- You can use Windows NT compression.
- You can use Windows NT file sharing and fully control remote access to files and directories.
- You can use long file names (file and directory names with up to 255 characters).

File Naming

Windows NT file naming conventions apply to both files and directories. For simplicity, the term "file naming" is often used to refer to both files *and* directories. Although Windows NT file names are case-aware, they are not case-sensitive. This means you can save a file named MyBook.doc and the file name will be displayed in the correct case. However, you can't save a file called mybook.doc to the same directory.

Both NTFS and FAT support long file names—up to 255 characters. You can name files using just about any of the available characters, including spaces. However, there are some characters you can't use. They include

? * / \ : ; < >

> **Tip** Using spaces in file names can cause access problems. Anytime you reference the file name, you may need to enclose the file name within quotation marks. Also, if you plan to publish the file on the Web, you may need to remove the spaces from the file name or convert them to the underscore character (_) to ensure that Web browsers have easy access to the file.

The following file names are all acceptable:

- My Favorite Short Story.doc
- My_Favorite_Short_Story.doc
- My..Favorite..Short..Story.doc
- My Favorite Short Story!!!.doc

Accessing Long File Names Under MS-DOS

Under MS-DOS and 16-bit FAT file systems, file and directory names are restricted to eight characters with a three-character file extension, such as CHAPTER4.TXT. This naming convention is often referred to as the 8.3 file-naming rule or the standard MS-DOS file-naming rule. Because of it, when you work with files at the Command prompt you may have problems accessing files and directories.

To support access to long file names, abbreviated file names are created for all files and directories on a system. These file names conform to the standard MS-DOS file-naming rule. You can see the abbreviated file names using the command

```
dir /X
```

A typical abbreviated file name looks like this:

```
PROGRA~1.DOC
```

How Windows NT Creates an Abbreviated File Name

When Windows NT creates an abbreviated file name from a long file name, the following rules are used:

- Any spaces in the file name are removed. The file name, My Favorite Short Story.doc, becomes MyFavoriteShortStory.doc.
- All periods in the file name are removed (with the exception of the period separating the file name from the file extension). The file name, My..Favorite..Short..Story.doc, becomes MyFavoriteShortStory.doc.
- Invalid characters under the standard MS-DOS naming rule are replaced with the underscore character (_). The file name, My[Favorite]ShortStory.doc, becomes My_Favorite_Short_Story.doc.
- All remaining characters are converted to uppercase. The file name, My Favorite Short Story.doc, becomes MYFAVORITESHORTSTORY.DOC.

The Rules of Truncation

To make the file conform to the 8.3 naming convention, the file name and file extension are truncated if necessary. The rules for truncation are as follows:

- The file extension is truncated to the first three characters. The file name Mary.text becomes MARY.TEX.
- The file name is truncated to the first six characters (this is the file's root name) and a unique designator is appended. The unique designator follows the convention ~n, where *n* is the number of the file with the six-character file name. Following this, the file name, My Favorite Short Story.doc, becomes MYFAVO~1.DOC. The second file in this directory that is truncated to MYFAVO becomes MYFAVO~2.DOC.

Note The file name truncation rule described here is the one you'll usually see, and you won't often have to worry about anything else. However, if you have lots of files with similar names, you may see another convention used to create the short file name.

Specifically, if more than four files use the same six-character root, additional file names are created by combining the first two characters of the file name with a four-character hash code and then appending a unique designator. A directory could have files named MYFAVO~1.DOC, MYFAVO~2.DOC, MYFAVO~3.DOC, and MYFAVO~4.DOC. Additional files with this root could be named MY3140~1.DOC, MY40C7~1.DOC, and MYEACC~1.DOC.

Manipulating Files and Directories

Microsoft Windows NT Explorer is the tool of choice for working with files and directories. You can also use My Computer and Network Neighborhood to perform many file manipulation tasks. Access My Computer and Network Neighborhood by double-clicking on their icons on the Windows NT desktop.

> **Note** For brevity, this section focuses primarily on using Windows NT Explorer. However, you can apply similar techniques to My Computer and Network Neighborhood.

Using Windows NT Explorer

To run Windows NT Explorer, go to Start, then select Programs, and then select Windows NT Explorer. As shown in Figure 9-1, Windows NT Explorer has two panes:

- **All Folders** Shows special top-level folders as well as other accessible resources, such as drives.
- **Contents** Shows the contents of a folder selected in the All Folders pane.

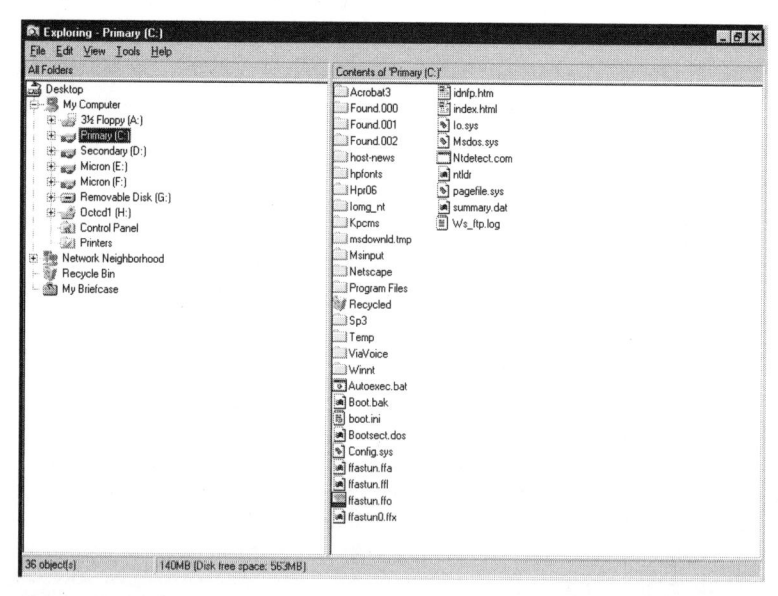

Figure 9-1. *Windows NT Explorer has two panes: All Folders and Contents. All Folders shows drives and folders. Contents shows what's in a folder selected in the All Folders pane.*

Understanding Windows NT Explorer Icons
Each icon displayed in Windows NT Explorer has a purpose. Key icons displayed in the All Folders pane are used as follows:

- **Desktop** The top-level folder for the system. The folder is at the same level in the hierarchy as Network Neighborhood.
- **My Computer** A top-level folder containing all local resources and folders available to the computer.
- **Network Neighborhood** The top-level folder for the network. Click on this to browse network resources.
- **Recycle Bin** A folder that stores files and directories that have been deleted. If the system is configured to use the recycle bin, files can be recovered from this folder before they are permanently removed.
- **My Briefcase** A folder designed to help you keep personal files up-to-date even if you work on several computers. You can use this folder to automatically update copies of your personal files.
- **Drives** Storage devices that are identified with unique icons and drive letters. Windows NT shows hard drives, floppy drives, removable drives, and CD-ROMs.
- **Network Drives** A remote network resource that is connected to the system.
- **Open Folders** Folders that have been accessed by clicking on them. Open folders show their contents in the Contents pane.
- **Closed Folders** Folders that have not been accessed. Closed folders do not display their contents.

Tip To expand folders without displaying their contents in the Contents pane, click on the + symbol next to the folder. This technique allows you to browse folders on remote systems faster than usual.

You can also use this technique when you are copying files. Here, you display the contents of the folder you want to copy in the Contents pane and then browse for the destination folder in the All Folders pane. When you find it, you copy the source files to the folder.

Customizing the Windows NT Explorer Display
Windows NT Explorer can be customized in many ways. Figure 9-2, on the following page, shows Windows NT Explorer with details enabled. The detailed view adds file size, file type, modification date, and file attributes to the Contents panel.

To change the settings for the main view panels, you use the View menu. Checked items are enabled. Unchecked items are disabled. The main options on this menu are used as follows:

- **Toolbar** Adds a toolbar where you'll find icons for quickly performing common tasks.

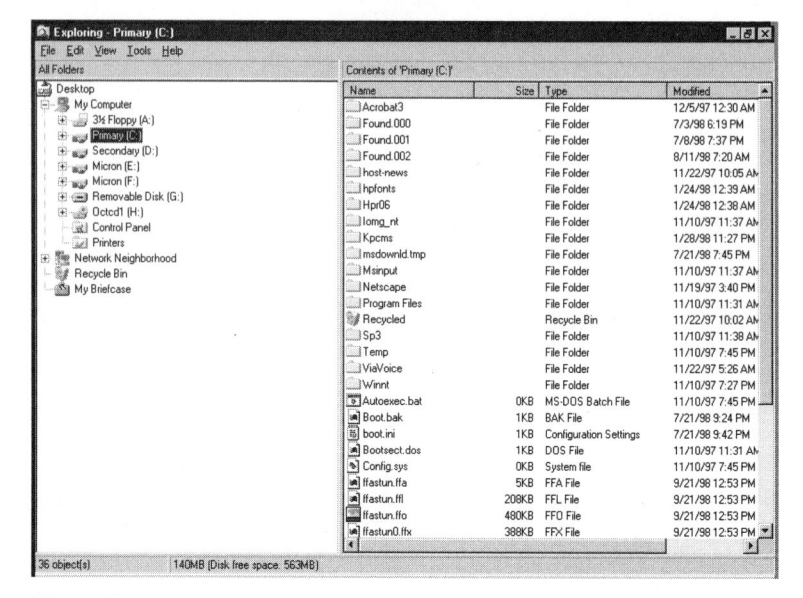

Figure 9-2. *The detailed view adds extra information to the Contents panel. Select Details from the View menu to enable or disable this option.*

- **Status Bar** Adds a status bar that displays information about objects that are selected.
- **List** Displays a list of files and folders, rather than the detailed listings or file icons.
- **Details** Displays detailed listings for files and folders.
- **Small Icons** Displays small icons for files and folders.
- **Large Icons** Displays large icons for files and folders.
- **Arrange Icons** Allows you to arrange files and folders by name, type, size, and date. In detailed view, clicking on the column headers has the same effect.

Displaying Hidden Files and File Extensions in Windows NT Explorer

As an administrator, you'll often want to see file extensions and system files, such as DLLs. By default, however, Windows NT Explorer doesn't display file extensions or hidden file types. To override the initial settings, select Options from the View menu and then configure new settings using the dialog box shown in Figure 9-3.

- To display hidden files, click the Show All Files button.
- To always display file extensions, deselect the Hide File Extensions For Known File Types check box.

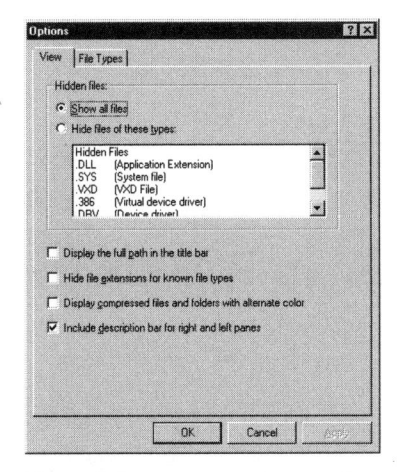

Figure 9-3. *Set options for Windows NT Explorer by selecting Options from the View menu.*

Searching for Files

Finding files on a network isn't easy, especially if the files are located on a remote system. Fortunately, you can use the Windows NT Explorer to search for files anywhere on the network—provided you have appropriate access to remote systems. The feature you'll use to do this is called Find.

Using Find, you can search for files

- By name and location
- By creation and modification date
- By file contents (text within a file)
- By file size

Searching by file name and location The most basic search is by name and location. To search for files by name and location, follow these steps:

1. In Windows NT Explorer, right-click on the folder or drive where you want to begin the search. The search will begin at the location you select and will continue to the bottom of the directory tree for the selected item.
2. Select the Find option on the pop-up menu. This opens the Find: All Files dialog box shown in Figure 9-4, on the following page.
3. Use the Name & Location tab to set up the search parameters. In the Named field, enter a file name. You can use the wildcards * and ? to match partial file names. For example, enter **sp*.doc** to find all Word documents that start with sp. Enter **sp????.doc** to find all Word documents that start with sp and have four additional characters in the filename.

168 | Part III Windows NT Data Administration

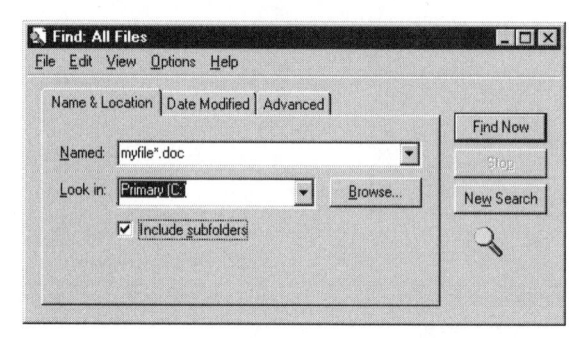

Figure 9-4. *Search by file name by using the Name & Location tab.*

4. Click on the Find Now button to begin the search. When the search is complete, Find displays all files that match the search parameters. You can view, copy, or delete any of the matching files. For example, to access a file directly, double-click on its file name.

Searching by creation date and modification date To search for files by creation date or modification date, follow these steps:

1. In Windows NT Explorer, right-click on the folder or drive where you want to begin the search and then select the Find option on the pop-up menu. The search will begin at the location you select and will continue to the bottom of the directory tree for the selected item.
2. Select the Date Modified tab shown in Figure 9-5.
3. Click on the Find All Files Created Or Modified radio button.
4. Use the additional radio buttons to refine the search. These radio buttons provide three ways to search by date:
   - Between a known start date and known end date by selecting the Between radio button then entering a start and end date.
   - Going back in time by months by selecting the During The Previous X Months radio button and then using the list box to set the number of months.

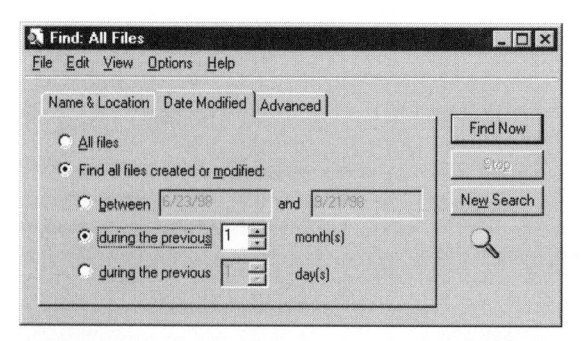

Figure 9-5. *Search by creation date and modification date by using the Date Modified tab.*

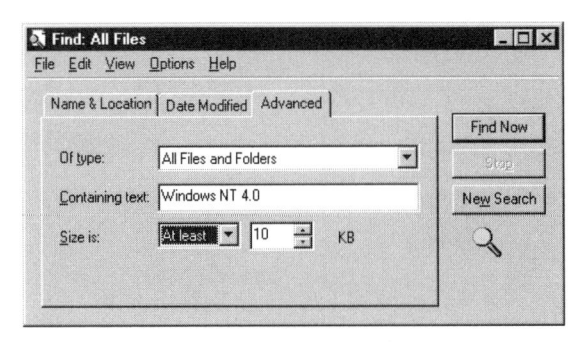

Figure 9-6. *Search by file size or contents, or both, by using the Advanced tab.*

- Going back in time by days by selecting the During The Previous X Days radio button and then using the list box to set the number of days.

5. If desired, click on the Name & Location tab and use its fields to set a complete or partial file name.
6. Click on the Find Now button to begin the search. When the search is complete, Find displays all files that match the search parameters. You can view, copy, or delete any of the matching files. For example, to access a file directly, double-click on its file name.

Searching by file size and contents   To search by file size or contents, follow these steps:

1. In Windows NT Explorer, right-click on the folder or drive where you want to begin the search and then select the Find option on the pop-up menu. The search will begin at the location you select and will continue to the bottom of the directory tree for the selected item.
2. Select the Advanced tab shown in Figure 9-6.
3. To narrow the search to a specific file type, use the Of Type selection list. For example, select Microsoft Word Document to search for Word document files.
4. To search for a specific string of text within files, enter the text in the Containing Text field.
5. To search by file size, select At Least or At Most using the Size Is selection list. Then specify a file size using the KB field.
6. Click on the Find Now button to begin the search. When the search is complete, Find displays all files that match the search parameters. You can view, copy, or delete any of the matching files. For example, to access a file directly, double-click on its file name.

Formatting Floppy Disks and Removable Disks

Windows NT Explorer makes it easy to work with floppy and removable disks. You can format disks by doing the following:

1. Insert the floppy or removable disk you want to format.

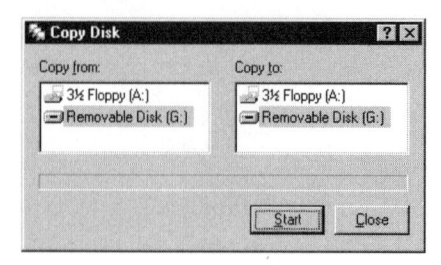

Figure 9-7. *Use the Copy Disk dialog box to select the source and destination drives.*

2. Right-click on the floppy or removable disk icon in Windows NT Explorer's All Folders pane.

3. Select Format from the pop-up menu, then use the Format dialog box to set the formatting options. For floppy disks, the only available file system type is FAT. For removable disks, such as Zip and SyJet, you can use FAT or NTFS.

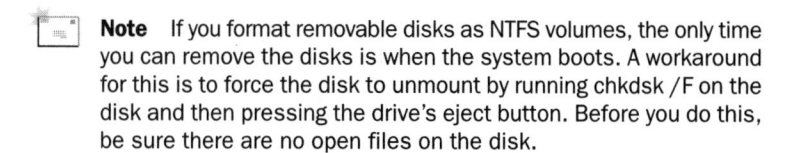

> **Note** If you format removable disks as NTFS volumes, the only time you can remove the disks is when the system boots. A workaround for this is to force the disk to unmount by running chkdsk /F on the disk and then pressing the drive's eject button. Before you do this, be sure there are no open files on the disk.

4. Click on the Start button to begin formatting the floppy or removable disk.

Copying Floppy Disks and Removable Disks

To copy a floppy or removable disk, follow these steps:

1. Right-click on the floppy or removable disk icon in Windows NT Explorer's All Folders pane, then select Copy Disk from the pop-up menu.

2. If the system has a single floppy/removable drive, insert the floppy disk you want to copy when prompted, then follow the prompts to copy the disk.

3. If the system has multiple floppy/removable drives, you'll see the Copy Disk dialog box shown in Figure 9-7. Use this dialog box to select the source and destination drives. In the Copy From area, select the drive you want to use as the source. In the Copy To area, select the drive you want to use as the destination. Click the Start button when you are ready to begin copying, then insert the source and destination disks when prompted.

Selecting Files and Directories

In Windows NT Explorer, you can select individual and multiple files in a variety of ways.

To select individual files

- Click on them with the mouse.

- Use the Tab key to switch between the All Folders pane (on the left side of Windows NT Explorer) and the Contents pane (on the right side of Windows NT Explorer) and then use the arrow keys to highlight the desired item.

To select multiple files:

- Hold down the Ctrl key and then click the left mouse button on each file or folder you want to select.
- Hold the Shift key, select the first file or folder, and then click on the last file or folder.

Copying and Moving Files

Windows NT provides many different ways to copy and move files. You can copy or move them within windows—such as within Windows NT Explorer—and between windows—such as copying a file from Windows NT Explorer to the Network Neighborhood window. You can also copy or move files to and from the desktop.

Copying Files By Dragging

The way Windows NT handles a file copy operation depends on the type of file and the location you are copying to.

Here are some rules you should know before you try to copy files:

- If you try to copy a file to a new location on the same drive, Windows NT will try to move the file instead and ask you to confirm this. To prevent this, hold down the Ctrl key as you drag the file.
- If you try to copy an executable file, Windows NT creates a shortcut to the file instead. To *copy* the file, you'll need to hold down the Ctrl key as you drag the executable file to its new location. To *move* the file, you need to hold down the Shift key as you drag the executable file to its new location.
- To avoid using Ctrl and Shift or having to remember what happens when, hold the right mouse button instead of the left mouse button when you drag files. Now when you release the mouse button at the new location, you'll see a pop-up menu that asks if you want to copy, move, or create shortcuts.

Copying or moving items to displayed areas To copy or move items to any open window or visible area on the desktop, do the following:

1. Select the item(s) you want to copy or move.
2. Hold down the mouse button and drag the item(s) to the new location. If this is a regular file, the file will be copied. If it's an executable file, a shortcut is created.

> **Note** The source and destination location must be visible. This means you may need to open multiple versions of Windows NT Explorer or multiple windows and expand the folders within these windows as necessary.

Copying items to locations that aren't displayed You may also need to copy items to locations that aren't currently displayed. To do this, follow these steps:

1. Select the item(s) you want to copy.
2. Hold down the mouse button and drag the item(s) into the All Folders pane.
3. Slowly drag the items up to the last visible folder at the top of the pane (or down to the last visible folder at bottom of the pane). You should be able to scroll up or down slowly through the existing tree structure.
4. When you find the destination folder, release the mouse button. If this is a regular file, the file will be copied. If it's an executable file, a shortcut is created.

Moving Files By Dragging

To move files, you follow the same steps as with copying files. The key difference is that you should hold down the Shift key as you drag the file to its new location. This ensures that the file is always moved—regardless of location and file type.

Copying and Pasting Files

I prefer to move files around by copying and pasting. When you copy and paste files, you don't have to worry about whether you are copying to a location on the same drive or whether you are copying an executable file. You simply copy files to the clipboard and paste them anywhere you like. You can even paste copies of files in the same folder—something you can't do by dragging.

To copy and paste files, follow these steps:

1. Select the item(s) you want to copy.
2. Right-click and select Copy from the pop-up menu. You could also select Copy from the Edit menu or press Ctrl+C.
3. Access the destination location, then right-click and select Paste from the pop-up menu. You could also select Paste from the Edit menu or press Ctrl+V.

> **Note** Windows NT may not let you copy files and folders to special windows. For example, you generally can't copy a file and then paste it into the My Computer window. Similarly, you may not be able to copy items in special folders and paste them into other windows.

Chapter 9 Managing Files and Directories | 173

Moving Files By Cutting and Pasting

To move files by cutting and pasting, follow these steps:

1. Select the item(s) you want to move.
2. Right-click and select Cut from the pop-up menu. You could also select Cut from the Edit menu or press Ctrl+X.
3. Access the destination location, then right-click and select Paste from the pop-up menu. You could also select Paste from the Edit menu or press Ctrl+V.
4. When prompted to move the selected items, click OK.

Note When you use the Cut and Paste commands, Windows NT doesn't delete the item(s) from the original location immediately. The Cut command simply places a copy of the item(s) on the clipboard. After you use the Cut command to paste the file to the new location, the file is deleted from the old location.

Renaming Files and Directories

To rename a file or directory, follow these steps:

1. Right-click on the file or directory name and then select Rename from the pop-up menu. Or select the file or directory name and then select Rename from the File menu.
2. The resource name is now editable. Enter the new name for the resource.
3. Press Enter or click on the resource's icon.

Deleting Files and Directories

To delete files and directories, follow these steps:

1. Select the items to be deleted.
2. Press the Delete key or choose Delete from the File menu.

Note By default, Windows NT puts deleted items in the Recycle Bin. To delete the files permanently, you need to empty the recycle bin. To delete a file immediately and bypass the recycle bin, press down the Shift key and then press the Delete key or choose Delete from the File menu.

Creating Folders

In Windows NT Explorer, you can create a folder by doing the following:

1. In the All Folders pane, select the directory that will contain the new folder.

2. In the Contents pane, right-click and then select Folder from the New menu. A new folder is added to the Contents pane. The folder name is initialized to New Folder and selected for editing.
3. Edit the name of the folder and press Enter.

Examining Drive Properties

Windows NT Explorer, My Computer, and Network Neighborhood all let you examine the properties of your drives. This includes

- Logical drives
- Floppy drives
- Removable drives
- Network drives
- CD-ROM drives

To examine drive properties you can do either of two things:

- Right-click on the drive's icon and then select Properties from the pop-up menu.
- Select the drive by clicking on it and then select Properties from the File menu.

Figure 9-8 shows the Properties dialog box for a logical drive. The Security tab shown in the figure is only available for NTFS. You can use this tab to set access permissions, auditing, and ownership. Click on the quick access tabs (Tools, Web Sharing, Sharing, and Security) to access other property windows.

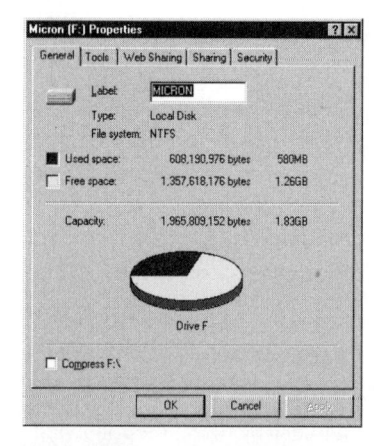

Figure 9-8. *The Properties dialog box provides a quick overview of the drive. The number of tabs available depends on the type of drive.*

The exact number of tabs available depends on the type of drive. Table 9-1 provides a quick overview of how the tabs are used and when they are available.

Table 9-1. Availability and Description of Drive Property Tabs

Tab	Availability	Description
General	All drive types	Provides an overview of drive configuration and drive space.
Security	NTFS drives	Use this tab to set access permissions, auditing, and ownership.
Sharing	All local drives	Allows you to share the drive with remote users.
Tools	Hard drives, floppy drives, and removable drives	Provides access to drive tools for error checking, defragmentation, and backup.
Web Sharing	All drive types	Allows you to share the drive with a local Web server. (Available when the system has Internet Information Server or Personal Web Server installed.)

Examining File and Folder Properties

Windows NT Explorer, My Computer, and Network Neighborhood all let you examine the properties of files and folders. There are two ways you can do this:

- Right-click on the file or folders icon and then select Properties from the pop-up menu.
- Select the file or folder by clicking on it and then select Properties from the File menu.

Figure 9-9, on the following page, shows the Properties dialog box for a folder on NTFS. The General tab provides an overview of the folder and allows you to set its attributes. Folder and file attributes include:

- **Read-only** Shows whether the file or folder is read-only. Read-only files and folders can't be modified or accidentally deleted.
- **Archive** Shows whether the file or folder should be archived. If set, the backup utility will copy the file to the archive and then turn off the check box.
- **Compress** Shows whether the file is compressed. This is only available for NTFS.
- **Hidden** Determines whether the file is displayed in file listings. You can override this by telling Windows NT Explorer to display hidden files.
- **System** Shows whether the file is used by the operating system. For non-system files, this box is usually shaded.

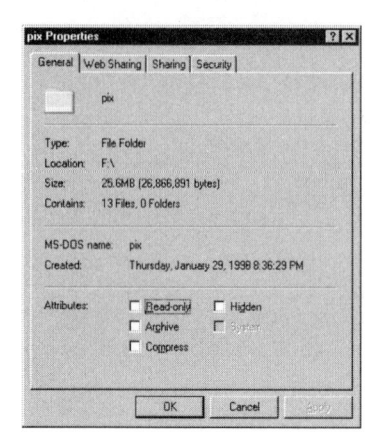

Figure 9-9. *The file and folder Properties dialog boxes are similar. As with drives, the availability of tabs depends on the file system type.*

With file and folder properties, the availability of tabs depends on the type of file or folder. Table 9-2 provides a quick overview of how the common tabs are used and when they are available.

Table 9-2. Availability and Description of Common File and Folder Tabs

Tab	Availability	Description
General	All files and folders	Provides an overview of the item and lets you set its attributes.
Security	NTFS files and folders	Use this tab to set access permissions, auditing, and ownership.
Sharing	All local folders	Allows you to share the folder with remote users.
Version	Win32 DLL and executable files	Allows you to check the file version, description, copyright, and other key information.
Web Sharing	All local folders	Allows you to share the folder with a local Web server. (Available when the system has Internet Information Server or Personal Web Server installed.)

Note When you register a new file type, the file type can create entries that add and remove property tabs. For example, with most image files, you'll see additional tabs. These tabs include Keywords, Description, Caption, Origin, and Credits. Photoshop adds another tab called Photoshop Image, which can provide a thumbnail for the image that allows you to view it without having to open it.

Chapter 10

Sharing Files, Directories, and Drives

Sharing files, directories, and drives allows remote users to access these resources on a network or the Web. When you share a directory or a drive, you make all its files and subdirectories available to a specified set of users. If you want to control access to specific files and subdirectories within a shared directory, you can only do this with NTFS volumes. On NTFS volumes, you use Microsoft Windows NT access control lists to grant or deny access to files and directories.

Sharing Directories on Local and Remote Systems

Shares are used to control access for remote users. Permissions on shared directories have no effect on users who log on locally to a server.

- To grant remote users access to files *across the network*, you use standard directory sharing.
- To grant remote users access to files *from the Web*, you use Web sharing. This is only available if the system has Internet Information Server or Personal Web Server installed from the Microsoft Windows NT Option Pack.

Creating Shared Directories

Windows NT provides two ways to share directories:

- You can share local directories using Microsoft Windows NT Explorer.
- You can share local and remote directories using Server Manager.

Because Server Manager allows you to work with and manage shared resources on any of your network computers, it's usually the best tool to use. Keep in mind that to share directories you must be a member of the Administrators or Server Operators group.

To share a directory, follow these steps:

1. In Server Manager, select the computer on which you want to set up the share.
2. Select Shared Directories from the Computer menu.

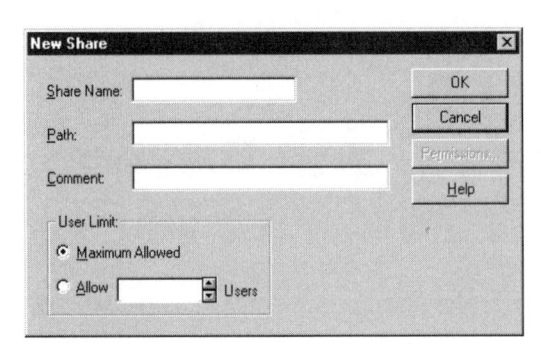

Figure 10-1. *Use the New Share dialog box to create a new share on the selected computer.*

3. In the Shared Directories dialog box, click on the New Share button to open the dialog box shown in Figure 10-1.
4. Enter a name for the share. Share names must be unique for each system and can be up to 12 characters long.

> **Note** MS-DOS and Windows 3.1 computers only access shares that follow the standard 8.3 naming convention. To ensure that the share is accessible to users on these systems, you should follow the 8.3 naming convention. For example, instead of using the name PrimaryShare, you would use PRIMARY.SHR or something similar. See Chapter 9 for more information on this naming convention.

5. Enter the local file path to the directory you want to share. The file path must be exact, such as **C:\Data\CorpDocuments**.
6. If you like, you can enter a comment to describe the share. In Windows NT Explorer, users will see the comment when connecting to the shared directory.
7. If you like, you can set a maximum number of users who can connect to the share at one time. You do this by clicking on the Allow radio button and then entering the user limit.
8. Click OK when you're finished.

By default, everyone on the network has full control over the share. If you want to restrict access to the share, follow the steps outlined in the section of this chapter titled "Managing Share Permissions."

> **Note** If you view the shared directory in Windows NT Explorer, you'll see that the folder icon now includes a hand to indicate a share. Through Server Manager, you can also view shared resources. To learn how, see the section of this chapter titled "Viewing Shares on Local and Remote Systems."

Creating Additional Shares on an Existing Share

Individual directories can have multiple shares. Each share can have a different name and a different set of access permissions. To create additional shares on an existing share, simply follow the steps for creating a share outlined in the previous section—with these changes:

- In Step 4: when you name the share, make sure that you use a different name.
- In Step 6: when you add a comment to the share, use a comment that explains what the share is used for (and how it is different from the other share(s) for the same directory).

Creating a Web Share

If the system you are currently logged on to has Internet Information Server or Personal Web Server installed on it, you can create shares that are accessible from Web browsers. To create Web shares, follow these steps:

1. In Windows NT Explorer, right-click on the local directory you want to share and then select Sharing from the pop-up menu.
2. In the Properties dialog box, click on the Web Sharing tab, which is shown in Figure 10-2.
3. Use the Share On drop-down list box to select the Web server on which you want to share the directory.
4. If this is the first share for this folder, select the Share This Folder radio button to display the Edit Alias dialog box. Otherwise, click on the Add button. Figure 10-3, on the following page, shows the Edit Alias dialog box.

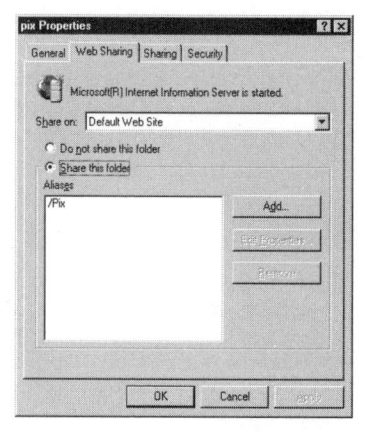

Figure 10-2. *Use the Web Sharing tab to create a Web share.*

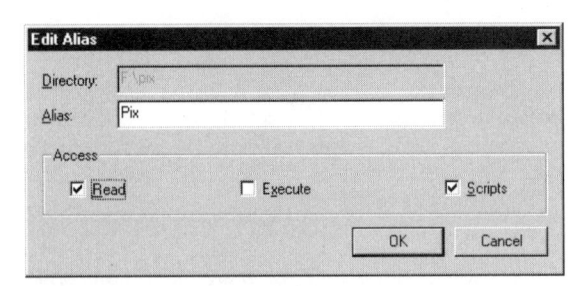

Figure 10-3. *The Edit Alias dialog box allows you to set the alias and access permissions for the directory.*

5. In the Alias field, enter an alias for the directory. The alias is the name you'll use to access the folder on the Web server. This name must be unique and must not conflict with existing directories used by the Web server. For example, if you enter the alias **MyDir**, you could access the directory as *http://localhost/MyDir/*.
6. Use the check boxes in the Access area to set permissions for the directory. These check boxes are used as follows:
    - **Read** Sets Read permission on the directory.
    - **Execute** Allows programs in the directory to be executed from the Web.
    - **Scripts** Allows scripts in the directory to be run from the Web.
7. Click OK when you're finished.
8. To further restrict access to contents of the shared directory on an NTFS volume, set file and directory permissions as outlined in the section of this chapter titled "Managing Share Permissions."

> **Note** Web shares are subject to the access controls enforced by the Web server and Windows NT. If you have problems accessing a share, check the Web server permissions first and then the Windows NT file and directory permissions.

Managing Share Permissions

Share permissions set the maximum allowable actions available within a shared directory. By default, when you create a share everyone with access to the network has full control over the share's contents. With NTFS volumes, you can use file and directory permissions to further constrain actions within the share as well as share permissions. With FAT volumes, share permissions provide the only access controls.

The Different Share Permissions

Share permissions available, from the most restrictive to the least restrictive, are

- **No Access**   No permissions are granted for the share.
- **Read**   With this permission, users can
  - View file and subdirectory names.
  - Access the subdirectories of the share.
  - Read file data and attributes.
  - Run program files.
- **Change**   Users have Read permissions and the additional ability to
  - Create files and subdirectories.
  - Modify files.
  - Change attributes on files and subdirectories.
  - Delete files and subdirectories.
- **Full Control**   Users have Read and Change permissions, as well as the following additional capabilities on NTFS volumes:
  - Change file and directory permissions.
  - Take ownership of files and directories.

Note   Only NTFS volumes have file and directory permissions, or (sometimes and) file and directory ownership.

Share permissions can be assigned to users and groups. You can even assign permissions to these implicit groups: EVERYONE, SYSTEM, NETWORK, INTERACTIVE, and CREATOR OWNER. For details on implicit groups, see Chapter 4.

Viewing Share Permissions

To view share permissions, follow these steps:

1. In Server Manager, select the computer on which the share is created.
2. Select Shared Directories from the Computer menu.
3. In the Shared Directories dialog box, click on the share you want to view and then click on the Properties button.
4. In the Share Properties dialog box, click on the Permissions button to open the dialog box shown in Figure 10-4, on the following page. You can now view the users and groups that have access to the share and the type of access they have.

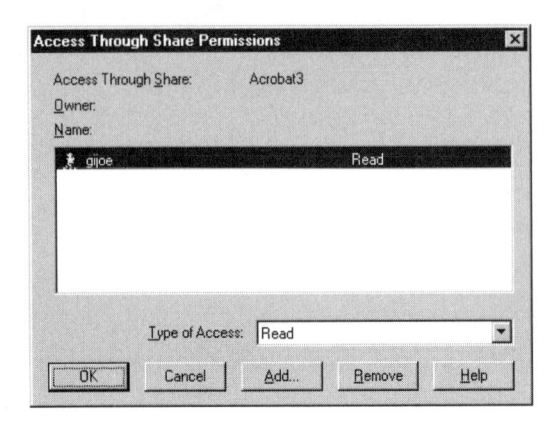

Figure 10-4. *The Access Through Share Permissions dialog box shows which users and groups have access to the share and what type of access they have.*

Adding User and Group Permissions to Shares

To add user and group permissions to shares, follow these steps:

1. In Server Manager, select the computer on which the share is created and then select Shared Directories from the Computer menu.

2. In the Shared Directories dialog box, select the share you want to modify, then click on the Properties button to open the Share Properties dialog box. Then click on the Permissions button to open the Access Through Share Permissions dialog box.

3. Choose Add in the Access Through Share Permissions dialog box. This opens the Add Users and Groups dialog box shown in Figure 10-5. You can now grant access to users and groups. The fields of this dialog box can be used as follows:

   - **List Names From** To access account names from other domains, click on the List Names From drop-down list box. You should now see a list that shows the current domain, trusted domains, and other computers that you can access.
   - **Names** Shows the available accounts on the currently selected domain or computer. For a domain, user accounts and global group accounts are shown. For a computer, only user accounts are shown.
   - **Add** Add selected names to the Add Names list.
   - **Show Users** Shows user accounts in the current domain.
   - **Members** Shows the members of a global group. When you select a global group in the Names list box, you can use this button to show group members. You can then select individual members of the group and add them to the Add Names list.
   - **Search** Allows you to search for a user or group name.

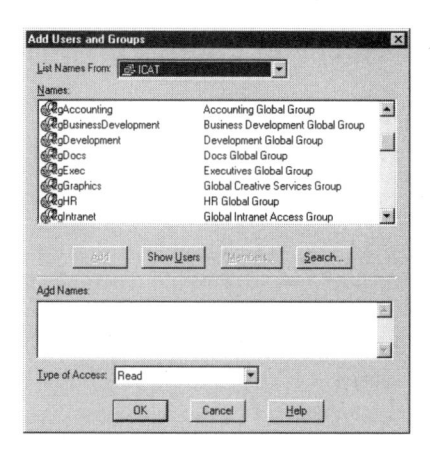

Figure 10-5. *Add users and groups to the share using the Add Users And Groups dialog box.*

- **Add Names**   The list of users and groups to add to the local group.
- **Type Of Access**   The type of access the user or group is granted.

4. Select the user(s) or group(s) you want to have share permissions.
5. Use the Type Of Access drop-down list box to select the access to be granted to the users and groups in the Add Names area.
6. Click OK. The users and groups are added to the Names list for the share.

Modifying Existing Share Permissions for Users and Groups

Share permissions you assign to users and groups can be changed using the Access Through Share Permissions dialog box. To do this, follow these steps:

1. In Server Manager, select the computer on which the share is created and then select Shared Directories from the Computer menu.
2. In the Shared Directories dialog box, select the share you want to modify, then click on the Properties button. This will open the Share Properties dialog box. Then click on the Permissions button to open the Access Through Share Permissions dialog box.
3. Select the user or group you want to modify in the Name list box.
4. Use the Type Of Access drop-down list box to set the new access permission.
5. Repeat for other users or groups, then click OK when you are finished.

Removing Share Permissions for Users and Groups

You remove share permissions assigned to users and groups using the Access Through Share Permissions dialog box. To do this, follow these steps:

1. In Server Manager, select the computer on which the share is created, then select Shared Directories from the Computer menu.
2. In the Shared Directories dialog box, select the share you want to modify, then click on the Properties button. This will open the Share Properties dialog box. Then click on the Permissions button to open the Access Through Share Permissions dialog box.
3. Select the user or group you want to remove in the Name list box.
4. Choose Remove.
5. Repeat for other users or groups as necessary, then click OK when you are finished.

Managing Existing Shares

As an administrator, you'll often have to manage shared directories. The common administrative tasks of managing shares are covered in this section.

Understanding Special Shares

When you install Windows NT, the operating system creates special shares automatically. These shares area also known as Administrative shares and Hidden shares. These shares are designed to help make system administration easier. You can't set access permissions on special shares; Windows NT assigns access permissions. However, you can delete special shares if you are certain the share isn't needed.

Which special shares are available depends on system configuration. Table 10-1 shows special shares you may see and how they are used.

Table 10-1. Special Shares Used by Windows NT

Special Share Name	Description	Usage
ADMIN$	A share used during remote administration of a system. Provides access to the operating system *%SystemRoot%*.	On workstations and servers, Administrators and Backup Operators can access these shares. On domain controllers, Server Operators also have access.
IPC$	Supports named pipes during remote IPC access.	Used by programs when performing remote administration and when viewing shared resources.
NETLOGON	Supports the Net Logon service and access to logon scripts.	Used by the Net Logon service. Everyone has Read access.

(continued)

Chapter 10 Sharing Files, Directories, and Drives | 185

Table 10-1. *(continued)*

Special Share Name	Description	Usage
PRINT$	Supports shared printer resources by providing access to printer drivers.	Used by shared printers. Everyone has Read access. Administrators, Server Operators, and Printer Operators have full control.
REPL$	Supports directory replication. Required for exporting directories that are replicated.	Used by the replication service.
driveletter$	A share that allows adminstrators to connect to the root directory of a drive. These shares are shown as C$, D$, E$, and so on.	On workstations and servers. Administrators and Backup Operators can access these shares. On domain controllers, Server Operators also have access.

Connecting to Special Shares

Special shares end with the $ symbol. While these shares are not displayed in Windows NT Explorer, administrators and certain operators can connect to them. To connect to a special share, follow these steps:

1. In Windows NT Explorer, select Map Network Drive from the Tools menu. This opens the dialog box shown in Figure 10-6.
2. In the Drive field, select a free drive letter. This drive letter is used to access the special share.
3. In the Path field, enter the UNC path to the desired share. For example, to access the D$ share on a server called TWIDDLE, you would use the path **TWIDDLE\D$**.
4. Click OK.

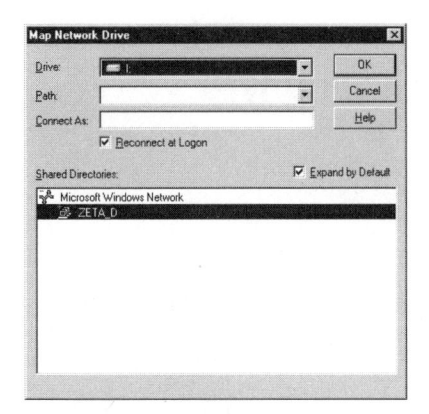

Figure 10-6. *Connect to special shares by mapping them with the Map Network Drive dialog box.*

Once you connect to a special share, you can access it as you would any other drive. Because special shares are protected, you don't have to worry about ordinary users accessing these shares and running amuck. The first time you connect to the share, you may be prompted for a user name and password. If you are, provide that information.

Viewing Shares on Local and Remote Systems

Using Server Manager, you can view all the shares on a Windows NT server or workstation. There are two ways to do this:

- In Server Manager, select the computer on which the share is created and then select Shared Directories from the Computer menu.
- In Server Manager, select the computer on which the share is created and then select Properties from the Computer menu. Then click on the Shares button.

Stop Sharing Files and Directories

To stop sharing a directory, follow these steps:

1. In Server Manager, select the computer on which the share is created and then select Shared Directories from the Computer menu.
2. Select the share you want to remove.
3. Choose Stop Sharing.

> **Caution** Windows NT does not ask you to confirm that you want to remove a share. Further, you should never delete a directory containing shares without first stopping the shares. If you fail to stop the shares, Windows NT will attempt to reestablish the share the next time the computer is started, and the resulting error will be logged in the System event log.

Connecting to Network Drives

Users can connect to a network drive and to shared resources available on the network. This connection is shown as a network drive that users can access like any other drive on their system.

> **Note** When users connect to network drives, they are subject not only to the permissions set for the shared resource, but also to Windows NT file and directory permissions. Differences in these permission sets are usually the reason users may not be able to access a particular file or subdirectory within the network drive.

Mapping a Network Drive

On Windows NT you connect to a network drive by mapping to it. On other systems, you connect to a network drive using the procedure specific to the operating system.

To connect to a shared resource on Windows NT, follow these steps:

1. While the user is logged on, start Windows NT Explorer on the user's computer.
2. Select Map Network Drive from the Tools menu. This opens the Map Network Drive dialog box.
3. In the Drive field, select a free drive letter. This drive letter is used to access the share.
4. In the Path field, enter the UNC path to the desired share. For example, to access a share called DOCS on a server called ROMEO, you would use the path **\\ROMEO\DOCS**.
5. Click OK.

Tip On other operating systems, such as Novell NetWare, you could use the Universal Naming Convention (UNC) from the command line as follows:

Net Use K: \\Server1\Public

If you would like to make this mapping permanent, then add the /Persistent:yes to the end of the Net Use statement:

Net Use K: \\Server1\Public /Persistent:yes

This will ensure that the system will try to access the Public folder on the Server1 every time you log on to the system.

Disconnecting a Network Drive

To disconnect a network drive, follow these steps:

1. While the user is logged in, start Windows NT Explorer on the user's computer.
2. Select Disconnect Network Drive from the Tools menu. This opens the Disconnect Network Drive dialog box.
3. Select the drive you want to disconnect, then click on the OK button.

Managing Directory and File Permissions

With NTFS volumes, you can set directory and file permissions. These permissions can be used to control access with precision.

Taking Ownership of Files

It's important to understand the concept of file ownership. File and folder owners have direct control over their files and folders. File owners can grant access permissions and can give other users permission to take ownership of these resources. But they can't assign ownership to other users. This prevents users from creating files and then making it look like they belong to someone else.

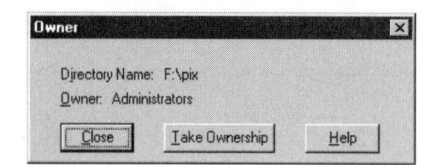

Figure 10-7. *The Owner dialog box tells you the owner of the file or directory.*

As an administrator, you can take ownership of any files and directories on the network. This ensures that administrators can't be locked out of files. Once you take ownership of files, however, you can't return ownership to the original owner. This prevents administrators from accessing files and then trying to hide this fact.

To take ownership of a file or directory, follow these steps:

1. In Windows NT Explorer, right-click on the file or directory you want to take ownership of.
2. Select Properties from the pop-up menu and then click on the Security tab in the Properties dialog box.
3. If you are an administrator (or have Take Ownership permission), the Take Ownership button is displayed. Click on it. You'll see the Owner dialog box shown in Figure 10-7, which tells you the name of the file or directory you are working with and the identity of the owner.
4. Click on the Take Ownership button.
5. If you are taking ownership of a directory or are attempting to take control of a resource you don't have permission to view, you'll see dialog boxes asking you to confirm the action. Click Yes if you wish to proceed.

File and Directory Permissions

Each file and directory on an NTFS volume has an associated ACL (access control list). Entries in the ACL define the access permissions for users and groups on the network. You can view and modify ACL entries using the File Permissions and Directory Permissions dialog boxes, which are accessed as follows:

1. In Windows NT Explorer, right-click on the file or directory you want to work with.
2. Select Properties from the pop-up menu, then click on the Security tab in the Properties dialog box.
3. Click on the Permissions button.

Assigning Permissions to Files and Directories

The basic permissions that you can assign to any file or directory are shown in Table 10-2. Anytime you work with file and directory permissions, you should keep the following in mind:

- Execute is the only permission needed to execute program files. Users don't need Read access.

- Read is the only permission needed to run scripts. Execute permission doesn't matter.
- Read access is required to access a shortcut and its target.
- Giving a user permission to write to a file but not to delete it doesn't prevent the user from deleting the file's contents. A user can still delete the contents.
- Basic permissions are usually combined to form the access types available in the File Permissions and Directory Permissions dialog boxes.

Table 10-2. Basic Permissions Used by Windows NT

Permission	Code Letter	Meaning for Directories	Meaning for Files
Read	R	Permits listing files and subdirectories	Permits viewing or accessing the file's contents
Write	W	Permits adding files and subdirectories	Permits file editing
Execute	X	Permits accessing subdirectories in the directory	Permits running executable files
Delete	D	Permits deleting the directory	Permits deleting the file
Change Permissions	P	Permits changing the directory's permissions	Permits changing the file's permissions
Take Ownership	O	Permits taking ownership of the directory	Permits taking ownership of the file

The basic permissions shown in Table 10-2 are combined to form the basic access types you can assign to files and directories. For example, Read and Execute permissions are combined to form the List access type for directories.

Note You can assign the basic access permissions to files and directories individually, if necessary. For directories, open the Directory Permissions dialog box, then select Special Directory Access or Special File Access from the Type Of Access drop-down list. For files, open the File Permissions dialog box, then select Special Access from the Type Of Access drop-down list.

Access Types for Files

Table 10-3, on the following page, lists the access types for files. As you read the access types, note which basic permissions are combined to form a specific access type. These basic permissions tell you the actions users and groups can perform. As you study the access types, keep the following in mind:

- If no access is specifically granted or denied, the user is denied access.
- Actions that users can perform are based on the sum of all the permissions assigned to the user and to all the groups the user is a member

of. For example, if the user GIJOE has Read access and is a member of the group TECHIES that has Change access, GIJOE will have Change access. If TECHIES is in turn a member of ADMINISTRATORS, which has Full Control, GIJOE will have complete control over the file.

- The exception to the permission rule is the No Access type. If a user or any group the user is a member of is specifically denied access to a file with the No Access type, the user is denied access to the file.
- If the No Access type is assigned to the group EVERYONE, no one is allowed to access the file and the file is locked. To unlock the file, you'll need to take ownership of the file and then change the access permissions.

Table 10-3. Access Types Used with Files

Access Type	Associated Basic Permissions	Description
No Access	None	Denies access to the file
Read	RX	Provides permissions necessary to read files and to execute scripts and programs
Change	RWXD	Provides permissions needed for creating, editing, and deleting files
Full Control	RWXDPO	Provides complete control over the file
Special Access	Variable	Enables you to assign the basic permissions individually

Access Types for Directories

Table 10-4 lists the access types for directories. As you study the access types, keep the following in mind:

- When you set permissions for directories, you can force all files and subdirectories within the directory to inherit the permissions. You do this with the check boxes labeled Replace Permissions On Subdirectories and Replace Permissions On Existing Files.
- When you create files in directories, these files can inherit certain permission settings. These permission settings are shown in the Default File Permissions column.

Table 10-4. Access Types Used with Directories

Access Type	Associated Basic Permissions	Default File Permissions	Description
No Access	None	None	Denies access to the file.
Read	RX	RX	Provides permissions necessary to list directory contents and access subdirectories.

(continued)

Table 10-4. (continued)

Access Type	Associated Basic Permissions	Default File Permissions	Description
Add	WX	Not Specified	Provides permission to create files and subdirectories. However, users have no access to existing files or to newly created files.
Add & Read	RWX	RX	Provides permission to create and access files and subdirectories.
Change	RWXD	RWXD	Provides permissions needed for creating and deleting directories.
Full Control	RWXDPO	RWXDPO	Provides complete control over the directory.
Special Directory Access	Variable	N/A	Enables you to assign the basic permissions individually for directories.
Special File Access	N/A	Variable	Enables you to assign the basic permissions individually for files created in the directory.

Setting File and Directory Permissions

To set permissions for files and directories, follow these steps:

1. In Windows NT Explorer, right-click on the file or directory you want to work with.
2. Select Properties from the pop-up menu and then click on the Security tab in the Properties dialog box. .
3. Click on the Permissions button to open the File Permissions dialog box or the Directory Permissions dialog box. Figure 10-8, on the following page, shows the Directory Permissions dialog box.
4. Users or groups that already have access to the file or directory are listed in the Name field. You can change permissions for these users and groups by doing the following:
   - Select the user or group you want to change.
   - Use the Type Of Access drop-down list box to change the access permissions.
5. To grant access permissions to additional users or groups, click on the Add button and then use the Add Users and Groups dialog box to grant access permissions.

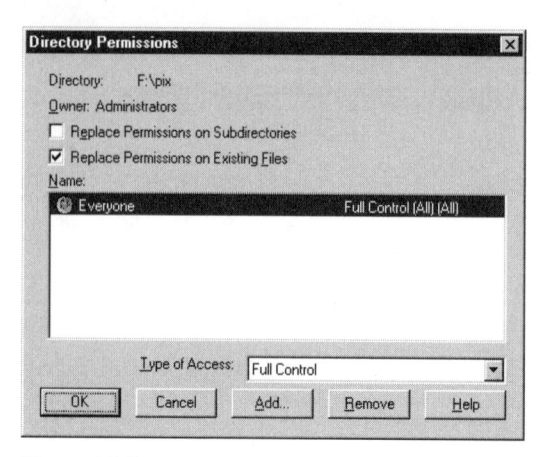

Figure 10-8. *You can view and modify directory permissions with the Directory Permissions dialog box.*

6. You can now grant access to users and groups. The fields of this dialog box are used as follows:

    - **List Name From** To access account names from other domains, click on the List Name From drop-down list box. You should now see a list that shows the current domain, trusted domains, and other computers that you can access.

    - **Names** Shows the available accounts on the currently selected domain or computer. For a domain, user accounts and global group accounts are shown. For a computer, only user accounts are shown.

    - **Add** Add selected names to the Add Names list.

    - **Members** Shows the members of a global group. When you select a global group in the Names list box, you can use this button to show group members. You can then select individual members of the group and add them to the Add Names list.

    - **Search** Allows you to search for a user or group name.

    - **Show Users** Shows user accounts in the current domain.

    - **Add Names** The list of users and groups to add to the local group.

    - **Type Of Access** The type of access the user or group is granted.

7. Select the user(s) and group(s) you want to have access permissions.

8. Use the Type Of Access drop-down list box to select the access to be granted to the users and groups in the Add Names area.

9. Choose OK. The users and groups are added to the Names list for the file or directory.

Chapter 11
Data Backup and Recovery

Data is the heart of the enterprise, and to protect your organization's data, you need to implement a data backup and recovery plan. Backing up files can protect against accidental loss of user data, database corruption, hardware failures, and even natural disasters. It's your job as an administrator to make sure that backups are performed and that backup tapes are stored in a secure location.

Creating a Backup and Recovery Plan

Think of data backup as an insurance plan. Important files are accidentally deleted all the time. Mission-critical data can become corrupt. Natural disasters can leave your office in ruin. With a solid backup and recovery plan, you can recover from any of these situations. Without one, you're left with nothing to fall back on.

Figuring Out a Backup Plan

Creating and implementing a backup and recovery plan takes time. You'll need to figure out what data needs to be backed up, how often the data should be backed up, and more. To help you create a plan, consider the following:

- **How important is the data on your systems?** The importance of data can go a long way in determining if you need to back it up, as well as when and how it should be backed up. For critical data, such as a database, you'll want to have redundant backup sets that extend back for several backup periods. For less important data, such as daily user files, you won't need such an elaborate backup plan, but you'll need to back up the data regularly and ensure that the data can be recovered easily.

- **What type of information does the data contain?** Data that doesn't seem important to you may be very important to someone else. Thus, the type of information the data contains can help you determine if you need to back up the data—as well as when and how the data should be backed up.

- **How often does the data change?**   The frequency of change can affect your decision on how often the data should be backed up. For example, data that changes daily should be backed up daily.
- **How quickly do you need to recover the data?**   Time is an important factor in creating a backup plan. For critical systems, you may need to get the system back online swiftly and to do this, you may need to alter your backup plan.
- **Do you have the equipment to perform backups?**   If you don't have backup hardware, you can't perform backups. To perform timely backups, you may need several backup devices and several sets of backup media. Backup hardware includes tape drives, optical drives, and removable disk drives. Generally, tape drives are less expensive but slower than other types of drives.
- **Who will be responsible for the backup and recovery plan?** Ideally, someone should be a primary contact for the organization's backup and recovery plan. This person may also be responsible for performing the actual backup and recovery of data.
- **What is the best time to schedule backups?**   You'll want to schedule backups when system use is as low as possible. This will speed the backup process. However, you can't always schedule backups for off-peak hours. So you'll need to carefully plan when key systems are backed up.
- **Do you need to store backups off-site?**   Storing copies of backup tapes off-site is essential to the recovery of your systems in the case of a natural disaster. In your off-site storage location, you should also include copies of the software you may need to install to reestablish operational systems.

The Basic Types of Backup

As you'll find when you work with data backup and recovery, there are many techniques for backing up files. The techniques you use will depend on the type of data you are backing up, how convenient you want the recovery process to be, and more.

If you view the properties of a file or directory in Explorer, you'll note an attribute called Archive. This attribute often is used to determine whether a file or directory should be backed up. If the attribute is on, the file or directory may need to be backed up. The basic types of backups you can perform include:

- **Normal/full backups**   All files that have been selected are backed up, regardless of the setting of the archive attribute. When a file is backed up, the archive attribute is cleared. If the file is later modified, this attribute is set, which indicates that the file needs to be backed up.
- **Copy backups**   All files that have been selected are backed up, regardless of the setting of the archive attribute. Unlike a normal backup, the archive attribute on files is not modified. This allows you to perform other types of backups on the files at a later date.

- **Differential backups** Designed to create backup copies of files that have changed since the last normal backup. The presence of the archive attribute indicates that the file has been modified and only files with this attribute are backed up. However, the archive attribute on files is not modified. This allows you to perform other types of backups on the files at a later date.
- **Incremental backups** Designed to create backups of files that have changed since the most recent normal or incremental backup. The presence of the archive attribute indicates that the file has been modified and only files with this attribute are backed up. When a file is backed up, the archive attribute is cleared. If the file is later modified, this attribute is set, which indicates that the file needs to be backed up.
- **Daily backups** Designed to back up files using the modification date on the file itself. If a file has been modified on the same day as the backup, the file will be backed up. This technique does not change the archive attribute of files.

In your backup plan, you'll probably want to perform full backups on a weekly basis and supplement this with daily, differential, or incremental backups. You may also want to create an extended backup set for monthly and quarterly backups that include additional files that aren't being backed up regularly.

Tip You'll often find that weeks or months can go by before anyone notices that a file or data source is missing. This doesn't mean the file isn't important. Some types of data aren't used often but are needed just the same. So don't forget that you may also want to create extra sets of backups for monthly or quarterly periods, or both, to ensure that you can recover historical data over time.

Differential and Incremental Backups

The difference between differential and incremental backups is extremely important. To understand the distinction between them, examine Table 11-1. As it shows, with differential backups you back up all files that have changed since the last full backup (which means the size of the differential backup grows over time). With incremental backups, you only back up files that have changed since the most recent full or incremental backup (which means the size of the incremental backup is usually much smaller than a full backup).

Table 11-1. Incremental and Differential Backup Techniques

Day of Week	Weekly Full Backup with Daily Differential Backup	Weekly Full Backup with Daily Incremental Backup
Sunday	A full backup is performed.	A full backup is performed.
Monday	A differential backup contains all changes since Sunday.	An incremental backup contains changes since Sunday.

(continued)

Table 11-1. *(continued)*

Day of Week	Weekly Full Backup with Daily Differential Backup	Weekly Full Backup with Daily Incremental Backup
Tuesday	A differential backup contains all changes since Sunday.	An incremental backup contains changes since Monday.
Wednesday	A differential backup contains all changes since Sunday.	An incremental backup contains changes since Tuesday.
Thursday	A differential backup contains all changes since Sunday.	An incremental backup contains changes since Wednesday.
Friday	A differential backup contains all changes since Sunday.	An incremental backup contains changes since Thursday.
Saturday	A differential backup contains all changes since Sunday.	An incremental backup contains changes since Friday.

Once you determine what data you're going to back up and how often, you can select backup devices and media that support these choices. These are covered in the next section.

Selecting Backup Devices and Media

Many solutions are available for backing up data. Some are fast and expensive. Others are slow but very reliable. The backup solution that's right for your organization depends on many factors, including

- **Capacity** The amount of data that you need to back up on a routine basis. Can the backup hardware support the required load given your time and resource constraints?
- **Reliability** The reliability of the backup hardware and media. Can you afford to sacrifice reliability to meet budget or time needs?
- **Extensibility** The extensibility of the backup solution. Will this solution meet your needs as the organization grows?
- **Speed** The speed with which data can be backed up and recovered. Can you afford to sacrifice speed to reduce costs?
- **Cost** The cost of the backup solution. Does it fit into your budget?

Common Backup Solutions

Capacity, reliability, extensibility, speed, and cost are the issues driving your backup plan. If you understand how these issues affect your organization, you'll be on track to select an appropriate backup solution. Some of the most commonly used backup solutions include

- **Tape drives** Tape drives are the most common backup devices. Tape drives use magnetic tape cartridges to store data. Magnetic tapes are relatively inexpensive but aren't highly reliable. Tapes can break or stretch. They can also lose information over time. The average capacity of tape cartridges ranges from 100 MB to 2 GB. Compared with other backup solutions, tape drives are fairly slow. Still, the key selling point is the low cost.

- **DAT drives** DAT (Digital Audio Tape) drives are quickly replacing standard tape drives as the preferred backup devices. DAT drives use 4mm and 8mm tapes to store data. DAT drives and tapes are more expensive than standard tape drives and tapes but offer better speed and more capacity. DAT drives that use 4mm tapes typically can record over 30 MB per minute and have capacities of up to 16 GB. DAT drives that use 8mm tapes typically can record more than 10 MB per minute and have capacities of up to 36 GB (with compression).
- **Auto-loader tape systems** Auto-loader tape systems use a magazine of tapes to create extended backup volumes capable of meeting the high-capacity needs of the enterprise. With an auto-loader system, tapes within the magazine are automatically changed as needed during the backup or recovery process. Most auto-loader tape systems use DAT tapes. The typical system uses magazines with between 4 and 12 tapes. The key drawback to these systems is the high cost.
- **Magnetic optical drives** Magnetic optical drives combine magnetic tape technology with optical lasers to create a more reliable backup solution than DAT. Magnetic optical drives use 3.5-inch and 5.25-inch disks that look similar to floppies but are much thicker. Typically, magnetic optical disks have capacities of between 1 GB and 4 GB.
- **Tape jukeboxes** Tape jukeboxes are similar to auto-loader tape systems. Jukeboxes use magnetic optical disks rather than DAT tapes to offer high-capacity solutions. These systems load and unload disks stored internally for backup and recovery operations. The key drawback to tape jukeboxes is the high cost.
- **Removable disks** Removable disks, such as Iomega Jaz and SyQuest SyJet, are increasingly being used as backup devices. Removable disks offer good speed and ease of use for a single drive or single system backup. However, the disk drives and the removable disks tend to be more expensive than standard tape or DAT drive solutions.

Buying and Using Tapes

Backup device selection is an important step toward implementing a backup and recovery plan. However, it is not the only step. You also need to purchase the tapes or disks, or both, that will allow you to implement your backup and recovery plan. The number of tapes you need depends on

- How much data you'll be backing up
- How often you'll be backing up the data
- How long you'll need to keep additional data sets

The typical way to use backup tapes is to set up a rotation schedule whereby you rotate through two or more sets of tapes. The idea is that you can increase tape longevity by reducing tape usage and at the same time reduce the number of tapes you need to ensure that you have historic data on hand when necessary.

One of the most common tape rotation schedules is the 10-tape rotation. With this rotation schedule, you use 10 tapes divided into two sets of 5 (one for each weekday). As shown in Table 11-2, the first set of tapes is used one week and the second set of tapes is used the next week. From Monday through Thursday, incremental backups are performed. On Fridays, full backups are performed. If you add a third set of tapes, you can rotate one of the tape sets to an off-site storage location on a weekly basis.

Table 11-2. Using Incremental Backups

Day of Week	Tape Set 1	Tape Set 2
Monday	Incremental backup on Tape 1	Incremental backup on Tape 1
Tuesday	Incremental backup on Tape 2	Incremental backup on Tape 2
Wednesday	Incremental backup on Tape 3	Incremental backup on Tape 3
Thursday	Incremental backup on Tape 4	Incremental backup on Tape 4
Friday	Full backup on Tape 5	Full backup on Tape 5

Tip The 10-tape rotation schedule is designed for the 9 to 5 workers of the world. If you are in a 24x7 environment, you'll definitely want extra tapes for Saturday and Sunday. In this case, use a 14-tape rotation with two sets of 7 tapes. Perform incremental backups Monday through Saturday. On Sundays, perform full backups.

Installing Backup Devices

Before you can use a backup device, you must install it. When you install backup devices other than standard tape and DAT drives, you need to tell the operating system about the controller card and drivers that the backup device uses. You do this by using the SCSI Adapters utility in the Control Panel.

When you install standard tape and DAT drives, you install the drivers for the drive and control the drive using the Tape Devices utility in the Control Panel.

Installing a SCSI Adapter and Backup Device Driver

The controller card and drivers for backup devices are installed using the SCSI adapter utility in the Control Panel. This is true even if you are installing an IDE device.

To install the controller and drivers for the backup device, follow these steps:

1. Double-click on the SCSI Adapters utility in Control Panel. This opens the dialog box shown in Figure 11-1.
2. Select the Drivers tab, then click on the Add button to display the Install Driver dialog box shown in Figure 11-2.
3. Scroll through the list of manufacturers to find the manufacturer of your backup device, then choose the appropriate adapter in the SCSI Adapters panel.

Chapter 11 Data Backup and Recovery | 199

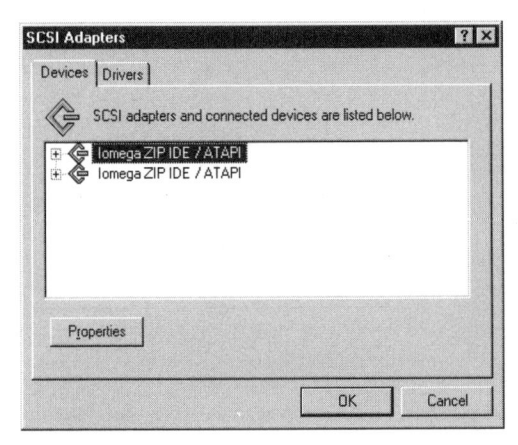

Figure 11-1. *The SCSI Adapters dialog box lets you install SCSI devices and drivers.*

Note If the manufacturer or adapter isn't listed, click on the Have Disk button and follow the prompts. Afterward, select the appropriate adapter. (You can skip this procedure by inserting the driver disk into the floppy disk drive before accessing the Drivers tab.)

4. Click OK.
5. If the Microsoft Windows NT Setup dialog box is displayed, select Current. This tells the system to use the current driver installed on your system, which is usually preferable unless you know specifically that the driver on the disk is newer than the currently installed driver.
6. When Windows NT finishes installing the driver, you'll need to reboot your system. Choose Yes when prompted.

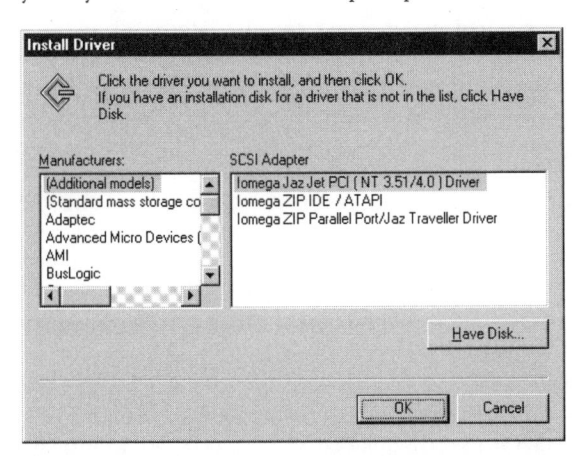

Figure 11-2. *Select the backup device driver in the Install Driver dialog box.*

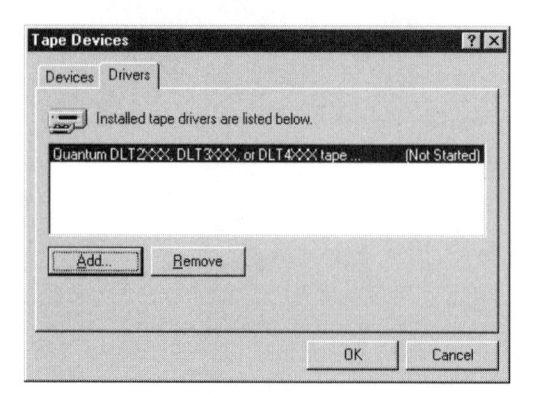

Figure 11-3. *The Tape Devices dialog box lets you install drivers and examine the properties of tape devices.*

Installing a Tape Device

You install drivers for a tape device using the Tape Devices utility. If you haven't configured a tape device yet, the Tape Devices utility tells you that it can't find any tape devices. You can remedy this situation by installing the drivers for the tape device as follows:

1. Double-click on the Tape Devices utility in Control Panel. This opens the dialog box shown in Figure 11-3.
2. Select the Drivers tab, then click on the Add button to display the Install Driver dialog box shown in Figure 11-4.
3. Scroll through the list of manufacturers to find the manufacturer of your tape drive, then choose the appropriate device in the Tape Devices panel.

> **Note** If the manufacturer or adapter isn't listed, click on the Have Disk button and follow the prompts. Afterward, select the appropriate tape device. (You can skip this procedure by inserting the driver disk into the floppy disk drive before accessing the Drivers tab.)

4. Click OK.
5. If the Windows NT Setup dialog box is displayed, select Current. This tells the system to use the current driver installed on your system, which is usually preferable unless you know specifically that the driver on the disk is newer than the currently installed driver.
6. When Windows NT finishes installing the driver, you'll need to reboot your system. Choose Yes when prompted.

When you finish installing the tape device, you'll be able to use the buttons on the Devices tab. The Properties button lets you view the properties of the drive, such as its drive number. The Detect button lets you detect

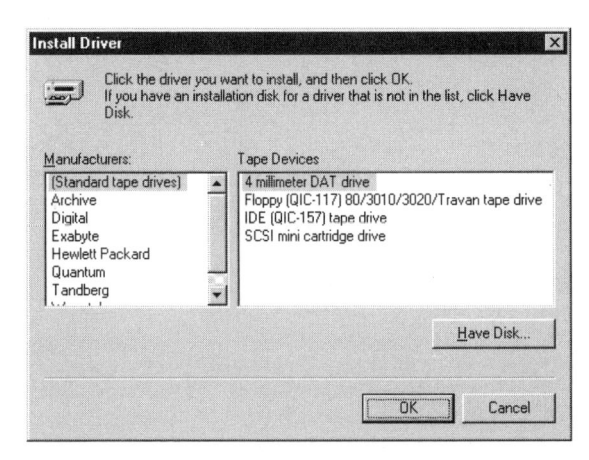

Figure 11-4. *Select the tape device driver in the Install Driver dialog box.*

an installed tape device. This is handy if you recently inserted a tape into the device and you want to check its status.

Using the Windows NT Backup Utility

Windows NT provides a backup utility, called Backup, for creating backups on a local tape drive. You can't use this utility to create backups on a device other than a tape drive. You access Backup by going to Start, selecting Programs, then Administrative Tools (Common), and then Backup. Only Administrators and Backup Operators can run the backup utility.

Figure 11-5, on the following page, shows the main window for the backup utility. Here, Backup has a control window with a main menu and two smaller windows labeled Tapes and Drives.

The Tapes window is used

- To select the desired tape drive for backup
- To view backup sets and their contents
- To select backup sets that you want to recover

The Drives window is used

- To select the file systems/drives that are being backed up
- To drill down to the folders and files contained on a drive so they can be individually selected or deselected for backup

Note On your system, you may see additional windows. For example, if you have installed Exchange Server, you'll see a window for Microsoft Exchange Server.

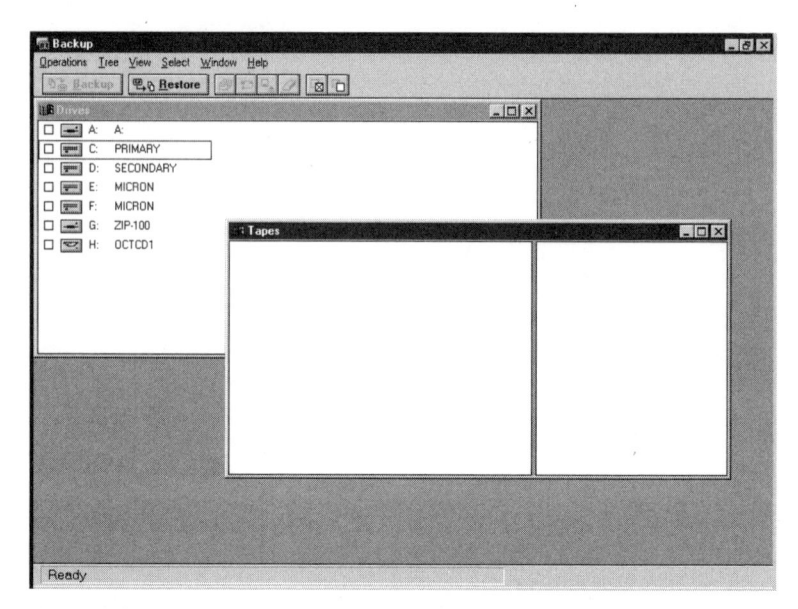

Figure 11-5. *The Windows NT backup utility has subwindows for working with tapes and drives.*

Backing Up File Systems, Directories, and Files

You can back up files with the Windows NT backup utility. Start the utility by going to Start, then choosing Programs, then Administrative Tools (Common), and then Backup. In the Tapes window, select the tape drive you want to use for the backup. In the Drives window, select the files you want to back up.

- You make selections by selecting or deselecting the check boxes associated with a particular file system. When you select a file system's check box, all files and directories on the file system are selected. When you deselect a file system's check box, all files and directories on the file system are deselected.

- If you want to work with individual files and directories on a file system, double-click on the drive's icon. This opens a folder view such as the one shown in Figure 11-6. You can now select and deselect individual directories and files by clicking on their associated check boxes. When you do this, the file system's check box becomes shaded. This shows that you haven't selected all the files on the file system.

Configuring the Backup

When you are finished selecting the files you want to back up, click on the Backup button or choose Backup from the Operations menu. You can now configure the backup using the Backup Information dialog box. Table 11-3 shows how the fields in the dialog box are used as well as the

Chapter 11 Data Backup and Recovery | 203

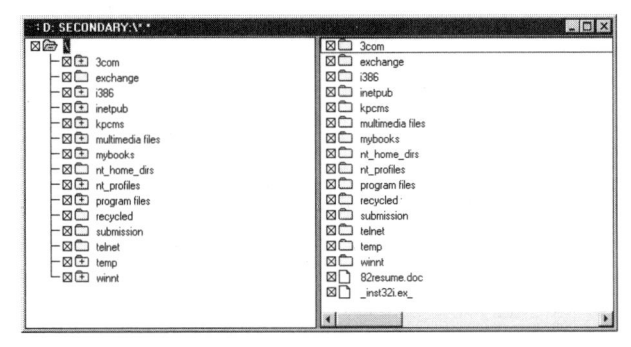

Figure 11-6. *The Folder view lets you select and deselect individual folders and files for backup.*

corresponding flag for Backup's command-line interface (if available). Running Backup from the command line is covered in the section of this chapter titled "Automating and Scheduling Backups."

Note The Backup button is only available if the Drives window or one of its subwindows is open. Select a related window to enable this option.

Table 11-3. Options in the Backup Information Dialog Box

Field	Usage	Command-Line Mode
Current Tape	Displays the name of the tape that is currently installed in the tape device. If the tape is blank or not available, the field displays an appropriate value, such as The Tape In The Drive Is Blank.	N/A
Creation Date	Displays the date the backup set was created.	N/A
Owner	Displays the name of the person who created the backup set.	N/A
Tape Name	Allows you to enter a name for the tape. Tape names can contain up to 32 characters and are set by default to the creation date.	N/A
Verify After Backup	Instructs the tape device to verify data after the backup procedure is completed. If selected, every file on the backup tape is compared to the original file. Verifying data can protect against write errors or failures.	/v
Backup Local Registry	If selected, the tape device backs up the Windows NT registry on the local system. The utility can access the registry files even when they are in use.	/b

(continued)

Table 11-3. *(continued)*

Field	Usage	Command-Line Mode
Restrict Access to Owner or Administrator	If selected, only the tape's owner, Administrators, and Backup Operators can access the tape to view its contents, recover files, or write new backup archives. Use this option to provide additional protection to data.	/r
Hardware Compression	If selected, data is compressed as it is written to the tape. However, the option is only available if the tape device supports hardware compression. Only compatible tape drives can read the compressed information on the drive, which may mean that only a tape drive from the same manufacturer can recover the data.	/hc:on – Turn on /hc:off – Turn off
Operation	Lets you specify how data is written to the tape. If you select Append, data is added to the end of the tape, preserving any current contents.	/a – append /r – restrict
Drive Name	The designator(s) for the drive(s) you are backing up.	/tape:n where *n* is the number of the drive you are backing up. You can view drive numbers using the Properties button of the Tape Devices utility.
Description	Allows you to enter a description of the backup set. If you are creating more than one backup set, you'll be able to enter additional descriptions using the scroll bar provided. Descriptions can be up to 32 characters long.	/d description where *description* is the text of the description.
Backup Type	Allows you to specify the type of backup using a drop-down menu. The utility supports the following types of backups: Normal (Full), Copy, Incremental, Differential, and Daily. For details on these backup techniques, see the section of this chapter titled "Creating a Backup and Recovery Plan."	/t type where *type* is either normal, copy, incremental, differential, or daily.
Log File	Determines where the log file for the backup is stored. If you select an existing log file, the data is appended to the end of the file. Click on the button showing the ellipses to browse for a location or existing log file.	/l filename where *filename* is the full path to the log file.

(continued)

Table 11-3. *(continued)*

Field	Usage	Command-Line Mode
Log Detail	Allows you to select the detail of the logging. Full Detail provides detailed entries for each file including path, file name, file attributes, file size, and file modification date and time. Summary Only entries only provide path and file name information. Don't Log turns off logging.	

When you are finished selecting options for the backup, click on the OK button to begin the backup. The backup utility creates one backup set for each file system you've selected. The backup set is contained in a single file. Later, you can access the backup sets to recover files, directories, or even the entire file system.

During backup operations, the backup utility behaves differently depending on the type and status of a file. If a file is open, the utility generally attempts to back up the last saved version of the file. However, if the file is locked by an exclusive lock, the file is not backed up at all. The utility also doesn't back up certain system files, such as temporary files being used for paging in virtual memory.

Recovering Data from Backups

You can restore files with the Windows NT backup utility by doing the following:

1. Insert the backup tape into the tape drive. This tape should contain any files or directories that you want to recover.

2. Display the list of backup sets (called catalogs) on the tape by double-clicking on the tape's entry in the Tapes window or by selecting Catalogs from the Operations menu. The tape device will go out to the tape and find all of the available catalogs.

3. Using the right-hand pane of the Tapes windows, browse through the available catalogs. Double-click on a catalog to access its contents. Afterward, designate files and directories for recovery by selecting or deselecting their check boxes.

Tip The tape logs provide another way to find files you want to recover. These files are written as standard ASCII text and can be searched in a word processor, like any other text file. You can also use the Find feature of Windows NT Explorer as described in the "Searching by File Size and Contents" section of Chapter 9.

4. When you are finished selecting files, click the Restore button or choose Restore from the Operations menu. You can now specify how the selected files and/or directories are to be restored.

> **Note** The Restore button is only available when you are working with tapes or catalogs. Select a tape or catalog window to enable this option.

Table 11-4 provides details on the options in the Restore Information dialog box. By default, the backup utility restores files to their original location. If you aren't entirely sure that you want to overwrite the files in the original location, use the Alternate Path field to specify a new location for the files, such as C:\temp. Once the files are in the temp directory, you can compare them to the existing files and determine if you want to recover them. Other options of the Restore Information dialog box let you customize the backup process.

Table 11-4. Options in the Restore Information Dialog Box

Field	Usage
Tape Name	Displays the name of the tape that is currently installed in the tape device.
Backup Set	Displays the name of the currently selected backup set. This is the backup set that will be used to restore files and directories.
Creation Date	Displays the date the backup set was created.
Owner	Displays the name of the person who created the backup set.
Restore to Drive	Allows you to specify the drive where the files and directories will be restored. This defaults to the location specified in the catalog.
Alternate Path	Allows you to specify an alternative file path for recovering files, such as C:\temp.
Restore Local Registry	If selected, the tape device restores the Windows NT registry on the local system. The utility can restore the registry files even when they are in use.
Restore File Permission	If selected, file access permissions and ownership are restored with the files. Otherwise, permissions are assigned according to the directory in which files are restored and ownership is assigned to the person restoring the files.
Verify After Restore	Instructs the tape device to verify the data after the restore procedure is completed. If selected, the restored files are compared to the files on the backup tape to make sure that they are written properly. Verifying data can protect against read errors or failures.
Log File	Determines where the log file for the restore is stored. If you select an existing log file, the data is appended to the end of the file. Click on the button showing the ellipses to browse for a location or existing log file.
Log Detail	Allows you to select the detail of the logging. Full Detail provides detailed entries for each file, including the restore path, file name, file attributes, file size, and file modification date and time. Summary Only entries provide only the restore path and file name information. Don't Log turns off logging.

Backing Up and Restoring the Windows NT Registry

The backup utility can be used to back up and restore the Windows NT registry. You can back up the registry by doing the following:

1. Follow the instructions in the section of this chapter titled "Backing Up File Systems, Directories, and Files."
2. Make sure that the Backup Local Registry check box is selected before you begin the backup operation.

You can restore the registry by doing the following:

1. Follow the instructions in the section of this chapter titled "Recovering Data from Backups."
2. Make sure that the Restore Local Registry check box is selected before you begin the backup operation.

The backup utility can back up and restore the registry while the registry files are being used. This allows you to better manage the registry of a live system.

Backing Up and Restoring Data on Remote Systems

The Windows NT backup utility can be used to back up data on remote systems. To do this, you must create network drives for the remote file systems before you begin the backup or restore procedure. You create network drives by following the instructions provided in the section of Chapter 10 titled "Mapping a Network Drive."

Automating and Scheduling Backups

The Windows NT backup utility has a command-line interface, which makes it possible to automate and schedule backups. The command-line interface for backup uses the following syntax:

```
ntbackup   operation   path   [options]
```

where *operation* is either backup to begin a backup procedure or eject to eject a tape, and *path* is the list of file systems and/or directories to be backed up. The options for the command-line interface correspond to fields in the Backup Information dialog box. Use Table 11-3 to help you determine which options to use for your backups.

The following command tells Backup to back up the C and D file systems and append the files to the end of the tape:

```
ntbackup  backup  C:  D:  /a
```

You automate backups by placing commands to the backup utility in batch files and then executing those batch files. If you want, you can use the

Windows NT scheduling service to schedule unattended backups. Here, you set up an At command to run the batch files containing the backup commands.

The following At commands schedule incremental backups for Monday to Thursday and full backups on Fridays:

```
AT   \\ZETA   00:05
/every:Monday,Tuesday,Wednesday,Thursday INC.BAT"
AT   \\ZETA   00:05   /every:Friday   "FULL.BAT"
```

> **Note** If you find the At command difficult to use, you're not alone. Most administrators have problems using the At command; this is why Microsoft developed the WINAT utility—a GUI version of At. WINAT is available in the Windows NT Resource Kit.

The corresponding entry in the incremental batch file might look like this:

```
ntbackup   backup   C:/working/docs   D:/employee/records   /a
/d "Daily Incremental" /b /t incremental /l
"D:\logs\backuplogs\inc\inc.log"
```

The corresponding entry in the full backup batch file might look like this:

```
ntbackup   backup   C:   D:   /a   /d   "Friday Full Backup"   /b   /t
normal    /l    D:\logs\backuplogs\full\full.log"
```

As you can see, the combination of batch files and the Windows NT scheduler allows you to schedule unattended backups on a regular basis. To learn more about the scheduler and the At command, see Chapter 3.

Part IV

Windows NT Network Administration

This part covers advanced network administration tasks. Chapter 12 provides the essentials for installing, configuring, and testing TCP/IP networking on Microsoft Windows NT 4.0 systems. Chapter 13 begins with a troubleshooting guide for common printer problems, then goes on to cover tasks for installing and configuring local printers and network print servers. Chapter 14 provides details on managing DHCP clients and servers. Chapter 15 explores tasks for configuring WINS clients and servers. Finally, Chapter 16 covers tasks for setting up DNS on Windows NT networks.

Chapter 12

Managing TCP/IP Networking

As an administrator, you enable networked computers to communicate by using the basic networking protocols built into Microsoft Windows NT 4.0. The key protocols you'll use are TCP/IP and NetBEUI.

- TCP/IP (Transmission Control Protocol/Internet Protocol) is actually a collection of protocols and services used for communicating over a network and is the primary protocol used for internetwork communications. Configuring TCP/IP communications is fairly complicated compared to the other networking protocols, but it's the most versatile.
- NetBEUI (NetBIOS Enhanced User Interface) is the standard Microsoft protocol for network communications and is designed for use on simple networks. You'll use NetBEUI in conjunction with the NetBIOS Interface service to enable the standard Microsoft network computer browsing features, such as Network Neighborhood.

In this chapter you'll learn about configuring and managing TCP/IP networking. Whenever you work with TCP/IP networking, you must tell the computer about the network. You do this by telling the computer how to route information on the network and how to access other computers. Once you configure TCP/IP, you also need to make the computer a member of the network so it can access network resources.

This chapter also provides an introduction to NetBEUI and the NetBIOS Interface service. For a more detailed discussion see Chapter 15, "Managing WINS and NetBIOS over TCP/IP."

Installing TCP/IP Networking

TCP/IP networking relies on network adapters and the TCP/IP protocol. To access the network using TCP/IP, you'll need to install one or more network adapters on the computer and then set up the TCP/IP protocol.

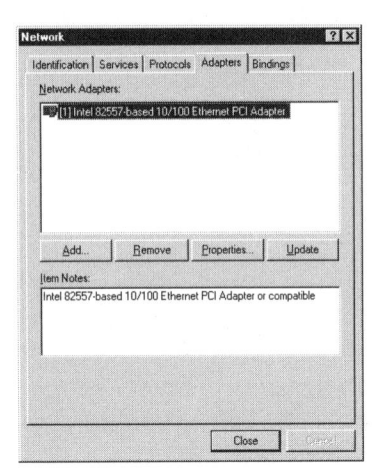

Figure 12-1. *The Adapters tab of the Network dialog box displays a list of currently installed network adapters.*

Installing Network Adapters

Network adapters are hardware devices, such as network interface cards, that are used to communicate on networks. You can install and configure network adapters by doing the following:

1. Configure the network adapter card following the manufacturer's instructions. For example, you may need to set jumpers on the adapter board.

2. Disconnect the computer and unplug it, then install the adapter board into the appropriate slot on the computer. When you're finished, boot the system.

3. Tell Windows NT about the new network adapter card by means of the Network Control Panel utility. Start the utility by double-clicking on the Network icon in the Control Panel.

4. Select the Adapters tab to display the dialog box shown in Figure 12-1. The fields of this tab are used as follows:

    - **Network Adapters** Shows the currently installed network adapters.
    - **Add** Adds network adapters to the system.
    - **Remove** Removes network adapters.
    - **Properties** Sets the properties of the currently selected network adapter.
    - **Update** Updates the drivers for an adapter card. If you have difficulty updating an adapter's drivers, you may want to remove the adapter and then put it back. This ensures that the adapter's new drivers are properly installed.
    - **Item Notes** Shows additional information for the currently selected adapter.

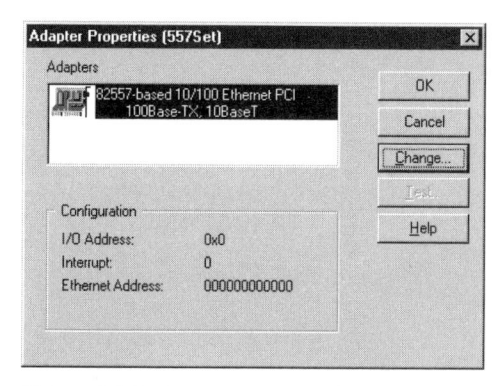

Figure 12-2. *The Adapter Properties dialog box lets you change the adapter's basic settings and test it. The test only works if you've installed the TCP/IP protocol service.*

5. If the new network adapter isn't shown in the Network Adapters list box, click on the Add button.

6. Using the Select Network Adapter dialog box, select the appropriate network adapter. If you don't see the adapter you installed, click on the Have Disk button and insert the adapter's installation disk when prompted.

Note Adding the adapter also installs the drivers for the adapter. Because of this, be sure that you use the correct installation disk.

7. The dialog box you see next depends on the type of adapter you're installing. With most network interface cards, you see the Adapter Properties dialog box shown in Figure 12-2.

8. Click on the Change button, then configure the adapter's basic settings, such as network speed and duplex mode. If you've already configured the TCP/IP protocol service and the computer is attached to the network, you can use the Test button to test the network card. Click OK to continue.

9. Close the Network properties dialog box by clicking on the Close button. Windows NT installs the network bindings for the network adapter. Afterward, if TCP/IP is installed on the computer, you'll see the Microsoft TCP/IP Properties dialog box. You use this dialog box to configure the TCP/IP protocol service as detailed in the section of this chapter titled "Configuring TCP/IP Networking."

Installing the TCP/IP Protocol Service

TCP/IP networking is normally installed during Windows NT installation. You can also install TCP/IP networking by using the Network Control Panel utility.

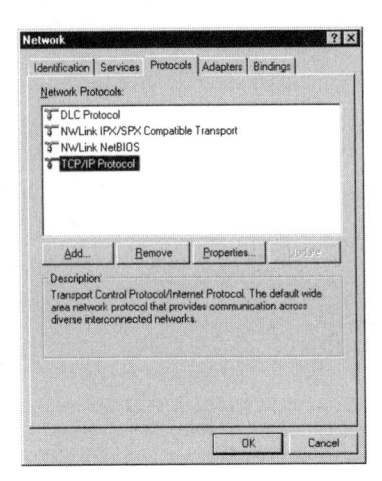

[Screenshot of Network dialog box, Protocols tab]

Figure 12-3. *The Protocols tab displays a list of the currently installed protocols.*

If you're installing TCP/IP after the installation of Windows NT, log on to the computer using an account with Administrator privileges and then follow these steps:

1. Start the Network utility in the Control Panel by double-clicking on the Network icon.
2. Click on the Protocols tab to display the dialog box shown in Figure 12-3. If the TCP/IP protocol is not listed in the Network Protocols list box, you need to add it.
3. To add or reinstall TCP/IP, click on the Add button. This opens the Select Network Protocol dialog box shown in Figure 12-4.
4. Choose TCP/IP Protocol and then click OK.

[Screenshot of Select Network Protocol dialog box]

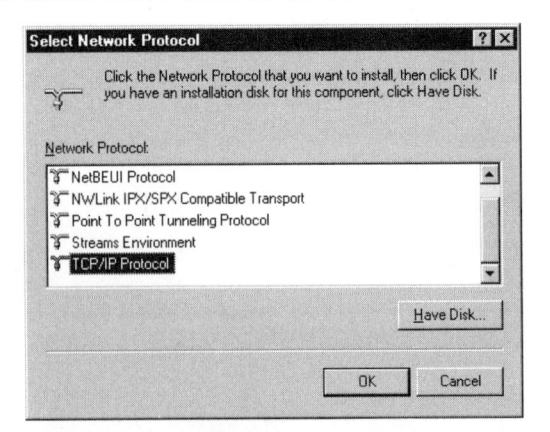

Figure 12-4. *In the Select Network Protocol dialog box, choose TCP/IP Protocol in the list box.*

5. You should now see a dialog box that allows you to obtain an IP address from a DHCP server or to manually configure the IP address. With DHCP (Dynamic Host Configuration Protocol), you can dynamically assign an IP address to the computer. To learn more about DHCP, see Chapter 14.

   Choose Yes to install the necessary services for DHCP. Choose No to assign an IP address manually.

Note DHCP-assigned IP addresses are referred to as dynamic IP addresses. Manually entered IP addresses are referred to as static IP addresses. With DHCP, you have centralized control over IP addressing and TCP/IP default settings. With static IP addresses, you ensure that your computers always have the same IP address, but you have to manually configure all TCP/IP settings.

6. Next, you'll need the Windows NT distribution CD-ROM. When prompted, insert the disk and then enter the path for the distribution files, such as **e:\i386**. Afterward, click Continue to allow Windows NT to retrieve the files necessary to install DHCP on the computer. Once the files are transferred, Windows NT will complete the installation process for TCP/IP.

7. Follow the instructions in the next section for configuring TCP/IP for the computer.

Configuring TCP/IP Networking

Installing TCP/IP doesn't enable networking. To enable networking, you need to tell the computer how to access the network, how to find other computers on the network, and how to relay information to other segments on the network if necessary. You configure networking properties with the Microsoft TCP/IP Properties dialog box. The following sections describe how to use it.

Configuring Static IP Addresses

Computers use IP addresses to communicate over TCP/IP. Windows NT provides two ways to configure IP addressing:

- **Manually**   Manually assigned IP addresses are fixed and don't change unless you change them.
- **Dynamically**   Dynamic IP addresses are assigned at startup by a DHCP server (if one is installed on the network) and may change over time.

When you assign a static IP address, you need to tell the computer the IP address you want to use, the subnet mask for this IP address, and, if necessary, the default gateway to use for internetwork communications. The IP address is a numeric identifier for the computer. IP addressing schemes vary depending on how your network is configured, but they're normally assigned from a range of addresses for a particular network segment. For example, if you're working with a computer on the network segment 192.55.10.0, the address range you have available for computers is usually from 192.55.10.1 to 192.55.10.254.

Using "Ping" to Check an Address

Before assigning an IP address, you should make sure that the address isn't already in use or reserved for use with DHCP. You can check to see if an address is in use with "ping." Open a command prompt and type **ping** followed by the IP address you want to check. To test the IP address 192.55.10.12, you would use the following command:

```
ping    192.55.10.12
```

Assigning a Static IP Address

You assign a static IP address by doing the following:

1. In the Network Control Panel utility, select the Protocols tab. This opens the dialog box shown in Figure 12-5.
2. Open the Microsoft TCP/IP Properties dialog box shown in Figure 12-6 by double-clicking on TCP/IP Protocol in the Network Protocols list box. Or you could select TCP/IP Protocol and then click on the Properties button.
3. In the IP Address tab, select the network adapter you want to configure using the Adapter drop-down list. Multiple selections are only available if the computer has more than one network card/adapter installed.
4. Select the Specify An IP Address button, then enter the IP address in the IP Address field. The IP address you assign to the computer must not be used elsewhere on the network.
5. The Subnet Mask field ensures that the computer communicates over the network properly. Windows NT should insert a default value for

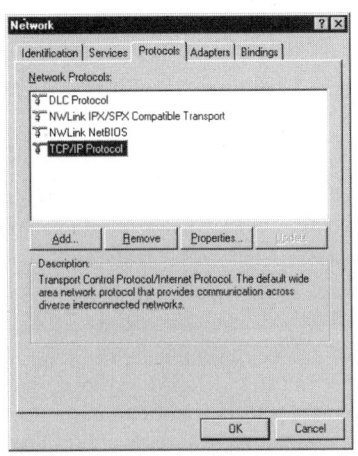

Figure 12-5. *The currently installed protocols are listed in the Protocols tab of the Network dialog box.*

the subnet mask into the Subnet Mask field. If the network doesn't use subnets, the default value should suffice. But if it does use subnets, you'll need to change this value as appropriate for your network.

6. If the computer needs to access other TCP/IP networks, the Internet, or other subnets, you must specify a default gateway. Enter the IP address of the network's default router in the Default Gateway field.

7. Repeat this process for other network adapters you want to configure. Keep in mind that each network adapter must have a unique IP address.

8. Configure DNS, WINS, and Routing as necessary.

9. Close the Network dialog box with the Close button when you're done. Afterward, Windows NT installs the necessary TCP/IP bindings, protocols, and services. When prompted, click Yes to reboot the computer, which will complete the configuration.

Configuring Dynamic IP Addresses

DHCP gives you centralized control over IP addressing and TCP/IP default settings. If the network has a DHCP server, you can assign a dynamic IP address to any of the network adapter cards on a computer. Afterward, you rely on the DHCP server to supply the basic information necessary for TCP/IP networking. Because the dynamic IP address can change, you shouldn't use a dynamic IP address for Windows NT servers.

You configure dynamic IP addressing by completing the following steps:

1. Select the Protocols tab of the Network Control Panel utility, then double-click on TCP/IP Protocol in the Network Protocols list box. This opens the dialog box shown in Figure 12-6.

2. In the IP Address tab, select the network adapter you want to configure using the Adapter drop-down list. Multiple selections are only

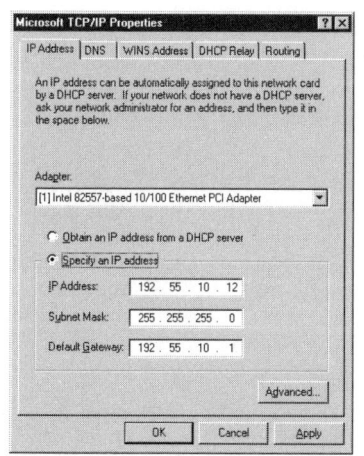

Figure 12-6. *Use the IP Address tab to configure dynamic and static IP addressing.*

available if the computer has more than one network card/adapter installed.

3. Select the button labeled Obtain An IP Address From A DHCP Server.
4. You should see a warning telling you that any settings in the TCP/IP Properties dialog box override the DHCP default settings. Click Yes when prompted.
5. Repeat this process for other network adapters you want to configure. Keep in mind that each network adapter must have a unique IP address.
6. If you want to override the default TCP/IP settings for DNS, WINS, and Routing, insert these settings now.
7. When you're finished, close the Network dialog box with the Close button. Afterward, Windows NT installs the necessary TCP/IP bindings, protocols, and services. When prompted, click Yes to reboot the computer, which will complete the configuration.

Configuring Multiple IP Addresses and Gateways

Windows NT computers can have multiple IP addresses—even if the computers only have a single network adapter card. Multiple IP addresses are useful in several situations:

- You want a single computer to appear to be several different computers. For example, if you're installing an intranet server, you may also want the server to provide Web, FTP, and SMTP services. You can use a different IP address for each service, and you can use different IP addresses for the intranet and the FTP services.

- If your network is divided into multiple logical IP networks (subnets) and the computer needs access to these subnets to route information or provide other internetworking services, you may want a single network adapter card to have multiple IP addresses. For example, the address 192.55.10.8 could be used for workstations accessing a server from the 192.55.10.0 subnet and the address 192.55.11.8 could be used for workstations accessing a server from the 192.55.11.0 subnet.

Caution When you use a single network adapter, IP addresses must be assigned to the same network segment or segments that are part of a single logical network. If your network is divided into multiple physical networks, you must use multiple network adapters, with each network adapter being assigned an IP address in a different physical network segment.

Assigning Addresses and Gateways

Each network adapter installed on a computer can have up to five IP addresses (a sixth IP address is configurable in some Windows NT installations). These addresses can also be associated with up to five default

Chapter 12 Managing TCP/IP Networking | 219

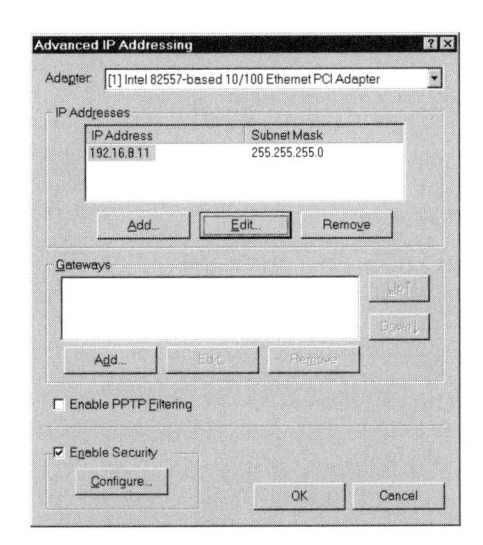

Figure 12-7. *Configure multiple IP addresses using the Advanced IP Addressing dialog box. Each network adapter can have up to five IP addresses and five gateways.*

gateways. You assign multiple IP addresses and gateways to a single network adapter card by doing the following:

1. Select the Protocols tab of the Network Control Panel utility, then double-click on TCP/IP Protocol in the Network Protocols list box.

2. In the IP Address tab, click on the Advanced button to open the dialog box shown in Figure 12-7.

3. Select the network adapter you want to configure using the Adapter drop-down list. Multiple selections are only available if the computer has more than one network card/adapter installed.

4. Choose Add in the IP Addresses area, then enter the IP address in the IP Address field and the subnet mask in the Subnet Mask field. Repeat this step for each IP address you want to add to the network adapter card.

5. You can enter additional default gateways as necessary. Click on the Add button in the Gateways area and then enter the gateway address in the TCP/IP Gateway Address field. Repeat this step for each gateway you want to add.

Tip Make sure that gateways are assigned in the correct order. The gateway listed at the top of the Gateways list box is always used first. Additional gateways are used only when a gateway is unavailable. If the computer can't communicate with the first gateway, Windows NT tries to use the next gateway in the list. You can change the priority of a gateway by clicking on it and then using the Up or Down button to change the gateway order in the list box.

Configuring DNS Resolution

DNS (Domain Name Service) is a host name resolution service. You use DNS to determine the IP address of a computer from its host name. This allows users to work with host names, such as *www.centraldrive.com* or *www.microsoft.com*, rather than an IP address, such as 207.250.162.104 or 207.250.162.107. DNS is the primary name service for the Internet and is also used extensively with UNIX networks. Consequently, if a computer with a static IP address accesses resources on the Internet or on UNIX networks, you should configure DNS.

> **Tip** A DNS server must be installed on the network (or be available to the network) for DNS to function properly. Managing DNS servers is covered in Chapter 16.

The DNS Tab of the Microsoft TCP/IP Properties Dialog Box

You configure DNS using the DNS tab of the Microsoft TCP/IP Properties dialog box shown in Figure 12-8. The fields of the DNS tab are used as follows:

- **Host Name** Enter the TCP/IP host name of the computer, which is usually the same as the computer name. If you want to use a different TCP/IP host name, enter this name instead of the computer name.

    Host names can use alphanumeric characters (A to Z and 0 to 9) as well as hyphens and periods. Host names can't use other characters. A valid host name is *www*.

- **Domain** This optional field allows you to enter the DNS domain name to associate with a host. DNS domain names follow the normal hierarchy for DNS and are different from Windows NT domains.

    Domain names are subject to the same naming rules as host names. A valid domain name is centraldrive.com.

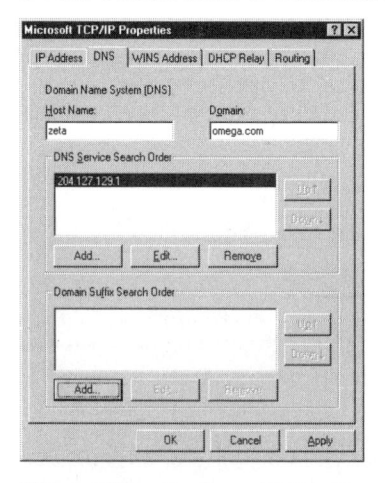

Figure 12-8. *Configure DNS settings using the DNS tab in the Microsoft TCP/IP Properties dialog box.*

Note To determine the fully qualified domain name for a host, the host name and domain name are combined. For example, the fully qualified domain name for the host *www* with a domain of centraldrive.com is *www.centraldrive.com*.

- **DNS Service Search Order** Allows you to specify the IP address of the DNS servers that are used for domain name resolution. Use the Add button to add a server IP address to the list. Use the Remove button to remove a server from the list. Use the Edit button to edit the currently selected entry.

  You can specify up to three servers to use for DNS resolution. These servers are used in priority order. If the first server can't resolve a particular host name, DNS attempts to use the next server on the list. If this server fails to resolve the name, the next server is used, and so on. To change the position of a server in the list box, click on it and then use the Up or Down button.

- **Domain Suffix Search Order** Allows you to enter common domain suffixes in the Domain Suffix Search Order list box. If users fail to use a fully qualified host name, domain name suffixes can be appended to the host name during domain name resolution. A domain suffix of yahoo.com would allow the host name Quote to be resolved to quote.yahoo.com. Use the Add button to add a domain suffix to the list. Use the Remove button to remove a domain suffix from the list. Use the Edit button to edit the selected entry.

  You can specify up to six domain suffixes. These suffixes are used in priority order. If the first suffix doesn't resolve properly, DNS attempts to use the next suffix in the list. If this fails, the next suffix is used, and so on. To change the order of the domain suffixes, select the suffix and then use the Up or Down button to change its position.

Configuring WINS Resolution

WINS (Windows Name Services) is used to resolve NetBIOS computer names to IP addresses. You can use WINS to help computers on a network determine the address of other computers on the network. If a WINS server is installed on the network, the server can be used to resolve computer names. WINS is only supported on computers running Microsoft Windows 3.1, Microsoft Windows 95, Microsoft Windows 98, and Windows NT.

NT computers can also be configured to use the local files LMHOSTS and HOSTS to resolve computer names. LMHOSTS can be used to resolve NetBIOS computer names. HOSTS can be used to resolve TCP/IP host names. However, these files are consulted only if normal name resolution methods fail. In a properly configured network these files are rarely used. Thus, the preferred method of NetBIOS computer name resolution is WINS in conjunction with a WINS server, and the preferred method of TCP/IP host name resolution is DNS in conjunction with a DNS server.

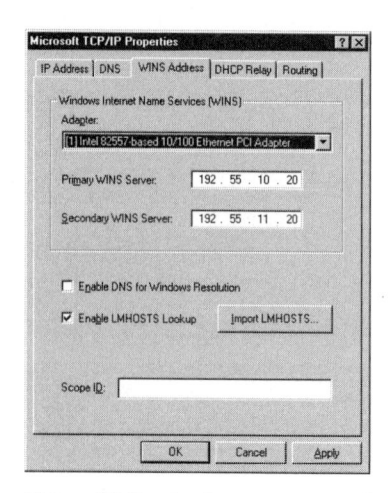

Figure 12-9. *Configure WINS resolution for NetBIOS computer names using the WINS Address tab.*

You can configure WINS by completing the following steps:

1. Select the Protocols tab of the Network Control Panel utility, then double-click on TCP/IP Protocol in the Network Protocols list box.

2. Click on the WINS Address tab. This displays the window shown in Figure 12-9.

3. WINS resolution is configured only for the currently selected network adapter. Select the network adapter you want to configure for WINS resolution with the Adapter drop-down list box.

   Note When a computer uses DHCP, WINS resolution is automatically enabled. While settings you make in this tab may override the settings used by DHCP, blank settings do not turn off WINS resolution. Further, if the computer you're configuring is a WINS server, WINS resolution is always handled locally.

4. Enter the IP address of the primary and secondary WINS servers. The optional secondary server is only used if the primary server can't respond.

   Tip Windows 95 requires you to enter a primary and secondary WINS server. If the network doesn't have a secondary WINS server, simply assign the IP address of the primary server to both fields.

5. To enable DNS for Windows name resolution, select the Enable DNS For Windows Resolution check box. DNS For Windows Resolution is used in addition to the currently defined computer name resolution methods and is really only useful when the DNS server is configured with Windows NetBIOS computer name to IP address mappings.

6. To enable LMHOSTS lookups, select the Enable LMHOSTS Lookup check box. If you want the computer to use an existing LMHOSTS file defined somewhere on the network, you can retrieve this file with the Import LMHOSTS button. Generally, LMHOSTS is used only when other name resolution methods fail.

Best Practice LMHOSTS files are maintained locally on a computer-by-computer basis, which can eventually make them unreliable. Rather than relying on LMHOSTS, you should ensure that your DNS and WINS servers are configured properly and are accessible to the network. This way, you can ensure centralized administration of name resolution services.

7. The SCOPE ID sets the scope identifier for a computer. To limit access to a computer for NetBIOS over TCP/IP, set a SCOPE ID. Then only computers with a matching SCOPE ID will be able to communicate with the computer using NetBIOS over TCP/IP. The SCOPE ID can be a keyword or a string identifier.

Tip The concept of scope is a difficult one. It's helpful to think of a scope as a somewhat limited mechanism for restricting access to computers on a network. Using a scope, you can allow computers A, B, and C to communicate using NetBIOS over TCP/IP while preventing all other computers on the network from communicating with them using this technique. NetBIOS is used for computer browsing in Network Neighborhood, WINS, and other related services.

8. Repeat this process for other network adapters as necessary.

Configuring DHCP Relays

DHCP relays are used to relay BOOTP and DHCP messages to DHCP servers on different networks and subnets. Without this relay mechanism, BOOTP and DHCP messages will fail to transfer across network segments. You should configure a DHCP relay anytime DHCP clients are located on a different subnet or network from the DHCP server. Any computer that has physical connections to the needed network or subnet can act as a DHCP relay.

You can configure a DHCP relay by doing the following:

1. Select the Protocols tab of the Network Control Panel utility, then double-click on TCP/IP Protocol in the Network Protocols list box.
2. Click on the DHCP Relay tab. This displays the window shown in Figure 12-10, on the following page.
3. DHCP relays use the Seconds Threshold to determine which messages to relay. If a message is older than the threshold, it's discarded. Set a threshold for message aging using the Seconds Threshold field.

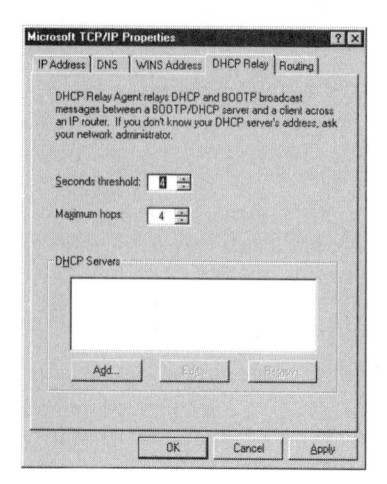

Figure 12-10. *DHCP relays are used to relay BOOTP and DHCP messages across networks and subnets.*

You can set the threshold to any value between 0 and 9999 seconds, but the default value, 4 seconds, is usually adequate. Use the Seconds and Maximum Hops thresholds together to ensure that messages aren't being relayed back and forth in an endless loop.

4. DHCP relays also count the number of computers that a message has passed through to get to its current position. If this number is greater than the Maximum Hops threshold, the message is discarded.

   You can set the maximum hops to any value between 0 and 16. The default value, 4 hops, works well on small-sized to mid-sized networks. If you have a large network with many subnets, you may want to increase this value.

5. Enter the IP addresses of the DHCP servers to which messages should be relayed.
6. Install the DHCP Relay Agent service on the computer.

Installing the DHCP Relay Agent Service

To install the DHCP Relay Agent service, follow these steps:

1. Access the Services tab of the Network Control Panel utility, then click on the Add button.
2. Choose DHCP Relay Agent in the Select Network Service dialog box and then click OK.
3. Now you'll need the Windows NT distribution CD-ROM. When prompted, insert the disk and then enter the path for the distribution files, such as **e:\i386**. Afterward, click Continue to allow Windows NT to retrieve the necessary files.

Configuring IP Forwarding and Dynamic Routing

When multiple network adapters are installed on a computer and those adapters are configured for separate subnets, you may want the computer to forward IP requests between the network segments. In this way, the computer can act as a simple router between the network segments.

IP Forwarding

To enable IP forwarding, follow these steps:

1. Select the Protocols tab of the Network Control Panel utility, then double-click on TCP/IP Protocol in the Network Protocols list box.
2. Click on the Routing tab, then select the Enable IP Forwarding check box.
3. This technique only works for static routing. If the network uses dynamic routing, you should install RIP (Routing Information Protocol).

Installing RIP for Dynamic Routing

To install the RIP service, follow these steps:

1. Access the Services tab of the Network Control Panel utility and then click on the Add button.
2. Select RIP For Internet Protocol in the Select Network Service dialog box, then click OK.
3. Now you'll need the Windows NT distribution CD-ROM. When prompted, insert the disk and then enter the path for the distribution files, such as **e:\i386**. Afterward, click Continue.
4. The RIP For Internet Protocol service is now installed on the computer. You must restart the computer to turn on dynamic routing with RIP.

Connecting Computers to a Domain

Before users can log on to a Windows NT domain from a new computer, the computer must be added to the domain. Computers can be added to a domain during installation of Windows NT. They can also be added to or removed from the domain after installation.

Adding a Computer to a Domain

After you install network adapters and configure TCP/IP, you can add the computer to the domain. You can do this using the Server Manager utility or you can do it from the new computer.

To add a computer to the domain using the Server Manager utility, follow these steps:

1. Start the Server Manager, then select Add To Domain from the Computer menu. This opens the dialog box shown in Figure 12-11, on the following page.

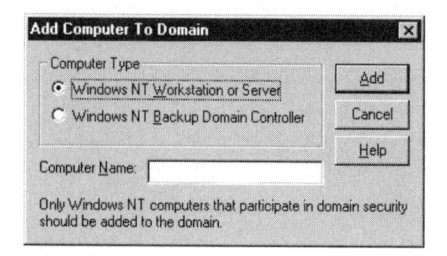

Figure 12-11. *Add computers to a domain using the Add Computer To Domain dialog box.*

2. Specify the computer type. Only servers that are installed as domain controllers can become backup domain controllers.
3. Enter the computer name in the Computer Name field.
4. Click on the Add button.

You've now created an account for the computer on the domain controller. The next step is to have the computer join the domain. You can do this in one of two ways:

- **From the computer's logon prompt**   Have users select the domain from the Domain drop-down list before logging on to the computer.
- **Using the Identification tab of the Network Control Panel utility**   With this tab open, click on the Change button. Enter the domain name, then click OK.

Another way to add a computer to a domain is to do so directly from the computer you're configuring. Do this by completing the following steps:

1. Access the Identification tab of the Network Control Panel utility, then click on the Change button.
2. In the Member Of area, select the Domain radio button, then enter the domain name in the field provided.
3. Select Create A Computer Account in the Domain.
4. Enter the user name and password for an account with domain administration privileges.
5. Click OK.

Removing a Computer from a Domain

Before you move a computer to a different domain or workgroup, you should remove the computer from the domain it's attached to. You do this by completing the following steps:

1. Access the Identification tab of the Network Control Panel utility, then click on the Change button. Remove the computer from the domain by making a new selection in the Member Of area. To add the computer to a workgroup, select the Workgroup radio button and then enter the name of the workgroup. To add the computer to a different domain, select the Domain radio button and then enter the new domain name.

2. Remove the computer account from the old domain by using Server Manager. Be sure to select the old domain in Server Manager before you proceed. To remove the computer account, select the computer name and then select Remove From Domain on the Computer menu.

Configuring Additional TCP/IP Services

Windows NT systems can be configured for additional TCP/IP services, such as RIP, DNS, or DHCP. When you add these services, Windows NT installs the service and binds the service to the currently installed protocols and adapters as necessary. Windows NT also installs any utilities that the service needs in order to operate. These utilities are installed in the Administrative Tools (Common) folder. For example, if you install DNS, the DNS Manager utility is added to this folder.

Table 12-1 provides a brief overview of the various network services you can install. The management of key network services, such as DNS and DHCP, is covered in later chapters.

Table 12-1. Network Services Available on Windows NT

Service Name	Description
BOOTP Relay Agent	Allows the computer to forward BOOTP messages across network segments. BOOTP is used to support the remote booting of diskless workstations.
Computer Browser	Allows browsing of network computers, such as through Network Neighborhood.
DHCP Relay Agent	Allows the computer to forward DHCP messages to DHCP servers in a different network segment.
Gateway (and Client) Services for NetWare	Allows the computer to access NetWare networks.
Microsoft DHCP Server	Allows the computer to be configured as a DHCP server.
Microsoft DNS Server	Allows the computer to be configured as a DNS server.
Microsoft Internet Information Server	Allows the computer to be configured as a Web/FTP server.
Microsoft TCP/IP Printing	Allows the computer to print over TCP/IP using the LPD facility.
NetBIOS Interface	Provides the basic functions needed for NetBIOS and services that use NetBIOS, such as WINS.
Network Monitor Agent	Allows the computer to collect network performance information for the computer.
Network Monitor Tools and Agent	Allows the computer to collect network performance information for the computer. Includes the utilities necessary for performance monitoring.
Remote Access Service	Allows the computer to use dial-up networking.
Remoteboot Service	Installs services needed to remotely boot diskless workstations.
RIP for Internet Protocol	Installs services needed for dynamic routing between subnets.

(continued)

Table 12-1. *(continued)*

Service Name	Description
RIP for NWLink IPX/SPC Compatible Transport	Installs services needed for dynamic routing to NetWare networks.
RPC Configuration	Installs the remote procedure call facilities.
RPC Support for Banyan	Allows for remote procedure calls to computers on Banyan Vines networks.
SAP Agent	Allows the computer to support the NetWare Service Advertising Protocol.
Server	Provides the services needed for the computer to act as a Windows NT server.
Services for Macintosh	Allows the computer to communicate with Macintosh clients.
Simple TCP/IP Services	Adds basic services and command-line tools for TCP/IP. Includes chargen, daytime, discard, echo, and quote.
SNMP Service	Installs the Simple Network Management Protocol used by most network management utilities.
Windows Internet Name Service	Allows the computer to be configured as a WINS server.
Workstation	Provides the services needed for the computer to act as a Windows NT workstation.

Using the Services Tab

The Services tab of the Network Control Panel utility allows you to configure TCP/IP services (see Figure 12-12). The Network Services list box shows the services that are currently installed on the computer. The buttons on the Services tab are used as follows:

- **Add** Used to add additional services. To add a service, click Add, select the service you want to add from the Select Network Service dialog box, and then click OK.

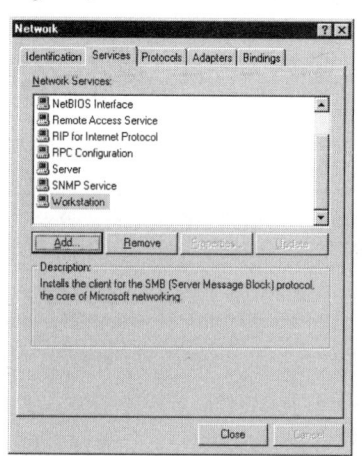

Figure 12-12. *Use the Services tab to view, add, and remove network services.*

- **Remove** Used to remove the currently selected service. To remove a service, click Remove and then confirm the action by selecting Yes when prompted.
- **Properties** Used to configure properties of the currently selected service. If this button is shaded, the service is not configurable through this dialog box.
- **Update** Used to update a service. If this button is shaded, the service can't be updated in this manner.

Testing the TCP/IP Configuration

Whenever you install a new computer or make configuration changes to the computer's network settings, you should test the configuration. The most basic TCP/IP test is to use the ping command to test the computer's connection to the network. Ping is a command-line utility and is used as follows:

```
ping host
```

where host is the host computer you're trying to reach.

On Windows NT, there are several ways to test the configuration using ping:

- **Try to ping IP addresses.** If the computer is configured correctly and the host you're trying to reach is accessible to the network, ping should receive a reply. If ping can't reach the host, ping will time out.
- **On domains that use WINS, try to ping NetBIOS computer names.** If NetBIOS computer names are resolved correctly, the NetBIOS facilities, such as WINS, are correctly configured for the computer.
- **On domains that use DNS, try to ping DNS host names.** If fully qualified DNS host names are resolved correctly, DNS name resolution is configured properly.

You may also want to test network browsing for the computer. If the computer is a member of a Windows NT domain and computer browsing is enabled throughout the domain, log on to the computer and then use the Windows NT Explorer or Network Neighborhood to browse other computers in the domain. Afterward, log on to a different computer in the domain and try to browse the computer you just configured. These tests tell you if the NetBIOS facilities, such as the Computer Browser service, are configured correctly. If you can't browse, check the configuration of the related services and protocols.

Chapter 13

Administering Network Printers and Print Services

As an administrator, there are two main things you need to do so users throughout a network can access print devices connected to a Microsoft Windows NT workstation or server:

- You need to set up a workstation or server as a print server.
- You then need to use the print server to share print devices on the network.

This chapter covers the basics of setting up shared printing and accessing it from the network. You'll also find help for administering printers and for troubleshooting printer problems, which is where we'll begin.

Note Under Windows NT, the terminology for printers and print devices is slightly different than what is used conventionally. In Windows NT, a print device is the actual hardware device that produces printed output. Print devices attached locally to print servers are known as local print devices. Print devices attached directly to a network are referred to as network interface print devices. A printer, on the other hand, is the software interface between the operating system and the print device. Printers are installed on print servers. Further, it is important to note these terms are sometimes used as if they were interchangeable in documentation and dialog windows. If this happens, focus on whether the developers are referring to a physical device (a print device) or a software interface (a printer).

Troubleshooting Printer Problems

An understanding of how printing works can go a long way when you're trying to troubleshoot printer problems. When you print documents, many processes, drivers, and devices work together so that the documents are printed. These include the following:

- **Printer driver** When you print a document in an application, your computer loads a printer driver. If the print device is attached to your computer physically, the printer driver is loaded from a local disk drive.

If the print device is located on a remote computer, the printer driver may be downloaded from the remote computer. Typically, this is done only if the driver on the remote computer is newer than the one installed on the local system.

The availability of printer drivers on the remote computer is configurable by operating system and chip architecture. If the computer can't obtain the latest printer driver, it's probably because an administrator hasn't enabled the driver for the computer's operating system. For more information, see the section of this chapter titled "Installing Network Print Devices."

- **Local print spool and print processor** The application you're printing from uses the printer driver to translate the document into a file format understandable by the selected print device. Then your computer passes the document off to the local print spooler. The local spooler in turn passes the document to a print processor, which creates the raw print data necessary for printing on the print device.

  The print processor is run through a DLL (Dynamic-link library) called WINPRINT.DLL. Problems with this DLL can sometimes lead to garbled printing or the inability to recognize the print job data type. However, before you replace this DLL, make sure that the printer driver is installed and configured properly. Additionally, some printing problems—such as the partial loss of formatting within a document—can be the result of incorrect settings for print job data types.

- **Print router and print spooler on the print server** The raw data is passed back to the local print spooler. If you're printing to a remote printer, the raw data is then routed to the print spooler on the print server. On Windows NT systems, the printer router, WINSPOOL.DRV, handles the tasks of locating the remote printer, routing print jobs, and downloading printer drivers to the local system if necessary. If any one of these tasks fails, the print router is usually the culprit. See the sections of this chapter titled "Solving Spooling Problems" and "Setting Printer Access Permissions" to learn possible fixes for this problem. If these procedures don't work, you may want to replace or restore WINSPOOL.DRV.

  The key reason for downloading printer drivers to clients is to provide a single location for installing driver updates. Thus, rather than having to install a new driver on all the client systems, you install the driver on the print server and allow clients to download the new driver. For more information on working with printer drivers, see the section of this chapter titled "Installing Network Print Devices."

- **Printer (print queue)** Next, the document goes into the printer stack—which in some operating systems is called the print queue—for the selected print device. Once in the queue, the document is referred to as a print job—a task for the print spooler to handle. The length of time the document waits in the printer stack is based on its priority and position within the printer stack. For more information, see the section of this chapter titled "Scheduling and Prioritizing Print Jobs."

- **Print monitor** When the document reaches the top of the printer stack, the print monitor sends the document to the print device, where it's actually printed. If the printer is configured to notify users that the document has been printed, you see a message confirming this.

  The specific print monitor used by Windows NT depends on the print device configuration and type. The default monitor is LOCALMON.DLL. You may also see monitors from the print device manufacturer, such as HPMON.DLL, which is used with most Hewlett-Packard print devices. This DLL is required to print to the print device. If it's corrupted or missing, you may need to reinstall it.

- **Print device** The print device is the physical device that prints documents on paper. Common print device problems and display errors include:
  - **Insert Paper Into Tray X** Print device is looking for paper in a specific tray. Add paper to it.
  - **Low Toner** When a laser print device gets low on toner, you may need to remove the toner cartridge, shake it several times, and put it back into the print device. Shaking the cartridge moves the toner around and sometimes allows you to print additional documents.
  - **Out Of Paper** Print device is out of paper (or thinks it is). Add paper.
  - **Out Of Toner; Out Of Ink** Print device is out of toner or ink. Replace the toner cartridge or ink cartridge.
  - **Paper Jam** Paper is stuck in the print device. Open the print device, remove the jammed paper, and then put the print device back on line.
  - **Printer Off-Line** Print device may be warming up or initializing. If so, the print device should come on line when finished. Otherwise, you'll need to put the print device back on line using the print device control buttons.

Installing and Configuring Printers

Two types of print devices are used on a network:

- **Local print device** A print device that is physically attached to the user's computer and employed only by the user who's logged on to that computer.
- **Network print device** A print device that is set up for remote access over the network. This can be a print device attached directly to a print server or a network-attached print device.

To install or configure a new printer, you must be a member of one of the privileged groups shown in Table 13-1, on the following page. On Windows NT servers, as you can see, Administrators, Printer Operators, and Server Operators can configure printers. On Windows NT workstations, Administrators and Power Users can configure printers.

Table 13-1. Groups That Can Configure Printers, According to System Type

Group	Windows NT Workstation	Windows NT Server
Administrators	X	X
Power Users	X	
Print Operators		X
Server Operators		X

To connect to and print documents to the printer, you must have the appropriate access permissions. See the section of this chapter titled "Setting Printer Access Permissions" for details.

The sections that follow describe procedures for installing and configuring printers. You install new network printers on print servers. You connect to network printers on remote systems, such as a user's workstation.

Installing Network Print Devices

Print devices can connect directly to the network or to an actual system on the network by way of a parallel or serial port. Regardless of which is used, print servers are used to manage network printing. Any Windows NT workstation or server can be configured as a print server. The primary job of the print server is to share the print device out to the network and to handle print spooling.

You install new network printing as follows:

1. Log on locally to the print server.
2. Follow the print device manufacturer's instructions for installing printer services and protocols on the print server as necessary. For example, to use a network print device that is physically attached to the network rather than to a computer printer port, you may need to install the DLC (Data Link Control) protocol. To do this, follow these steps:
   - Double-click on the Network icon in the Control Panel.
   - In the Network dialog box, select the Protocols tab and then click on the Add button.
   - In the Select Network Protocol dialog box, select DLC Protocol from the Network Protocol list.
   - Choose OK.
   - When prompted, insert the appropriate disk or disks and specify the location of the protocol drivers.
   - Close the Network dialog box and reboot the print server when prompted.
3. Double-click on the Printers icon in the Control Panel or select Settings in the Start menu and then choose the Printers option. This opens the Printers folder shown in Figure 13-1. You should see the Add Printer icon and an icon for each additional printer configured for the system.
4. Double-click on the Add Printer icon to open the Add Printer Wizard shown in Figure 13-2.

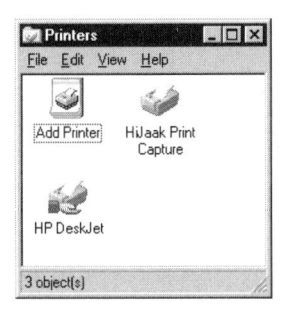

Chapter 13 Administering Network Printers and Print Services | 235

Figure 13-1. *The Printers folder allows you to add printers, update currently configured printers, and manage print server properties.*

5. Select the My Computer radio button, then click on the Next button.
6. Next, you need to configure the port or ports used by the printer (see Figure 13-3, on the following page).

    - For a print device physically connected to the print server, select the appropriate LPT or COM port. If you select more than one port, Windows NT prints to the first available port. You can also print to a file. If you do, Windows NT prompts users for a file name each time they print.

    - For a print device physically connected to the network, click on the Add Port button. This opens the Printer Ports dialog box. You can now select the appropriate port type for the printer you're configuring, such as Digital Network Port, Lexmark DLC Network Port, or Lexmark TCP/IP Port. If necessary, click on the New Monitor button to specify a new print monitor. Then complete the process by clicking on the New Port button to create the new port. Once the port is defined, you can select it from the Available Ports list.

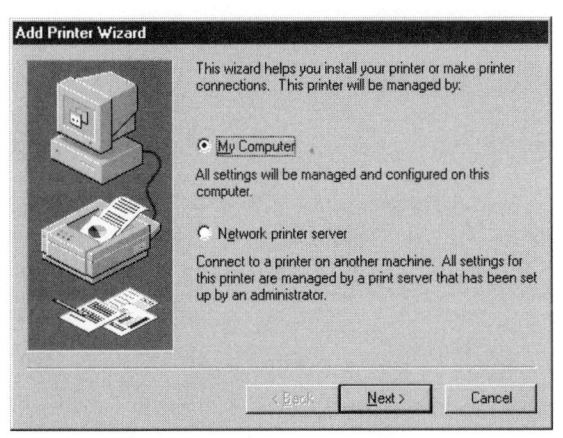

Figure 13-2. *The Add Printer Wizard lets you configure local print devices and remote access to network printer servers.*

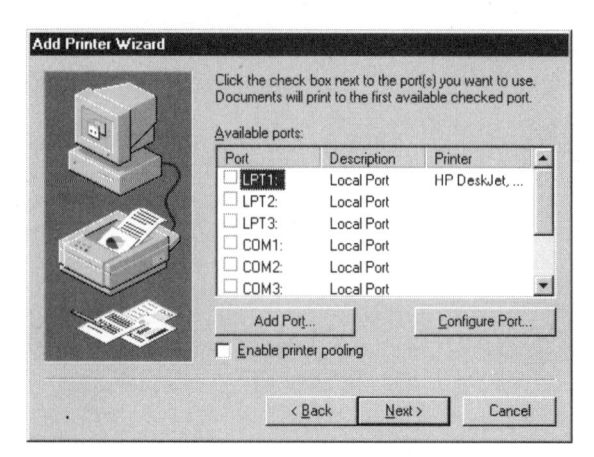

Figure 13-3. *In the Add Printer Wizard window, select a printer port for a local printer or click on the Add Port button for a network-attached printer.*

> **Note** The appropriate port type should be specified in the print device's documentation. Digital Network Port is used with DECNet and DEC printers. LPR port is used to create a print gateway to a UNIX system. DLC Network Port is used with Lexmark and HP print devices (and you may see Lexmark DLC Network Port or Hewlett-Packard DLC Network Port).

7. When you're finished configuring ports, click on the Next button to display the window shown in Figure 13-4. You must now specify the print device manufacturer and model. This allows Windows NT to assign a printer driver to the print device. After you choose a print device

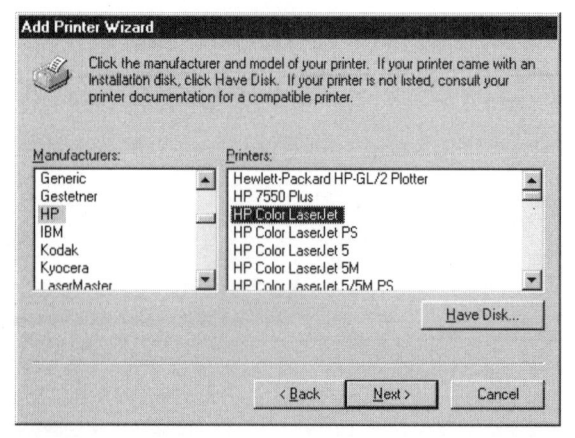

Figure 13-4. *Select a print device manufacturer and model with the Add Printer Wizard.*

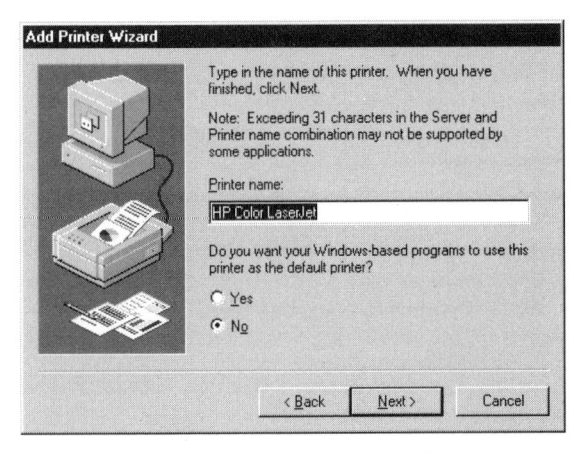

Chapter 13 Administering Network Printers and Print Services | 237

Figure 13-5. *Name the printer in the Add Printer Wizard.*

manufacturer, choose a printer model. If the print device manufacturer and model you're using isn't displayed in the list, choose Have Disk to install a new driver.

Note If a driver for the specific printer model you're using isn't available, you can usually select a generic driver or a driver for a similar print device. Consult the print device documentation for specific pointers.

8. Click on the Next button to assign a name to the printer, as shown in Figure 13-5. This is the name you'll see in the Printers folder of Control Panel. You can also specify whether the printer is the default used by the local system. Choose Yes or No and click on the Next button.
9. You can now specify whether the printer is available to remote users (see Figure 13-6, on the following page). To create a network printer that is accessible to remote users, click on the Shared radio button and enter a name for the shared resource. In a large organization, you'll want the share name to be logical and helpful in locating the printer. For example, you may want to name the printer that points to the print device in the northeast corner of the twelfth floor TwelveNE.

Note If Microsoft Windows 3.1 or MS-DOS systems will access the printer, be sure the printer name conforms to the standard MS-DOS naming rule. For example, use the name NORTH12.PRT rather than NORTH_PRINTER_FLOOR12.

10. In the same window, select the type of computers that will use the printer. The selections you make here are used to install printer drivers for other operating systems. When users from these systems access the printer, the driver can be downloaded to their systems. Normally, this is done if the driver on the print server is newer than the driver on the user's computer.

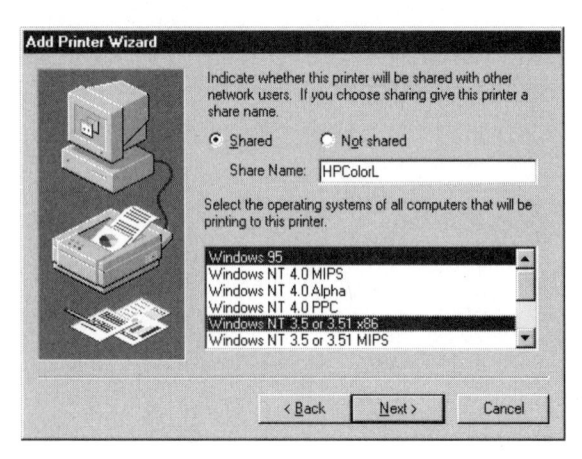

Figure 13-6. *Share the network printer and assign it a name in the Add Printer Wizard. Afterward, select the operating systems of computers that will use the printer.*

> **Note** If you make selections in this step, you'll need the Windows NT CD-ROM or the manufacturer's distribution disks.

11. The final window lets you test the installation by printing a test page to the print device. If you want to do this, select Yes. Otherwise, select No. When you're ready to install the printer, click on the Finish button.

When the Add Printer Wizard finishes installing the new printer, the Printers folder in the Control Panel will have an additional icon with the name set the way you previously specified. You can change the printer properties and status at any time. For more information, see the section of this chapter titled "Configuring Printer Properties."

> **Tip** If you repeat this process, you can create additional printers for the same print device. All you need to do is change the printer name and share name. Having additional printers for a single print device allows you to set different properties to serve different needs. For example, you could have a high priority printer for print jobs that need to be printed immediately and a low priority printer for print jobs that aren't as urgent.

Installing Local Print Devices

A local print device is physically connected to a user's computer and accessible only on that computer. Installing printing on a local system is much like installing network printing. The key difference is that the printer

Chapter 13   Administering Network Printers and Print Services | 239

isn't shared. Accordingly, follow the steps for creating a printer as specified in the section of this chapter titled "Installing Network Print Devices." Then in step 9, specify that the printer is *not* shared.

Note   A local printer can easily become a network printer. To learn how to do this, see the section of this chapter titled "Starting and Stopping Printer Sharing."

Connecting to Printers Created on the Network

Once you create a network printer, remote users can connect to it and use it much like any other printer. You'll need to set up a connection on a user-by-user basis or have users do this themselves. To create the connection to the printer on a Windows NT system, follow these steps:

1. With the user logged on, double-click on the Printers icon in the Control Panel or select Settings in the Start menu and then choose the Printers option. This opens the Printers folder shown in Figure 13-1.
2. Double-click on the Add Printer icon to open the Add Printer Wizard shown in Figure 13-2.
3. Select the Network Printer Server radio button, then click on the Next button.
4. Using the Connect To Printer dialog box shown in Figure 13-7, select the shared printer. Click on the items in the Shared Printers list to work your way down to the shared printer to which you want to connect. When the printer is selected, click OK.
5. Determine whether the printer is the default used by Windows applications. Choose Yes or No and then click on the Next button.
6. Choose Finish to complete the operation.

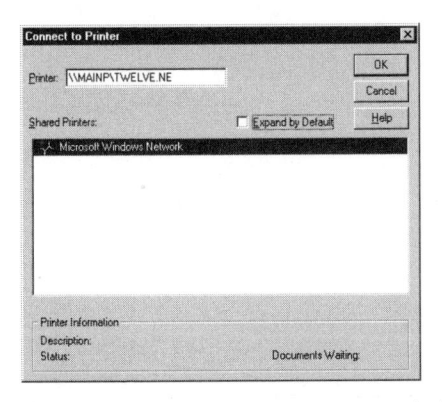

Figure 13-7.   *In the Connect To Printer dialog box, work your way down from Microsoft Windows Network to the shared printer.*

The user can now print to the network printer by selecting the printer in an application. The Printers tab on the user's computer shows the new network printer. You can configure local property settings using this icon.

> **Tip** As you might expect, Windows NT provides several different ways to connect to a network printer. You can also set up a printer by browsing to the print server in Network Neighborhood and then accessing the server's Printers folder by double-clicking on it. Next, double-click on the icon of the printer to which you want to connect. This opens a management window for the printer. Finally, select Install from the Printer menu.

Solving Spooling Problems

Windows NT uses a service to control the spooling of print jobs. If this service isn't running, print jobs can't be spooled. You can check the status of the Spooler using the Services utility in Control Panel. Follow these steps to check and restart the Spooler service:

1. Click Settings from the Start menu and then select Control Panel.
2. Double-click on Services.
3. Select the Spooler service as shown in Figure 13-8. The service status should read "Started." If it doesn't, click on the Startup button to restart the service. The Startup option should read Automatic. If it doesn't, click on the Startup button and change the startup type to Automatic.

> **Tip** Spoolers can become corrupted. Symptoms include a frozen printer or one that doesn't send jobs to the print device. Sometimes the print device may print pages of garbled data. In most of these cases, stopping and starting the Spooler service will resolve the problem.

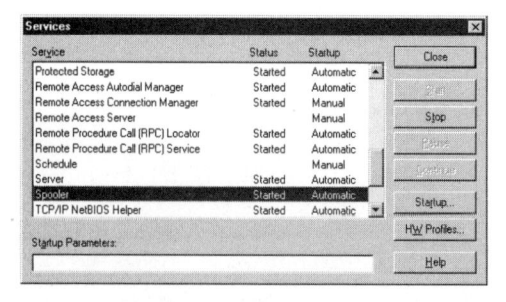

Figure 13-8. *The Spooler service handles print spooling.*

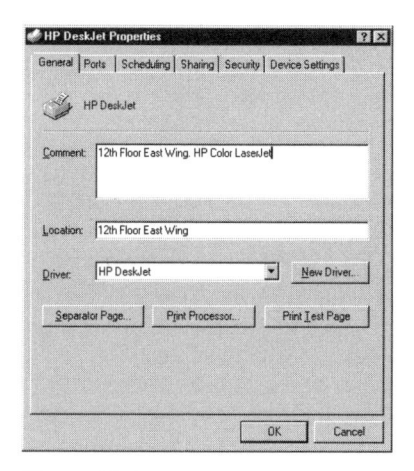

Figure 13-9. *Set printer properties with the dialog box for the printer you want to configure.*

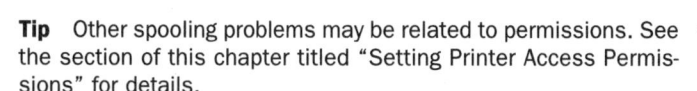

Tip Other spooling problems may be related to permissions. See the section of this chapter titled "Setting Printer Access Permissions" for details.

Configuring Printer Properties

Once you install network printing, you can use the Properties dialog box to set its properties. You access the Properties dialog box by doing the following:

1. Double-click on the Printers icon in the Control Panel or select Settings in the Start menu and then choose the Printers option.
2. Right-click on the icon of the printer you want to configure and select Properties from the pop-up menu.
3. This opens the dialog box shown in Figure 13-9. You can now set the printer properties.

The sections that follow explain how to set commonly used printer properties.

Adding Comments and Location Information

To make it easier to determine which printer to use when, comments and location information can be added to printers. Comments provide general information about the printer, such as the type of print device and who is responsible for it. Location describes the actual site of the print device.

Once set, these fields can be displayed by applications. For example, Microsoft Word displays this information when you select Print from the File menu in the Comment and Where fields, respectively.

Comments and location information can be added to a printer using the fields in the General tab of the printer's Properties dialog box. Enter your comments in the Comment field. Enter the printer location in the Location field.

Changing Printer Drivers

In a Windows NT domain, you should configure and update printer drivers only on your print servers. You don't need to update printer drivers on Windows clients. Instead, you configure the network printer to provide the drivers to client systems as necessary.

Updating a Printer Driver

You can update a printer's driver by doing the following:

1. Open the printer's Properties dialog box and select the General tab. The Driver field lets you select the driver from a list of currently installed drivers. Use the Driver drop-down list to select a new driver from a list of known drivers.

2. If the driver you need isn't listed or if you obtained a new driver, click on the New Driver button to install a driver from disk. Windows NT displays a prompt telling you that printer properties will change when you install the new driver and asking you to confirm that you want to continue. Click Yes. Then use the Add Printer Wizard dialog box to select and install the new driver.

Downloading a New Driver

After you install a new driver, you may want to select the operating systems that should download the driver from the print server. By allowing clients to download the printer driver, you provide a single location for installing driver updates. Thus, rather than having to install a new driver on all the client systems, you install the driver on the print server and allow clients to download the new driver.

You can allow clients to download the new driver by doing the following:

1. Open the printer's Properties dialog box. Click on the Sharing tab.

2. Use the Alternate Drivers list box to select operating systems that can download the new driver. When prompted, insert the distribution CD and/or printer driver disks for the selected operating systems.

Note If you want to install alternate drivers, you may need the installation disks for the selected operating systems and chip architectures. The Windows NT 4.0 distribution CD-ROM has drivers only for Windows NT version 4. For Microsoft Windows 95, Microsoft Windows 98, and Microsoft Windows NT 3.51 drivers, you'll need the appropriate distribution disks.

Setting a Separator Page and Changing Print Device Mode

Separator pages have two uses on Windows NT systems:

- They can be used at the beginning of a print job to make it easier to find a document on a busy print device.
- They can be used to change the print device mode, such as whether the print device uses PostScript or PCL (printer control language).

To set a separator page for a print device, follow these steps:

1. Access the General tab of the printer's Properties dialog box and then click on the Separator Page button.
2. In the Separator Page dialog box, click Browse and then select one of the three available separator pages:
   - **PCL.SEP**   Switches the print device to PCL mode and prints a separator page before each document.
   - **PSCRIPT.SEP**   Sets the print device to PostScript mode but doesn't print a separator page.
   - **SYSPRINT.SEP**   Sets the print device to PostScript mode and prints a separator page before each document.

To stop using the separator page, access the Separator Page dialog box and remove the file name.

Changing the Printer Port

The port used by a print device can be changed at any time by using the Properties dialog box for the printer you're configuring. Open the dialog box, then click on the Ports tab. You can now either add a port for printing by selecting its check box or remove a port by deselecting its check box. To add a new port type, click Add Port and then follow step 6 in "Installing Network Print Devices." To remove a port permanently, select it and then click Delete Port.

Scheduling and Prioritizing Print Jobs

Default settings for print job priority and scheduling are set using the Properties dialog box for the printer you're configuring. Open the dialog box and then click on the Scheduling tab. You can now set the default schedule and priority settings using the fields shown in Figure 13-10, on the following page. Each of these fields is discussed in the sections that follow.

Scheduling Printer Availability

Use the Available field of the Scheduling tab to set the printer availability. Printers are either always available or available only during the hours specified using the From list box and the To list box.

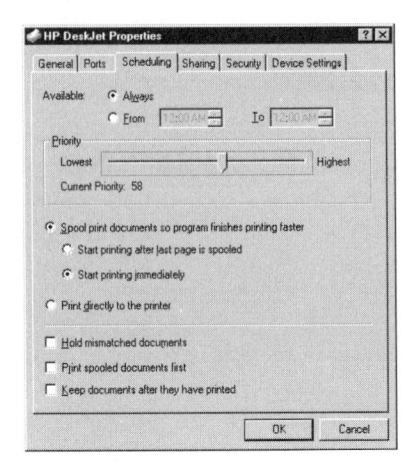

Figure 13-10. *Configure printer scheduling and priority using the Scheduling tab.*

Scheduling Printer Priority

Use the Priority slider of the Scheduling tab to set the default priority for print jobs. Print jobs always print in order of priority. Jobs with higher priority print before jobs with lower priority.

Configuring Printer Spooling

For print devices attached to the network, you'll usually want the printer to spool files rather than print files directly. Print spooling makes it possible to use a printer to manage print jobs.

Enabling spooling   To enable spooling, use one of the following methods:

- Select the radio button labeled Spool Print Documents So Program Finishes Printing Faster.

- Select Start Printing Immediately if you want printing to begin immediately when the print device is not already in use. This option is preferable when you want print jobs to be completed faster or when you want to ensure that the application returns control to users as soon as possible.

- Select Start Printing After Last Page Is Spooled if you want the entire document to be spooled before printing begins. This option ensures that the entire document makes it into the print queue before printing. If for some reason printing is canceled or not completed, the job won't be printed.

Other spooling options   You can disable spooling by selecting the Print Directly To The Printer radio button. Additional check boxes let you configure other spooling options. These check boxes are used as follows:

- **Hold Mismatched Documents**   If selected, the spooler holds print jobs that don't match the setup for the print device. Selecting this option is a good idea if you frequently have to change printer form or tray assignments.

- **Print Spooled Documents First** If selected, jobs that have completed spooling will print before jobs in the process of spooling—regardless of whether the spooling jobs have higher priority.
- **Keep Documents After They Have Printed** Normally documents are deleted from the queue after they're printed. To keep a copy of documents in the printer, select this option. Use this option if you're printing files that can't easily be recreated. In this way, you can reprint the document without having to recreate it. For details, see the section of this chapter titled "Pausing, Resuming, and Restarting Individual Document Printing."

Starting and Stopping Printer Sharing

Printer sharing is set using the Properties dialog box of the printer you're configuring. Open the dialog box and then click on the Sharing tab. You can use this tab to change the name of a network printer as well as to start sharing or stop sharing a printer. Printer sharing tasks that you can perform include

- **Sharing a local printer (thus making it a network printer)** To share a printer, select Shared and specify a name for the shared resource. If Windows 3.1 or MS-DOS systems will access the printer, be sure the printer name conforms to the standard 8.3 naming rule, such as SOUTHEAS.PRT rather than SOUTHEAST_PRINTER. Click OK when you're finished.
- **Changing the shared name of a printer** To change the shared name, simply enter a new name in the Share Name field and click OK.
- **Quit sharing a printer** To quit sharing a printer, select the Not Shared radio button. Click OK when you're finished.

Setting Printer Access Permissions

Network printers are a shared resource, and as such, you can set access permissions for them. You set access permissions by using the Properties dialog box of the printer you're configuring. Open the dialog box and then click on the Security tab. Next, open the Printer Permissions dialog box by clicking on the Permissions button.

Table 13-2, on the following page, shows the available printer permissions and their meaning. These permissions are assigned to users and groups with the same technique you use for other shared resources, such as files. To print documents, a user must have Print permission for the printer and Change permission on the local spool directory. See the section of this chapter titled "Locating the Spool Folder and Enabling Printing on NTFS" for details.

Table 13-2. Printer Permissions Used by Windows NT

Permission	Description	Actions Permitted
Full Control	User/group has complete control over printer configuration, print spooling, and document settings.	Print documents. Administer printer, printer properties, and printer permissions. Control settings for documents. Pause, resume, restart, and cancel print jobs.
Manage Documents	User/group can control spooling and settings for print jobs.	Print documents. Control settings for documents. Pause, resume, restart, and cancel print jobs.
Print	User/group can print documents. User/group has no control over the spooling or settings of documents.	Print or delete his or her own documents only.
No Access	User/group can't use the printer or access the printer queue.	None.

Figure 13-11 shows the default settings of the Printer Permissions dialog box. These settings are used for any new network printer you create:

- Administrators, Print Operators, and Server Operators have full control over the printer by default. This allows you to administer the printer and its print jobs.

- Creator or Owner of the document can manage his or her own document. This allows the person who printed a document to change its settings and to delete it.

- Everyone can print to the printer. This makes the printer accessible to all users on the network.

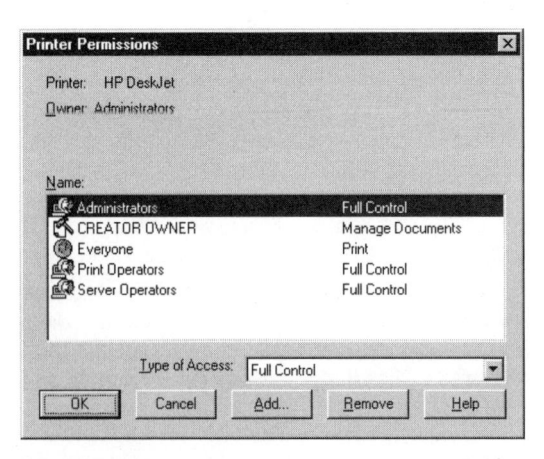

Figure 13-11. *The default settings of the Printer Permissions dialog box are used for any new network printer.*

Auditing Print Jobs

Windows NT lets you audit common printer tasks. To do this, follow these steps:

1. Open the printer's Properties dialog box, then click on the Security tab. Open the Printer Auditing dialog box by clicking on the Auditing button.
2. In the Printer Auditing dialog box, add the names of users or groups you want to audit with the Add button and remove names of users or groups with the Remove button.
3. Select the events you want to audit by selecting the check boxes under the Success and Failure headings as appropriate. You can track both success and failure. These events are used as follows:
   - **Print** Log events related to document printing and the changing of print job settings.
   - **Full Control** Log events related to printer sharing, modifying printer properties, and modifying the status of print jobs (through Pause, Restart, Resume, and Cancel, as well as changing the position of a print job in the printer stack).
   - **Delete** Log events related to deleting a printer.
   - **Change Permissions** Log events related to changing the printer access permissions.
   - **Take Ownership** Log events related to taking ownership of a printer.
4. Click OK when you're finished.

Setting Document Defaults

Document default settings are only used when you print from non-Windows applications, such as when you print from the MS-DOS prompt. You can set document defaults by doing the following:

1. Double-click on the printer's icon in the Printers folder.
2. In the Printer Management window, select Document Defaults from the Printer menu.
3. Use the fields in the Page Setup tab and the Advanced tab to configure the default settings.

Configuring Print Server Properties

Windows NT allows you to control global settings for print servers by using the Print Server Properties dialog box. You can access this dialog box by doing the following:

1. Double-click on the printer's icon in the Control Panel or select Settings in the Start menu and then choose the Printers option.
2. In the Printers window, select Server Properties from the File menu.

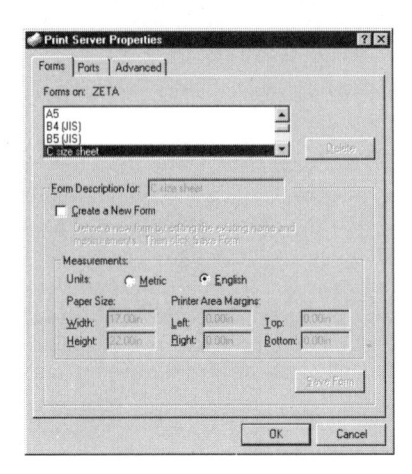

Figure 13-12. *Use the Forms tab of the Print Server Properties dialog box to view printer forms.*

Viewing and Creating Printer Forms

Forms are used by the print server to define the standard sizes for paper, envelopes, and transparencies. To view the current settings for a printer form, follow these steps:

1. Open the Print Server Properties dialog box and then click on the Forms tab as shown in Figure 13-12.
2. Use the Forms On list box to select the form you want to view.
3. The form settings are shown in the Measurements area. You can't change or delete the default system forms.

To create a new form, follow these steps:

1. Access the Forms tab of the Print Server Properties dialog box.
2. Use the Forms On list box to select the existing form on which you want to base the new form.
3. Select the Create A New Form check box.
4. Enter a new name for the Form in the Form Description For field.
5. Use the fields in the Measurements area to set the paper size and margins.
6. Choose the Save Form button to save the form.

Locating the Spool Folder and Enabling Printing on NTFS

The Spool folder holds a copy of all documents in the printer spool. By default, this folder is located at *%SystemRoot%*\spool\PRINTERS. On NTFS, all users who access the printer must have Change permission on this directory. If they don't, they won't be able to print documents. To check the permission on this directory if you're experiencing problems, follow these steps:

1. Double-click on the Printers icon in the Control Panel or select Settings in the Start menu and then choose the Printers option.
2. In the Printers window, select Server Properties from the File menu.
3. Select the Advanced tab. The location of the Spool folder is shown in the Spool folder field. Note this location.
4. Right-click on the Spool folder in Windows NT Explorer and then select Properties from the pop-up menu.
5. Select the Security tab, then click on Permissions.
6. Verify that the permissions are set appropriately.

Logging Printer Events

You can configure the logging of printer events using the Print Server Properties dialog box. Access the dialog box, then click on the Advanced tab. Use the check boxes provided to determine which spooler events are logged.

Removing Print Job Completion and Notification

By default, the print server notifies users when a document has finished printing. This can be annoying, so you may want to remove this feature. You do this by using the Advanced tab of the Print Server Properties dialog box. To disable notification, deselect the check box labeled Notify When Remote Documents Are Printed. You can enable notification later by selecting this check box again.

Managing Print Jobs on Local and Remote Printers

You manage print jobs and printers using the print management window.

If the printer is configured on your system, you can access the print management window as follows:

1. Double-click on the Printers icon in the Control Panel or select Settings in the Start menu and then choose the Printers option.
2. Double-click on the icon of the printer you want to work with.

If the printer isn't configured on your system, you can manage the printer remotely by doing the following:

1. Start Windows NT Explorer and then use Network Neighborhood to access the print server.
2. Access the Printers folder on the print server and then double-click on the icon of the printer you want to work with.

250 | Part IV Windows NT Network Administration

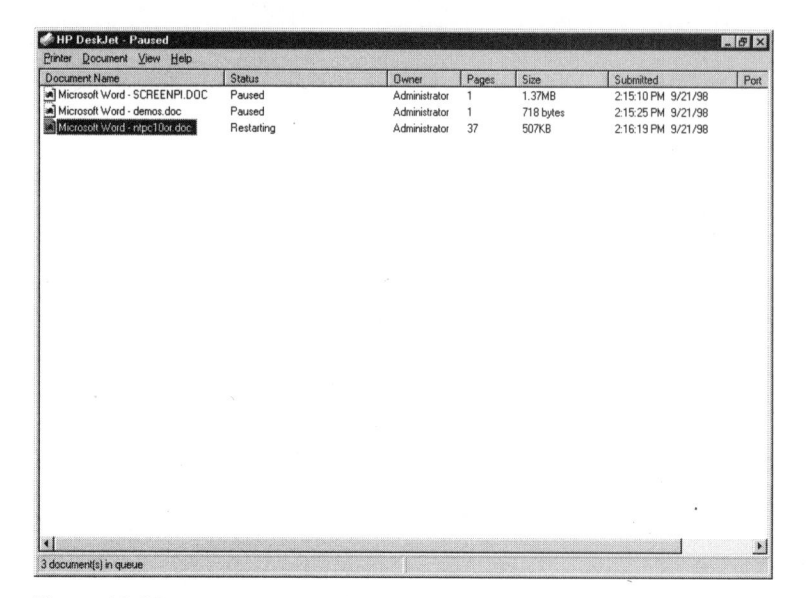

Document Name	Status	Owner	Pages	Size	Submitted	Port
Microsoft Word - SCREENPI.DOC	Paused	Administrator	1	1.37MB	2:15:10 PM 9/21/98	
Microsoft Word - demos.doc	Paused	Administrator	1	718 bytes	2:15:25 PM 9/21/98	
Microsoft Word - ntpc10or.doc	Restarting	Administrator	37	507KB	2:16:19 PM 9/21/98	

3 document(s) in queue

Figure 13-13. *Manage print jobs and printers using the print management window.*

Using the Print Management Window

You can now manage print jobs and printers using the print management window shown in Figure 13-13. The print management window shows information about documents in the printers. This information tells you

- **Document Name**   The document file name, which can include the name of the application that printed it.
- **Status**   The status of the print job, which can include the status of the document as well as the status of the printer. Document status entries you'll see include Printing, Spooling, Paused, Deleting, and Restarting. Document status can be preceded by the printer status, such as Printer Off-Line.
- **Owner**   The document's owner.
- **Pages**   The number of pages in the document.
- **Size**   The document size in kilobytes or megabytes.
- **Submitted**   The time and date the print job was submitted.
- **Port**   The port used for printing, such as LPT1, COM3, or File (if applicable).

Pausing the Printer and Resuming Printing

Sometimes you need to pause a printer. Using the print management window, you do this by selecting the Pause Printing option on the Printer menu (a check mark indicates that the option is selected). When you pause printing, the printer completes the current job and then puts all other jobs on hold.

To resume printing, select the Pause Printing option a second time. This should remove the check mark next to the option.

Emptying and Purging the Printer

You can empty the printer and delete all of its contents using the print management window. To do this, select the Purge Print Documents option on the Printer menu.

Pausing, Resuming, and Restarting Individual Document Printing

The status of individual documents is set using the Document menu in the print management window. To change the status of a document, follow these steps:

1. Select the document in the print management window.
2. Use the Pause, Resume, and Restart options on the Document menu to change the status of the print job.
   - Pause puts the document on hold and lets other documents print.
   - Resume tells the printer to resume printing the document from where it left off.
   - Restart tells the printer to start printing the document again from the beginning.

Removing a Document and Canceling a Print Job

To remove a document from the printer or cancel a print job, follow these steps:

1. Select the document in the print management window.
2. Select Cancel from the Document menu or press Del.

Note When you cancel a print job that's currently printing, the print device may continue to print part or all of the document. This is because most print devices cache documents in an internal buffer, and the print device may continue to print the contents of this cache.

Checking the Properties of Documents in the Printer

Document properties can tell you many things about documents that are in the printer, such as the page source, orientation, and size. You can check the properties of a document in the printer by doing either of the following:

- Select the document in the print management window and then select Properties from the Document menu.
- Double-click on the document name in the print management window.

Setting the Priority of Individual Documents

Scheduling priority determines when documents print. Documents with higher priority print before documents with lower priority. You can set the priority of individual documents in the printer by doing the following:

1. Select the document in the print management window and then select Properties from the Document menu.
2. In the General tab, use the Priority slider to change the priority of the document. The lowest priority is 1 and the highest is 99.

Scheduling the Printing of Individual Documents

In a busy printing environment, you may need to schedule the printing of documents in the printer. For example, you may want large print jobs of low priority to print at night. To set the printing schedule, follow these steps:

1. Select the document in the print management window and then select Properties from the Document menu.
2. In the General tab, select the Only From radio button and then specify a time interval. The time interval you set determines when the job is allowed to print. For example, you can specify that the job can print only between the hours of 12:00 midnight and 5:00 A.M.

Chapter 14

Running DHCP Clients and Servers

DHCP (Dynamic Host Configuration Protocol) is designed to simplify administration of Microsoft Windows NT 4.0 domains, and in this chapter you'll learn how to manage it. You use DHCP to dynamically assign TCP/IP configuration information to network clients. This not only saves you time during system configuration but also provides a centralized mechanism for updating the configuration. To enable DHCP on the network, you need to install and configure a DHCP server. This server is responsible for assigning the necessary network information.

Understanding DHCP

DHCP gives you centralized control over IP addressing and more. If the network has a DHCP server, you can assign a dynamic IP address to any of the network adapter cards on a computer. You do this by using the Identification tab of the TCP/IP Properties dialog box. Once DHCP is set up on a computer, you rely on the DHCP server to supply the basic information necessary for TCP/IP networking, which can include

- IP address, subnet mask, and default gateway
- Primary and secondary DNS servers
- Primary and secondary WINS servers

The DHCP Client and the IP Address

A computer that uses dynamic addressing is called a DHCP client. When you boot a DHCP client, an IP address is retrieved from a pool of IP addresses defined for the network's DHCP server and assigned for a specified time period known as a *lease*. When the lease is approximately 50% expired, the client tries to renew it. If the client can't renew the lease, it will try again before the lease expires, and if this attempt fails, the client will try to contact a new DHCP server. IP addresses that are not renewed are returned to the address pool. If the client is able to contact the DHCP server but the current IP address can't be reassigned, the DHCP server assigns a new IP address to the client.

Installing a DHCP Server

Dynamic IP addressing is only available if a DHCP server is installed on the network. Once a DHCP server is installed, you use the DHCP Manager utility to configure and manage dynamic IP addressing on the network. On a Windows NT server, you use the following steps to allow it to function as a DHCP server:

1. Access the Services tab of the Network Control Panel utility and then click on the Add button.
2. Choose DHCP Server in the Select Network Service dialog box and then click OK.
3. Now you'll need the Windows NT distribution CD-ROM. When prompted, insert the disk and then enter the path for the distribution files, such as: **e:\i386**. Click Continue.
4. Click OK at the prompt. If any of the server's network adapter cards currently uses dynamic addressing, Windows NT opens the TCP/IP Properties dialog box and you'll need to set up static IP addresses.
5. When you close the Network utility, the DHCP server is installed and you'll need to restart the computer.

From now on, the Microsoft DHCP Server service should start automatically each time you reboot the server. If it doesn't start, you'll need to start it manually with the Services utility in the Control Panel.

> **Tip** A single DHCP server can provide services to multiple network segments. However, DHCP relays must be configured to forward DHCP messages to the server. Configuring DHCP relays is covered in the section of Chapter 12 titled "Configuring DHCP Relays."

Managing DHCP Scopes

Once you install a DHCP server, you need to configure the scopes that the DHCP server will use. Scopes are pools of IP addresses that can be leased to clients. A single DHCP server can manage scopes for multiple network segments, provided that DHCP relays are set up on the network.

Using the DHCP Manager

You'll use the DHCP Manager utility to create and manage DHCP scopes. This utility is found in the Administrative Tools (Common) folder. The main window for DHCP Manager is shown in Figure 14-1. As you see, the main window is divided into two panes: DHCP Servers and Option Configuration.

The left pane lists the DHCP servers in the domain by the IP address as well as the local machine, if it's a DHCP server. By double-clicking on an

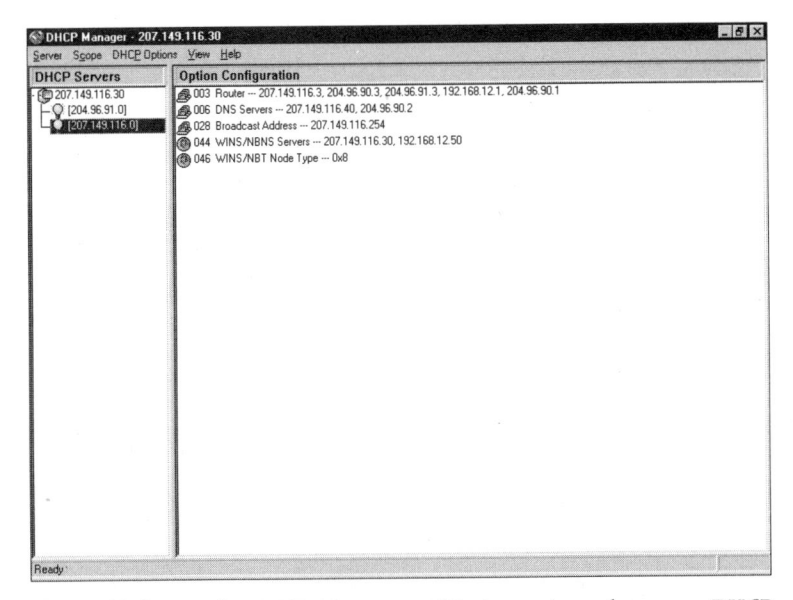

Chapter 14 Running DHCP Clients and Servers | 255

Figure 14-1. *Use the DHCP Manager utility to create and manage DHCP server configurations.*

entry, you can expand the listing to show the scopes defined for each DHCP server. Active scopes are shown with a yellow light bulb icon. Inactive scopes are shown with a gray light bulb icon. The right pane lists options that have been configured for the item selected in the left pane.

If the DHCP Manager utility doesn't list the DHCP server you want to configure, use the Add option on the Server menu to add the server. This opens the dialog box shown in Figure 14-2. Enter the IP address or computer name of the DHCP server you want to manage. Keep in mind that you can only manage DHCP servers in trusted domains.

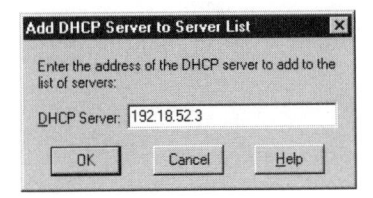

Figure 14-2. *If your DHCP server isn't listed, you'll need to add it to the DHCP Manager utility.*

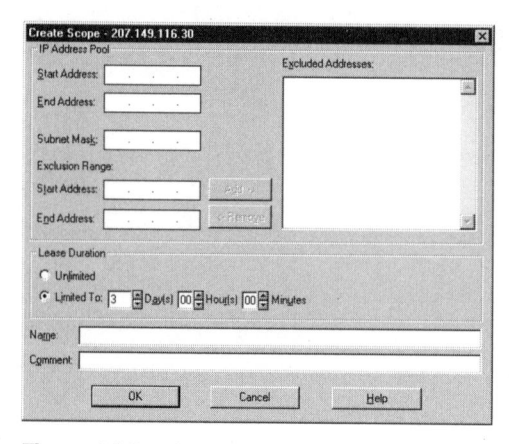

Figure 14-3. *The Create Scope dialog box is used to configure new DHCP scopes.*

Creating a Scope

Scopes provide a pool of IP addresses for DHCP clients. You can create a scope by doing the following:

1. Start the DHCP Manager and then double-click on the entry for the DHCP server you want to configure.
2. Choose Create from the Scope menu. This opens the dialog box shown in Figure 14-3.
3. The Start Address and End Address fields define the valid IP address range for the scope. Enter a start address and an end address in these fields.

   Note Generally, the scope does not include the x.0 and x.255 addresses, which are usually reserved for message broadcasts and routers, respectively. Accordingly, you would use a range of 192.55.10.1 to 192.55.10.254 rather than 192.55.10.0 to 192.55.10.255.

4. Enter a valid subnet mask in the Subnet Mask field.
5. Use the Exclusion Range fields to define IP address ranges that are to be excluded from the scope. Multiple address ranges can be excluded.
   - To define an exclusion range, enter a start address and an end address in the Exclusion Range's Start Address and End Address fields respectively and then click on the Add button.
   - To track which address ranges are excluded, use the Excluded Addresses list box.

- To delete an exclusion range, select the range in the Excluded Addresses list box and then select the Remove button.

6. Specify the duration of leases for the scope. You can assign an unlimited lease or a lease with a specific duration.

   - To assign a permanent lease to the clients, select the Unlimited option.

Best Practice Assigning permanent leases reduces the effectiveness of pooling IP addresses with DHCP. Permanent leases are not released unless you physically release them or deactivate the scope. As a result, you may eventually run out of addresses, especially as your network grows. A better alternative to unlimited leases is to use address reservations—and then only for specific clients that need fixed IP addresses.

   - To specify lease duration, select the Limited To radio button and then use the Day(s), Hour(s), and Minutes fields to set the duration.

Best Practice Take a few minutes to plan out the lease duration you use. A lease duration that is set too long can reduce the effectiveness of DHCP and may eventually cause you to run out of available IP addresses, especially on networks with mobile users or other types of computers that aren't fixed members of the network. A good lease duration for most networks is from one to three days.

7. In the optional Name field, enter a name for the scope if you like. Scope names can use alphanumeric characters (A to Z and 0 to 9) as well as hyphens and periods. Host names can't use other characters.
8. In the optional Comment field, enter a description of the scope if you like.
9. When you're finished configuring the scope, click OK. If possible, DHCP Manager will create the scope and display a prompt asking if you want to activate it. If you want to configure options for the scope, click No and follow the instructions for setting scope options given in the following section of this chapter. Otherwise, click Yes to activate the scope.
10. DHCP clients can now use the scope.

Setting Scope Options

Scope options allow you to precisely control the functioning of a scope and to set default TCP/IP settings for a scope. For example, you can use scope options to enable clients to automatically find WINS servers on the network. You can also define settings for default gateways, routers, DNS, and more. Scope options can be set in one of three ways:

- Globally for all scopes by choosing the Global selection on the DHCP Options menu
- On a per-scope basis by choosing the Scope selection on the DHCP Options menu
- By individual DHCP client by using the TCP/IP Properties dialog box

Scope options use a hierarchy to determine when certain options apply. Individual DHCP client settings always override other settings. Scope-specific options always override global options. Option settings are passed to the client in the DHCP message. To reduce network traffic, DHCP network packets allocate a maximum of 312 bytes for DHCP options. If the option settings exceed 312 bytes, some options may be lost.

> **Tip** A good indicator that you're exceeding the packet limit is that DHCP clients lose TCP/IP default settings or other information you've configured as a DHCP option. In this case, you'll need to remove some of the DHCP options.

Assigning DHCP Options

You can assign DHCP options by doing the following:

1. Start the DHCP Manager and then select the scope you want to configure.
2. On the DHCP Options menu, select Global to define global options or Scope to define scope-specific options. This opens a dialog box like the one shown in Figure 14-4.
3. The DHCP Options dialog box has two list boxes. The Unused Options list box shows options you haven't assigned to the scope yet. The Active Options list box shows options you've already assigned to the scope. Selecting an option in either list box displays, in the Comment field at the bottom of the dialog box, a comment related to the option.
4. If you want to add an option, select the option in the Unused Options list and click Add.

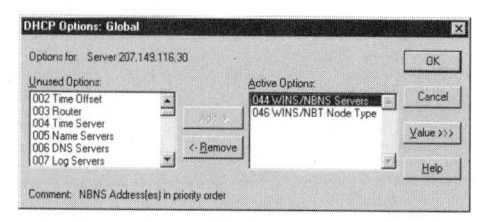

Figure 14-4. *Use the DHCP Options dialog box to set options for a scope.*

5. If you want to remove an option, select the option in the Active Options list and click Remove.
6. Next, you need to set values for each option you've added to the Active Options list. Select the option in the Active Options list box, then click Value. You can now configure the option.
7. Choose OK to save the option changes.
8. Changes in scope options become effective only when a lease is set initially or renewed.

Setting Default WINS Servers for DHCP Clients

Using the DHCP Manager, you can configure default WINS servers for all DHCP clients. To do this, follow these steps:

1. Start the DHCP Manager and then select the scope you want to configure.
2. On the DHCP Options menu, select Global to define global options or Scope to define scope-specific options.
3. Make sure that the WINS/NBNS Servers option is listed in the Active Options list box. If it is, select it and then click Value.

Note In order for WINS to function properly you must set option 46 (WINS/NBT Node Type), as detailed in the next section of this chapter.

4. Click the Edit Array button. This opens the dialog box shown in Figure 14-5. In the New IP Address field enter the IP address of the primary WINS server. Click Add. Repeat this process for other WINS servers.
5. Choose OK to save the option values.
6. Changes in scope options become effective only when a lease is initially set or when it is renewed.

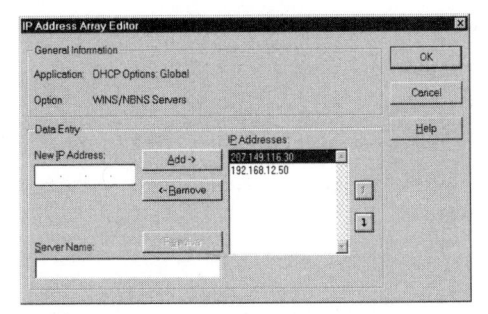

Figure 14-5. *Set the IP address for the WINS servers using the New IP Address field.*

Setting Default WINS Node Type for DHCP Clients

Using the DHCP Manager, you can configure the default WINS node type by doing the following:

1. Start the DHCP Manager and then select the scope you want to configure.
2. On the DHCP Options menu, select Global to define global options or Scope to define scope-specific options.
3. Make sure that the WINS/NBT Node Type option is listed in the Active Options list box. If it is, select it. The Comment field should display a list of valid node type values. Use these values to set a hexadecimal value for the node type you want to use in the Byte field. To change it, select Value and make changes in the Byte dialog box.
4. Choose OK to save the option values.
5. Changes in scope options become effective only when a lease is set initially or renewed.

Setting Default DNS Servers for DHCP Clients

Using the DHCP Manager, you can configure default DNS servers for all DHCP clients. To do this, follow these steps:

1. Start the DHCP Manager and then select the scope you want to configure.
2. On the DHCP Options menu, select Global to define global options or Scope to define scope-specific options.
3. Make sure that the DNS Servers option is listed in the Active Options list box. If it is, select it and then click Value.
4. Click the Edit Array button. In the New IP Address field enter the IP address of the primary DNS server. Click Add. Repeat this process for other DNS servers.
5. Choose OK to save the option values.
6. Changes in scope options become effective only when a lease is set initially or renewed.

Setting Default Routers and Gateways for DHCP Clients

Using the DHCP Manager, you can configure default routers and gateways for DHCP clients by following these steps:

1. Start the DHCP Manager and then select the scope you want to configure.
2. On the DHCP Options menu, select Global to define global options or Scope to define scope-specific options.
3. Ensure the Router option is listed in the Active Options list box. If it is, select it and then click Value.

4. Click the Edit Array button. In the New IP Address field enter the IP address of the primary default gateway. Click Add. Repeat this process for other default gateways.
5. Choose OK to save the option values.
6. Changes in scope options become effective only when a lease is set initially or renewed.

Modifying a Scope

You can modify an existing scope by doing the following:

1. Start the DHCP Manager and then double-click on the entry for the DHCP server you want to configure. This should display the currently configured scopes for the server.
2. Select the scope you want to modify and then choose Properties from the Scope menu. This opens a dialog box similar to the Create Scope dialog box shown in Figure 14-3.
3. Modify the scope as necessary and then close the Scope Properties dialog box by clicking OK. The changes are saved in the DHCP Manager.

Activating and Deactivating Scopes

In the DHCP Manager, active scopes are displayed with a yellow light bulb icon and inactive scopes are displayed with a gray light bulb icon.

You can activate an inactive scope by doing the following:

1. Select the scope you want to activate in the DHCP Manager.
2. Chose Activate from the Scope menu.

You can deactivate a scope by doing the following:

1. Select the scope you want to deactivate in the DHCP Manager.
2. Chose Deactivate from the Scope menu.

Tip Deactivating turns off a scope but doesn't terminate current client leases. If you want to terminate leases, follow the instructions in the section of this chapter titled "Managing Client Leases."

Removing a Scope

Removing a scope permanently removes the scope from the DHCP server. To remove a scope, follow these steps:

1. Select the scope you want to remove in the DHCP Manager and then choose Deactivate from the Scope menu.
2. Release any active leases used by the client by following the instructions in the section of this chapter titled "Managing Client Leases and Reservations."

3. Select Delete from the Scope menu.

Configuring Multiple Scopes on a Network

You can configure multiple scopes on a single network. A single DHCP server or multiple DHCP servers can serve these scopes. However, anytime you work with multiple scopes, it's extremely important that the address ranges used by different scopes don't overlap. Each scope must have its own unique address range. If it doesn't, the same IP address may be assigned to different DHCP clients, which can cause severe problems on the network.

To understand how you can use multiple scopes, consider the following scenario. On server A, you create a DHCP scope with an IP address range of 192.55.10.1 to 192.55.10.99. On server B, you create a DHCP scope with an IP address range of 192.55.10.100 to 192.55.10.199. On server C, you create a DHCP scope with an IP address range of 192.55.10.100 to 192.55.10.199. All of these servers will respond to DHCP discovery messages, and any of them can assign IP addresses to clients. If one of the servers fails, the other servers can continue to provide DHCP services to the network.

Managing Client Leases and Reservations

When you create a scope, you specify that client leases should be assigned either with a fixed expiration date or with an unlimited expiration date. A fixed expiration date is usually the best option. You can then supplement this with address reservations for clients that need semipermanent IP addresses.

Managing Client Leases

You manage active leases using the Active Leases dialog box shown in Figure 14-6. To open this dialog box, select the scope in the DHCP Manager and then choose Active Leases from the Scope menu. The primary fields of this dialog box are used as follows:

- **Total Addresses in Scope** Shows the total number of IP addresses assigned to the scope.

- **Active/Excluded** Shows the total number of active or excluded addresses as a numerical value and a percentage of the total available addresses.

> **Tip** Think of the Active/Excluded field as the number of addresses used up. If the percentage total reaches 85 percent or more, you may want to consider assigning additional addresses or freeing up addresses for use.

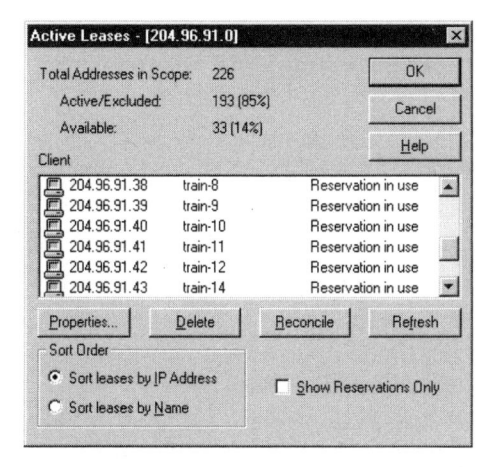

Figure 14-6. *The Active Leases dialog box allows you to view or modify lease settings.*

- **Available** Shows the total number of addresses available for use as a numerical value and a percentage of the total available addresses.
- **Client** Shows the active leases or reservations for the currently selected scope. Clients are listed by IP address and by client name. If the IP address is reserved, the listing is followed by the keyword Reservation. Select the Show Reservations Only check box to only display reservations in the Client list box.
- **Properties** Displays the properties of the lease or reservation selected in the Client list box.
- **Delete** Deletes the currently selected lease or reservation.
- **Reconcile** Reconciles the client leases and reservations against the DHCP database on the server. This is useful if you want to ensure that the list of leases shown is actually in use.
- **Refresh** Refreshes the listings in the Client list box.

Reserving DHCP Addresses

DHCP provides several ways to provide permanent addresses to clients. One way is to use the Unlimited setting in the Scope dialog box to assign permanent addresses to all clients that use the scope. Another way is to reserve DHCP addresses on a per-client basis. When you reserve a DHCP address, the client is always assigned the same IP address by the DHCP server, and you can do so without sacrificing the centralized management features that make DHCP so attractive.

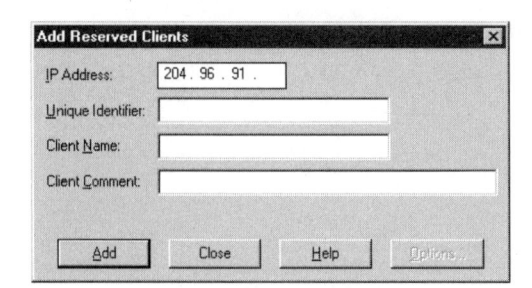

Figure 14-7. *Use the Add Reserved Clients dialog box to reserve an IP address for a client.*

To reserve a DHCP address for a client, follow these steps:

1. In the DHCP Manager, select the scope you want to work with and then choose Add Reservation from the Scope menu. This opens the dialog box shown in Figure 14-7.
2. In the IP Address field, enter the IP address you want to reserve for the client. Note that this IP address must be within the valid range of addresses for the currently selected scope.
3. The Unique Identifier field specifies the MAC (media access control) address for the client computer's network adapter card. You can obtain the MAC address by typing the command **net config wksta** at the Command prompt on the client computer. This value must be typed exactly for the address reservation to work.
4. In the Client Name field, enter the computer name for the client. This field is used for identification purposes only and doesn't affect the client's actual computer name.
5. Enter an optional comment in the Client Comment field if you like.
6. Select Add to create the address reservation.

Releasing Addresses and Leases

When you work with reserved addresses, there are a couple of caveats you should know about:

- Reserved addresses aren't automatically reassigned. So if the address is already in use, you'll need to release the address to ensure that the appropriate client can obtain it. You can force a client to release an address by terminating the client's lease or by logging on to the client and typing the command **ipconfig/release** at the Command prompt.
- Clients don't automatically switch to the reserved address. So if the client is already using a different IP address, you'll need to force the client to release the current lease and request a new one. You can do this by terminating the client's lease or by logging on to the client and typing the command **ipconfig/renew** at the Command prompt.

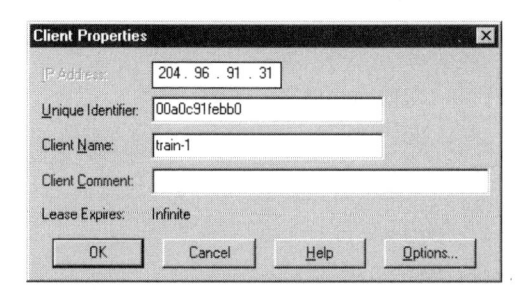

Figure 14-8. *The Client Properties dialog box allows you to modify lease and reservation properties. For details on the fields in this dialog box, see the section of this chapter titled "Reserving DHCP Addresses."*

Modifying Lease and Reservation Properties

You can modify the properties of leases and reservations by doing the following:

1. Select the scope that contains the lease or reservation you want to modify and then choose Active Leases from the Scope menu.
2. In the Active Leases dialog box, select the lease or reservation you want to modify in the Client list box and then select Properties. This opens the dialog box shown in Figure 14-8.
3. You can now modify lease and reservation properties. Fields that are shaded can't be modified. Other fields can be modified. These fields are the same fields described in the previous section.
4. To configure lease-specific or reservation-specific options, click on the Options button. You can now configure DHCP options that only apply to this lease or reservation.

Deleting Leases and Reservations

You can delete active leases and reservations by completing the following steps:

1. Select the scope that contains the lease or reservation you want to modify and then choose Active Leases from the Scope menu.
2. In the Active Leases dialog box, select the lease or reservation you want to delete and then click on the Delete button.
3. The lease or reservation is now removed from DHCP. However, the client isn't forced to release the IP address. To force the client to release the IP address, log on to the client that holds the lease or reservation and type the command **ipconfig/release** at the Command prompt.

Backing Up and Restoring the DHCP Database

DHCP servers store DHCP lease and reservation information in database files. By default, these files are stored in the *%SystemRoot%*\System32\dhcp directory. The key files in this directory are used as follows:

- **DHCP.MDB** The primary database file for the DHCP server.
- **DHCP.TMP** A temporary working file for the DHCP server.
- ***.LOG** Transaction log files used to recover incomplete transactions in case of a server malfunction.
- ***.CHK** Check files for the DHCP server.

The Backup Directory

The backup directory in the *%SystemRoot%*\System32\dhcp folder contains backup information for the DHCP configuration and the DHCP database. By default, the DHCP database is backed up every 60 minutes. Registry keys that control the location and timing of DHCP backups as well as other DHCP settings are located in the folder

```
HKEY_LOCAL_MACHINE
  \SYSTEM
    \CurrentControlSet
      \Services
        \DHCPServer
          \Parameters
```

Restoring the Database from Backup

If you want to force DHCP to restore the database from backup, follow these steps:

1. Stop the DHCP Server service by using the Services utility in the Control Panel.
2. Restore a good copy of the *%SystemRoot%*\System32\dhcp\backup directory from a tape or other archive source.
3. Use the Registry Editor to edit the key HKEY_LOCAL_MACHINE \SYSTEM \CurrentControlSet \Services \DHCPServer \Parameters. Set the key's RestoreFlag value to 1.
4. Start the DHCP Server service.

Chapter 15

Managing WINS and NetBIOS Over TCP/IP

WINS (Windows Internet Name Service) is a name resolution service that resolves computer names to IP addresses. Using WINS, the computer name OMEGA, for example, could be resolved to an IP address that enables computers on a Microsoft network to find one another and transfer information.

The underlying application programming interface, or API, that enables WINS name resolution and information transfers between computers is NetBIOS (Network Basic Input/Output System). The NetBIOS API contains a set of commands that applications can use to access session-layer services. Commonly used extensions for NetBIOS are NetBEUI (NetBIOS Enhanced User Interface) and NBT (NetBIOS over TCP/IP). This chapter focuses on WINS and NBT.

Understanding WINS and NetBIOS Over TCP/IP

WINS works best in client-server environments where WINS clients send queries to WINS servers for name resolution and WINS servers resolve the query and respond. To transmit WINS queries and other information, computers use NetBIOS. NetBIOS provides an API that allows computers on a network to communicate. When you install TCP/IP networking on a Microsoft client or server, NetBIOS over TCP/IP is also installed. NetBIOS over TCP/IP is a session-layer service that enables NetBIOS applications to run over the TCP/IP protocol stack. NetBIOS applications, such as the command-line NET utilities, rely on WINS or the local LMHOSTS file to resolve computer names to IP addresses.

Using DNS

WINS isn't the only name resolution service available. You can also use DNS (Domain Name Service). DNS is a name resolution service that resolves Internet host names to IP addresses. Using DNS, you can resolve the fully qualified domain name *www.centraldrive.com,* for example, to an IP address. While WINS is used with NetBIOS applications, DNS is used with Winsock applications that operate over the TCP/IP protocol stack, such as FTP or Telnet. DNS can be configured to work in conjunction with WINS.

Configuring WINS Clients and Servers

To enable WINS name resolution on a network, you need to configure WINS clients and servers. When you configure WINS clients, you tell the clients the IP addresses of WINS servers on the network. Using the IP address, clients can communicate with WINS servers anywhere on the network, even if the servers are on different subnets. WINS clients can also communicate using a broadcast method in which clients broadcast messages to other computers on the local network segment requesting their IP addresses. Because messages are broadcast, the WINS server isn't used. Any non-WINS clients that support this type of message broadcasting can also use this method to resolve computer names to IP addresses.

When clients communicate with WINS servers, they establish sessions that have three key parts:

- **Name registration**   During name registration, the client gives the server its computer name and its IP address and asks to be added to the WINS database. If the specified computer name and IP address aren't already in use on the network, the WINS server accepts the request and registers the client in the WINS database.

- **Name renewal**   Name registration isn't permanent. Instead, the client has use of the name for a specified period, which is known as a lease. The client is also given a time period within which the lease must be renewed, which is known as the renewal interval. The client must reregister with the WINS server during the renewal interval.

- **Name release**   If the client can't renew the lease, the name registration is released, allowing the computer name or IP address, or both, to be used by another system on the network. The names are also released when you shutdown a WINS client.

> **Note**   Configuring a WINS client is described in the section of Chapter 12 titled "Configuring WINS Resolution." Configuring a WINS server is described in this chapter under "Installing WINS Servers."

Name Resolution Methods

Once a client establishes a session with a WINS server, the client can request name resolution services. The method used to resolve computer names to IP addresses depends on how the network is configured. Four name resolution methods are available:

- **B-node (Broadcast node)**   B-node uses broadcast messages to resolve computer names to IP addresses. Computers that need to resolve a name broadcast a message to every host on the local network, requesting the IP address for a computer name.

    B-node has two strengths. First, you don't need to configure a WINS server to use this method. Second, some non-WINS clients support b-node and—in conjunction with at least one WINS client (acting as a proxy)—can resolve computer names using this method. Also, b-node can be used with a local LMHOSTS file, which would enable name resolution on subnets.

B-node has two weaknesses. The method isn't routable and you can't use it to resolve names across routers. Broadcast messages can generate a lot of traffic on the network, especially as the number of computers on the network grows.

- **P-node (Point-to-point node)**   P-node uses WINS servers to resolve computer names to IP addresses. As explained earlier, client sessions have three parts: name registration, name renewal, and name release. When a client needs to resolve a computer name to an IP address, the client sends a query message to the server and the server responds with an answer.

  The main strength of p-node is that it's point-to-point and doesn't use a lot of network bandwidth. P-node is also routable, which enables clients to query servers across routers. However, any time the server is down or otherwise unavailable, name resolution fails.

- **M-node (Modified node)**   M-node is a modified mode that combines b-node and p-node. With it, a WINS client first tries to use b-node for name resolution. If the attempt fails, the client then tries to use p-node. Because b-node is used first, this method has the same problems with network bandwidth usage as b-node.

- **H-node (Hybrid node)**   H-node also combines b-node and p-node. With it, a WINS client first tries to use p-node for point-to-point name resolution. If the attempt fails, the client then tries to use broadcast messages with b-node. Because point-to-point is the primary method, h-node offers the best performance on most networks. H-node is also the default method for WINS name resolution.

If WINS servers are available on the network, Microsoft Windows NT clients use the p-node method for name resolution. If no WINS servers are available on the network, Windows NT clients use the b-node method for name resolution. Windows NT computers can also use DNS and the local files LMHOSTS and HOSTS to resolve network names. Working with DNS is covered in the next chapter.

Tip   When you use DHCP to dynamically assign IP addresses, you should set the name resolution method for DHCP clients. To do this, you need to set DHCP scope options for the 046 WINS/NBT Node Type as specified in the section of Chapter 14 titled "Setting Default WINS Servers for DHCP Clients." The best method to use is h-node. You'll get the best performance and have reduced traffic on the network.

Installing WINS Servers

On Windows NT servers, install a WINS server by doing the following:

1. Access the Services tab of the Network Control Panel utility and then click on the Add button.
2. Choose Windows Internet Name Service in the Select Network Service dialog box and then click OK.
3. Now you'll need the Windows NT distribution CD-ROM. When prompted, insert the disk and then enter the path for the distribution files, such as **e:\i386**. Click Continue.
4. When you close the Network utility, the WINS server is installed and you'll need to restart the computer.

From now on, Windows Internet Name Service should start automatically each time you reboot the server. If the service isn't started, you'll need to start it manually with the Services utility in the Control Panel.

> **Best Practice** Although a single WINS server can provide services to multiple network segments, you'll usually want to install more than one WINS server. Additional servers can provide a fail-safe mechanism in case the primary WINS server is unavailable. When you install multiple WINS servers on a network, you must also set up WINS database replication. For details on database replication, see the section of this chapter titled "Configuring WINS Database Replication."

Using WINS Manager

When you install a new server, it is configured with default settings. You can view and change these settings at any time using the WINS Manager.

Getting to Know WINS Manager

To manage WINS servers on a network, you'll use the WINS Manager utility. This utility is found in the Administrative Tools (Common) folder. The main window for WINS Manager is shown in Figure 15-1. As you see, this window is divided into two panes: WINS Servers and Statistics. The left pane lists the WINS servers in the domain by IP address or computer name, or both. By double-clicking on these entries, you can display server statistics in the right pane.

The server statistics fields are used as follows:

- **Server Start Time** The time Windows Internet Name Service started on the server.
- **Database Initialized** The time the server's WINS database was initialized.
- **Statistics Cleared** The time the server's statistics were last cleared.
- **Last Replication Times** The time the server's WINS database was last replicated.

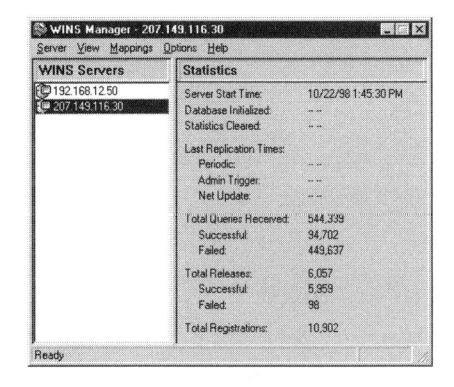

Chapter 15 Managing WINS and NetBIOS Over TCP/IP | 271

Figure 15-1. *Use the WINS Manager to manage WINS server configurations.*

- **Periodic** Indicates the time the WINS database was last replicated based on the replication interval set in the Pull Partner Properties dialog box.
- **Admin Trigger** Indicates the time the WINS database was last replicated by the administrator (using the Replicate Now button in the Replication Partners dialog box).
- **Net Update** Indicates the time the WINS database was last replicated based on a push notification message that requested propagation.
- **Total Queries Received** The total number of queries received by the server since it was last started. Successful indicates the number of queries successfully resolved. Failed indicates the number of queries that failed.
- **Total Releases** The total number of messages received that indicate a NetBIOS application has released its name registration and shut itself down. Successful indicates the number of successful releases. Failed indicates the number of failed releases.
- **Total Registrations** The total number of name registration messages received from WINS clients.

Adding a WINS Server to WINS Manager

If the WINS Manager doesn't list the WINS server you want to configure, use the Add WINS Server option on the Server menu to add the server. This opens the dialog box shown in Figure 15-2. Now enter the IP address or computer name of the WINS server you want to manage.

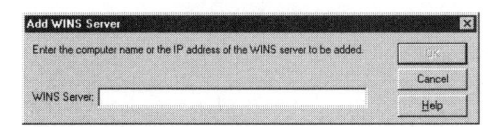

Figure 15-2. *If your WINS servers aren't listed, you'll need to add them to the WINS Manager.*

Refreshing and Clearing Server Statistics

Depending on the server preferences, WINS Manager may not automatically refresh server statistics. To refresh the statistics, select Refresh Statistics from the View menu or press F5.

In addition to refreshing the statistics, you may also want to reinitialize the related counters. You do this by selecting Clear Statistics from the View menu. When asked to confirm the operation, click Yes.

Viewing Detailed Server Information

You can view detailed information for a WINS server by completing the following steps:

1. Select the server you want to work with in WINS Manager.
2. Choose Detailed Information from the Server menu. This opens the dialog box shown in Figure 15-3. The fields of this dialog box are used as follows:
   - **WINS Server Address** Provides server naming information.
     - **Computer Name** Is the NetBIOS computer name of the server.
     - **IP Address** Is the IP address of the server.
     - **Connected Via** Is the protocol used to connect to the server, such as NetBIOS.
     - **Connected Since** Is the time you connected to the server in WINS Manager.
     - **Last Address Change** Is the time the server's WINS database change was last replicated.
   - **Last Scavenging Times** The times the server's database was last cleaned.
     - **Periodic** Indicates the last time a cleaning took place because of the renewal interval set in the WINS Server Configuration dialog box.
     - **Admin Trigger** Indicates the last time a cleaning was initiated by the administrator (using the Initiate Scavenging option on the Mappings menu).
     - **Extinction** Indicates the last time a cleaning took place because of the extinction interval set in the WINS Server Configuration dialog box.
     - **Verification** Indicates the last time a cleaning took place because of the verification interval set in the WINS Server Configuration dialog box.
   - **Unique Registrations** The total number of name registration messages received and accepted from WINS clients. Conflicts indicate the number of name conflicts encountered for each unique computer name. Renewals indicate the number of renewals received for each unique computer name.

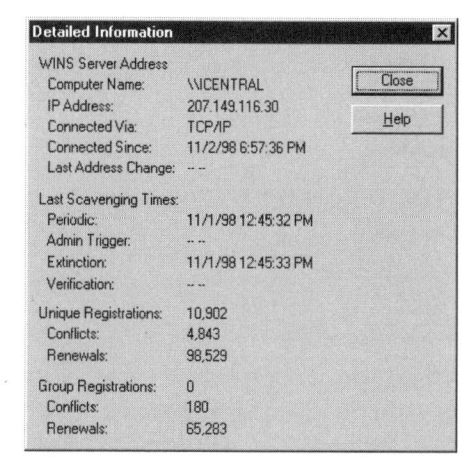

```
Detailed Information
WINS Server Address
  Computer Name:    \\CENTRAL
  IP Address:       207.149.116.30
  Connected Via:    TCP/IP
  Connected Since:  11/2/98 6:57:36 PM
  Last Address Change: --

Last Scavenging Times:
  Periodic:         11/1/98 12:45:32 PM
  Admin Trigger:    --
  Extinction:       11/1/98 12:45:33 PM
  Verification:     --

Unique Registrations: 10,902
  Conflicts:          4,843
  Renewals:           98,529

Group Registrations:  0
  Conflicts:          180
  Renewals:           65,283
```

Figure 15-3. *The Detailed Information dialog box provides additional details about the server that can help in administration.*

- **Group Registrations** The total number of name registration messages received and accepted from groups. Conflicts indicate the number of name conflicts encountered for group names. Renewals indicate the number of renewals received for group names.

Setting WINS Manager Preferences

Changing the default settings in WINS Manager can help you manage WINS servers according to your unique needs. To set WINS Manager preferences, select the Preferences command on the Options menu. This opens the dialog box shown in Figure 15-4, on the following page. You can now customize the setup for WINS Manager.

The key fields of the Preferences dialog box are used as follows:

- **Address Display** Use these fields to specify whether servers should be displayed in the main WINS Manager window by computer name, IP address, or a combination of the two. The default is to display IP addresses only.

- **Auto Refresh** Sets the refresh interval for server statistics. By default, this interval is set to 60 seconds.

- **LAN Manager-Compatible** Select this check box to use LAN Manager-compatible computer names. Because all Microsoft clients and servers use this name type, you should select this option. The only time you'll want to deselect this option is when the network receives NetBIOS names from non-Microsoft subnets and systems.

- **Validate Cache of "Known" WINS Servers at Startup Time** Used to check and validate the list of known WINS servers each time you start WINS Manager. If a server is no longer valid, WINS Manager may delete it from the list. In an extended network environment, selecting this option is a good idea.

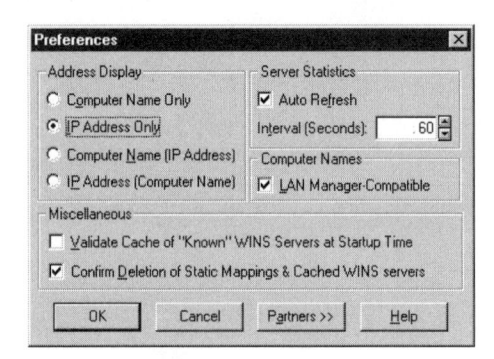

Figure 15-4. *Customize WINS preferences using the Preferences dialog box.*

- **Confirm Deletion of Static Mappings & Cached WINS Servers** If selected, WINS Manager will prompt you before deleting static mappings or the cached name of a WINS server. It's generally a good idea to select this option.

- **Partners** Click on this button to configure default options for database replication (push and pull partners).

Configuring WINS Servers

When you install a WINS server, the server is configured with default settings. You can change these settings by completing the following steps:

1. Select the server you want to work with in WINS Manager.

2. Choose the Configuration option on the Server menu. This opens the dialog box shown in Figure 15-5.

3. Set the WINS Server Configuration parameters. These parameters are used as follows:

    - **Renewal Interval** Sets the interval during which a WINS client must renew its computer name. It is also known as the lease period. Generally, clients attempt to renew when they reach 50 percent of the lease. The minimum value is 40 minutes. The default value is six days, meaning clients attempt to renew their lease every three days. A computer name that is not renewed is marked as released.

    - **Extinction Interval** Sets the interval during which a computer name can be marked as extinct. Once a computer name has been released, the next step is to mark it as extinct. The minimum value is 40 minutes.

    - **Extinction Timeout** Sets the interval during which a computer name can be purged from the WINS database. Once a computer name has been marked as extinct, the next step is to purge it from the database. The minimum value is 24 hours (one day).

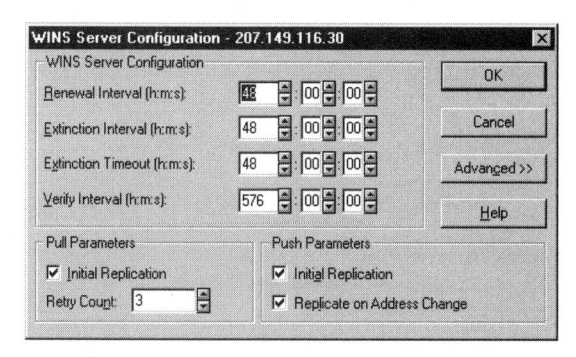

Figure 15-5. *Configure WINS Manager to customize server operation for your network needs.*

- **Verify Interval** Sets the interval after which a WINS server must verify old names it doesn't own. If the names aren't active, they can be removed. The minimum value is 576 hours (24 days). Generally, computer names registered in a different WINS server have a different owner, and thus they fall into this category.

Tip Think of these intervals as giving you a timeline for names listed in the WINS database. Renewal Interval affects when leases are renewed. Extinction Interval affects when names that aren't renewed are marked as extinct. Extinction Timeout affects when extinct names are purged from the database. If you set Renewal Interval to 24 hours, Extinction Interval to 48 hours, and Extinction Timeout to 24 hours, it could take as long as 96 hours for a record to clear out of the WINS database.

4. Pull and push partners are discussed in the section of this chapter titled "Configuring WINS Database Replication."
5. Click on the Advanced button to configure advanced WINS parameters. You can now set the following fields:
   - **Logging Enabled** Check this field to turn on event logging for the WINS server. WINS logs are placed in the *%SystemRoot%\system32\wins* folder.
   - **Log Detailed Events** Check this field to turn on detailed event logging for the WINS server.

Note Detailed logging on a busy network can cause a heavy load on the WINS server. Because of this, detailed logging should only be used during testing, troubleshooting, or optimization.

   - **Replicate Only With Partners** Check this field to ensure that replication is done only with push and pull partners. If this field is not selected, administrators can force push or pull replication on this server.

- **Backup On Termination** Check this field to ensure that the WINS database is backed up when the WINS service is stopped. This option isn't used when the WINS server is shutting down.
- **Migrate On/Off** Set this option when you're upgrading non-Windows systems to Windows NT. If set, this option allows records to be dynamically updated in the WINS database during migration.
- **Database Backup Path** Allows you to set the path used for database backup files. The default is *%SystemRoot%\system32\wins*.
- **Starting Version Count** Sets the starting version ID number for the WINS database. This value is set in hexadecimal format and the maximum value is 2^31. You only need to change this value if the WINS database becomes corrupt. If it does, you should set the ID to a value higher than the version number counter on all remote partners that have a replica of the server's database records. The version number is displayed in the Show Database dialog box.

6. Select OK to save the configuration settings.

Configuring WINS Database Replication

WINS servers can be configured to replicate their databases with each other. This ensures that each server's database is current and reflects changes on the network. As an administrator, you have many options for controlling when replication occurs. You can also force replication at any time.

Replication is handled with push partners and pull partners. Any WINS server can be configured as a push or pull partner, or both. A push partner is a WINS server that notifies other WINS servers of changes on the network. A pull partner is a WINS server that requests replicas from a push partner.

Setting Default Replication Parameters

On an extended network, you may want to set default parameters for all new push and pull partners. To do this, follow these steps:

1. Select the server you want to work with in WINS Manager and then choose the Preferences command on the Options menu.
2. In the Preferences dialog box, click on the Partners button. As shown in Figure 15-6, you should see a new area of the Preferences dialog box.
3. Set the default options for Pull Partners using the New Pull Partner Default Configuration area. Start Time sets the hour in the day when replication should begin, such as 7:00:00 A.M. Replication Interval sets the intervals at which scheduled replication should occur, such as every 30 minutes.
4. Set the default options for Push Partners using the New Push Partner Default Configuration area. Update Count specifies the number of registrations and changes that must take place before pull partners are

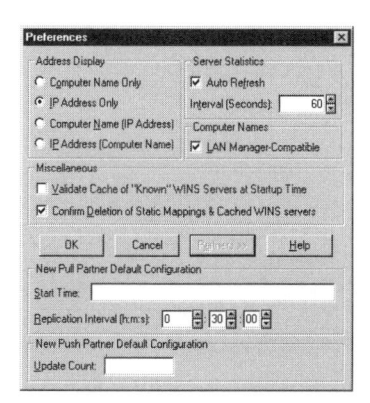

Figure 15-6. *Click on the Partners button on the Preferences dialog box to display an extended window for setting default push and pull partner parameters.*

notified, which triggers database replication. This counter is for local changes only and doesn't tally changes pulled from other partners.

5. Click OK to set the default values.

Best Practice The default values you use depend on your network's size. On a small network, you may want to have a fairly low update count and a higher replication interval, which accounts for fewer changes and less information needing replication. For example, use a count of 25 and an interval of 60 minutes. On a large network, you may want to have a higher update count and a lower replication interval, which accounts for more changes and a greater need to replicate information throughout the network. For example, use a count of 250 and an interval of 20 minutes. Keep in mind that if you set the replication interval or the update count too low, you may cause extra traffic to be generated on the network.

Creating Push and Pull Partners

Push and pull partners are needed to replicate WINS databases whenever there are multiple WINS servers on a network. You must configure replication separately for each WINS server on the network.

To configure push and pull partners, follow these steps:

1. Select the server you want to work with in WINS Manager. This server is the one for which you will configure replication partners.
2. Choose the Replication Partners option on the Server menu. This opens the dialog box shown in Figure 15-7, on the following page.
3. If the WINS servers you want to work with aren't listed in the WINS Server area, click on the Add button. This opens the Add WINS Server dialog box and you can now enter the computer name or IP address of a WINS server on the network. Repeat this step as necessary for additional WINS servers.

Figure 15-7. *The Replication Partners dialog box is used to configure push and pull partners.*

4. The WINS Servers To List area of the Replication Partners dialog box lets you control which types of WINS servers are displayed in the WINS Server list box. You'll usually want all three check boxes to be selected.

   - Push Partners is used to display push partners for this server.
   - Pull Partners is used to display pull partners for this server.
   - Other is used to display WINS servers that are neither push nor pull partners.

5. In the WINS Server list box, select the WINS server you want to make a replication partner. A single server can be a push or pull partner, or both. If the server is to be a push and pull partner, follow steps 6 and 7.

6. If the server is to be a push partner,

   - Select the Push Partner check box and choose the related Configure button. This opens the Push Partner Properties dialog box shown in Figure 15-8.
   - Now set the update count for the push partner. Update Count specifies the number of registrations and changes that must take place before pull partners are notified, which triggers database replication. This counter is for local changes only and doesn't tally changes pulled from other partners.
   - Click OK to close the dialog box.

Figure 15-8. *Use the Push Partner Properties dialog box to configure the push partner.*

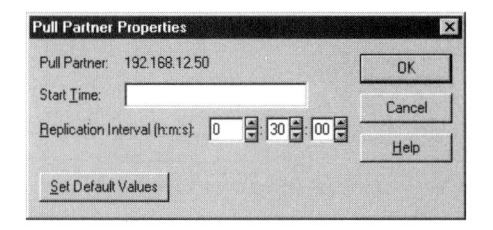

Figure 15-9. *Use the Pull Partner Properties dialog box to configure the pull partner.*

7. If the server is to be a pull partner,
   - Select the Pull Partner check box and choose the related Configure button. This opens the Pull Partner Properties dialog box shown in Figure 15-9.
   - Now set the options for pull partner. Start Time sets the hour in the day when replication should begin, such as 7:00:00 A.M. Replication Interval sets the intervals at which scheduled replication should occur, such as every 30 minutes.
   - Click OK to close the dialog box.
8. In the Replication Partners dialog box, you start replication immediately by clicking on the Replicate Now button.
9. Click OK to save the replication configuration.

Forcing Database Replication

Sometimes you may want to immediately update the WINS databases on replication partners. You can do this by forcing database replication with all partners or by triggering replication for a specific partner.

You can force replication by doing the following:

1. In WINS Manager, select the server whose database you want to replicate.
2. Choose the Replication Partners option on the Server menu and then click on the Replicate Now button.

Triggering Replication for a Specific Partner

To send a push or pull replication trigger to a specific partner, complete the following steps:

1. In WINS Manager, select the server whose database you want to replicate and then choose the Replication Partners option on the Server menu.
2. In the Replication Partners dialog box, select the push or pull partner on which you want to trigger replication.
3. In the Send Replication Trigger Now area, choose the Push or Pull button as appropriate for the trigger you want to send. If you want to propagate the push trigger to the selected server's partners, select the Push With Propagation check box before you click on the Push button.

Managing Static Mappings for Non-WINS Clients

Static mappings allow computer names for non-WINS clients to be resolved to IP addresses. A static map permanently lists a computer name to IP address mapping that can't be overridden or removed by the WINS server. Only an administrator can remove a static mapping.

Viewing Static Mappings

You can view static mappings for a server selected in WINS Manager by choosing the Static Mappings option on the Mappings menu. This opens the dialog box shown in Figure 15-10. You can now

- Set the listing order with the radio buttons in the Sort Order area.
- Set a filter for the listings by using the Set Filter button. Simply enter a filter parameter, such as **192.11.*.*** or **CLEO***, and click OK. Filters are useful when you have lots of static mappings and need to find a particular set of mappings.

Creating Static Mappings

You create static mappings for non-WINS clients on the network, which allows their computer names to be resolved to IP addresses. Static mappings are permanent and should not be created for WINS clients. Note also that if DHCP is used with WINS, reserved IP addresses in DHCP always override static mappings assigned in WINS.

You create static mappings by completing the following steps:

1. In WINS Manager, select the server on which you want to create static mappings and then choose Static Mappings from the Mappings menu.

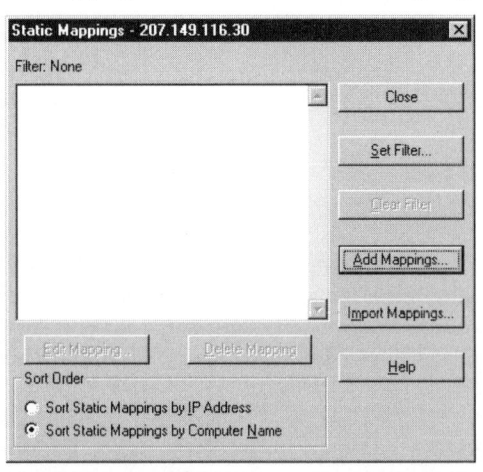

Figure 15-10. *Static mappings can be permanently assigned to non-WINS clients with the Static Mappings dialog box.*

Chapter 15 Managing WINS and NetBIOS Over TCP/IP | 281

2. In the Static Mappings dialog box, choose Add Mappings. This opens the dialog box shown in Figure 15-11.
3. Select the type of static mapping. The type selections available are
   - **Unique** Used for computer names that are unique on the network with a single IP address per name. With unique mappings, you need to set a computer name and IP address.
   - **Group** Used for computers on a subnet where individual addresses are not stored for members of the group. No IP address needs to be set for a group. You can define a group for any subnet and then register this group with any or all of the WINS servers on the network. If a WINS server receives a request for the group name, the request resolves to the broadcast address 255.255.255.255. WINS clients then use this broadcast address as the destination address in the message packet, which results in a local broadcast on a subnet.
   - **Domain Name** Creates a domain name for up to 25 NetBIOS computer names that have 0x1C as the sixteenth byte. You need to set the domain name in the Name field and then enter up to 25 IP addresses using the IP Address field.
   - **Internet Group** Creates an Internet group with up to 25 members. You need to set the Internet Group name in the Name field and then enter up to 25 IP addresses using the IP Address field.
   - **Multihomed** Creates a single name that maps to multiple IP addresses on a multihomed computer. Enter the computer name in the Name field and then enter the computer's IP address(es) in the IP Address field.
4. Make sure that you've entered the computer name and IP address(es) as specified in Step 3.
5. Choose Add to create the static mapping.

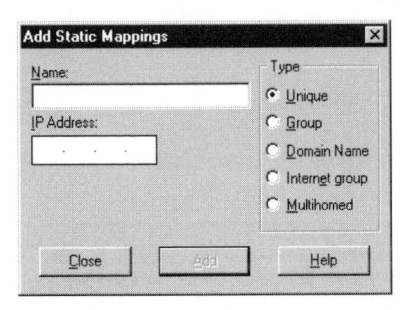

Figure 15-11. *Use the Add Static Mappings dialog box to create static mappings for non-WINS clients.*

Importing Static Mappings from Other WINS Servers

On a network, you only need to create static mappings on a single WINS server. Afterward, you can import the mappings to other servers as necessary.

You can import static mappings by doing the following:

1. In WINS Manager, select the server on which you want to create static mappings and then choose Static Mappings from the Mappings menu.
2. In the Static Mappings dialog box, choose Import Mappings. This opens the Select Static Mappings dialog box, which is generally the same as a File Open dialog box.
3. You can import static mappings from any LMHOSTS file or from any file formatted the same as LMHOSTS. All keywords in the LMHOSTS file are ignored, except the #DOM keyword. When the #DOM keyword is used, a special group is created.
4. Choose Open to import the file.

Editing Static Mappings

You can edit or delete static mappings at any time in the WINS Manager. To do this, follow these steps:

1. In WINS Manager, select the server on which you want to edit static mappings and then choose Static Mappings from the Mappings menu.
2. In the Static Mappings dialog box, choose the static mapping you want to edit or delete.
3. To edit the mapping, choose Edit Mapping.
4. To delete the mapping, choose Delete Mapping.

Managing the WINS Database

The WINS database should be actively managed to maintain the health of WINS name resolution on the network. The WINS database files are stored in the *%SystemRoot%*\system32\wins folder. While you should never modify or delete these files, you may want to back them up periodically. A good set of backups can enable you to restore the WINS database in case of failure. Table 15-1 provides an overview of the WINS files.

Table 15-1. WINS Database Files

File Name	Description
JET.LOG	The database transaction log, which can be used to recover incomplete transactions
SYSTEM.MDB	Stores information about the structure of the WINS database
WINS.MDB	The WINS database file
WINSTMP.MDB	A temporary database file created while WINS is running on the system

Showing WINS Database Mappings

You can view the WINS database for a server selected in WINS Manager by choosing Show Database from the Mappings menu. This opens the dialog box shown in Figure 15-12. You can now

- Set display options for all mappings or only for a specific owner.
- Set the listing order using the radio buttons in the Sort Order area.
- Set a filter for the listings by using the Set Filter button. Simply enter a filter parameter, such as **192.11.*.*** or **CLEO***, and click OK. Filters are useful when you have lots of static mappings and need to find a particular set of mappings.

The list box in the lower portion of the Show Database dialog box provides entries for static and active mappings. At the left side of the entry, you'll see one of two icons. An icon of a single computer shows that the mapping is for a unique name. An icon with multiple computers shows that the mapping is for a group, domain, Internet group, or multihomed entry. Mappings also show the following:

- **NetBIOS Computer Name** The complete NetBIOS name of the computer or group along with a numeric suffix. The numeric suffix indicates the service associated with this mapping, such as 00h for the Workstation service.
- **IP Address** The IP address associated with the mapping.
- **A/S** Shows whether the mapping is active or static.
- **Expiration Date** The time and date the mapping expires.
- **Version ID** A unique ID assigned during registration that is used to find new records during replication.

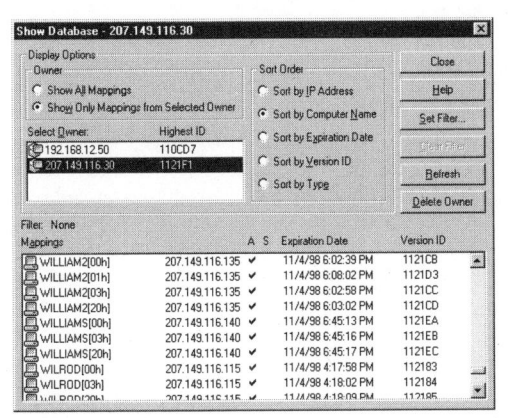

Figure 15-12. *The Show Database dialog box displays the current contents of the WINS database.*

Cleaning and Scavenging the WINS Database

The WINS database should be cleaned periodically to ensure that old computer names are removed. The process of cleaning the database, called scavenging, is initiated automatically according to the Extinction Timeout interval set in the WINS Server Configuration dialog box.

You can also initiate scavenging manually. To do this, select the server you want to work with in WINS Manager and then choose Initiate Scavenging from the Mappings menu.

Compacting the WINS Database

The size of the WINS database can grow substantially over time. To squeeze the extra space out of the database, you should periodically compact it. To do this, follow these steps:

1. Log on to the WINS server that contains the WINS database you want to compact.
2. Start the Services Control Panel utility.
3. In the Services dialog box, select Windows Internet Name Service and then click Stop.
4. Run JETPACK.EXE. This file is located in the *%SystemRoot%*\system32 folder.
5. In the Services dialog box, select Windows Internet Name Service and then click Start.

Backing Up and Restoring the WINS Database

Normally, the WINS database is backed up when Windows Internet Name Service is stopped (except when the WINS server is shutting down). You set this option by selecting the Backup On Termination check box in the WINS Server Configuration dialog box. The directory used for backups is set using the Backup Directory Path field of this same dialog box.

> **Note** If you do not see the Backup On Termination check box in the WINS Server Configuration dialog box, click on the Advanced button. This displays the advanced configuration area of the dialog box.

Manual Backup

You can also back up the WINS database manually. You do this by completing the following steps:

1. Log on to the WINS server on which you want to back up the database.
2. Start WINS Manager and then select Backup Database from the Mappings menu.
3. In the Select Backup Directory dialog box, select the directory you want to use for the backup and then choose OK. Because WINS databases can't be restored from mapped drives, the directory should be located on the local system.

Chapter 15 Managing WINS and NetBIOS Over TCP/IP | 285

4. WINS Manager creates a subdirectory called wins_bak and backs up the WINS database to this subdirectory.

Restoring the Database

To restore the WINS database, follow these steps:

1. Log on to the WINS server on which you want to restore the database.
2. Start WINS Manager and then select Restore Local Database from the Mappings menu.
3. Select the directory that contains the database backup and then click OK.

Chapter 16

Optimizing DNS

This chapter discusses the techniques you'll use to set up and manage DNS (Domain Name Service) on a network. DNS is a name resolution service that resolves Internet host names to IP addresses. Using DNS, the fully qualified domain name *www.tvpress.com*, for example, could be resolved to an IP address, which enables computers within DNS domains to find one another. DNS is used with Winsock applications that operate over the TCP/IP protocol stack, such as ping, and can be integrated with WINS.

Understanding DNS

DNS organizes groups of computers into domains. Unlike Microsoft Windows NT domains, which have a flat structure, DNS domains are organized into a hierarchical structure. This structure is defined on an Internet-wide basis, and the different levels identify individual computers, organizational domains, and top-level domains. For the fully qualified host name *www.tvpress.com*, *www* represents the host name for an individual computer, *tvpress* is the organizational domain, and *com* is the top-level domain.

Root Domains and Parent Domains

Top-level domains are at the root of the DNS hierarchy and are therefore also called root domains. These domains are organized

- Geographically, by using two-letter country codes, such as CA for Canada
- By organization type, such as *com* for commercial organizations
- By function, such as *shop* for online stores

Normal domains, such as tvpress.com, are also referred to as parent domains. They are called parent domains because they are the parents of an organizational structure. Parent domains can be divided into subdomains, which can be used for groups or departments within an organization. For example, the fully qualified domain name for a computer within a human resources group could be designated as jacob.hr.microsoft.com. Here, jacob is the host name, hr is the subdomain, and microsoft.com is the parent domain.

DNS and WINS

DNS domains are completely separate from Windows NT domains and are used to enable interactions with other DNS domains. If computers on the network don't need to access the Internet or other DNS domains, you don't need DNS. One of the key reasons to set up DNS on the network is to enable computers to access the Internet and to resolve host names properly when using Web browsers, Internet e-mail, or other Internet services. A local HOSTS file can also be used to resolve host names to IP addresses. You *could* use this file to enable name resolution on individual computers, but the HOSTS file has limited usefulness and is a poor way to manage DNS needs on the network.

DNS isn't the only name service available. You can also use WINS (Windows Internet Name Service). Within Windows NT 4.0 domains, WINS is the preferred name service. You'll use WINS to resolve NetBIOS computer names to IP addresses. For more information on WINS, see Chapter 15, "Managing WINS and NetBIOS Over TCP/IP."

The process of resolving fully qualified domain names is often referred to as a DNS lookup. When a network computer makes a request for a fully qualified domain name, a forward lookup is used to determine the IP address of the target computer. To ensure a valid response and deter spoofing (tricking users, often by making a transmission appear to come from an authorized source, into providing passwords and other information to allow unauthorized access to the network), the computer can use the IP address returned in the response to validate the host name. This process is called a reverse lookup.

Enabling DNS on the Network

To enable DNS on the network, you need to configure DNS clients and servers. When you configure DNS clients, you tell the clients the IP addresses of DNS servers on the network. Using this address, clients can communicate with DNS servers anywhere on the network, even if the servers are on different subnets. When the network uses DHCP, you should configure DHCP to work with DNS. To do this, you need to set the DHCP scope options for DNS servers as specified in the section of Chapter 14 titled "Setting Default DNS Servers for DHCP Clients."

Additionally, if computers on the network need to be accessible from other DNS domains, you need to create records for them in DNS. DNS records are organized into zones, where a zone is simply an area within a DNS domain.

Note Configuring a DNS client is described in the section of Chapter 12 titled "Configuring DNS Resolution." Configuring a DNS server is described in the following section of this chapter.

Installing DNS Servers

Microsoft Windows NT servers can be configured as DNS servers. Three types of DNS servers are available:

- **Primary server**   The main DNS server for a domain. This server stores a master copy of DNS records and the domain's configuration files.
- **Secondary server**   A DNS server that provides backup services for the domain. Secondary servers obtain their DNS information from the primary server when they are started, and they maintain this information until the information is refreshed or expired.
- **Forwarding-only server**   A server that caches DNS information after lookups and always passes requests to other servers. These servers maintain DNS information until it is refreshed or expired or the server is restarted. Unlike secondary servers, forwarding-only servers don't request full copies of a zone's database files.

Before you configure a DNS server, you must install the Microsoft DNS Server service. Afterward, you can configure the server to provide primary, secondary, or forwarding-only DNS services.

Installing the Microsoft DNS Service

You can install the Microsoft DNS Server by doing the following:

1. Access the Services tab of the Network Control Panel utility and then click on the Add button.
2. Choose Microsoft DNS Server in the Select Network Service dialog box and then click OK.
3. Now you need the Windows NT distribution CD-ROM. When prompted, insert the disk and enter the path for the distribution files, such as **e:\i386**. Afterward, click Continue.
4. When you close the Network utility, the DNS Server service is installed and you'll need to restart the computer.

From now on, Microsoft DNS Server service should start automatically each time you reboot the server. If the service isn't started, you'll need to start it manually with the Services utility in the Control Panel. Installing this service also installs Domain Name Service Manager, which you'll use to manage DNS on the network. You'll find this utility in the Administrative Tools (Common) folder.

Configuring a Primary Server

Every domain should have a primary DNS server. Once you install the Microsoft DNS Server service on the server, you can configure a primary server by completing the following steps:

1. Select Server List in the left window of DNS Manager and then choose the New Server option on the DNS menu.

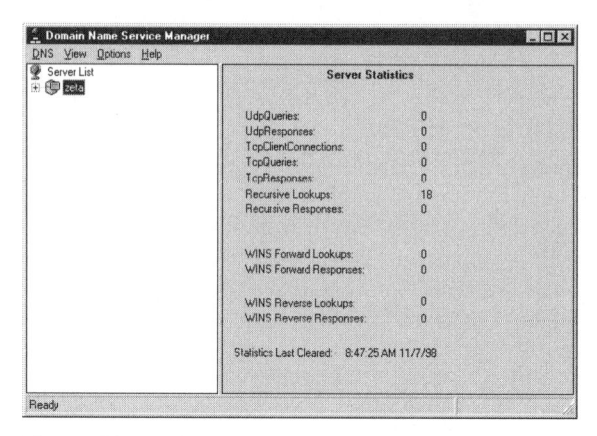

Figure 16-1. *The new DNS server is listed under the Server List in the Domain Name Service Manager dialog box.*

2. Enter the name or IP address of the server you're configuring and then click OK. As shown in Figure 16-1, an entry for the new server should be added to the left window of DNS Manager.
3. Right-click on the server entry and then choose New Zone from the pop-up menu. This opens the dialog box shown in Figure 16-2.
4. Select the Primary radio button and then click Next.
5. Enter the full DNS name for the zone and then click in the Zone File field. A default name for the zone's DNS database file should be filled in for you. You can use this name or enter a new file name.
6. Click Next and then click Finish to complete the process. The new zone is added to the server. Basic DNS records for the zone are created automatically.

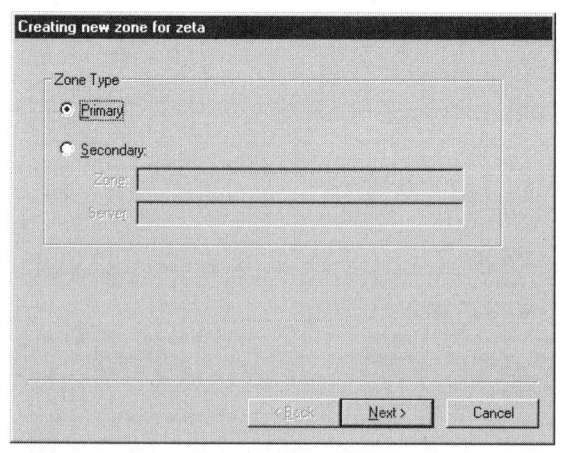

Figure 16-2. *Configure a primary zone with the Create New Zone dialog box.*

Note The zone name should help determine how the server/zone fits into the DNS domain hierarchy. For example, if you're creating the primary server for the tvpress.com domain, you should enter tvpress.com as the zone name.

7. Reverse lookups are necessary to authenticate DNS requests. If you want to enable reverse DNS lookups for the domain, you should create reverse lookup files for all primary zones now. Follow the steps listed in the section of this chapter titled "Configuring Reverse Lookups."

8. You need to create additional records for any computers that should be accessible to other DNS domains. Follow the steps listed in the section of this chapter titled "Managing DNS Records."

Configuring a Secondary DNS Server

Secondary servers provide backup DNS services on the network. On a small-sized or medium-sized network, you may be able to use your Internet service provider's name servers as secondaries, and in this case you should contact your Internet service provider to configure secondary DNS services for you. If you want to set up your own secondaries for backup services and load balancing, follow these steps:

1. Select Server List in the left window of DNS Manager and then choose the New Server option on the DNS menu.

2. Enter the name or IP address of the server you're configuring and then click OK. As shown in Figure 16-1, an entry for the new server should be added to the left window of DNS Manager.

3. Right-click on the server entry and then choose New Zone from the pop-up menu.

4. As shown in Figure 16-3, on the following page, select the Secondary radio button and then specify the zone whose files should be copied to create the secondary. Do this by entering the name of an existing zone and its primary server in the Zone field and the Server field respectively. Alternatively, you can drag the hand icon from the dialog box to the zone you want to use in DNS Manager's main window.

5. When you're finished, click Next and then enter the full DNS name for the zone and its database file in the Zone Name and Zone File fields respectively. Note that you may need to overwrite any existing entries.

6. Click Next to proceed and then enter the IP addresses of one or more master servers for the zone. The secondary server obtains DNS information from the master servers that you specify in this step.

7. Click Next and then click Finish.

Configuring Reverse Lookups

Forward lookups are used to resolve domain names to IP addresses. Reverse lookups are used to resolve IP addresses to domain names. You define information for forward lookups through standard zone and

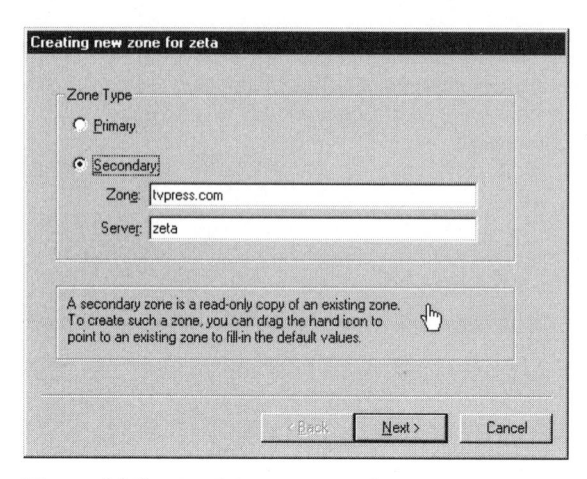

Figure 16-3. *Configure a secondary zone using the Create New Zone dialog box.*

domain records. You define information for reverse lookups through in-addr.arpa zone files.

Each segment on your network should have an in-addr.arpa database file. If present, the file must be in sync with the zone/domain database files for the network. If the files get out of sync, authentication may fail for the domain.

You create in-addr.arpa database files by doing the following:

1. In DNS Manager, right-click on the server entry.
2. Choose New Zone from the pop-up menu.
3. Select the Primary radio button and then click Next.
4. In the Zone Name field, enter the network or subnet portion of your IP address in reverse order followed by in-addr.arpa. For example, if you were on the 192.155.10 subnet, you would use 10.155.192.in-addr.arpa.

> **Note** If you have multiple subnets on the same network, such as 192.155.10 and 192.155.11, enter only the network portion for the file name. That is, you would use 155.192.in-addr.arpa and allow DNS Manager to create the necessary subnet database files when needed.

5. Click in the Zone File field. A default name for the zone's DNS database file should be filled in for you. You can use this name or enter a new file name.
6. Click Next and then click Finish.

Once you set up the in-addr.arpa zone files, you need to ensure that delegation for the zone is handled properly. Contact the Information Services department or your Internet service provider to ensure that the zones are registered with the parent domain.

Managing DNS Servers

DNS Manager is the tool you'll use to manage local and remote DNS Servers. As shown in Figure 16-4, the main window of DNS Manager is divided into two panes. The left pane allows you to access DNS servers and their database files. The right pane shows the details for the currently selected item. You can work with DNS Manager in several ways:

- Double-click on an entry in the left pane to expand the list of files for the entry.
- Select an entry in the left pane to display details such as Zone Info or Server Statistics in the right pane.
- Right-click on an entry to display a context menu with available options.

Adding Remote Servers to DNS Manager

Servers running Microsoft DNS can be managed from DNS Manager by doing the following:

1. Install Microsoft DNS Service on the remote server and make sure that the service is properly started.
2. Right-click on the Server List icon and select New Server from the pop-up menu.
3. Enter the fully qualified host name or IP address of the DNS server you want to manage and then click OK.

Note If the remote server can't be reached, a red X is displayed on top of the server's icon. Generally, this means that the server is offline or otherwise inaccessible due to security restrictions or problems with the RPC service. If you select the server, the Server Statistics pane shows the error message "RPC service is unavailable."

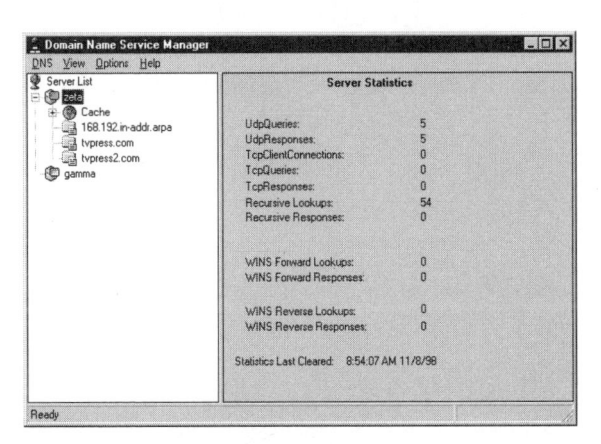

Figure 16-4. *The Domain Name Service Manager dialog box lets you manage local and remote DNS Servers.*

Working with the Cache Zone

DNS servers can have zones and domain files associated with them. When you create a new server, the only zone file available by default is the Cache zone. This zone lists authoritative name servers for root domains, such as arpa (used for reverse name lookups) and NET (used for top-level name services). If you create additional zones and name them so that they fit into the DNS domain hierarchy properly, you may see additional root domains, such as COM (if you create a zone called tvpress.com) or EDU (if you create a zone called tvpress.edu).

Normally, cache entries are updated automatically when you create, modify, or delete zone files and DNS records. Thus, in most cases you don't need to update cache entries. However, you may need to periodically update the ROOT-SERVERS zone for the NET domain. This domain contains entries for the top-level name servers on the Internet and can be accessed by doing the following:

1. Double-click on the DNS server you want to work with and then double-click on the Cache entry to display entries for root domains. Note the NS entries.

2. Double-click on the NET zone and then select ROOT-SERVERS. The address records for the root name servers should now be displayed in user manager as shown in Figure 16-5. Note these entries.

3. You can obtain a current list of root servers by entering *ftp://ftp.rs.internic.net/domain/named.root* into your Web browser.

4. If necessary, add entries for new root servers or change existing entries in the ROOT-SERVERS zone. Then select the Cache zone and add corresponding name server entries for new root servers.

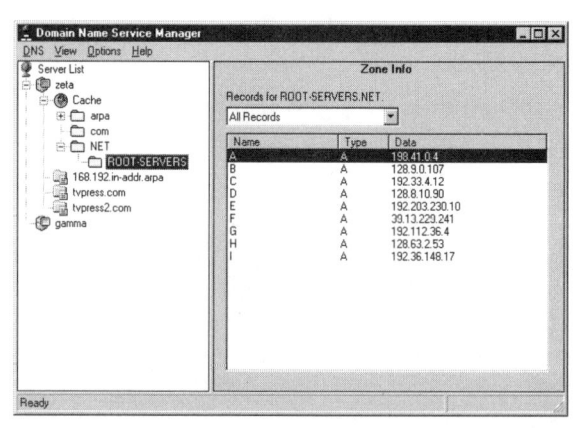

Figure 16-5. *Root name servers are defined in the Cache zone.*

Tip Updating the Cache zone isn't something you have to do often, but it is something you may need to do semiannually. For example, the version of Microsoft DNS installed on my system had information for root servers A to I. Since the installation, root servers J to M have been added. To update the Cache zone for these entries, I created address records in ROOT-SERVERS and name server records in Cache for each new server.

Examining Server Statistics

If you select a DNS server in the left pane, the right pane displays statistics for the server. Table 16-1 provides an overview of server statistics and how they are used.

Table 16-1. DNS Server Statistics

Statistic	Description
UdpQueries	Tracks the number of name server requests over UDP.
UdpResponses	Tracks the number of name server responses over UDP.
TcpConnections	Tracks the number of TCP connections to the server.
TcpQueries	Tracks the number of name server requests over TCP.
TcpResponses	Tracks the number of name server responses over TCP.
Recursive Lookups	Tracks the number of times the server has to query other servers to fulfill client's requests for recursive lookups.
Recursive Responses	Tracks the number of times the server responds to recursive lookups.
WINS Forward Lookups	Tracks the number of times a WINS name to IP address mapping is requested.
WINS Forward Responses	Tracks the number of responses to WINS forward lookups.
WINS Reverse Lookups	Tracks the number of times an IP address to WINS name mapping is requested.
WINS Reverse Responses	Tracks the number of responses to WINS reverse lookups.
Last Statistics Cleared	Specifies the date and time the server statistics were last cleared.

Removing a Server from DNS Manager

In DNS Manager, you can delete a server by selecting its entry and then pressing Delete. When prompted, click Yes to confirm the deletion. Deleting a server only removes it from the Server List and doesn't actually delete the server.

Deleting a Zone

Deleting a zone permanently removes it from the DNS server. To delete a zone, follow these steps:

1. In the DNS Manager, right-click on the zone's entry.
2. Select Delete Zone from the pop-up menu and then confirm the action by clicking Yes.

> **Note** Deleting a zone deletes all DNS records in the zone file but doesn't actually delete the zone file. You'll find that the actual zone file remains in the %SystemRoot%/system32/dns directory. If you want, you can delete this file.

Creating a Domain within a Zone

Using DNS Manager, you can create domains within a zone. For example, if you created the primary zone tvpress.com, you could create hr.tvpress.com and mis.tvpress.com subdomains for the zone. You create domains by completing the following steps:

1. In the DNS Manager, right-click on the zone's entry.
2. Select New Domain from the pop-up menu.
3. Enter the name of the new domain and click OK.

> **Note** When you create domains within zones, you must delegate authority to the domain to enable WINS integration with DNS.

Delegating an Existing Domain to a New Server

Moving DNS records from a domain on one server to a domain on another server is a fairly complex process. Because the process can be confusing, let's use a practical example where you're moving records from a domain on ServerA to a domain on ServerB. Using this scenario, you would move the records to the new server by doing the following:

1. Add ServerA and ServerB to DNS Manager.
2. In Server Manager, right-click on ServerA and then choose New Zone from the pop-up menu. Select Primary and then click Next.
3. In the Zone Name field, enter the name of the existing primary domain, such as ns.tvpress.com.
4. Afterward, click on the Zone File field to display the file name and then click Next. A new primary zone is created on ServerA.
5. Right-click on ServerB and choose New Zone from the pop-up menu.
6. Select Secondary and then drag the hand icon onto the new primary zone you just created on ServerA. Click Next.
7. The Zone Name and Zone File fields should be filled in for you. Don't change this information; it should exactly match the zone name and

file you just created on ServerA. Click Next. A new secondary zone is created.

8. Wait for the zone information to transfer from the primary zone. You'll know the transfer is complete when right-clicking the zone and clicking Refresh displays updated zone information.

9. Right-click the new secondary zone and choose Properties from the pop-up menu. On the General tab, click Primary to promote the zone to a primary zone. When prompted, click OK. Then click OK again to close the Zone Properties dialog box.

10. ServerB's secondary zone is now a primary zone. Double-click on this zone to display its records in the right pane.

11. In Zone Info, double-click the SOA record to display its properties. Next, in the Primary Name Server DNS Name field, replace the fully qualified domain name for ServerA with the fully qualified domain name for ServerB. Click OK.

12. In Zone Info, double-click the NS record to display its properties. Then in the Name Server DNS Name field, replace the fully qualified domain name for ServerA with the fully qualified domain name for ServerB. Click OK.

13. Right-click on ServerB's new primary zone and then select New Record. For Record Type, choose A Record to create an address record. Then enter the host name and IP address for ServerB.

14. Select the old primary zone on ServerA and then press Delete.

15. Create NS and A records for the new primary server in the parent domain. If you created the ns.tvpress.com domain, you would create these records in the tvpress.com domain.

16. Right-click on the parent domain and choose New Record. For Record Type, choose NS Record and then enter the fully qualified domain name for ServerB.

17. Right-click on the parent domain and choose New Record. For Record Type, choose A Record and then enter the fully qualified domain name and IP address for ServerB.

18. To complete the process, choose Update Server Data Files from the DNS menu.

Managing DNS Records

After you create the necessary zone files, you can add records to the zones. Computers that need to be accessed from other DNS domains must have DNS records. DNS records for other computers are optional and usually unnecessary. Although there are many different types of DNS records, most of these records types are not commonly used. So rather than focus on records types you probably *won't* use, let's focus on the ones you *will* use:

- **A (Address)** Maps a host name to an IP address. When a computer has multiple adapter cards and IP addresses, it should have multiple address records.

- **CNAME (Canonical Name)** Sets an alias for a host name. For example, using this record, zeta.tvpress.com can have an alias as *www.tvpress.com*.
- **MX (Mail Exchange)** Specifies a mail exchange server for the domain, which allows mail to be delivered to the correct mail servers in the domain.
- **NS (Name Server)** Specifies a name server for the domain, which allows DNS lookups within various zones. Each primary and secondary name server should be declared through this record.
- **PTR (Pointer)** Creates a pointer that maps an IP address to a host name for reverse lookups.
- **SOA (Start of Authority)** Declares the host that is the most authoritative for the zone and, as such, is the best source of DNS information for the zone. Each zone file must have an SOA record (which is created automatically when you add a zone).

Adding Address and Pointer Records

The A record maps a host name to an IP address and the PTR record creates a pointer to the host for reverse lookups. Address and pointer records can be created together using the New Host option or separately using the New Record option.

Create a new host entry with A and PTR records by doing the following:

1. In DNS Manager, right-click on the zone you want to update and then choose New Host from the pop-up menu. This opens the dialog box shown in Figure 16-6.
2. Enter the host name and IP address and then select the Create Associated PTR Record check box.

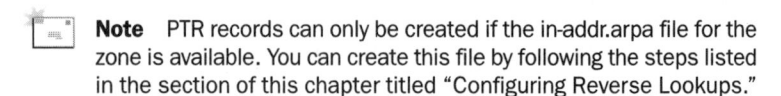

   Note PTR records can only be created if the in-addr.arpa file for the zone is available. You can create this file by following the steps listed in the section of this chapter titled "Configuring Reverse Lookups."

3. Click Add Host.
4. Repeat as necessary to add other hosts.
5. Click Done when you are finished.

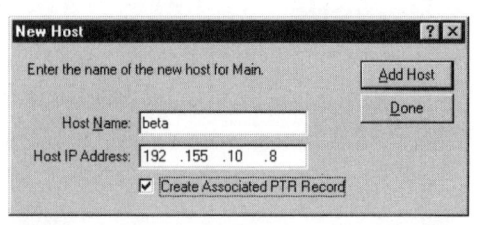

Figure 16-6. *Create A records and PTR records simultaneously with the New Host option.*

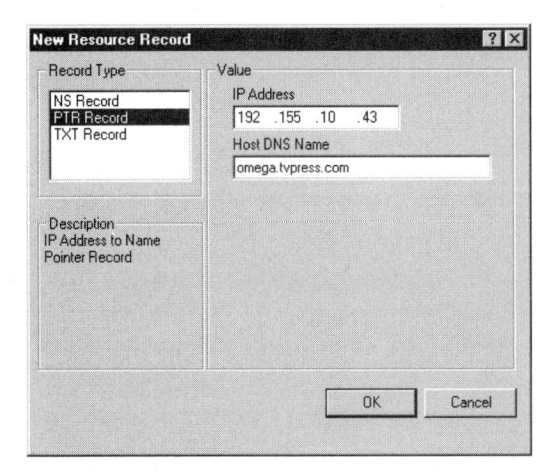

Figure 16-7. *PTR records can be added later, if necessary, with the New Resource Record dialog box.*

Adding a PTR Record Later

If you need to add a PTR record later, you can do so by completing the following steps:

1. In DNS Manager, right-click on the in-addr.arpa entry for the network or subnet you want to work with and then choose New Record from the pop-up menu. This opens the dialog box shown in Figure 16-7.
2. In the Record Type field, select PTR Record.
3. Enter the IP address and fully qualified host name in the fields provided.
4. Click OK.

Adding DNS Aliases with CNAME

You specify host aliases using CNAME records. Aliases allow a single host computer to appear to be multiple host computers. For example, the host gamma.tvpress.com can be made to appear as *www.tvpress.com* and *ftp.tvpress.com*.

To create a CNAME record, follow these steps:

1. In DNS Manager, right-click on the zone you want to update and then choose New Record from the pop-up menu.
2. If the address record for the host hasn't been created yet, select A Record and then enter a host name and IP address. Afterward, click OK.

   This creates the A record for the host. Now right-click on the zone again and choose New Record.

3. In the Record Type field, select CNAME Record. As shown in Figure 16-8, on the following page, you can now enter an alias for a designated host. Enter the alias in the Alias Name field and the fully qualified host name in the For Host DNS Name field.
4. Click OK.

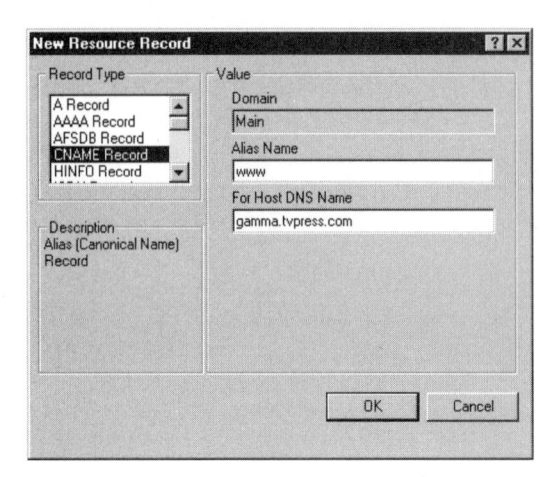

Figure 16-8. *When you create the CNAME record, be sure to use the fully qualified host name.*

Adding Mail Exchange Servers

MX records identify mail exchange servers for the domain. These servers are responsible for processing or forwarding mail within the domain. When you create an MX record, you must specify a preference number for the mail server. A preference number is a value from 0 to 65,535 that denotes the mail server's priority within the domain. The mail server with the lowest preference number has the highest priority and is the first to receive mail. If mail delivery fails, the mail server with the next lowest preference number is tried.

Create an MX record by doing the following:

1. In DNS Manager, right-click on the zone you want to update and then choose New Record from the pop-up menu.

2. If the address record for the host hasn't been created yet, select A Record and then enter a host name and IP address. Afterward, click OK.

   This creates the A record for the host. Now right-click on the zone again and choose New Record.

3. In the Record Type field, select MX Record. As shown in Figure 16-9, you can now create a record for the mail server by filling in these fields:

   - **Host Name (Optional)**   Enter the optional host name, such as mail.
   - **Mail Exchange Server DNS Name**   Enter the fully qualified host name, such as mail.tvpress.com.
   - **Preference Number**   Enter a preference number for the host from 0 to 65,535.

4. Click OK.

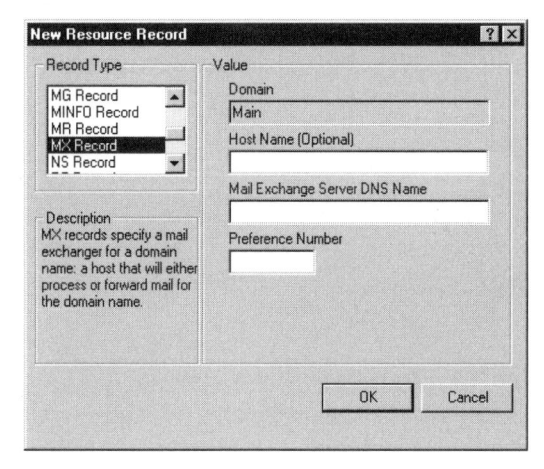

Figure 16-9. *Mail servers with the lowest preference number have the highest priority.*

Tip Assign preference numbers that leave room for growth. For example, use 10 for your highest priority mail server, 20 for the next, and 30 for the one after that.

Adding Name Servers

NS records specify the name servers for the domain. Each primary and secondary name server should be declared through this record. If you obtain secondary name services from an Internet service provider, be sure to insert the appropriate NS records.

Create an NS record by doing the following:

1. In DNS Manager, right-click on the zone you want to update and then choose New Record from the pop-up menu.
2. If the name server is located in the domain and its address record hasn't been created yet, select A Record and then enter a host name and IP address. Afterward, click OK.

    This creates the A record for the name server. Now right-click on the zone again and choose New Record.
3. In the Record Type field, select NS Record. As shown in Figure 16-10, on the following page, you can now create a record for the name server. Enter the fully qualified host name, such as names1.tvpress.com.
4. Click OK.

Viewing and Updating DNS Records

To view or update DNS records, follow these steps:

1. Double-click on the zone you want to work with. Zone Info should be displayed in the right pane.

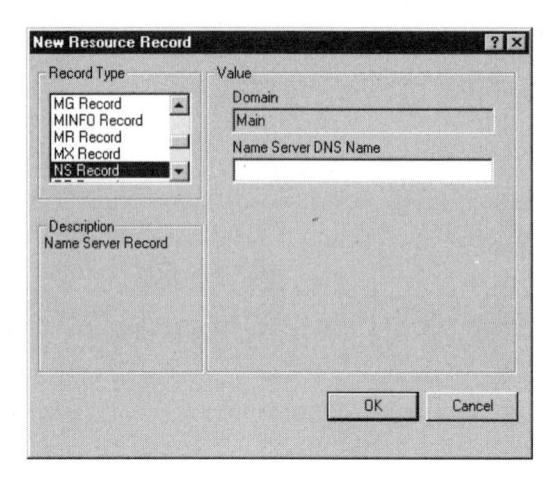

Figure 16-10. *Configure name servers for the domain with the New Resource Record dialog box.*

2. In Zone Info, double-click on the DNS record you want to view or update. This opens the record's Properties dialog box.
3. Make the necessary changes and click OK.

Updating Zone Properties and the SOA Record

Each zone has separate properties that you can configure. These properties set general zone parameters by using the SOA record, change notification, and WINS integration. In DNS Manager, you set zone properties by doing the following:

- Right-click on the zone you want to update and then choose Properties from the pop-up menu.
- Select the zone and then choose Properties from the DNS menu.

Selecting Properties opens the Zone Properties dialog box shown in Figure 16-11. Tasks you'll accomplish using this dialog box are covered in the sections that follow.

Modifying the Start of Authority Record

An SOA record designates the authoritative name server for a zone and sets general zone properties, such as retry and refresh intervals. You can modify this information by doing the following:

1. In DNS Manager, right-click on the zone you want to update and then choose Properties from the pop-up menu.
2. Click on the SOA Record tab and then update the fields shown in Figure 16-12.

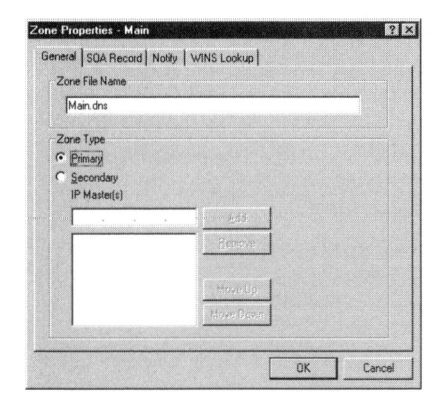

Figure 16-11. *Use the Zone Properties dialog box to set general properties for the zone and to update the SOA record.*

The fields of the SOA Record tab are used as follows:

- **Primary Name Server DNS Name** The fully qualified domain name for the name server, followed by a period. The period is used to terminate the name and ensure that the domain information is not appended to the entry.

- **Responsible Person Mailbox DNS Name** The e-mail address of the person in charge of the domain. The default entry is *administrator* followed by a period, meaning administrator@your_domain. If you change this entry, substitute a period in place of the @ symbol in the e-mail address and terminate the address with a period. For example, if william@tvpress.com is the responsible person, you would enter: **william.tvpress.com**.

- **Serial Number** A serial number that indicates the version of the DNS database files. The number is updated automatically whenever you

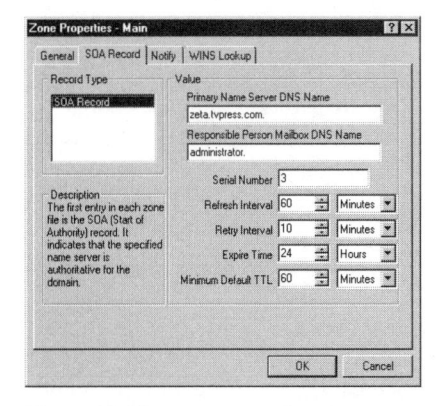

Figure 16-12. *Set zone and authority properties using the SOA Record tab.*

make changes to zone files. You can also update the number manually. Secondary servers use this number to determine if the zone's DNS records have changed. If the primary server's serial number is larger than the secondary server's serial number, the records have changed and the secondary server can request the DNS records for the zone. You can also configure DNS to notify secondary servers of changes (which may speed up the update process).

- **Refresh Interval**   The interval at which a secondary server checks for zone updates. If set to 60 minutes, NS record changes may not get propagated to a secondary server for up to an hour. You reduce network traffic by increasing this value.
- **Retry Interval**   The time the secondary waits after a failure to download the zone database. If set to 10 minutes and a zone database transfer fails, the secondary will wait 10 minutes before requesting the zone database once more.
- **Expire Time**   The period of time for which zone information is valid on the secondary. If the secondary can't download data from a primary server within this period, the secondary server lets the data in its cache expire and stops responding to DNS queries. Setting the Expire Time to seven days allows the data on a secondary server to be valid for seven days.
- **Minimum Default TTL**   Sets the minimum time-to-live value for cached records on a secondary server. When this value is reached, the secondary expires the associated record and discards it. The next request for the record will need to be sent to the primary for resolution. Set this value to a relatively high value, such as 24 hours, to reduce traffic on the network and increase efficiency. However, keep in mind that a higher value slows down the propagation of updates through the Internet.

Notifying Secondaries of Changes

You set properties for a zone with its Start of Authority Record. These properties control how DNS information is propagated on the network. You can also specify that the primary server should notify secondary name servers when changes are made to the zone database. To do this, follow these steps:

1. In DNS Manager, right-click on the zone you want to update and then choose Properties from the pop-up menu.
2. Click on the Notify tab shown in Figure 16-13 and then enter the IP addresses of secondary servers to notify them of changes.
3. Click OK.

> **Note**   Under normal DNS operations, you don't need to notify secondaries of changes to the primary zone database. However, if you want to restrict access to the primary zone database, you must configure the Notify List before you can set access restrictions.

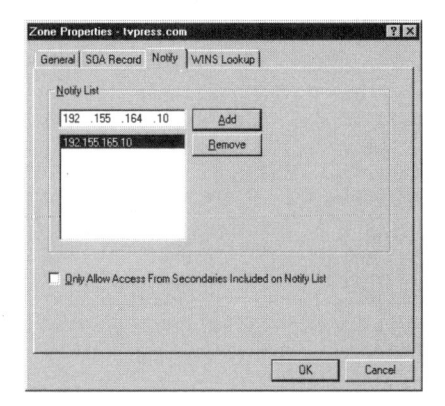

Figure 16-13. *Enter the IP addresses of servers in the Zone Properties dialog box to notify them when changes occur.*

Restricting Access to the Primary Zone Database

Restricting access to the primary zone database is a security precaution you may want to consider using on your network. When you restrict access to the primary zone database, only secondary servers that you've configured on the Notify List can request updates from the zone's primary server. This allows you to funnel requests through a select group of secondary servers, such as your Internet service provider's secondary name servers, and to hide the details of your internal network from the outside world.

To restrict access to the primary zone database, follow these steps:

1. In DNS Manager, right-click on the zone you want to update and then choose Properties from the pop-up menu.
2. Click on the Notify tab and then enter the IP addresses of secondary servers that should have access to the primary zone database.
3. Select Only Allow Access From Secondaries Included On Notify List and then click OK.
4. To enforce the changes immediately, select Update Server Data Files from the DNS menu.

Managing DNS Server Configuration and Security

The general configuration of DNS servers is managed through the Server Properties dialog box. Through it you can enable and disable IP addresses for the server and control access to DNS servers outside the organization.

Enabling and Disabling IP Addresses for a DNS Server

By default, multihomed DNS servers respond to DNS requests on all available network adapters and the IP addresses they're configured to use.

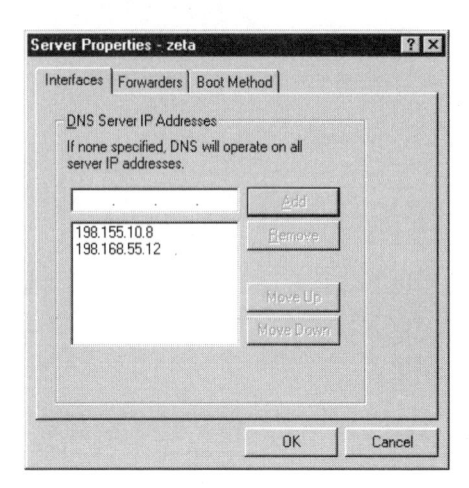

Figure 16-14. *Set the IP addresses that should handle DNS requests and responses by using the Interfaces tab.*

Through DNS Manager, you can specify that the server can only answer requests on specific IP addresses. To do this, follow these steps:

1. In DNS Manager, right-click on the server you want to configure and then choose Properties from the pop-up menu.
2. In the Interfaces tab shown in Figure 16-14, enter the IP addresses that should respond to DNS requests.
3. Only these IP addresses will be used for DNS. All other IP addresses on the server will be disabled for DNS.

Controlling Access to DNS Servers Outside the Organization

Restricting access to the primary zone database allows you to specify which internal and external servers can access the primary server. For external servers, this controls which servers can get in from the outside world. You can also control which DNS servers within your organization can access servers outside it. To do this, you need to set up DNS forwarding within the domain.

With DNS forwarding, you configure DNS servers within the domain as

- **Nonforwarders**   Servers that must pass DNS queries they can't resolve on to designated forwarding servers.
- **Forwarding-only**   Servers that can only cache responses and pass requests on to forwarders. This is also known as a caching-only DNS server.
- **Forwarders**   Servers that receive requests from nonforwarders and forwarding-only servers. Forwarders use normal DNS communication methods to resolve queries and to send responses back to other DNS servers.

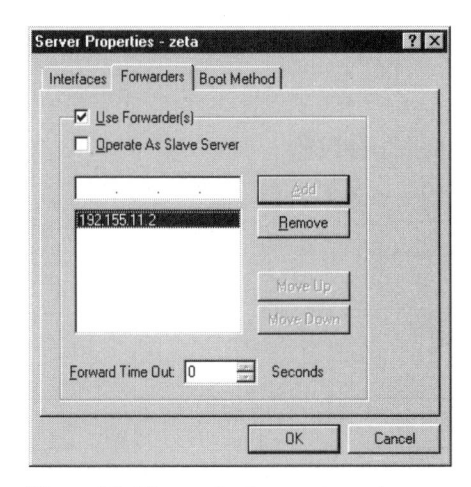

Figure 16-15. *Use the Forwarders tab to enter the IP addresses of the network's forwarders.*

Creating Nonforwarding DNS Servers

To create a nonforwarding DNS server, follow these steps:

1. In DNS Manager, right-click on the server you want to configure and then choose Properties from the pop-up menu.
2. In the Forwarders tab shown in Figure 16-15, select Use Forwarder(s).
3. Enter the IP addresses of the network's forwarders.
4. Set the Forward Time Out. This value controls how long the server tries to query the server if it gets no response. When the Forward Time Out interval passes, the server tries the next forwarder on the list. The default is 0 seconds.
5. Click OK.

Creating Forwarding-Only Servers

To create a forwarding-only server, follow these steps:

1. In DNS Manager, right-click on the server you want to configure and then choose Properties from the pop-up menu.
2. In the Forwarders tab, select Use Forwarder(s) and then select Operate As Slave Server.
3. Enter the IP addresses of the network's forwarders.
4. Set the Forward Time Out. This value controls how long the server tries to query the server if it gets no response. When the Forward Time Out interval passes, the server tries the next forwarder on the list. The default is 0 seconds.
5. Click OK.

Creating Forwarders

Any DNS server that is not designated as a nonforwarder or a forwarding-only server will act as a forwarder. Thus, on the network's designated forwarders, you should ensure that Use Forwarder(s) and Operate As Slave Server are *not* selected.

Integrating WINS with DNS

A Windows NT DNS server can be integrated with WINS. WINS integration allows the server to act as a WINS server or to forward WINS requests to specific WINS servers. When you configure WINS and DNS to work together, you can configure

- Partial integration with forward lookups using NetBIOS computer names.
- Partial integration with reverse lookups using NetBIOS computer names.
- Caching and timeout values for WINS resolution.
- Full integration with lookups resolved using NetBIOS computer names and NetBIOS scopes.

Configuring WINS Lookups in DNS

When you configure WINS lookups in DNS, the leftmost portion of the fully qualified domain name can be resolved using WINS. The procedure works like this:

> The DNS server looks for an address record for the fully qualified domain name. If a record is found, the server uses the record to resolve the name using only DNS. If a record is not found, the server extracts the leftmost portion of the name and uses WINS to try to resolve the name (as a NetBIOS computer name).

You configure WINS lookups in DNS by doing the following:

1. In DNS Manager, right-click on the zone you want to update and then choose Properties from the pop-up menu.
2. Click on the WINS Lookup tab shown in Figure 16-16.
3. Select Use WINS Resolution and then enter the IP addresses of the network's WINS servers. At least one WINS server must be specified.
4. Click OK.

Configuring Reverse WINS Lookups in DNS

When you configure reverse WINS lookups in DNS, the IP address of the host can be resolved to a NetBIOS computer name. The procedure works like this:

> The DNS server looks for a pointer record for the specified IP address. If a record is found, the server uses the record to resolve the fully qualified domain name. If a record is not found, the server sends a request to WINS, and, if possible, WINS returns the NetBIOS computer name for the IP address and the host domain is appended to this computer name.

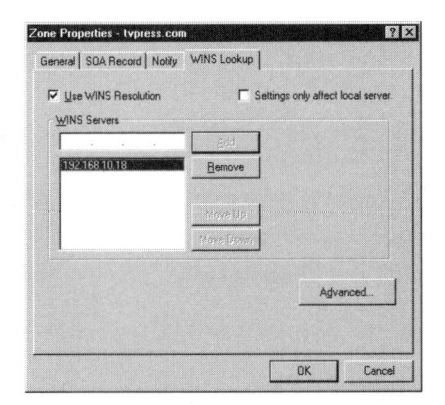

Figure 16-16. *Use the WINS Lookup tab to configure WINS lookups in DNS.*

You configure reverse WINS lookups in DNS by doing the following:

1. In DNS Manager, right-click on the in-addr.arpa zone for the domain and then choose Properties from the pop-up menu.
2. Click on the WINS Reverse Lookup tab shown in Figure 16-17.
3. Select Use WINS Reverse Lookup and then enter the IP addresses of the network's WINS servers.
4. In the DNS Host Domain field, enter the host domain information. The domain is appended to the computer name returned by WINS. For example, if you enter **tvpress.com** and WINS returns the NetBIOS computer name gamma, the DNS server will combine the two values and return gamma.tvpress.com.
5. Click OK.

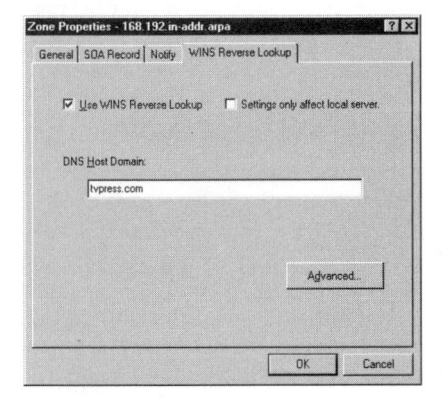

Figure 16-17. *Use the WINS Reverse Lookup tab to configure WINS reverse lookups in DNS.*

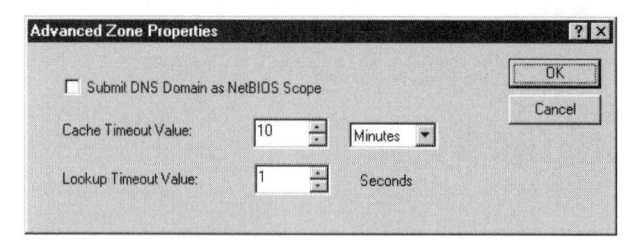

Figure 16-18. *In the Advanced Zone Properties dialog box, set caching and timeout values for WINS in DNS.*

Setting Caching and Timeout Values for WINS in DNS

When you integrate WINS and DNS, you should also set WINS caching and timeout values. The caching value determines how long records returned from WINS are valid. The timeout value determines how long DNS should wait for a response from WINS before timing out and returning an error. These values are set for both forward and reverse WINS lookups.

You set caching and timeout values for WINS in DNS by doing the following:

1. In DNS Manager, right-click on the zone you want to update and then choose Properties from the pop-up menu.
2. Select the WINS Lookup tab and then choose the Advanced button. This opens the dialog box shown in Figure 16-18.
3. Set the caching and timeout values using the Cache Timeout Value field and the Lookup Timeout Value field. By default, DNS caches WINS records for 10 minutes and times out after 1 second. For most networks, you should increase these values. Sixty minutes for caching and three seconds for timeouts may be better choices.
4. Repeat this process for the in-addr.arpa zone for the domain.

Configuring Full WINS and DNS Integration

When you configure full WINS and DNS integration, lookups can be resolved using NetBIOS computer names and NetBIOS scopes. Here, a forward lookup works like this:

> The DNS server looks for an address record for the fully qualified domain name. If a record is found, the server uses the record to resolve the name using only DNS. If a record is not found, the server extracts the leftmost portion of the name as the NetBIOS computer name and the remainder of the name as the NetBIOS scope. These values are then passed to WINS for resolution.

You configure full integration of WINS and DNS by doing the following:

1. In DNS Manager, right-click on the zone you want to update and then choose Properties from the pop-up menu.
2. Select the WINS Lookup tab and then choose the Advanced button.

3. In the Advanced Zone Properties dialog box, select Submit DNS Domain As NetBIOS Scope.
4. Click OK.

Before you fully integrate WINS and DNS, you should make sure that the NetBIOS scope is properly configured on the network. You should also ensure that a consistent naming scheme is used for all network computers. Because NetBIOS is case-sensitive, queries resolve only if the case matches exactly. Note also that if the domain has subdomains, the subdomains must be delegated the authority for name services in order for WINS and DNS integration to work properly.

Index

Note to the reader: Italicized page numbers refer to figures, tables, and illustrations.

A

abbreviated file names, 163
access. *See also* permissions; security
   dial-in privileges, 106, 120
   granting and denying, 59
   logon hours, 103-04
   logon workstations, 104-05
   passwords for, 80-86
   printer, 245-46, *246*
   restricting to the primary zone database, 305-07
   share permissions and, 180-84, 186, 191-92
Access Through Share Permissions dialog box, *182*, 183, 184
access types
   for directories, 190, *190-91*
   for files, 189-90, *190*
Account Information dialog box, 105-06, 119-20, *120*
Account Operators group, 74-75
Account Policy dialog box, 81-85, *81*
accounts. *See also* group accounts; user accounts
   built-in, 64-68
   dial-in privileges for, 106
   expiration date for, 105
   managing multiple, 115-20
   privileges and permissions, 68-73, 180-84
   tools for working with, 61-64
   updating, 107-12
Active Leases dialog box, 262-63, *263*
Adapter Properties dialog box, 213, *213*
adapters
   diagnostic information on, 53-54
   installing, 212-13
Adapters tab (Network dialog box), 212-13, *212*
Add Computer to Domain dialog box, 225-26, *226*
adding
   computers to a domain, 225-26
   group accounts, 91-94
   hard drives, 127-34
   share permissions, 182-83
   user accounts, 89-91
   users to a group, 95
Add Printer Wizard, 234-38, *235*, *236*, *237*, *238*
Add Reserved Clients dialog box, 264, *264*
address (A) records, 296, 297
addresses. *See* DHCP addresses; IP addresses
Add Static Mappings dialog box, 281, *281*
Add Users and Groups dialog box, 92-93, *93*, 182-83, *183*, 191-92
administering. *See* managing
administrative tools, 7-10, *8*
   installing on Windows NT workstations, 9-10
   system configuration and, 8-10
Administrative Wizards, 10, *10*
Administrator account, 64-65
administrators
   groups used by, 73-74
   passwords for, 65
Administrators group, 73-74
Advanced IP Addressing dialog box, *219*
Advanced Zone Properties dialog box, *309*
alerts, 20
aliases, 297, 298
All Folders pane (NT Explorer), 164
application performance, 24
applications
   administering, 36-37
   right-clicking on listings for, 37
Applications tab (Task Manager), 36-37, *36*
archiving event logs, 51-52
Assign Drive Letter dialog box, 138-39, *139*
assigning
   DHCP options, 258-59
   drive letters, 133-34, 138-39
   home directories, 102-03
   IP addresses and gateways, 218-19
   local profiles, 114

assigning, *continued*
　share permissions, 180-84, 188-89, 191-92
　static IP addresses, 216-17
auditing system resources, 43-47
　directory and file security, 45-46
　printer security, 46-47
　setting security policies, 43-45
Audit Policy dialog box, 44-45, *44*
AutoAdminLogon option, 122
auto-loader tape systems, 197
automatic backups, 207-08
automatic logon option, 122
automatic reboot option, 29

B

background processes, 35
backup device driver, 198-200
backup directory, 266
backup domain controller (BDC), 3, 21
Backup Information dialog box, 202-03, *203-05*
Backup Operators group, 75
backups, 193-208
　automating and scheduling, 207-08
　configuring, 202-05
　devices and media for, 196-98
　DHCP database, 266
　differential, 195-96
　incremental, 195-96
　installing devices for, 198-201
　making a plan for, 193-94
　restoring data from, 205-07
　tapes used for, 197-98
　types of, 194-95
　Windows NT utility for, 201-08
　of WINS database, 284
Backup utility, 201-08
bad sectors, 141-43
BIOS version, 53
B-node (broadcast node) name resolution, 268-69
Boost slider, 24
booting your system
　creating an emergency boot disk, 145
　recovering a boot failure, 146-47, 158-59
BOOT.INI file, 145
breaking mirrored sets, 157
built-in accounts, 64-68
　group accounts, 67-68, 73-78
　user accounts, 64-67

built-in capabilities
　for domain controllers, 70-71
　for non-domain controllers, 72-73

C

Cache zone, 293-94
caching values, 309
canceling print jobs, 251
CD-ROM drives, 174-75
Check Disk utility, 141-43, *143*
Client Properties dialog box, 265, *265*
clients. *See* DHCP clients; WINS clients
CNAME aliases, 297, 298, *299*
command-line utilities, 11
　Backup, 207-08
　Convert, 140-41
　NET tools, 11
　ping, 216, 229
comments, printer, 241-42
compacting the WINS database, 284
Compact utility, 145
compressing directories and files, 143-44
computer name resolution, 221-23, 267, 268-69
configuring
　alerts, 20
　backups, 202-05
　DHCP relays, 223-24
　DNS forwarding, 305-07
　DNS resolution, 220-21
　DNS servers, 289-91
　dynamic IP addresses, 217-18
　environment variables, 26-27
　hardware profiles, 29-31
　IP forwarding, 225
　multiple DHCP scopes, 262
　multiple IP addresses and gateways, 218-19
　printer properties, 241-47
　printers, 233-41
　reverse lookups, 291-92
　services logon options, 43
　services startup options, 42
　static IP addresses, 215-17
　system startup and recovery, 27-29
　TCP/IP networking, 215-25, 229
　testing the configuration, 229
　user profiles, 31
　virtual memory, 25-26

configuring, *continued*
  WINS and DNS integration, 309-10
  WINS resolution, 221-23
  WINS servers, 268, 274-76
connecting
  computers to a domain, 225-26
  to network drives, 186-87
  to network printers, 239-40
Connect To Printer dialog box, 239, *239*
Contents pane (NT Explorer), 164
Control Panel utilities, 6-7, *6*
Convert utility, 140-41
copy backups, 194
copying
  files, 171-73
  floppy and removable disks, 170
  user and group accounts, 109
  user profiles, 114-15
CPU clock speed, 53
Create Extended Partition dialog box, 136
Create Logical Drive dialog box, 136
Create Primary Partition dialog box, 135, *135*
Create Scope dialog box, 256-57, *256*
creating
  DHCP scopes, 256-57
  domains within zones, 295
  emergency boot disk, 145
  environment variables, 27
  event log archives, 51-52
  extended partitions, 136
  folders, 173-74
  group accounts, 91-94
  logical drives, 136
  logon scripts, 101-02
  mirror sets, 154-55
  primary partitions, 135
  printer forms, 248
  shared directories, 177-80
  static mappings, 280-81
  stripe sets, 153-54
  user accounts, 79-91
  user profiles, 98-101
  volume sets, 149-50
Creator Owner group, 78
customizing Windows NT Explorer display, 165-66

D

daily backups, 195
data
  backing up, 193-205, 207-08
  compressing, 143-45
  recovering from backups, 205-07
databases
  backing up/restoring the DHCP database, 266
  backing up/restoring the WINS database, 284-85
  configuring WINS database replication, 276-79
  managing the WINS database, 282-85
  restricting access to the primary zone database, 304
DAT drives, 197
date searches, 168
default system services, 41
defragmenting hard drives, 143
deleting. *See also* removing
  environment variables, 27
  files and directories, 173
  leases and reservations, 265
  local profiles, 113-14
  print jobs, 251
  servers from DNS Manager, 294
  user and group accounts, 110
  volume label for a drive, 139
  volume sets, 150
  zones from DNS servers, 295
Dependencies tab (Diagnostics utility), 55
Desktop key, 121, 123-24
Detailed Information dialog box (WINS Manager), 272-73, *273*
DHCP (Dynamic Host Configuration Protocol), 253-66
  backing up/restoring the DHCP database, 266
  configuring relays for, 223-24
  dynamic IP addressing with, 215, 217-18
  explained, 253
  managing client leases and reservations, 262-65
  managing scopes, 254-62
  Relay Agent service installation, 224
  server installation, 254
DHCP addresses
  releasing, 264
  reserving, 263-64
DHCP clients, 253
  default DNS servers for, 260

Index

DHCP clients, *continued*
   default routers and gateways for, 260-61
   default WINS node type for, 260
   default WINS servers for, 259
   managing leases and reservations for, 262-65
DHCP Manager utility, 254-55, *255*
DHCP Options dialog box, 258-59, *258*
DHCP Relay tab (Microsoft TCP/IP Properties dialog box), 223-24, *224*
DHCP scopes, 254-62
   activating and deactivating, 261
   configuring multiple, 262
   creating, 256-57
   modifying, 261
   removing, 261-62
   setting options for, 257-59
DHCP servers
   backing up/restoring the server database, 266
   configuring scopes for, 254-62
   installing, 254
Diagnostics utility, 52-56, *53*
dial-in privileges, 106
   setting for multiple accounts, 120
dialog boxes. *See names of specific dialog boxes*
differential backups, 195-96
directories. *See also* folders
   access types for, 190, *190-91*
   assigning permissions to, 180-84, 188-89, 191-92
   auditing, 45-46
   backing up, 202-05
   compressing and expanding, 143-45
   deleting, 173
   exporting, 33
   importing, 33-34
   managing replication of, 31-34
   renaming, 173
   selecting, 170-71
   sharing, 177-86
Directory Auditing dialog box, 45-46, *45*
Directory Permissions dialog box, 191, *192*
Directory Replication Service, 31-34
   configuring, 32
   creating replication accounts, 31-32
   exporting directories, 33

Directory Replication Service, *continued*
   importing directories, 33-34
disabled user accounts
   enabling, 110-11
   logon problems and, 111-12
disconnecting
   network drives, 187
   users, 18, 103
Disk Administrator utility, 129-32
   assigning drive letters with, 133-34, 138-39
   changing/deleting volume label with, 139
   Check Disk utility and, 142
   color-coding partitions with, 134
   mirrored sets and, 154-55, 157
   partitioning hard drives with, 134-38
   stripe sets and, 153-54, 156, 160
Disk Administrator window, 129-30, *130*
disk drives. *See also* floppy drives; hard drives; network drives; removable drives
   assigning drive letters to, 133-34, 138-39
   diagnostic information on, 54
   examining properties of, 174-75
   general information on, 130-31
Disk Keeper utility, 143
disk mirroring, 154-55
disk striping, 152-54
   with parity, 155-56
DMA usage information, 55-56
DNS (Domain Name Service), 267, 287-310
   client configuration, 220-21
   configuring reverse lookups, 291-92
   domain organization, 287
   enabling on the network, 288
   explained, 287-88
   forwarding capabilities, 305-07
   installing, 289
   managing DNS records, 296-301
   managing DNS servers, 292-96
   modifying the SOA record, 301-03
   security issues, 304-07
   server configuration, 289-91, 304-07
   updating zone properties, 301-04
   WINS integration with, 307-10

DNS forwarding, 305-07
DNS Manager, 292-96
  adding remote servers to, 292
  Cache zone and, 293-94
  creating domains within zones, 295
  delegating domains to new servers, 295-96
  deleting zones, 295
  examining server statistics, 294
  managing DNS records, 296-301
  modifying the SOA record, 301-03
  removing servers from, 294
  updating zone properties, 301-04
DNS Manager dialog box, *292*
DNS records, 296-301
  address and pointer records, 297-98
  CNAME aliases, 298, *299*
  mail exchange server records, 299-300
  name server records, 300
  types of, 296-97
  viewing and updating, 300-301
DNS servers
  adding to DNS manager, 292
  configuring, 289-91, 304-07
  creating domains within zones, 295
  delegating domains to, 295-96
  deleting zones from, 295
  enabling/disabling DNS addresses for, 204-05
  examining statistics for, 294
  forwarding capabilities on, 305-07
  installing, 289
  managing, 292-96
  primary, 289-91
  removing from DNS manager, 294
  restricting access to outside servers, 305-07
  reverse lookups on, 291-92
  secondary, 291
  security and access management, 304-07
  setting for DHCP clients, 260
DNS tab (Microsoft TCP/IP Properties dialog box), 220-21, *220*
docked profiles, 29
  configuring a computer for, 30-31
documents
  checking properties of, 251
  pausing and resuming printing of, 251
  prioritizing in the printer, 252
  removing from the printer, 251
  scheduling printing of, 252
  setting printer defaults for, 247
Domain Admins group, 74
domain controllers, 3, 21-22
  built-in capabilities for, 70-71
  promoting, 22
  synchronizing, 22
  types of, 21-22
  user rights for, 69-70
Domain Guests group, 77-78
domain names, 220
Domain Name Service Manager dialog box, *290*
domains
  adding computers to, 225-26
  creating within zones, 295
  delegating to new servers, 295-96
  removing computers from, 226-27
  root and parent, 287
Domain Users group, 76-77
DontDisplayLastUserName option, 121
downloading printer drivers, 242
dragging, moving files by, 172
drivers
  for backup devices, 198-200
  for printers, 231-32
  for tape devices, 200-201
dump file, 29
dynamic IP addresses, 215
  configuring, 217-18
  enabling IP forwarding for, 225
dynamic routing, 225

E

Edit Alias dialog box, 179-80, *180*
editing
  environment variables, 27
  static mappings, 282
emergency boot disk, 145, 158
emergency repair disk, 145-47
enabling
  IP addresses for DNS servers, 304-05
  printer spooling, 244
  user accounts, 110-11
Environment tab (System utility), 26, *27*

environment variables
    configuring, 26-27
    user account setup and, 97-98
errors. *See also* problems
    checking hard drives for, 141-43
event logs, 48-52
    accessing and using, 48-49
    archiving, 51-52
    clearing, 51
    events monitored through, 48
    printer, 249
    setting options for, 49-50
Event Log Settings dialog box, *50*
events
    monitoring, 48-52
    printer, 249
    viewing on remote computers, 52
Event Viewer, 48-52, *48*
Everyone group, 78
expanding compressed files/directories, 144-45
Expand utility, 145
expiration date
    resetting, 111
    setting for accounts, 105
    setting for multiple accounts, 119-20
exporting directories, 33
extended partitions, 132
    assigning drive letters to, 133-34
    color-coding, 134
    creating, 136
    deleting, 140
extending volume sets, 150-51
Extend Volume Set dialog box, 151, *151*
extinction interval, 274
extinction timeout, 274

F

FAT file system, 137, 161-63
    converting to NTFS, 140-41
    file naming conventions, 162
    major features of, 161
file extensions
    displaying hidden extensions, 166-67
    rules of truncation for, 163
file names
    accessing long file names under MS-DOS, 162-63
    conventions applicable to, 162
    rules of truncation for, 163

file names, *continued*
    searching for files by, 167-68
files. *See also* directories; documents
    access types for, 189-90, *190*
    assigning permissions to, 188-89, 191-92
    auditing, 45-46
    backing up, 202-05
    compressing and expanding, 143-45
    copying and moving, 171-73
    deleting, 173
    displaying hidden files, 166-67
    dump, 29
    examining properties of, 175-76
    naming conventions for, 162
    ownership of, 187-88
    paging, 24-26
    renaming, 173
    searching for, 167-69
    selecting, 170-71
    sharing, 177-86
file systems, 127, 161-63
    backing up, 202-05
    comparison of features, 161-62
    converting a volume to NTFS, 140-41
    file naming conventions, 162
    specifying when formatting partitions, 137
filtering, password, 85-86
Find: All Files dialog box, 167-69, *168*, *169*
Find feature (Windows NT Explorer), 167-69
floppy disks
    copying, 170
    emergency boot disk, 145
    emergency repair disk, 145-47
    formatting, 169-70
floppy drives. *See also* disk drives
    assigning drive letters to, 133
    examining properties of, 174-75
folders. *See also* directories
    creating, 173-74
    examining properties of, 175-76
    expanding without displaying contents, 165
Forcibly Disconnect Remote Users From Server...option, 84-85
foreground processes, 35
Format dialog box, 137-38, *137*
formatting
    floppy and removable disks, 169-70
    partitions, 136-38

forms, printer, 248
forwarding
   DNS, 305-07
   enabling for IP addresses, 225
forward lookups, 291-92

G

gateways
   configuring multiple, 218-19
   setting for DHCP clients, 260-61
General tab
   Diagnostics utility, 55
   Properties dialog box, 130-31, *131*
   System utility, 23
global groups, 93-94
global scope, 63
graphical administrative tools, 7-10, *8*
   installing on Windows NT workstations, 9-10
   system configuration and, 8-10
graphs, Task Manager, 38-40
group accounts, 60-61
   adding, 91-94
   administrators and, 73-74
   built-in, 67-68, 73-78
   changing/resetting passwords, 110
   copying, 109
   deleting, 110
   global, 93-94
   handling group membership, 94-96
   implicit, 78
   local groups, 91-93
   operators and, 74-76
   privileges and permissions, 68-73, 182-84
   share permissions for, 182-84
   tools for working with, 61-64
   updating, 107-12
   users and, 76-78
group membership
   managing, 94-96
   setting for multiple accounts, 117-18
Group Memberships dialog box, 94-96, *95*, 117, *117*
Guest account, 66
Guests group, 77

H

hard drives
   adding, 127-34

hard drives, *continued*
   assigning drive letters to, 133-34, 138-39
   changing/deleting volume labels, 139
   checking for errors and bad sectors, 141-42
   compressing, 143-45
   defragmenting, 143
   diagnostic information on, 54
   emergency boot disk for, 145
   emergency repair disk for, 145-47
   examining properties of, 174-75
   managing, 138-47
   partitioning, 134-38
   preparing for use, 129-32
   primary vs. extended partitions on, 132-34
   recovering a boot failure on, 146-47
   types of, 128-29
hardware profiles, 29-31
Hardware Profiles tab (System utility), 29
H-node (hybrid node) name resolution, 269
home directories, 102-03
host names, 220
hot fixes for Windows NT, 5

I

icons, Windows NT Explorer, 165
IDE drives, 129
implicit groups, 78
importing
   directories, 33-34
   static mappings, 282
incremental backups, 195-96
   tape rotation schedule for, *198*
Install Driver dialog box, 198-99, *199*
installing
   backup devices, 198-201
   DHCP Relay Agent service, 224
   DHCP server, 254
   DNS server, 289
   local print devices, 238-39
   network adapters, 212-13
   network print devices, 234-38
   printers, 233-41
   tape devices, 200-201
   TCP/IP networking, 211-15
   WINS servers, 270
Interactive group, 78
interactive processes, 35

Interfaces tab (Server Properties dialog box), *305*
I/O ports, diagnostic information on, 55-56
IP addresses
  configuring multiple, 218-19
  DHCP client and, 253
  dynamic, 215, 217-18, 254
  enabling/disabling for DNS servers, 304-05
  enabling forwarding for, 225
  ping command for checking, 216
  static, 215-17
IP Address tab (Microsoft TCP/IP Properties dialog box), 217-18, *217*
IP forwarding, 225
IRQs, diagnostic information on, 55-56

L

leases
  deleting, 265
  managing client leases, 262-63
  modifying properties of, 265
  releasing, 264
LegalNoticeCaption option, 122-23
LegalNoticeText option, 123
LMHOSTS files, 223
local file systems, 127
local groups, 91-93
local home directory, 102
local print devices, 233
  installing, 238-39
local print spooler, 232
local profiles, 98-99
  assigning new, 114
  changing to roaming profiles, 115
  deleting, 113-14
  managing, 112-13
local scope, 63
location, printer, 241-42
locked-out user accounts, 110-11
Lockout After X Bad Logon Attempts option, 83-84
Lockout Duration option, 84
logging events. *See* event logs
logical drives
  creating, 136
  examining properties of, 174-75
  extending, 150-51
logon hours
  managing, 103-04

logon hours, *continued*
  setting for multiple accounts, 119
Logon Hours dialog box, 103-04, *104*
logon process
  configuring service logon, 43
  customizing for users, 120-24
  troubleshooting problems with, 111-12
logon scripts, 101-02
logon workstations
  setting for multiple accounts, 119
  setting permissions for, 104-05
Logon Workstations dialog box, 105, *105*, 119
long file names, 162-63
lookups
  reverse lookup configuration, 291-92
  WINS, configuring in DNS, 307-08

M

magnetic optical drives, 197
mail exchange (MX) servers, 297, 299-300
managing
  client leases, 262-63
  DNS servers, 292-96
  group membership, 94-96
  hard drives, 138-47
  logon hours, 103-04
  multiple user accounts, 115-20
  open resources, 19-20
  print jobs, 249-52
  properties, 15-21
  RAID arrays, 157-60
  replication, 31-34
  shared resources, 17-18
  share permissions, 180-84
  system services, 40-43
  TCP/IP networking, 211-29
  user connections, 17-18
  user profiles, 112-15
  WINS database, 282-85
mandatory profiles, 98, 101
Map Network Drive dialog box, *185*
mappings
  for network drives, 186-87
  static, 280-82
  viewing for WINS database, 283
Maximum Password Age option, 82
memory, virtual, 24-26

Index | 321

messages, sending to users, 21
Microsoft DNS Server. *See* DNS servers
Microsoft TCP/IP Properties dialog box
   DHCP Relay tab, 223-24, *224*
   DNS tab, 220-21, *220*
   IP Address tab, 217-18, *217*
   WINS Address tab, 222-23, *222*
Microsoft Windows NT. *See* Windows NT
Minimum Password Age option, 82-83
Minimum Password Length option, 83
mirrored sets
   boot failures and, 158-59
   breaking, 157
   creating, 154-55
   repairing, 157
M-node (modified node) name resolution, 269
moving files, 171-73
MS-DOS
   accessing long file names under, 162-63
   printer names and, 237
   shared directories and, 178
multiple accounts
   dial-in privileges for, 120
   expiration date for, 119-20
   group membership for, 117-18
   logon hours for, 119
   logon workstations for, 119
   managing, 115-20
   setting account type for, 119-20
   user profiles for, 118

N

name registration, 268
name release, 268
name renewal, 268
name resolution services. *See* DNS; WINS
names. *See also* file names; user names
   domain, 220
   printer, 237, 238
   share, 16-17
name server (NS), 297, 300
NetBEUI protocol, 211
NetBIOS, 267
   computer name resolution, 221-23
   running over TCP/IP, 267

NET commands, 11
network adapters, installing, 212-13
Network Control Panel utility, 213-15
Network dialog box
   Adapters tab, 212-13, *212*
   Protocols tab, 214, *214*, 216-17, *216*
network drives
   connecting to, 186-87
   disconnecting, 187
   examining properties of, 174-75
   mapping, 186-87
Network group, 78
network home directory, 103
network print devices, 233
   installing, 234-38
   setting access permissions for, 245-46, *246*
network services on Windows NT, 227-29, *227-28*
New Local Group dialog box, 92, *92*
New Resource Record dialog box, *301*
New Share dialog box, *178*
New User dialog box, 89-91, *90*
non-domain controllers
   built-in capabilities for, 72-73
   user rights for, 71-72
normal/full backups, 194
NTFS file system, 137, 161-63
   compression feature, 143-45
   converting FAT volumes to, 140-41
   file naming conventions, 162
   major features of, 162

O

open resources, managing, 19-20
Open Resources dialog box, 19-20, *19*
operators, groups used by, 74-76
OS build version, 53
Owner dialog box, 188, *188*
ownership, file, 187-88

P

paging files, 24-26
   diagnostic information on, 54-55
parent domains, 287
parity
   disk striping with, 155-56

parity, *continued*
  regenerating stripe sets with, 159-60
partitioning hard drives, 134-38
  color-coding partitions, 134
  creating extended partitions, 136
  creating primary partitions, 135
  deleting partitions and drives, 140
  formatting partitions, 136-38
  types of partitions, 132-34
Password Age options, 82-83
Password Length options, 83
passwords
  for Administrator account, 65
  changing and resetting, 110
  filtering, 85-86
  for Guest account, 66
  setting policies for, 81-86
  for user accounts, 80-86
Password Uniqueness options, 83
pasting files
  copying and, 172
  moving and, 173
pausing
  print jobs, 250-51
  system services, 42
performance
  monitoring system performance, 38-40
  setting for applications, 24
Performance tab
  System utility, 23, *24*
  Task Manager, 38-40, *39*
permissions, 68-73, 189. *See also* access; security
  file and directory, 187-92
  logon workstation, 104-05
  printer, 245-46, 248-49
  share, 180-84, 245-46
ping command, 216, 229
P-node (point-to-point node) name resolution, 269
pointer (PTR) records, 297-98
policies
  for passwords and accounts, 80-86
  for user names, 79-80
  for user rights, 86-89
ports
  configuring for printers, 235-36, 243
  diagnosis of I/O, 55-56
PowerdownAfterShutdown option, 121-22
Power Users group, 77

Preferences dialog box (WINS Manager), 273-74, *274*, 277
primary DNS servers, 289-91
  notifying secondary servers of changes, 303, *304*
primary domain controller (PDC), 3, 21
primary groups, 96
primary partitions, 132
  assigning drive letters to, 133-34
  color-coding, 134
  creating, 135
  deleting, 140
primary zones, 290-91, *290*
  restricting database access, 304, 305-07
print devices, 233
  installing, 234-39
  local, 233, 238-39
  network, 234-38
  separator pages for, 243
Printer Auditing dialog box, 47, *47*
printer drivers, 231-32
  downloading, 242
  updating, 242
printer events, 249
Printer Permissions dialog box, 246, *246*
printer port
  changing, 243
  configuring, 235-36
printers, 231-52
  auditing, 45-46, 247
  configuring properties for, 241-47
  connecting to, 239-40
  installing and configuring, 233-41
  managing print jobs, 249-52
  purging, 251
  removing documents from, 251
  setting access permissions for, 245-46, *246*
  Spooler service, 240
  troubleshooting, 231-33, 240-41
Printers folder, *235*
printer sharing
  setting access permissions for, 245-46, *246*
  starting and stopping, 245
print jobs
  auditing, 45-46, 247
  canceling, 251
  disabling job completion notification, 249
  managing, 249-52
  pausing and resuming, 250-51

Index | 323

print jobs, *continued*
   scheduling and prioritizing, 243-45, 252
Print Management window, 249-50, *250*
print monitor, 233
Print Operators group, 75
print processor, 232
print queue, 232
print router, 232
print server, 231
   configuring properties for, 247-49
   enabling Spool folder permissions, 248-49
   logging printer events, 249
   removing print job completion notification, 249
   viewing and creating printer forms, 248
Print Server Properties dialog box, 247-49, *248*
print spooler, 232
   enabling, 244
   options, 244-45
   troubleshooting, 240
priority, printer, 244, 252
privileges, 68-73
   dial-in, 106, 120
problems. *See also* troubleshooting
   checking hard drives for, 141-43
   diagnosing, 52-56
   logon, 111-12
processes
   administering, 37-38
   interactive, 35
   tool for managing, 36
Processes tab (Task Manager), 37-38, *38*
processors, diagnostic information on, 53
profiles
   changing type of, 115
   copying, 114-15
   hardware, 29-31
   local, 98-99, 112-14
   mandatory, 98, 101
   roaming, 98, 99-100
   setting for multiple accounts, 118
   user, 31, 96-103, 112-15
promoting domain controllers, 22
properties
   disk drive, 174-75
   document, 251
   file and folder, 175-76

properties, *continued*
   lease and reservation, 265
   managing, 15-21
   printer, 241-47
   print server, 247-49
   replication, 20
   retained when copying accounts, 109
   system startup and recovery, 27-29
Properties dialog box, 15, *15*
   for directory replication, *33*
   for disk drive information, 130-31
   for drive properties, 174-75
   for file and folder properties, 175-76
Protocols tab (Network dialog box), 214, *214*, 216-17, *216*
Pull Partner Properties dialog box, 279, *279*
Push Partner Properties dialog box, 278, *278*
push and pull partners, 277-79

R

RAID arrays, 149, 151-60
   disk mirroring, 154-55, 157-59
   disk striping, 152-54, 159
   disk striping with parity, 155-56, 159-60
   implementing on NT servers, 152-56
   managing, 157-60
   overview of, 151-52
RAM (random access memory), and virtual memory, 24-26
rebooting your system
   automatic reboot, 29
   emergency boot disk for, 159
recovering data from backups, 205-07
recovery options, 28-29
regenerating stripe sets with parity, 159-60
registry
   backing up and restoring, 207
   customizing user logons through, 120-24
   setting a size limit on, 26
remote file systems, 127
   backing up and restoring data on, 207
remote servers, 292

removable disks
  for backups, 197
  copying, 170
  formatting, 169-70
removable drives. *See also* disk drives
  examining properties of, 174-75
removing. *See also* deleting
  access to shared file and directories, 186
  computers from a domain, 226-27
  DHCP scopes, 261-62
  servers from DNS Manager, 294
  users from a group, 95
renaming
  files and directories, 173
  user accounts, 108
renewal interval, 274
repair disk, 145-47
Repair Disk Utility, 146
repairing
  mirrored sets, 157
  stripe sets, 159
  system failures, 146-47
replication
  creating replication accounts, 31-32
  forcing database replication, 279
  managing, 31-34
  viewing replication properties, 20
  of WINS database, 276-79
Replication Partners dialog box, 277-78, *278*
Replicator group, 76
reservations
  deleting, 265
  for DHCP addresses, 263-64
  modifying properties of, 265
Reset Count After option, 84
Restore Information dialog box, *206*
restoring data from backups, 205-07
  for DHCP database, 266
  for WINS database, 285
reverse lookups
  configuring, 291-92
  WINS, configuring in DNS, 307-08
right-clicking, on application listings, 37
RIP (Routing Information Protocol), 225
RISC-based computer systems, 141

roaming profiles, 98, 99-100
  changing to local profiles, 115
root domains, 287
routers
  print, 232
  setting for DHCP clients, 260-61
RunLogonScriptSync option, 122

S

scheduling
  backups, 207-08
  print jobs, 243-45, 252
SCOPE ID, 223
scopes, 63, 254-62
  activating and deactivating, 261
  configuring multiple, 262
  creating, 256-57
  modifying, 261
  removing, 261-62
  setting options for, 257-59
ScreenSaveActive option, 123
screen saver options, 123-24
ScreenSaveTimeOut option, 123
SCSI adapters, 198-99
SCSI Adapters dialog box, *199*
SCSI drives, 128
searching for files, 167-69
  by creation and modification date, 168-69
  by file name and location, 167-68
  by file size and contents, 169
secondary DNS servers, 291
  notifying of zone property changes, 303, *304*
secondary zones, 291, *292*
secure passwords, 81
security. *See also* access; permissions
  components, 59
  dial-in privileges, 105-06, 120
  directory, 45-46, 188-92
  DNS server, 204-07
  file, 45-46, 188-92
  granting and denying access, 59
  logon hours, 103-04
  logon workstations, 104-05
  printer, 46-47, 245-46
  setting auditing policies for, 43-45
Select Network Protocol dialog box, *214*
Select Users dialog box, 116, *116*
sending messages to users, 21
separator pages, 243

Server Manager, 13-22
  configuring alerts, 20
  main window display, 14
  managing domain controllers,
    21-22
  managing Windows NT
    properties, 15-21
  selecting a computer/domain to
    manage, 15
  sending messages to users, 21
  starting, 13
  tasks handled by, 13
Server Operators group, 75
Server Properties dialog box, 304
  Interfaces tab, *305*
  WINS Lookup tab, 307-08, *308*
servers. *See also* DHCP servers;
    DNS servers; Windows NT
    Servers; WINS servers
  mail exchange, 297, 299-300
  name, 297, 300
  print, 231, 247-49
  remote, 292
  stand-alone, 71-73
service packs for Windows NT,
    4, 49
  determining version of, 53
services, 40-43
  list of default services, *41*
  logon configuration, 43
  managing, 40-43
  Spooler, 240
  starting, stopping, and
    pausing, 42
  startup configuration, 42
Services dialog box, 40, *40*
Services tab (Network dialog box),
    228-29, *228*
Services utility, 40-43
shared directories
  adding to existing shares, 179
  assigning permissions, 180-84,
    188-89
  creating, 177-78
  managing, 184-86
  removing access to, 186
  Web shares, 179-80
Shared Directories dialog box, 178
shared resources, 177-92
  assigning share permissions,
    180-84, 188-89
  connecting to network drives,
    186-87
  creating shared directories,
    177-80
  file ownership and, 187-88
  managing, 17-18, 184-86

shared resources, *continued*
  removing access to, 186
  special shares, 184-86
  starting/stopping printer
    sharing, 245
  viewing user connections to,
    16-17, 186
Shared Resources dialog box, 17,
    17
share name, 16-17
share permissions, 180-84. *See also*
    permissions; security
  adding, 182-83
  assigning, 180-84, 188-89,
    191-92
  modifying, 183-84
  removing, 184, 186
  types of, 181
  viewing, 181-82, 186
Share Permissions dialog box, 181
Show Database dialog box,
    283, *283*
ShutdownWithoutLogon
    option, 121
SIDs (security identifiers), 108
size
  searching for files by, 169
  setting for the registry, 26
SOA (Start of Authority) record,
    301-04
SOA Record tab (Zone Properties
    dialog box), 302-03, *302*
special shares, 184-86
  connecting to, 185-86
  explained, 184-85
Spooler service, 240
Spool folder, 248-49
stand-alone servers
  built-in capabilities for, 72-73
  user rights for, 71-72
Start of Authority (SOA) record,
    301-04
starting. *See also* booting your
    system
  Server Manager, 13
  Services utility, 40
  System utility, 22
  Windows NT Explorer, 164
startup options
  setting, 28
  for system services, 42
Startup/Shutdown tab (System
    utility), 27, *28*
static IP addresses, 215
  assigning, 216-17
  configuring, 215-17
  enabling IP forwarding for, 225

static mappings, 280-82
  creating, 280-81
  editing, 282
  importing, 282
  viewing, 280
Static Mappings dialog box, 280-81, *280*
static routing, 225
statistics
  examining for DNS servers, 294
  Task Manager Performance tab, 39-40
STOP error, 28
stopping
  printer sharing, 245
  system services, 42
stripe sets, 152-54
  creating with parity, 156
  repairing and regenerating, 159-60
synchronizing domain controllers, 22
System account, 67
system environment variables
  configuring, 26-27
  user account setup and, 97-98
System group, 78
System Idle Process, 38
system information, 23
System partition, 134
system performance monitoring, 38-40
system problems
  diagnosing, 52-56
  troubleshooting, 55
system processes. *See* processes
System Properties dialog box, *113*
system resources
  auditing, 43-47
  monitoring usage of, 38-40
system services. *See* services
System utility, 13, 22-31
  configuring environment variables, 26-27
  configuring hardware profiles, 29-31
  configuring system startup and recovery, 27-29
  configuring user profiles, 31
  general system information, 23
  managing local profiles, 112-13
  setting application performance, 24
  setting registry size, 26
  setting virtual memory, 24-26
  starting, 22

T

tape backups
  buying and using tapes for, 197-98
  installing devices for, 200-201
  tape drives for, 196
  tape jukeboxes for, 197
Tape Devices utility, 200-201
Task Manager, 36
  Applications tab, 36-37, *36*
  Performance tab, 38-40, *39*
  Processes tab, 37-38, *38*
TCP/IP networking, 211-29
  adding computers to a domain, 225-26
  additional services for, 227-29, *227-28*
  configuring, 215-25
  defined, 211
  installing, 211-15
  removing computers from a domain, 226-27
  running NetBIOS over, 267
  testing the configuration, 229
TileWallPaper option, 124
timeout values, 309
tools. *See* utilities
troubleshooting
  hard drive errors, 141-43
  logon problems, 111-12
  printer problems, 231-33
  service and device problems, 55
  spooler problems, 240-41

U

undocked profiles, 29
  configuring a computer for, 30-31
Universal Naming Convention (UNC), 187
updating
  accounts, 107-12
  DNS records, 300-301
  printer drivers, 242
  zone properties, 301-04
user accounts, 60
  adding, 89-91
  built-in, 64-67
  changing/resetting passwords, 110
  copying, 109
  deleting, 110
  dial-in privileges, 106
  enabling, 110-11

user accounts, *continued*
  expiration date on, 105
  logon hours, 103-04
  logon workstations, 104-05
  managing multiple, 115-20
  password and account policies, 80-86
  privileges and permissions, 68-73, 180-84
  renaming, 108
  setup and organization, 79-89
  share permissions, 182-84
  system environment variables and, 97-98
  tools for working with, 61-64
  updating, 107-12
  user name policies, 79-80
  user rights policies, 86-89
user connections
  managing, 17-18
  viewing, 16-17
User Environment Profile dialog box, 96-98, *96*, *97*, *118*
user environment variables, 26-27
User Manager, 61, *64*
  adding group accounts, 91-94
  adding user accounts, 89-91
  updating accounts, 107-12
User Manager for Domains, 62-63, *64*
user names
  policies and guidelines for, 79-80
  viewing user connections by, 16
user profiles, 96-103, 112-15
  assigning new, 114
  changing type of, 115
  configuring, 31, 96-103
  copying, 114-15
  deleting, 113-14
  environment variables and, 97-98
  home directories and, 102-03
  local, 98-99
  logon scripts and, 101-02
  managing, 112-15
  mandatory, 98, 101
  roaming, 98, 99-100
  setting for multiple accounts, 118
User Profiles tab (System utility), 112-13
User Properties dialog box, *66*, 116, *117*, 119
user rights, 68
  administering policy for, 88-89

user rights, *continued*
  for domain controllers, 69-70
  for non-domain controllers, 71-72
  overview of basic and advanced, *86-88*
  policies for, 86-89
User Rights Policy dialog box, 88-89, *89*
users
  adding to groups, 95
  customizing logon process for, 120-24
  dial-in privileges for, 106
  disconnecting, 18, 103
  groups used by, 76-78
  logon hours for, 103-04
  logon workstations for, 104-05
  removing from groups, 95
  sending messages to, 21
  setting primary groups for, 96
  share permissions for, 182-84
User Sessions dialog box, 16, *16*
Users group, 76
Users Must Log On In Order To Change Password option, 85
utilities, 5
  Administrative Wizards, 10
  Backup, 201-08
  Check Disk, 141-43, *143*
  command-line, 11
  Compact and Expand, 145
  Control Panel, 6-7, *6*
  Convert, 140-41
  DHCP Manager, 254-55
  Diagnostics, 52-56
  Disk Administrator, 129
  Disk Keeper, 143
  graphical administrative tools, 7-10, *8*
  Network, 213-15
  ping, 216, 229
  Repair Disk, 146
  Services, 40-43
  System, 13, 22-31
  Tape Devices, 200-201
  WINS Manager, 270-74

V

verify interval, 275
video drivers, 53-54
viewing
  DNS records, 300-301
  events on remote computers, 52
  log archives, 52

328 | Index

viewing, *continued*
  printer forms, 248
  replication properties, 20
  share permissions, 181-82, 186
  static mappings, 280
  system performance, 38-40
  user connections, 16-17
  WINS database mappings, 283
virtual memory, 24-26
  configuring, 25-26
  diagnostic information on, 54-55
volumes
  changing/deleting volume labels, 139
  converting to NTFS, 140-41
  extending, 150-51
  features of FAT, 161
volume sets, 149-51
  creating, 149-50
  deleting, 150
  extending, 150-51
Volumes window (Disk Administrator), 131, *132*

W

WallPaper option, 124
Web share, creating, 179-80
Windows 3.1
  printer names and, 237
  shared directories and, 178
Windows NT
  access types, 189-91
  auditing system resources in, 43-47
  Backup utility, 201-07
  creation of abbreviated file names by, 163
  diagnosing system problems in, 52-56
  directory replication, 31-34
  environments, profiles, and properties, 22-31
  event logging and viewing, 48-52
  formats, 3
  managing network systems in, 13-22
  network services available on, 227-29, *227-28*
  performance monitoring, 38-40
  permissions used by, *189*
  processes, 35-38
  properties, 15-21
  security model, 59
  services, 40-43
  special shares used by, *184-85*

Windows NT, *continued*
  utilities for administering, 5, 6-11, 13
Windows NT Convert utility, 137
Windows NT Diagnostics, 52-56
Windows NT Explorer, 164-70
  changing/deleting volume label with, 139
  Check Disk utility and, 142
  copying floppy and removable disks with, 170
  customizing the display in, 165-66
  displaying hidden files and file extensions in, 166-67
  formatting floppy and removable disks with, 169-70
  icons displayed in, 165
  searching for files with, 167-69
  selecting files and directories in, 170-71
  starting, 164
Windows NT Option Pack, 4
Windows NT Resource Kit, 4
Windows NT Servers, 3
  implementing RAID arrays on, 152-56
  managing network systems on, 13-22
  utilities for administering, 5, 6-11, 13
Windows NT Workstations, 3
  built-in capabilities for, 72-73
  logon permissions for, 104-05, 119
  user rights for, 71-72
  utilities for administering, 5, 6-11, 13
Winlogon key, 120, 121-23
WINS (Windows Internet Name Services), 267-85, 288
  client configuration, 221-23, 268
  database replication configuration, 276-79
  DNS integration with, 307-10
  installing WINS servers, 270
  managing static mappings, 280-82
  managing the WINS database, 282-85
  name resolution services, 221-23, 267, 268-69
  server configuration, 268, 274-76
  using WINS Manager, 270-74

WINS Address tab (Microsoft TCP/
        IP Properties dialog box),
        222-23, *222*
WINS clients, configuring,
        221-23, 268
WINS database
    backing up and restoring,
        284-85
    cleaning and scavenging, 284
    compacting, 284
    configuring replication, 276-79
    creating push and pull partners,
        277-79
    forcing database replication, 279
    managing, 282-85
    overview of files in, *282*
    setting default replication
        parameters, 276-77
    viewing database mappings, 283
WINS Manager, 270-74, *271*, *275*
    adding a WINS server to, 271
    overview of, 270-71
    refreshing and clearing
        statistics, 272
    setting preferences in, 273-74
    viewing detailed server
        information, 272-73
WINS node type, 260
WINS servers
    adding to WINS Manager, 271

WINS servers, *continued*
    configuring, 268, 274-76
    database replication, 276-79
    importing static mappings
        from, 282
    installing, 270
    refreshing and clearing statistics
        on, 272
    setting for DHCP clients, 259
    viewing detailed information
        on, 272-73
workstations, 3
    built-in capabilities for, 72-73
    logon permissions for,
        104-05, 119
    user rights for, 71-72

Z

Zone Properties dialog box,
        301-04, *302*, *304*
zones
    Cache, 293-94
    creating domains within, 295
    deleting from DNS servers, 295
    primary, 290-91, *290*
    secondary, 291, *292*
    updating properties for, 301-04

About the Author

William R. Stanek (nt-consulting@tvpress.com) has a master of science in information systems degree and more than a decade of hands-on experience with advanced programming and development. He is a leading network technology expert and an award-winning author. Over the years, his practical advice has helped programmers, developers, and network engineers all over the world. He is also a regular contributor to leading publications like *PC Magazine*, where you'll often find his work in the "PC Tech" section.

The author served in the Persian Gulf War as a combat crew member on an electronic warfare aircraft. He flew on numerous combat missions into Iraq and was awarded nine medals for his wartime service, including one of the United States of America's highest flying honors, the Air Force Distinguished Flying Cross.

The manuscript for this book was prepared and submitted to Microsoft Press in electronic form. Text files were prepared using Microsoft Word 97 for Windows. Pages were composed by nSight, Inc., using Adobe PageMaker 6.5 for Windows, with text in Garamond Light and display type in ITC Franklin Gothic. Composed pages were delivered to the printer as electronic prepress files.

Cover Designer
Tim Girvin Design

Cover Illustrator
Tom Draper

Interior Illustrator
Javier Amador-Peña

Layout Artist
Tara L. Murray

Project Manager
Sarah Kimnach

Tech Editors
Richard and Darian Taha

Copy Editor
Joseph Gustaitis

Proofreaders
Pauline Chin and Elissa Leclerc

Indexer
James Minkin

The *ultimate companion to* Microsoft **Windows NT Workstation**
version 4.0

U.S.A.	**$69.95**
U.K.	£64.99 [V.A.T. included]
Canada	$94.95
ISBN 1-57231-343-9	

This exclusive Microsoft kit, written in cooperation with the Microsoft Windows NT Workstation development team, provides the complete technical information and tools you need to understand and get the most out of Microsoft Windows NT Workstation version 4.0. The comprehensive technical guide and a CD-ROM containing more than 100 useful tools help you take full advantage of the power of Microsoft Windows NT Workstation version 4.0. Administrators will especially like the section that describes strategies for deployment in large organizations and compatibility with other network and operating systems. Get the MICROSOFT® WINDOWS NT® 4.0 WORKSTATION RESOURCE KIT—and get *the* essential reference for installing, configuring, and troubleshooting Microsoft Windows NT Workstation version 4.0.

Microsoft Press® products are available worldwide wherever quality computer books are sold. For more information, contact your book retailer, computer reseller, or local Microsoft Sales Office.

To locate your nearest source for Microsoft Press products, reach us at http://mspress.microsoft.com, or call 1-800-MSPRESS in the U.S. (in Canada: 1-800-667-1115 or 416-293-8464).

To order Microsoft Press products, call 1-800-MSPRESS in the U.S. (in Canada: 1-800-667-1115 or 416-293-8464).

Prices and availability dates are subject to change.

Microsoft®

mspress.microsoft.com

This is how Microsoft Windows NT pros become incredibly resourceful.

This three-volume kit provides the valuable technical and performance information and the tools you need for handling rollout and support issues surrounding Microsoft Windows NT Server 4.0. You get a full 2500 pages—plus a CD-ROM—loaded with essential information not available anywhere else. For support professionals, MICROSOFT® WINDOWS NT® 4.0 SERVER RESOURCE KIT is more than a guide. It's a natural resource.

U.S.A. $149.95
U.K. £140.99 [V.A.T. included]
Canada $199.95
ISBN 1-57231-344-7

Microsoft Press® products are available worldwide wherever quality computer books are sold. For more information, contact your book or computer retailer, software reseller, or local Microsoft Sales Office, or visit our Web site at mspress.microsoft.com. To locate your nearest source for Microsoft Press products, or to order directly, call 1-800-MSPRESS in the U.S. (in Canada, call 1-800-268-2222).

Prices and availability dates are subject to change.

Microsoft®
mspress.microsoft.com

http://mspress.microsoft.com/reslink/

Look beyond the kits!

If you deploy, manage, or support Microsoft® products and technologies, here's a hot link to the hottest IT resources available—http://mspress.microsoft.com/reslink/. Microsoft Press® ResourceLink is an essential online information resource for IT professionals—the most complete source of technical information about Microsoft technologies available anywhere. Tap into ResourceLink for direct access to the latest technical updates, tools, and utilities—straight from Microsoft—and help maximize the productivity of your IT investment.

For a **complimentary 30-day trial CD** packed with Microsoft Press IT products, order via our Web site at http://mspress.microsoft.com/reslink/.

Microsoft Press
Resource Link

Microsoft®
mspress.microsoft.com

OWNER REGISTRATION CARD

0-7356-0574-2

MICROSOFT® WINDOWS NT® SERVER 4.0 ADMINISTRATOR'S POCKET CONSULTANT

FIRST NAME   MIDDLE INITIAL   LAST NAME

INSTITUTION OR COMPANY NAME

ADDRESS

CITY   STATE   ZIP

E-MAIL ADDRESS   (   ) PHONE NUMBER

U.S. and Canada addresses only. Fill in information above and mail postage-free. Please mail only the bottom half of this page.

start faster go farther

Register Today!

Return this
MICROSOFT® WINDOWS NT®
SERVER 4.0 ADMINISTRATOR'S
POCKET CONSULTANT
registration card today

***Microsoft*Press**

mspress.microsoft.com

start faster go farther

For information about Microsoft Press® products, visit our Web site at mspress.microsoft.com

Microsoft Press

BUSINESS REPLY MAIL
FIRST-CLASS MAIL   PERMIT NO. 108   REDMOND WA

POSTAGE WILL BE PAID BY ADDRESSEE

MICROSOFT PRESS
PO BOX 97017
REDMOND, WA 98073-9830

NO POSTAGE
NECESSARY
IF MAILED
IN THE
UNITED STATES